The Formulas of
Popular Fiction

ALSO BY ANNA FAKTOROVICH
AND FROM McFARLAND

*Rebellion as Genre in the Novels of
Scott, Dickens and Stevenson* (2013)

The Formulas of Popular Fiction

*Elements of Fantasy,
Science Fiction, Romance,
Religious and Mystery Novels*

ANNA FAKTOROVICH

McFarland & Company, Inc., Publishers
Jefferson, North Carolina

LIBRARY OF CONGRESS CATALOGUING-IN-PUBLICATION DATA

Faktorovich, Anna, 1981–
The formulas of popular fiction : elements of fantasy, science fiction, romance, religious and mystery novels / Anna Faktorovich.
      p.   cm.
Includes bibliographical references and index.

ISBN 978-0-7864-7413-4 (softcover : acid free paper) ∞
ISBN 978-1-4766-1585-1 (ebook)

1. Fiction genres.   I. Title.

PN3427.F35 2014   808.3—dc23   2014032196

BRITISH LIBRARY CATALOGUING DATA ARE AVAILABLE

© 2014 Anna Faktorovich. All rights reserved

No part of this book may be reproduced or transmitted in any form or by any means, electronic or mechanical, including photocopying or recording, or by any information storage and retrieval system, without permission in writing from the publisher.

Front cover image: "Charles Frohman presents William Gillette in his new four act drama, *Sherlock Holmes*," Metropolitan Printing Co., New York, 1900 (Library of Congress)

Printed in the United States of America

McFarland & Company, Inc., Publishers
Box 611, Jefferson, North Carolina 28640
www.mcfarlandpub.com

Table of Contents

Chronology of Works Discussed vii

Introduction 1

Chapter 1
Formulaic Fiction Writing
and the History of Literary Genres 11

Chapter 2
Fantasy, Science Fiction and Horror 45

Chapter 3
Romance 95

Chapter 4
Religious and Inspirational 141

Chapter 5
Mystery and Detective 160

Conclusion 195

Chapter Notes 201

Bibliography 209

Index 213

Chronology of Works Discussed

This chronology shows the key works in the development of the formulas and genres discussed in this book. It is useful for those who want to understand the timeline of these literary developmentss. The relationships among these works also says a lot about originality and mimicry.

2030 BC	*Pyramid Texts*
1200–900 BC	*Vedas, The Rig Veda*
868 BC	*The Diamond-Cutter Sutra*
722–444 BC	*Torah*
411 BC	Aristophanes, *Lysistrata*
1021	Murasaki Shikibu, *Tale of Genji*
1508	Garci Rodríguez de Montalvo, *Amadis de Gaula*
1605–1615	Miguel de Cervantes, *Don Quixote*
1726	Jonathan Swift, *Gulliver's Travels*
1814	Walter Scott, *Waverley*
1819	E. T. A. Hoffmann, *Mademoiselle de Scuderi*
1831	Honoré de Balzac, *The Wild Ass's Skin*
1833	George Sand, *Lavinia*
1839	Stendhal, *The Charterhouse of Parma*
1841	Edgar Allan Poe, "The Murders in the Rue Morgue"
1844	Alexandre Dumas, *The Three Musketeers*
1845	Alexandre Dumas, *Twenty Years After*
1845	George Sand, *The Devil's Pool*
1847	Alexandre Dumas, *The Vicomte of Bragelonne: Ten Years Later*
1856	Gustave Flaubert, *Madame Bovary*
1858	George MacDonald, *Phantastes*
1859	Wilkie Collins, *The Woman in White*
1860	Wilkie Collins, *The Moonstone*
1862	Ellen Wood, *The Channings*
1863	Mary Braddon, *Lady Audley's Secret*
1872	George MacDonald, *The Princess and the Goblin*
1874	Thomas Hardy, *Far from the Madding Crowd*
1886	Marie Corelli, *A Romance of Two Worlds*
1886	Robert Louis Stevenson, *Kidnapped*
1886	Arthur Conan Doyle, *A Study in Scarlet*
1889	Arthur Conan Doyle, *Micah Clarke*

Chronology of Works Discussed

1890	Arthur Conan Doyle, *The Sign of the Four*
1891	Arthur Conan Doyle, "A Scandal in Bohemia"
1891	Florence Louisa Barclay, *Guy Mervyn*
1895	H. G. Wells, *The Time Machine*
1895	Marie Corelli, *The Sorrows of Satan*
1896	H. G. Wells, *The Island of Doctor Moreau*
1896	William Morris, *The Well at the World's End*
1897	Bram Stoker, *Dracula*
1902	Arthur Conan Doyle, *The Hound of the Baskervilles*
1903	Arthur Conan Doyle, "The Adventure of the Dancing Men"
1905	Lloyd Douglas, *More Than a Prophet*
1905	Lord Dunsany, *The Gods of Pegana*
1909	Florence Louisa Barclay, *The Rosary*
1915	Arthur Conan Doyle, *The Valley of Fear*
1916	James Joyce, *A Portrait of the Artist as a Young Man*
1918	James Joyce, *Ulysses*
1920	Agatha Christie, *The Mysterious Affair at Styles*
1920	Lloyd Douglas, *Wanted—A Congregation*
1921	Edith M. Hull, *The Sheik*
1921	Georgette Heyer, *The Black Moth*
1921	Marie Corelli, *The Secret Power*
1922	Barbara Cartland, *Jigsaw*
1926	Georgette Heyer, *These Old Shades*
1928	D. H. Lawrence, *Lady Chatterley's Lover*
1929	Lloyd Douglas, *Magnificent Obsession*
1930	Agatha Christie, *Murder at the Vicarage*
1933	George Orwell, *Down and Out in Paris and London*
1934	Agatha Christie, *Murder on the Orient Express*
1936	Margaret Mitchell, *Gone with the Wind*
1937	J. R. R. Tolkien, *The Hobbit*
1939	James Joyce, *Finnegans Wake*
1942	Lloyd Douglas, *The Robe*
1945	George Orwell, *Animal Farm*
1949	George Orwell, *1984*
1950–1956	C. S. Lewis, *The Chronicles of Narnia*
1954–1955	J. R. R. Tolkien, *The Lord of the Rings*
1955	Vladimir Nabokov, *Lolita*
1961	C. S. Lewis, *An Experiment in Criticism*
1962	Stanley Kubrick, dir., Kathleen Woodiwiss, *The Flower and the Flame* (film)
1966	Jacqueline Susann, *Valley of the Dolls*
1966	Larry Niven, *World of Ptavvs*
1966–1976	Mao Zedong, *Quotations from the Works of Mao Zedong*
1967	Mark Robson, dir., Jacqueline Susann, *Valley of the Dolls* (film)
1972	Barbara Cartland, *Knaves of Hearts*
1972	Kathleen E. Woodiwiss, *The Flame and the Flower*
1974	Stephen King, *Carrie*

Chronology of Works Discussed

1976	Anne Rice, *Interview with the Vampire*
1977	Henning Mankell, *Vettvillingen*
1981	Nora Roberts, *Irish Thoroughbred*
1982	Alice Walker, *The Color Purple*
1983–1985	Anne Rice, *The Sleeping Beauty Trilogy*
1997	J. K. Rowling, *Harry Potter and the Philosopher's Stone*
1997	Rick Riordan, *Big Red Tequila*
2001	Stephen King, *Black House*
2003	Dan Brown, *The Da Vinci Code*
2005	J. K. Rowling, *Harry Potter and the Half-Blood Prince*
2005	Stephenie Meyer, *The Twilight Saga: Twilight*
2006	Larry Niven, *Draco's Tavern*
2008	Stephenie Meyer, *Breaking Dawn*
2008	Rick Riordan, *Percy Jackson & the Olympians: The Battle of the Labyrinth*
2012	Nora Roberts, *Inn BoonsBoro Trilogy: Last Boyfriend*
2012	Henning Mankell, *The Troubled Man: A Kurt Wallander Mystery*

Introduction

"It is impossible to distinguish exactly the different classes of literature. This is due largely to the fact that most literature is not written with a view to classification; but, even if it were, there are so many possible classifications and the border between two classes is so indefinite that careful distinction would fill a volume."—*A History of English Literature* (1915)[1]

Back in 1915, when *A History of English Literature* was written, most of the best-selling genres of the twentieth century had not yet formed, and even popular literature was viewed as an artistic construction based on complex, mixed generic techniques, unlike the present set of established formulas that have been designed by marketers, publishers, and profit-minded authors throughout the past century. Today popular genres are divided according to "style, theme or content,"[2] unlike the Aristotelian definition of "genre" commonly accepted in earlier centuries, which had broad categories such as poetry, dramatic tragedies, comedies, and epics. The primary distinction between the classic genres of comedy and tragedy is their endings or the overall effect of the story on the viewers. Genres today are divided into specific formulaic categories and subcategories that take several elements into account when calculating the genre a given work belongs in. "Before the First World War there was simply too little popular fiction to need categorizing, almost all popular writing being designated with the vague title of 'romance.'"[3] With a few exceptions, like Sir Walter Scott's historical novel genre and H. G. Wells' science fiction novel genre, most popular genres discussed in this book (i.e., Agatha Christie's detective genre) were developed after World War I. This is a volume that attempts to do just what *A History of English Literature* believed was impossible—to classify, define, and dissect popularly used literary genres.

The U.S. publishing industry, represented by 35,800 publishers registered with Bowker, earned $27.9 billion in net revenue from selling 2.57 billion books in 2010.[4] Half of these books were trade publications; of these, adult and juvenile fiction comprised around $6.8 billion, or 24 percent.[5] Of these fiction titles, there were several categories or genres that clearly had the best sales records. In 1999, adult fiction was the best-selling genre, followed by juvenile fiction, and finally poetry and drama, the latter two constituting a sixth of the total sales of adult fiction.[6] Adult fiction further breaks into four genres that lead in sales, with romance fiction being in the lead ($1.3 billion), followed by religious and inspirational fiction ($759 million), then mysteries ($682 million), and finally science fiction and fantasy ($559 million). In a different study, from 2002, romances made up "54.5 percent of all paperback titles sold in the

U.S.," while "mystery/thrillers held a 26.6 percent share of the market."[7] From this perspective, romances have an overwhelming lead in the paperback market, with mysteries and thrillers a lagging second, and no other major competitors with their majority market share. Classical fiction in all genres, with works by dead authors, accounts for a smaller percentage, at $455 million in 2010.[8] While these statistics are not astronomical compared with Microsoft's profit of $6.7 billion in 2010,[9] or with the U.S. film industry's $10.47 billion in revenue in 2010,[10] they are still large enough to make popular fiction writing into a major business endeavor.

The publishing industry has exploded since the beginning of near-universal literacy around the world at the end of the nineteenth century. This study focuses on the age of widespread literacy from the end of the nineteenth century to the present day (2013). Popular literature developed across the twentieth century, or "*the* century of literary production and consumption, the supremely *literate* century" in which "authorship is very big business," but also a period in which "we may no longer treasure books," as other mediums are competing with them, and books are no longer the "supreme expressive form."[11] In most countries, students are now compelled by law to stay in school for up to twelve years. During mandatory schooling regular book reading is required, and most people continue to read for entertainment throughout their lives. The reading public buys books for pleasure or individual use mostly in the above-mentioned genres: romance fiction, religious and inspirational, mystery, science fiction and fantasy, classical fiction, juvenile fiction, poetry and drama. The masses see generic writing as "entertainment" and find "pleasure" in "wanting to know what happened next"—they do not expect to find "genius" in the stories, but just hope that the writer did the best he or she could have done; in turn, the writers do their best to satisfy these basic needs.[12] While there is an enormous generic diversity if one looks at all published books, only a few genres are consistently bought by readers. Generic tastes have changed across the centuries, but have remained relatively stable in the last thirty years. Bookstores shelve their books based on the Book Industry Study Group (BISG) subject index, and book buyers look for books in the major sections of the store based on their individual preferences, and these sections are typically dedicated to the best-selling genres.

While potentially great amateur literary writers might have learned during their masters of fine arts studies about the Bildungsroman, political novels, postmodern genre mixing, or historical semi-biographies, they will probably quickly realize that writing in any genre outside of the best-selling genres is not likely to generate a sale to a publisher. Some conform and write in the best-selling genres, while others write "literary fiction" (the type of fiction they learned about during their MFA program and simultaneously take on academic positions to pay the rent. The worst part of this dilemma is that a great deal of popular fiction is written to a strict formula that unintentionally stifles the writer's creativity and leads to dry, unreadable prose.

The "formula" is frequently blamed for the deterioration of the literary marketplace, as the term "formulaic fiction" has gained a negative connotation, as something that is hacked and nearly plagiarized from earlier stories. A distinction should between hack and literary formulaic writing. Over the millennia, literary critics and literary giants from Aristotle to Sir Walter Scott have defined and utilized literary elements and formulaic conventions. Formulaic problems occur when a publishing factory takes prescribed rules and applies them in a mechanic mass-production process that stamps out copies of the formula, without respecting the principles of originality and literary quality that the founders of these conventions valued.

At the root of the problem is not the "formula" writers use, but rather the failure to properly edit the formula to satisfy its originality requirements. In the nineteenth century, writers including Charles Dickens, Sir Walter Scott and Benjamin Disraeli either outright invented new genres or made major modifications to earlier genres, mixing and mutating the formulas that had worked in the past. Formulaic fiction, in its best sense, means using literary formulas to build foundations for structurally and linguistically strong fiction. The term "formula" should be understood in the traditional sense, as a set of literary component elements simplified into basic calculable terms. Just like $E = mc^2$, genres can be broken down into formulas, such as Structure of Fiction = Plot + Characters + Setting. While pure calculus might be stumped by some of fiction's natural inconsistencies, formulas of this type can help writers to see the tools at their disposal and allow them to engage in generic innovation.

Anti-formulaic novels like *Lolita* and *The Color Purple* show the contrast between lowbrow, highly formulaic best-selling fiction of the twentieth century and the technic and anti-formulaic nature of highbrow, dense, classical fiction that was written before near-universal literacy and is still composed, occasional with a bestseller status, today. I use the term "anti-formulaic" as a description of novels that are written against the most popular best-selling formula in a given genre. Anti-formulaic fiction might have a formula behind it, but this formula is not simplistic and does not closely mimic a set of previously created plotlines, themes, character types, and other elements of a popularized generic formula, such as historical romance or whodunit detective novels. For example, the historical romance might have an $a + b + c = x$ formula, and the whodunit detective might have a $d + e + f = y$ formula; in contrast, *Lolita* has a formula that's $\Sigma ab^2 + cd\infty - px\Pi / \sqrt{2}v - 56 \neq v$. This latter formula makes no mathematical sense and it definitely is not the actual formula for *Lolita*, but it shows the variety and complex relationships between the different elements in *Lolita*. Simple, mimicked formulas are more common among best-sellers, but there cannot be any mimicry without somebody coming up with a new formulaic variation to be mimicked in its elemental parts. Even Stephen King once stated frankly in an interview that "good writing ... is ... antigenre. Good writing is not mystery writing, it's not western writing, horror writing, science fiction writing."[13] In the modern publishing industry, bad formulaic writing is commercial and good anti-generic writing is anti-commercial. Conglomerates have a pure profit goal, so in following this theory they avoid good writing and consistently buy bad writing.

The top best-selling writer in America today exemplifies the trouble with modern formulaic writing. Stephen King embraces the term "hack," seeing that he once replied in an interview, "I've done a lot of hack stuff."[14] In an interview at the 1984 World Fantasy Convention, King elaborated on this concept, saying that he and Peter Straub are "professional writers. We do this for a living ... there's a tendency to want to find art or try to find some kind of a holy divination ... we're doing something like making a coat, and we were careful to try and dye all the pieces so they were pretty much the same."[15] While in most interviews, King attempts to convince readers that there is some "art" or "holy divination" behind his stories, here he clearly explains that formulaic writing is closer to mechanic coat-making than to artistic production. *Playboy* and several other magazines that interviewed Stephen King have asked about the frequent criticisms that his work is "derivative." King has accepted this criticism, with a few insults thrown back at the critics:

> I've never considered myself a blazingly original writer in the sense of conceiving totally new and fresh plot ideas. Of course, in both genre and mainstream fiction, there aren't really too many of those left, anyway, and most writers are essentially reworking a few basic themes, whether it's the angst-ridden introspection and tiresome identity crises of the aesthetes, the sexual and domestic problems of the John Updike school of cock contemplators, or the traditional formulas of mystery and horror and science fiction. What I try to do ... is to pour new wine from old bottles ... *Carrie* ... derived ... from a terrible grade-B movie called *The Brain from Planet Arous*.[16]

In another interview, Stephen King summarized the formulaic and repetitive nature of most of his writing by saying, "If you write popular literature and you repeat a theme, the idea is that your head is so empty it produced an echo."[17] King is not alone in blatantly admitting to engaging in "empty" formulaic and derivative writing when he writes best-selling novels. Across this study, you will find similar views expressed by many best-selling novelists. That these writers perceive their craft as a formulaic and mechanic process, unlike the literary art it was in centuries past, expresses significant points about the current state of unliterary popular formulaic writing.

As literature speedily becomes more and more unliterary, the last decade saw an unusual explosion in studies of popular current literary genres and generic formulas. Some of these are useful for literature professors who are researching genre theory, including Christopher Booker's *The Seven Basic Plots* and Clive Bloom's *Bestsellers: Popular Fiction Since 1900*. Others attempt to be relevant for both college fiction writers and linguistic professors and generally fail in both of these extremes (i.e., Robert N. St. Clair's *Literary Structures, Character Development, and Dramaturgical Scenarios in Framing the Category Novel*). One of the less successful examples is the most recent, Ken Gelder's *Popular Fiction: The Logics and Practices of a Literary Field*. In it Anne Rice is called an "undead" author, when compared to most popular writers who, Gelder writes, seem to have "disappeared" because they are overshadowed by the genres they represent. And J. R. R. Tolkien is explained in terms of how his *Lord of the Rings* novels are used by George W. Bush and other politicians to justify the "war on terror." Gelder only looks at four focal writers, and some of these are not included in Bloom's *Bestsellers* list, so the selection isn't representative of the genres, which are all vaguely defined.[18] What these critical books have in common is that they attempt to zero in on the basic elements of generic structure universal to "high" and "low" literature from around the world within each of the covered categories. Formulaic genre theory and categorization began growing earlier, across the twentieth century; the distinction between this theorizing in the twentieth and nineteenth centuries is that during the latter period the critics writing the theory frequently also wrote professional, well-structured novels themselves. Twentieth-century genre theory made some pretty logical strides in the field that helped literature teachers to explain distinctions in literary forms. In 1960, Leslie Fiedler wrote *Love and Death in the American Novel*, which looked at genre categories in American novels and explained how they are different from the novel traditions in other nations. Categorizing fiction into genres is at least as old as Aristotle's theories on tragedy and comedy, and the numbers of generic categories have been growing since that time. George Polti came up with thirty-six dramatic situations in 1921, and several others beat that number. The term one uses to describe the categories frequently changes the resulting number, so that there might be seven to nine basic plots, but thirty-six dramatic situations. However, several other critics have derived different numbers for the same term "basic plots." For example, Karen M. Hubert focuses her book on four popular genres and plot lines (horror, adventure, mystery and romance), but she writes, "Jakov Lind once said to me that only twelve basic plots exist. If this is true then a remarkable amount of literature is repetition."[19] Hubert studies these repetitions in her four genre sections. The number of plots a researcher sees depends on the type of study they are conducting, their hypothesis, their evidence, and the structure of their final book. But all studies that reduce basic plot lines to a number are studying statistical or literary repetitions, which are more numerous if you divide stories into more basic plot lines (i.e., fifty-five, as opposed to twelve); however, when one uses wider and more general plotlines, one can study the common patterns in the major popular genres (romance, mystery), rather than in narrower story types that are less likely to reflect the majority of the works in any given genre.

While it is a cliché to say that "academics ... tend to regard category fiction as subliterary 'hack work,'"[20] there have not been any serious studies that classify and explain the workings of popularly read hack writers. In *Literary Structures*, Michael Williams and Robert N. St. Clair merge what St. Clair calls novels with "literary value" intended for "high culture" and genre novels written for the "masses" or "low culture"[21] into the same generic categories and argue that they are linguistically and structurally the same, and that they only vary by degrees rather than types—thus, to make a distinction between the two is a form of "class prejudice."[22] What I do in this book is show the difference between authors who founded new genres and those who repeat the established formulas, using repetitive elements that destroy the goals of the initial techniques, as their lack of originality fails to create suspense or tension for readers. The novels I look at in this study are the best-selling works in the genres and the novels that initially developed the formulas that are now being repeated. By definition, the founding novelists must go against prior generic rules to create a new genre. By definition, current hack writers must write books that are, statistically speaking, extremely similar to many other best-selling books in their subcategory of a genre. Writers who have recently created outstanding novels that bend the rules of the highly formulized novel in their genre are writing against formulas, and therefore do not fall into my categories of formulas within the current best-selling genres. I will argue that a novelist cannot write an outstanding, suspenseful, descriptive and well-structured novel if they simply copy somebody else's formula.

I only found a few recent novels that had both "popularity and quality."[23] A popular writer and critic, Michael Williams, explains the reason for hack writers' inability to write "quality" work, revealing that when he did "work-for-hire" he wasn't allowed to "kill off" characters, and that there were many other "subtle do's and don'ts in projects of this kind."[24] Even later in his career, he was given information about the "invented world" that was to serve "as the setting for a number of fictions," where the "subsequent" novels after the first "fill in the blanks" of their individual stories with a formulaic mechanical approach that is a kind of print making or reproduction, rather than original creative invention. Williams even confesses that his "editor" told him that "'these books are rather conventional—it won't take you that much time or effort.'"[25] This is an unusually honest confession despite the opposite sentiments expressed around it. He explains that he made it more complicated (but does not say that he spent more time due to this shift) by changing the "standard coming-of-age tale"[26] from having a sympathetic protagonist to an unsympathetic one. He then goes on to congratulate himself on this success. The villain-hero structure that Williams proposes is one of the standard twists to the fundamental plots that Christopher Booker discusses in *The Seven Basic Plots*. It is not an original plot; it is just a different plot from the one that he initially decided to work on. This example is a warning to those who think they will be able to learn about "genre-crossing" or an "inventive mixture of the conventions of one category with the setting and conventions of another"[27] from this book.

Plot is the most commonly reproduced element for modern formulaic writers. Robert St. Clair comments, "Copyrights last only fifty years and then they must be renewed. Plots, however, do last forever. They cannot be renewed. Since plots differ from story lines, the same plot can be told in different ways. This can be done by changing the location of the event, the historical period, the ages of the characters, the time of year that the events took place, and so on."[28] An indicator of this trend is the *Percy Jackson* series, which imitates the plot of *Harry Potter* and then nonsensically changes the "historical period," "characters," and the other noted components. The outcome can only be defined as hack work, regardless of whether it is the lower or the upper class that ends up spending money on these books. There is no sense in congratulating hacks for selling a lot of copies. Academics and independent literary scholars, including some outstanding classical novelists, have previously come forward to discuss the problems in formulaic novels and now is the best time for re-engaging such criticism.

Before Darwin explained the branches of the evolutionary tree, people could not connect dinosaur skeletons to the idea that human genetics had a connection to monkeys and apes. Modern writers are similarly blinded by confusing or incomplete generic groupings. The field of genre studies developed in the last couple of decades, but it has previously existed under other names, including structural studies. Most studies in these fields focus on determining the generic or structural components/formulas used in one work, or in a short list of works. These studies are helpful to graduate students in the narrow fields that they focus on. However, how-to books designed for writers, such as *The Writer's Digest's Genre Writing Series*, with titles such as *How to Write Science Fiction and Fantasy*,[29] offer commentary on a given genre. These how-to books form a genre of their own, and when one reads enough of them, they seem to say very similar things. In the first chapter, the genre is defined, and after this there is a discussion of generic elements, like setting and character types, followed by a chapter or more on the structure of this type of generic story, and finally a bit about writing style in general and on the publishing market. These how-to books assume that writers who pick them up have never read a book in the covered genre, and have not read all the other books about writing in that genre.

Nineteenth-century literary writers learned about literary formulas by closely studying and breaking down their successful predecessors' formulas. Now, many current struggling writers begin with simplistic formulas, such as mimicking exact character types, and assume that if they follow these tricks, they will sell their work. This mimicry can come in the form of repetition, plagiarism, borrowing, homage or pastiche. The latter can be seen in Sherlock Holmes–like characters reappearing in texts by other writers to celebrate the works they are imitating, in contrast to literary parody, such as *Don Quixote*. These borrowings might come in the form of neither flattery nor ridicule, but as thefts of characters (Harry Potter, Oliver, Bella) and entire "fictional universes," such as Tolkien's Middle Earth or Stoker's version of Transylvania. Some current hacks do succeed in selling this skeleton fiction, but at the cost of depleting literary quality. Instead of offering simple skeleton formulas, this book aims to show the variety of character types and character interactions, settings, and plot structures that have been used successfully by best-selling writers.

To explain why I am focusing on best-sellers, I should give some additional statistics and history on the world publishing industry. James Patterson, best known for his thrillers, but also as the author of a few romances, sold the most adult books (200 million copies), making $70 million in 2010 (if multiplied by the 20 years that he has been a popular author, it appears as if he is also a billion-dollar author, but he must be below this mark due to slower sales at the start of his career).[30] Because of his popularity, Patterson was also the "first author to sell more than 1 million e-books," at 1.14 million copies in 2010.[31] The award for the most prolific published hack writing, or for the "most published works by one author," goes to the founder of Scientology, L. Ron Hubbard, who primarily published in fantasy and science fiction, with a total of 1,084 works between 1934 and 2006 (he died in 1986).[32] Another popular fantasy writer holds the record for being the "youngest author of a bestselling book series"— Christopher Paolini published his first book as a teenager after being homeschooled, and then he was picked up by Knopf and followed with several other books in the series.[33] The most profitable single book for a current organization or person that holds the copyright to it, or the "best selling copyright book," is the *Guinness Book of World Records* itself, with over 100 million copies sold as early as 2003, after being in print since 1955.[34]

Out of spiritual and religious books, the best-sellers are devotional and historical books. Of these, the honor of being the "oldest mechanically printed book" goes to the Gutenberg Bible, printed in Mainz, Germany, in 1455 by Johann Laden[35]; this event is better known as the beginning of the printing press age. The spread of the Bible went hand-in-hand with the spread of the Christian religion across the world and marked the beginning of the growth of the publishing industry that initially developed to spread the holy word and only later became a tool for the spread of various forms of knowledge and fiction. Therefore, it is not surprising that the Bible is also recognized as the "best-selling book of non-fiction," with around 2.5 billion copies printed between 1815 and 1975. The Bible was typically the only book in the homes of the lower classes before 1815, so it is likely that the total sales would be much higher if earlier printings were included in this estimate, so some recent studies have put the total at over 5 billion copies. The only book that approaches this number is the Communist "little red book," *Quotations from the Works of Mao Zedong*, which was mandatory reading during China's Cultural Revolution, a period between 1966 and 1976 (but the book went out of print due to its publisher's death in a plane crash in 1971).[36] Both the Bible and the "little red book" were required by their respective establishments, as those who didn't believe in the Christian God or in the Communist system in China were executed, so these sales don't reflect consumer tastes as much as the force of propaganda and threats in consumer buying habits.

While some authors have focused on producing the most novels for the highest profit, one novelist, Marcel Proust, spent three years writing a single novel, until 1912, and published it at his own expense between 1913 and 1927. The first volume didn't sell very well, so Proust spent even more time editing the work, and the outcome is known not just for its length but also as a masterpiece of French modernism, winning major critical awards immediately after the release of the second volume. The outcome was *Remembrance of Things Past,* which has the distinction of being the "longest novel" in the world.[37] *Remembrance* is an anti-formulaic and autobiographical novel that has extreme digressions and numerous dropped plot lines that never reach climaxes. Proust is not among the top best-selling authors, but he is highly regarded by critics; still, as literacy continues to be a major problem around the world, the writers who are the most read are of greater statistical interest than those who are the most criticized.

This book is divided into four main chapters (2, 3, 4 and 5), each focusing on one of the key genres under examination: fantasy/science fiction, romance, religious/inspirational and mystery/detective. Each of these chapters gives some general genre information, presents three or more key best-selling authors in the genre, and explains the structural elements (plot, characters and setting) that define it. This introduction and Chapter 1 give some background information on the significance of the study of formulaic writing within popular (literary and unliterary) genres. Chapter 1 also explains the writing methodology that popular writers across these four genres have in common, and looks at literacy trends from around the world and the concept of the unliterary among both readers and publishers. In addition, before the plots, characters and settings common to each of these genres can be dissected, the meanings of these terms have to be established. A full section is offered on Christopher Booker's seven basic plot types because they are the foundation for the plot groupings made in this study. These four key genres did not suddenly appear with the dawn of literacy, so some background on the roots of these genres explains what happened in the generic tree before each of these genres crystalized.

This study discusses the formulaic writing in popular genres in general, and also focuses on a few key best-selling authors. The authors were chosen from several sources, including recent 2013 *New York Times* best-seller lists, lists of best-sellers from across the twentieth century in books such as *Bestsellers: Popular Fiction Since 1900,* and lists of authors in the *Guinness Book of World Records* for their sales records, as well as authors who are frequently cited in academic and reference books as the best-known trend-setters and best-selling authors. Sales records were not the only criteria for selection, as authors who founded or established a major genre were typically included in the discussion, even if their sales were lower than those of their imitators. Typically, the trend-setters are also the best-sellers, as the fact that they founded the new popular genre makes them appealing to readers. It should be noted that the sales records of some of the discussed "best-sellers" have been doubted and scrutinized by various parties. "Paper records of sales did not get collated for statistical and comparative purposes until the late 1970s."[38] Even today, while Amazon and some other sources publicize sales records for best-sellers, publishers do not open their accounting books for the public to examine, and most companies have policies that require them to destroy old records, unless they want to keep them in a house museum for posterity, but, according to Bloom, this is almost never the case in the mainstream publishing industry. Inflating sales records early on by having a marketing firm purchase copies of your own book and thereby creating the appearance that the book is about to become a best-seller can turn a book into a best-seller because consumers assume that it must be good if it is selling well.

Will the publishing industry and the reading public become more literary or regress further into unliterary and hyper-formulaic hack work over the upcoming decades? I will not attempt to make predictions as H. G. Wells would have done, but I believe that if these trends are put under the microscope by more literary scholars, they can still be reversed.

I would like to acknowledge the University of Arizona Library for allowing me to use its enormous collection as part of my research.

Chapter 1

Formulaic Fiction Writing and the History of Literary Genres

To effectively write with the use of literary formulas, one has to understand the foundations of these formulas. Some, such as the basic formulas of poetry and drama, have remained unchanged since nearly the beginning of structured writing. Poetic meter and rhyme were invented even earlier than the first Greek written texts, as oral poets used rhythm and rhyme to better remember the lines of their long epic poems so as to perform them before audiences. Aristotle wrote rhetoric defining tragedy and comedy millennia ago, which still influences modern tragedies and comedies. In times when writers were patronized by kings and queens, they created literary formulas that suited monarchic interests. Today, when popular writers are supported by the oligopolic publishing industry and by the unliterary book-buying readers market, writers' formulas are based on the demands of this much broader market. When reading was first popularized, writers such as Charles Dickens and Benjamin Disraeli wrote condition of England and realist novels that represented the interests of the poor, who made up the majority of their public. Over the two centuries that have passed since the 1814 publication of what can be regarded as the first international best-seller, *Waverley,* the publishing industry has shifted away from portraying poverty and political corruption to primarily portraying idyllic romances, mad detectives, and other escapist worlds for "Weary Giants." As literary tastes and demands on the writers changed, so did the formulas writers use. Whenever a major change in tastes occurred, writers who survived in the market were those who adapted to new demands with revitalized generic formulas, or revived, relevant, old and nearly forgotten formulas. Frequently writers, who had the logical ability to create new formulas, also wrote rhetorical essays, diaries or letters that explained their inspirations or the genres and works on which they built their new genres. Since the major genres discussed in this book have undergone drastic revisions in the last couple of centuries, and some were even invented within this previous century, there are many critical and writer-penned explanations for generic origins and development.

Popular Writing Methodology and Story Building Techniques

There are a few repeated comments that hack, formulaic and best-selling writers frequently make when talking about their writing methods. William Nolan, a popular writer and critic, puts a few of these in the form of commands: "You must prepare fully fleshed-out biographies for your main characters"—the "protagonist," "villain," "subsidiary ... (good *or* evil) ... characters"—but not "minor characters." In addition to these bios, he "suggests" that writers write questions and answers about each character's background on color-coded cards.[1] These biographies can be a part of an "outline" of "twenty or thirty typed pages," which might also include a detailed plot, possibly with some "dialogue, miniscenes, and a chapter-by-chapter breakdown of the book's action," as Nolan states Stephen King and Peter Straub did for their *Talisman* horror novel.[2] Several other writers mention writing a detailed outline in interviews and essays, typically before saying that detailed outlining is an exception rather than their standard procedure. "*Divide and Conquer* is the first book I wrote from a detailed outline and so every day I sat down at my desk, I knew exactly what to write," Carrie Ryan, a best-selling young adult fiction writer, replied in an interview with *Pennsylvania Literary Journal*.[3] It is interesting to note that she specifically said the outline was detailed enough for her to have a specific section to write daily, so it must have been broken down into sixty or so sections (assuming that a writer under contract spends a couple of months writing a short young adult novel and then goes through the revision stages with the editor). In order to know exactly what to write, her initial outline had to include the basic structural, plot, character and setting elements to be introduced in each chapter, so that she would not have to re-read to determine her direction and could just sit down and write the set-out content for the day.

The catalyst-question technique is another common strategy modern writers use to start a new story. For example, Larry Niven (a best-selling science fiction writer who will be examined in more detail later on) writes that for his short story "Rammer," because he had noticed that his "favorite characters were all tourists," he asked himself, "What would a Niven character do if I put him where they wouldn't let him be a tourist?"[4] I asked him in a *Pennsylvania Literary Journal* interview, "Is it typical for you to begin developing a new character by asking a question? What is usually involved in your character building process? Do you draw diagrams? Write a paragraph biography? Do research on related subjects?" Niven replied, "I usually start with a question, yes, but it doesn't have to be about a character. And I usually have an answer before I start [to write]. *Destiny's Road* started with a map. But 'Rammer' (which expanded into *World Out of Time*) began and stayed with a character. 'Once there was a dead man.'"[5] Here the question acts like a hypothesis in a scientific experiment. The question is essential in science fiction and mysteries (whodunit?), while romantic comedies or spiritual narratives can begin with a unique character type or a concept (among many other possibilities).

Another brainstorming strategy that Larry Niven has used is doing "homework" for a new story by conducting "extensive" research into things such as "weaving, balloon flight, magic in anthropology."[6] This is the research approach to character and story building, in which the science fiction and fantasy characters have to be based on complex human anthropological behaviors or on behavioral studies of animals, insects or other things that have some symbolic parallels. When asked about this, Niven replied, "I read up on most of these things, but for fun. Reading generates the stories. I don't usually plot, then read ... though it happens."[7]

Working from assumptions and beliefs similar to those of Niven, after making this extensive plot line, Nolan recommends that writers keep writing until they finish the entire book: "*Never stop to revise.*" Stopping apparently interrupts Nolan's "basic flow" or "creative momentum," so that stopping for "revisions" means "your book will likely never be completed." And worse still, instead of having "fun" with writing, it will become "drudgery."[8] In other words, Nolan (and perhaps most hack writers) is paid to not edit his work and to not revise his plots if there is something wrong with them.

The term "hack" is used in this book as a technical term for a writer who writes with the goal of finishing a book as quickly as possible and making the most money possible from it, regardless of the genre in which he or she is writing. In addition, a "hack" writer's final product is always a mimicry of an established formula in their narrow genre, and its quality is always lowbrow and, as Georgette Heyer called it, "illiterate." The term "hack" was used in the nineteenth century to separate the two main groups of authors: an "anonymous hack" from the "anonymous 'lady' or gentleman' whose interest in fiction might be serious."[9] In this earlier period, fiction writing was not a suitable or culturally acceptable profession, and those from the upper class who engaged in this pastime typically used pseudonyms, or "Anonymous," as their bylines. "Hacks" from the lower and middle classes wrote fiction for money, rather than as an exercise of their intellect or as a way to spend their leisure time. A change in this pattern came when middle-class authors, including Sir Walter Scott and Charles Dickens, became popular and started treating fiction writing as a professional craft that had to meet stylistic conventions and quality standards. While some authors broke out into professional literary writing, other writers from all classes wrote lowbrow or unliterary fiction solely for a paycheck, and this group continues to be called "hacks" to this day.

Nolan further explained that the original plot line must be followed speedily until the end, as stopping to review progress is likely to lead to a revision that might make for great literature. Great works of art are always self-reflective. It takes more effort to revise a novel than to write a draft without stopping, but the latter route cannot result in anything but hack writing for profit alone. On the other hand, Nolan insists, "your ending must *satisfy* the reader." An ending to a novel that has not been reread and studied from a distance is one that cannot satisfy the reader because the writer has not become a reader himself to check for the degree of satisfaction he might receive from the narrative. Nolan goes on to say that the ending "must be a logical extension of the narrative, the inevitable result of events that you set in motion earlier. Readers must be emotionally prepared for your ending. It cannot feel forced; rather, it must grow from the soil of your narrative, from your characters, and from their problems and conflict."[10] This is a recipe for a hyper-predictable and hyper-formulaic happy ending. Millennia of classical world literature have proven that tragic endings can be cathartic and more satisfying than happy ones. All happy endings to horror novels should appear forced to a critical reader. After depicting a few, or hundreds, or even millions of deaths, a lone, naked hero overcomes the forces of nature or hell to rescue humanity and win the sexual favor of his "love" interest? Is this seriously a natural and believable happy ending?

The trouble with modern formulaic writing is not that it has too few rules, but rather that the rules are numerous and dictate the dimensions of elements that are much more complex than the boundaries they are allowed. For example, Nolan explains that he pays particular attention to names because "psychological studies have repeatedly proved that people have definite perceptions of particular names.... The menace in your story should sound mean," with a "hard and edged" name. Rhyming names, like "Dick/Rick," should be avoided because they are confusing as are "highly recognized public names" like "Elvis." He also explains that different racial, social, religious and class groups have different names, and that before creating a name one should search through a phonebook from the region where the story is taking place. "Newspapers are also good sources, especially for geographically correct names. Upper-class names are found in the society pages; middle-class names are found in the listings of community activities; working- and lower-class names (and names for elderly people) are found in the obituaries and legal columns."[11] The last comment is a bit funny, a bit offensive, and I doubt it can be statistically proven—or can it? Poor people probably die more frequently than rich people, and it is likely that poor people end up in legal notices pretty frequently. However, aren't legal notices typically for houses that are up for foreclosure or new wills that offer a fortune to a distant relative? And what about all those people who go from rags to riches from the time they are named to the time they end up in the society pages? This illogical method for finding the "right" names is one of the problems with formulaic popular fiction.

Another piece of advice frequently repeated in how-to creative writing books is that writers should try an experiment to gather dialogue content. "Sit down at the counter of a crowded coffee shop and listen to the conversations going on around you. The talkers ramble. They stray from the point. They are repetitive, shallow, and often boring. A great many words are used to say very little." In contrast to this type of dialogue, writers are asked to "compress" dialogue so that it is full of "action," "points," and "truths," all under the "mast of realistic conversation."[12] Typically, the formulaic outcome of making "points" within "realistic dialogue" is a yes/no conversation about trivial disagreements between the main characters or with opponents. The conversation goes on and on in a circular way, with two argumentative sides being presented in the middle of a deadly action scene. As a result, the conversations are both unrealistic and slow, or else they freeze the action in the middle of what was previously a boiling point. Sir Walter Scott and Charles Dickens listened to dialogues in pubs in order to mimic the regional and class accents, dialects and other variations in the speech of their characters. Only a few formulaic best-selling novelists nowadays attempt to accurately represent regional speech patterns, and those who make the attempt typically borrow regionalisms formulaically from the best-selling writers that preceded them. Most formulaic fictional conversations do indeed sound as if they could have been overheard in a coffee shop, without the writer making an attempt to edit the content down to only relevant lines for the main storyline. However, formulaic dialogue can simply move the plot along without being of interest even to the characters engaged in the "debate." Nolan gives an example of this, taken from a story called "The Wind":

> "Hello."
> "Hello, Herb?"
> "Oh, it's you, Allin."
> "Is your wife home, Herb?"
> "Sure. Why?"
> "Damn it."[13]

The windy emptiness of this part of the exchange is followed by details that further the plot by explaining future and past actions. The repetition of the word "hello" is perhaps the most common one in modern formulaic dialogues. In contrast, classical authors, as a group, have an extremely low rate of reoccurring of "hellos" in two consecutive lines of dialogue. It is a classical convention that interesting dialogue has to avoid coffee shop chatter, as well as repetitions that fail to further the story.

One of the repeated explanations for the linguistic similarities among most modern writers' best-selling novels is the current popularity of the "minimalist" style. When a work by Franz Kafka is compared to a chapter from Charles Dickens, one can see the clear distinctions in style. Even if we take two novels written in the same year, let's say 1890, we are likely to see clear linguistic, descriptive and other patterns that distinguish the individual styles of the two authors. Style is more apparent and recognizable in the work of classical well-known authors because their popularity stems from their distinctive stylistic characteristics. In contrast, if one does a comparative linguistic and descriptive study of two best-selling novels from 2009, it is likely that the styles will be very similar, and you might not be able to tell the two authors apart, even if you have read novels by both of them. They will both be "minimalists." Larry Niven mentioned this term in an interview with the *Pennsylvania Literary Journal*, when he was asked about one item from his earliest 1984 version of "Niven's Laws": "It is a sin to waste the reader's time."[14] Niven was asked, "Can you comment on how some current genre writers 'waste the reader's time' and describe what you do to avoid this?" To which he answered, "It's called padding. I'm a minimalist."[15] Across numerous interviews with and essays by currently popular writers, the common sentiment is that readers are "Weary Giants" and that writers must not "waste" their time. This law typically contributes to the writers' minimalist style, which has so many common ingredients that popular formulaic writing becomes a linguistically simplified formula, not just a structurally simplified formula. In one of the other "Niven's Laws," specifically targeted "for writers," Niven covers minimalism in more detail: "If you've nothing to say, you can say it any way you like. Stylistic innovations, contorted story line or none, exotic or genderless pronouns, internal inconsistencies: feel free. If what you have to say is important and/or difficult to follow, use the simplest language possible. If the reader doesn't get it then, let it not be your fault."[16] Unlike most popular minimalist writers, Niven manages to refrain from simplifying his stories so much that the "something" that he has to say is entirely lost in ultra-limited vocabulary and an extremely simplified plot. The philosophy that most minimalist popular writers use is different from Niven's, as they typically do not have a specific political or cultural message to convey and so can minimize their style to a much simpler formula than a writer who wants to convey a significant message in simple terms.

In summary, formulaic, best-selling writers recommend that those who want to mimic their techniques should write character biographies and detailed outlines, ask catalyst-questions to decide on the plot structure, do a minimal amount of research, never stop to revise, use standard naming rules, use coffee shop dialogue, and adopt the minimalist-to-nil style. New writers who attempt to follow these rules end up with very similar hacked, formulaic fiction.

Skeleton Stories and Computerized Formulas

A skeleton story is a basic plot line with a set of questions that guide or prompt the writer on what he or she should write next. The use of similar skeleton stories leads to plot repetitions in both classical and popular fiction. On the other hand, complex skeleton stories can be used by professional writers to create an innovative generic formula for a new fiction project. Innovation happens when the basic plot and the questions asked are original; conformity and repetition happen when they are borrowed from an earlier work or a genre of works. Writing outside of the standard skeleton stories (with or without variations) might be labeled "experimental," "absurd," or postmodern. If a new skeleton story leads to a best-seller and it is mimicked by dozens of other writers, it becomes a standard generic formula.

In a book on teaching and writing popular fiction, Karen M. Hubert encourages her students to use the "skeleton stories" that she provides across the book, stating that they give "students valuable experience with shape and form, with beginning, middle and end. Skeleton stories are like bones without flesh; they are merely plot lines.... They have roughly the same relation to fiction as a coloring book does to art." Sadly, today too many writers take the coloring book, or an established popular "skeleton story," and base entire novels on its exact dimensions, instead of only practicing on it before moving on to constructing their own newly formulated and more complex plots.

Hubert gives an example of a "romance skeleton": "Boy meets girl. Boy and girl fall in love. Boy proposes, and girl accepts. Something happens to prevent their marriage. Boy and girl overcome the problem. Boy and girl marry."[17] Hubert's book was published in 1976, so the formula is noticeably different from most romance novels published in the last decade. Still, many of the movements in the beginning and middle are the same today, and were the same back in the days of chivalry tales. Of course, this is a very basic skeleton. For popular writers who produce several books per year, this skeleton is frequently expanded into an "outline," which in its entirety might be thirty pages long, and which might include all of the minor and major plot movements, events, and character developments that occur across the novel. In addition to the plot line points, such as "girl meets boy," there are also character and setting conventions standard to formulaic romance novels. For example, in an interview, Anne Rice, the author of several best-selling vampire fantasy/horror novels, confessed that the "absolute truth" was that she could not "get through the whole book" when asked about Bram Stoker's *Dracula*: "I've read the first chapters with Jonathan Harker and some stuff in the middle and the end, and I've read plot descriptions."[18] Jonathan Harker was the protagonist in *Dracula*, the classic tale in which Count Dracula and his brides ravish Transylvania. Rice summarizes here that her technique is to study a character type and the plot line of a classical work in the genre she hopes to join. Thus, she had the plot outline of *Dracula* in mind as she composed her *Interview with the Vampire*, the first book in the Vampire Chronicles. In general, plot outlines and character studies help novelists to replicate or develop a generic formula.

Hubert gives one of the best slightly expanded versions of a skeleton outline. It is better than the outlines and skeletons provided in most how-to books written over the last couple of decades because teaching writing as a formulaic process has gone out of style, since writing for a mass audience with strict formulas has become enormously popular. This particular example is an expanded skeleton plot line for a mystery. Hubert names a plot point, and then follows it with questions that should be answered by each individual writer to create a more complex story, by adding "details that are personal and original" to the skeleton.

> *A crime is committed.* (What? A kidnapping? Murder? Theft?) *It is discovered.* (How and by whom?) *Someone decides to try to solve the mystery.* (Who and why? For money? For love? Out of curiosity?) *The crime solver suspects certain people.* (Who? What are their backgrounds? Their relationship to the deceased, victim, or stolen object?) *The crime solver looks for clues.* (Where? Does she find any? What? What do the clues suggest?) *She follows the suspects.* (Do they see her? What does she discover?) *Suddenly she finds herself in a dangerous position.* (Describe in detail. Is she caught? Is she hanging from a cliff? Stuck in an elevator in a burning building?) *She escapes, or gains control.* (How? In an elaborate way, in a simple way?) *She solves the mystery. The criminal confesses.* (What does he say?) *The mystery is solved.* (How does the mystery solver feel?)[19]

With the onset of the computer age, formulas in fiction have become more detailed and more repetitive than they were in the world of the printing press or the typewriter. John Huntington commented on H. G. Wells in 1982, "I do not mean that Wells has a machine that produces art or thought, much less answers. A small repertory of essential images of opposition permits Wells to pose in various ways central puzzles of evolution and ethics, civilization and nature."[20] Prior to the introduction of the printing press, only a small group of wealthy intellectuals could access the ancient classics and literary theory that explained the proper movements of plot in tragedy, comedy or tragicomedy. They followed the prescribed plot arcs closely, but filled in the content from historical or dramatic stories that surrounded them. After literacy spread to the lower classes at the end of the nineteenth century, the creation of stories became a profitable business, and hack writers who wanted to capitalize on this swooped into the field. They started to reproduce the plots and formulas of the most popularly successful novels in extraordinary numbers, not fearing being discovered for the repetition even in basic storylines or character names (i.e., Sherlock Holmes). Then, when computers became widely used, from the 1980s to the present day, popular novels became so formulaic that clearly computerized formulas are now used to create a plot line and major incidents, and even some minor repeating elements. Computer programs, and especially Final Draft, with its standard templates for different genres, make generating hack work easier than ever. The computerization of formulaic writing is evident in statistically significant repetitions in the character description format, among other unliterary elements. Formulaic character descriptions frequently follow the approximate formula in which a few adjectives are filled into a line of the same body portions, as in "hair ... face ... body ... clothing ... eyes." I will give examples of these formulaic repetitions from several individual writers in later chapters.

On the Unliterary

The question of literacy comes up in the field of formulaic writing and genre studies in terms of both the literacy of the formulaic writers and that of their readers. While today it is less in vogue to discuss the semi-literate in a negative light, and the modern focus is on helping to improve their literacy skills, this perspective only developed in the last few decades. Yet even recent critics typically cannot avoid talking about a popular genre or popular reading in general without touching on the role literacy plays. In addition, both literary critics and fellow authors frequently accuse popular writers themselves of being "illiterate." In this sense of the term, "illiterate" refers to anything from not being able to sign your name all the way up to an extremely poorly written popular novel. In order to explain reading habits around the world, the question of literacy has to be addressed. Why do certain people buy and read certain books, and do not buy other books? Why do some types of books sell better than others? The ability of the reader to comprehend the content in the book is a crucial element in their purchase decision, and therefore in selecting which writers and novels become best-sellers.

Lewis, James and Others on Unliterary Readers

One of the bluntest studies on the distinction between the reading habits of the "literary" and those of the "unliterary" or illiterate is C. S. Lewis' *An Experiment in Criticism*. The book was published in 1961, when he first fell ill (he died two years later in 1963). Perhaps because Lewis knew that his health was deteriorating, he wrote a biting critique like nothing else he had written. He published other short articles of criticism and some literary studies, but focused most of his writing on fiction; he is currently best known for the *Chronicles of Narnia*, due to the recent release of three popular film adaptations. While the Narnia books have sold over 100 million copies, C. S. Lewis is not listed as one of the top best-selling authors of the twentieth century in Bloom's *Bestsellers*. Lewis' *Experiment*, however, is written in a distinctly angry tone, with many negative references to the students he had taught over the decades at Oxford and Cambridge, and against numerous other groups; an especially harsh attack is made against evaluative critics, who he indirectly mentions harshly criticized his children's books. When describing the difference between literary and illiterate readers, Lewis writes:

> The first reading of some literary work is often, to the literary, an experience so momentous that only experiences of love, religion, or bereavement can furnish a standard of comparison. Their whole consciousness is changed. They have become what they were not before. But there is no sign of anything like this among the other sort of readers. When they have finished the story or the novel, nothing much, or nothing at all, seems to have happened to them.[21]

Many professors have probably thought something along these lines about the majority of students (even in prestigious schools like Oxford), who fail to fully benefit from reading good literature. As students, those who love literature are so engulfed in learning that they might not notice the apathetic student body that makes up the majority, but professors have to fight against apathy and illiterate reading on a daily basis in class. The challenge is either somehow inspiring a love for closely reading literature or giving up on the majority and primarily teaching the minority that shares an obsession with reading, as if they are communing with the dead authors they read.

Lewis' antagonism is felt when he refers to the apathetic segment among students as "them," a group that is guilty of "illiteracy, barbarism, 'crass, 'crude' and 'stock' responses."[22] One of Lewis' descriptions of the reading traits of the "majority" explains

1. Formulaic Fiction Writing and the History of Literary Genres 19

the basic principles on which the modern book publishing industry's selections and marketing are based:

    1. They never, uncompelled, read anything that is not narrative. I do not mean that they all read fiction. The most unliterary reader of all sticks to "the news." ...
    2. They have no ears. They read exclusively by eye. The most horrible cacophonies and the most perfect specimens of rhythm and vocalic melody are to them exactly equal....
    3. Not only as regards the ear but also in every other way they are either quite unconscious of style, or even prefer books which we should think badly written.... You give them, it would seem, just the sort of matter they want, but all far better done: descriptions that really describe, dialogue that can produce some illusion, characters one can distinctly imagine. They peck about at it and presently lay the book aside. There is something in it that has put them off.
    4. They enjoy narratives in which the verbal element is reduced to the minimum— "strip" stories told in pictures, or films with the least possible dialogue.
    5. They depend swift-moving narrative. Something must always be "happening." Their favorite terms of condemnation are "slow," "long-winded," and the like.[23]

These five points are exactly what separate C. S. Lewis' and J. R. R. Tolkien's illustrated books for children and adults from the appropriate literary reading material that Lewis describes. These are also the critical principles behind most of popular and formulaic literature. Today descriptions like "slow" and "long-winded" are so common in criticisms of classical and highbrow literature that even literary critics frequently engage them. Popular writers, like Stephen King, utilize these criticisms regularly to explain their anti-literary style: "I want to talk too much about the characters and that slows the story down. So I say, 'Hey, people want to find out what's going to happen next.'" King deflects the criticism that he has poor "characterization" by pointing out that readers want "plot," citing his own quote to prove this point, as if he is a large enough survey of his reading public.[24] The popularity of films and other visual and auditory arts today has further programmed the public to expect that art should be narrative- and event-focused, with minimum dialogue and narrator descriptions, and that it should go by quickly and never be seen again.

    "The hackneyed *cliché* for every appearance or emotion (emotions may be part of the Event) is for him the best because it is immediately recognizable."[25] This key statement by Lewis explains why popular literature doesn't just have a core plot line formula, but also a formula for how the words are put together, and this formula encourages the use of as many clichés and simple repeating phrases and descriptions as possible. If a writer keeps talking about "the black horse" and "the pink sunset" and exclaiming that things are "in my black book," then the unliterary reader feels at home and secure because without reading these words closely he recognizes them as familiar and therefore good. In other words, "What they therefore demand is a decent pretense of description and analysis, not to be read with care but sufficient to give them the feeling that the action is not going on in a vacuum—a few vague references to trees, shade and grass for a wood, or some allusion to popping corks and 'groaning tables' for a banquet."[26] While it seems that Lewis is upset with the unliterary, the fact is that both he and Tolkien applied this theory to create literature that the unliterary could digest by using just these sorts of basic or bare descriptions across most of their Narnia and Lord of the Rings stories.

    Recognizing that his own books were just as "escapist" as works by many other popular fantasy and science fiction writers, Lewis quantified the difference between different types of escapism:

> Now there is a clear sense in which all reading whatever is an escape. It involves a temporary transference of the mind from our actual surroundings to things merely imagined or conceived. This happens when we read history or science no less than when we read fiction. All such escape is *from* the same thing; immediate concrete actuality. The important question is what we escape *to*. Some escape into egoistic castle-building ... using escape as a substitute for action where action is appropriate, and thus neglecting real opportunities and evading real obligations.[27]

The good form of escapism is into myths or religion, or into the active acquisition of knowledge from the books being read. Thus, he classifies his "mythological" Narnia stories as a positive escape, but formulaic women's romances and mysteries as a negative escape.

The biggest contradiction in Lewis' argument is that he ridicules people who are unliterary, but while criticizing them he also makes an argument against criticism that separates things into good and bad categories. He even points out, "Inevitably all this will seem to some an elaborate device for protecting bad books from the castigation they richly deserve. It may even be thought I have an eye to my own darlings or those of my friends. I can't help that. I want to convince people that adverse judgments are always the most hazardous." He adds, "A negative proposition is harder to establish than a positive," saying it's easier to prove there is a spider in the room than that there isn't one.[28] The contradiction becomes clearer when one returns to the earlier quote about those who are unliterary—that they are guilty of "illiteracy, barbarism, 'crass,' 'crude' and 'stock' responses." Lewis is a critic criticizing criticism, while also criticizing unenthusiastic unliterary readers. This contradiction is explained by the nature of this entire book—it is an explanation behind the thought process of a writer who writes for the unliterary audience that wants events, speed, and cliché descriptions. At the same time, the explanation is made by a bitter academic who is hyper-aware of his decision to cut down on detailed descriptions and other complex story elements, despite having the natural ability to utilize these at the level of the best classical writers. As a writer, Lewis wanted the majority of readers (the unliterary) to buy his books; as an academic, Lewis wanted his students to appreciate classical, highbrow literary works. These divided interests created the structure of Lewis' argument in *An Experiment in Criticism*. Putting his biases aside, this book is a very helpful look at the thought process of a popular formulaic novelist and into the mind of the unliterary reader.

Lewis applied his theories on the unliterary to his children's literature, and especially in his best-known Narnia series. There are several key elements that make *The Lion, the Witch and the Wardrobe* accessible to unliterary readers. First, the vast majority of the words in the story are monosyllabic, especially in descriptions: "and after that was a room all hung with green, with a harp in one corner; and then came three steps down and five steps up."[29] The only words that have two syllables are "after" and "corner." Second, the same quote uses simple descriptive adjectives like "green" and basic numbers like "five," vocabulary intended for supposedly very young children or for those who are semi-literate. Simplicity of description also applies to concepts and specific historical events—for example, there is a reference on the first pages to "the war,"[30] which is neither capitalized nor numbered, thus leaving a modern-day reader uncertain which of the two world wars Lewis is referring to. The use of the term "war" refrains from confusing children and illiterate readers who might not have heard of either of these two wars. Third, the conversations the four children have at the beginning of the story express formulaic concerns common to most Western children's stories: they discuss whether they have the freedom to be noisy and do whatever they want or if the old professor they are staying with will be strict. Fourth, Lewis only offers seven large-font pages before Lucy crawls through the wardrobe and discovers snow and Narnia; thus the writer jumps into the middle of the event and action, without excessive preliminary background. Fifth, while readers are told that the professor was elderly, they are not informed of the ages (or any other characteristics) of the four heroic children, aside from their names in the first chapter, "Lucy Looks into a Wardrobe."

Finally, a very clear-cut good versus evil religious story is at the center of the narrative, which echoes the religious objectives of the Inklings group of which Lewis and Tolkien were members at Oxford. However, this can be a contested point, as Lewis mixes Christian theology with pagan mythology. In this Narnia story, Lucy encounters a creature that, according to Christian mythology, is a devil: "From the waist upwards he was like a man, but his legs were shaped like a goat's (the hair on them was glossy black) and instead of feet he had goat's hoofs. He also had a tail."[31] While we are told that he is a "Faun," this really means that he is the pagan god, Pan, on which the Christian devil imagery is based. In chapter 2, "What Lucy Found There," the Faun asks Lucy if she is "a Daughter of Eve." This question and the conclusion that Lucy is a Daughter of Eve and "human"[32] implies that she has entered a hellish dimension where devils live, most of whom have never seen a human before. The four children later become kings and queens of Narnia with the help of these devils and a Lion, which in Christian theology typically is symbolic for either Jews or Jesus; the latter makes more sense in the Narnian theology, as the Lion later dies and then is resurrected. The concept who somebody that is a staunch believer in Christian theology can invert pagan devils into friendly assistants of Christ goes over my head, and yet many Christian spiritualists argue that stretching the Christian theology with some new mythological characters is Christian, while portraying witches and wizards, as done in *Harry Potter*, is "devil's work." But, to return to formulaic writing, Lewis simplifies larger religious and moral concepts into mythological characters to dramatize the battle between good and evil, and, in theory, to explain to kids the meaning of goodness (or how to gain supreme powers in a backward world). Either way, these examples from Lewis' children's literature for the unliterary exemplify most of the rules he explained in *An Experiment in Criticism*.

Lewis is not alone in his opinions on unliterary readers, for a similar argument has been made by recent critics, such as Alan Bloom in *The Closing of the American Mind: How Higher Education Has Failed Democracy and Impoverished the Souls of Today's Students* (1987) and Neil Postman in *Amusing Ourselves to Death: Public Discourse in the Age of Show Business* (1985). Bloom's book was published by Simon and Schuster and Postman's by Penguin Books, two companies that have a strong financial and cultural interest in the survival of literary reading.

Among the classical, literary writers who rebelled against the changes that eventually led to the current publishing oligopoly and repetitive formulaic writing was Henry James (1843–1916), who is best known for his realist novels: *The Portrait of a*

Lady (1880) and *The Turn of the Screw* (1898). James saw the trend toward formulaic crowd-pleasing fiction in 1884, when he wrote in his essay "The Art of Fiction" about what people typically consider to be "good" fiction: "'happy endings' … a distribution at the last of prizes, pensions, husbands, wives, babies, millions, appended paragraphs and cheerful remarks," and "being full of incident and movement, so that we shall wish to jump ahead, to see who was the mysterious stranger, and if the stolen will was ever found, and shall not be distracted from this pleasure by any tiresome analysis or 'description.'" James judged that for the common reader, the

> "artistic" idea would spoil some of their fun. One would hold it accountable for all the description, another would see it revealed in the absence of sympathy. Its hostility to a happy ending would be evident, and it might even, in some cases, render any ending at all impossible. The "ending" of a novel is, for many persons, like that of a good dinner, a course of dessert and ices, and the artist in fiction is regarded as a sort of meddlesome doctor who forbids agreeable aftertastes.

Lewis mentioned some of these repetitions in formulaic fiction, but he also practiced these techniques in his own writing. However, James was sincere in his disdain for "happy endings" and other anti-literary formulaic conventions and shunned them in his own work because he believed they did not reflect the "reality" of peoples' lives. Henry James was possibly the most outspoken literary critic and theorist from the realist movement. He gives several general rules about the "formulation" of realist fiction "The Art of Fiction": "In proportion as in what she offers us we see life *without* rearrangement do we feel that we are touching the truth; in proportion as we see it *with* rearrangement do we feel that we are being put off with a substitute, a compromise and convention."[33] On the other hand, James shared a belief in literary conventions with his contemporary literary novelists: "If there are exact sciences there are also exact arts," such as the "grammar of painting." Yet James insists that the science of the novel cannot be simplified to a

> factitious, artificial form, a product of ingenuity, the business of which is to alter and arrange the things that surround us, to translate them into conventional, traditional moulds. This … view … condemns the art to an eternal repetition of a few familiar *clichés*, cuts short its development, and leads us straight up to a dead wall. Catching the very note and trick, the strange irregular rhythm of life, that is the attempt whose strenuous force keeps Fiction upon her feet.[34]

Henry James offers prophetic advice. Because the art of the popular novel is hyper-formulaic today, best-selling novels are "repetitions of a few familiar clichés," which stopped developing after reaching a point of minimalist descriptions of both actions and characters, and with only the bones of suspense to support their progress.

The Unliterary Oligopoly

Lewis explained the correlation between unliterary readers and writers in terms of popular demand from an unliterary mass public and supply by a circle of unliterary formulaic novelists who create the type of fiction that an unliterary readership can read. A more recent, and an even more biting, study of this phenomenon was made by Arthur Vanderbilt in *The Making of a Bestseller: From Author to Reader*. Unlike Lewis, Vanderbilt spends less time on explaining the minds of apathetic unliterary readers, and more on the process that goes into making best-selling popular novels by authors and their publishing assistants. Vanderbilt offers many quotes on the technically brilliant writing processes from great classical novelists, like Fitzgerald and Hemingway, but shows that most of these best-selling literate authors died in obscurity before the grandeur of their writing was immortalized and their post-life sales were guaranteed to stretch over the following century. Then he shows the completely horrendous process that goes into "the making" of an unliterary best-seller. He investigates some of the key factors that have brought unliterary authors to the top of the publishing industry over the last half-century. The numbers argue that literary, classical authors are likely to enrich a company in the long run more than unliterary authors do for the companies that chase these best-sellers. For example, between 2000 and 2001, Pearson, McGraw-Hill, Scholastic and Random House were among the top five publishers with the best sales numbers in the business, totaling between 4.9 and 1.8 billion in 2001; meanwhile, Harlequin Books (romance novels) and AOL/Time Warner (movies and the Internet) were at the bottom of this list of the top twenty, with sales between .4 and .3 billion in 2001.[35] However, Random House and some of these other traditionally literary houses have started publishing enormous quantities of romance and other generic and unliterary novels. So, the question of whether literary classics or formulaic best-sellers sell more over the lifetime of the top titles is not a simple one. Why are most of the top best-selling authors from the twentieth century in the "unliterary," formulaic category?

In order for the market to be inundated with unliterary writers, literary writers have to somehow be prevented from entering and competing. The first hurdle that literary writers face in their attempts to succeed in literature is the gates of the publishers' acquisition process: "Authors have always felt that unless a writer is known to a publishing house, a proven name, a submission receives only the most perfunctory attention. Some interesting literary experiments certainly justify this sort of paranoia." These experiments include several attempts to put a different title and author's name on a manuscript that has previously been successful as a work of art, or commercially, and them submit it to publishers and producers, who all (according to these experiments) refuse publication or production, without realizing the similarity, or the work's value, because it was submitted by an unknown writer.[36] In addition, most of the major oligopoly publishers today have gotten rid of their "slush pile" by instituting policies that forbid the submission of "unsolicited" manuscripts and require that all writers who want to work with them go through one of the top few "literary" agents. The trend against unsolicited manuscripts and the slush pile began in 1974, when Doubleday started returning these "unopened."[37]

The second hurdle for literary writers is that they have a difficult time finding celebrity politicians or other popular figures who are able to read a well-constructed, dense, literary work and give praise or a blurb to support it. Praise from celebrities frequently catapults sales of almost any unliterary, hack work that is thus advertised. "It is ... endorsements from outside of the book world—especially by a leader of the free world—that can have the most dramatic effect on sales." Among politicians who have significantly multiplied sales are President Ronald Reagan, Prime Minister Stanley Baldwin, President Theodore Roosevelt, President Woodrow Wilson and even Eleanor Roosevelt. "You don't even need those few words if the president doesn't really like your book or doesn't have time to read it; just have him hold it."[38] For over three decades, Oprah Winfrey was a key media celebrity who boosted book sales, but she has been less influential since her daytime talk show went off the air in 2011. Oprah's support of President Barack Obama's campaign was one of the key elements that pushed him toward victory. Thus, the relationship between the success of politicians and the success of a media product is a very reciprocal one. Best-selling authors, talk-show hosts and politicians receive prime airtime to sell themselves or their work to the public. A brilliant unknown author has no chance of being interviewed by a host like Oprah, or to sell his or her book on national television. The one exception to this rule is that some entrepreneurial unknown authors have bought airtime on programs like shopping networks. Thus, money or celebrity is required in order to gain more money and celebrity.

Unknown and poorer writers and publishers also have difficulty breaking into the *New York Times* best-seller list and thus reaching an audience for their writing because wealthy publishers and writers can manipulate the list by creating an artificial initial spike in sales through purchasing a few thousand books from the bookstores that the list surveys, or the list can count books that are "in print" instead of books "sold." Vanderbilt explains that out of the 250 million people who make up the U.S. population, "in a slow season, the sale of 50,000 books may be enough to propel a new title onto the national best-sellers list."[39] Despite the doubling of the population, between 1923 and the present day the top best-sellers have continued to sell between 200,000 and 2 million copies per year, with some extremes on both ends. For a struggling new writer or a small independent publisher, buying 50,000 copies of their own book, or even just doing a print run of this many copies, is an enormous fiscal loss, which would bankrupt them if the scheme fell short of a best-seller. Even buying as few as 2,000 copies in 1990 of *Confessions of an S. O. B.* landed the work on the *NYT* list.[40] However, the top publishing companies have merged into a handful of conglomerates that can invest and lose a few million dollars without feeling the damage among their billions. Best-seller lists have been "scrutinized" by numerous other critics and compared with wholesale and bookstore sales records, but the major best-seller lists continue the practice of "statistical sampling," in which "each week staff members contact independent and chain bookstores" and then make use of "a statistically weighted evaluation of sales to determine bestsellers."[41] Similar strategies are used by *Publishers Weekly* and *USA Today*, despite numerous studies that have found how these types of calculations can be easily manipulated. Because the *New York Times*, *Publishers Weekly* and *USA Today* also make enormous revenue from running the "best-selling" publishers' ads, it is a mystery why consumers continue to trust these rankings.

Literary writers primarily fail to succeed because they fail to find literary readers. Publishing companies have merged and become an oligopoly, which prevents smaller competitors' successful entry into the market, and as a result overall book sales and literacy have declined in America. "The wave of mergers, consolidations and acquisitions by foreign corporations has left the publishing industry with just a handful of major houses that can grab a seat at the table and bid on the megadeals that now dominate the business."[42] Albert Greco offers the bare numbers to quantify this trend: "Between 1960 and 1989, there were a reported 573 mergers and acquisitions in the U.S. book publishing industry.... Although this is a staggering total, the pace between 1990 and 2002 was absolutely frenetic. There were an estimated 300 mergers and acquisitions between 1990 and 1995" and "380 mergers between 1996 and 2001."[43]

In contrast to this publishing oligopoly, "old line publishers—the Scribners, the Doubledays, the Knopfs—were proud of publishing books that they considered of literary value."[44] In an oligopoly, the top publishers do not have competitors that can change their business policies, so they can reduce overhead by "cutting staff, cutting promotion budgets, and raising the price of books, all of which can lessen the quality of books and shrink their market."[45] Since there are few players in an oligopoly and each of them is grabbing billions of dollars in revenue, the gradual decline in book purchases and the deterioration into unliterary formulaic fiction is ignored by these giants, as if these problems are flies on a Cyclops.

One of the chief causes of the financial problems that caused publishers to merge is the extremely high return rate for books shipped to bookstores and distributors. "Today, a publisher is jubilant if its returns are 20 percent or less, with a 42 percent return being average for hardcover fiction today, a return rate of 60 percent for fiction by unknown authors, and a 40 to 50 percent return just about average for mass market titles. Twenty years ago [in 1979] a return rate of 10 to 15 percent was standard."[46] Albert N. Greco gives more precise percentages for return rates: "Between 1996 and 2002, the mass-market paperback segment withstood the greatest onslaught of returns, ranging from an unacceptable 42.3 percent rate in 1995 to a Herculean 50 percent pace in 2001." Greco concludes, "The data is clear and unequivocal; this is a hit-driven, 'crapshoot' business with staggering title output and equally staggering returns."[47] For an unknown literary author, a return of 60 or more percent of their books means that they either barely break even against their advance or fail to reach it (if the initial order was small to begin with). The loss of these printed books counts as a deduction from the author's profits. If the books were not returnable, as they were before Richard Simon invented consignment sales to bookstores in the 1920s, these losses would be far less devastating.

The problem of the growth of a publishing oligopoly, or, as Jason Epstein calls them, "tyrannies,"[48] in America and other major world literary markets is better addressed by an insider. Epstein reflects on the more than fifty years he spent working in the New York publishing industry, after graduating from Columbia University and trying a year of graduate school before he turned twenty-two. He first joined Doubleday and worked there for eight years, and then resigned and worked for Random House for the remainder of his career. Epstein, in part, left Doubleday because he realized its stand on censorship. Doubleday became stringent in the 1940s, when it lost a Supreme Court case and had to withdraw Edmund Wilson's *Memoirs of Hecate County* because in it "a woman puts her hand on or near a man's private parts."[49] During Epstein's time with Doubleday, a friend introduced him to Vladimir Nabokov and gave him a copy of *Lolita* to review, which Epstein recommended for publication and released in parts in the journal *The Anchor Review*, but Doubleday refused to publish, to Epstein's great dismay and disappointment, resulting in his eventual exit from Doubleday. He explains that the bulk of his job for these publishing houses was acquiring and editing books, but that across these decades he also tried to start his own independent ventures, with varying degrees of success. These ventures included his foundation of the *New York Review of Books* in 1963 to compete with the *New York Times* book review section. Epstein's historically most significant achievement was the founding of Doubleday's Anchor Books, "the intellectually oriented series of paperbacks that precipitated what to my surprise became known as the paperback revolution."⁵⁰ This "paperback revolution" later led to the explosion of cheap paperbacks that allowed romance and mystery publishers to dominate the publishing world with their "trash" novels. Epstein left Doubleday for Random House as he saw this revolution running out of control, without a significant profit from his "invention" of cheap paperbacks. Then, in the mid–1980s Epstein helped to finalize the creation of the Library of America, after a nearly violent competition for a National Endowment for the Humanities grant with the Modern Languages Association. Just as the Library of America came together, Epstein started working on a new idea, *The Reader's Catalog,* "a two-thousand-page list of more than forty thousand titles,"⁵¹ but this venture, after a decade in the works, did not take off because of competition from another popular catalog-like database that sells books online: Amazon.

Epstein explains how the small literary publishing houses with extremely low overhead gradually merged, due to overestimating their earning potential, with larger and larger ventures, which in turn quickly realized that publishing is an extremely risky business and abandoned their investments to be picked up by bigger-still conglomerates. These mergers began early on, so that "by 1969, Random House had acquired Alfred A. Knopf, had been acquired in turn by RCA,"⁵² and that was only the beginning. Many of the other American publishers merged with CBS, ABC, and MCA Universal. When Random House went public and allowed public confidence to determine its capital investment in 1959, a year after Epstein joined it, its stock price started to plummet and its profitability became very risky. But, after holding the hot potatoes of literary publishing for a few decades, these "conglomerates" eventually dropped them. "When General Electric ... acquired RCA in 1986, it immediately expelled two divisions that didn't meet its standard of profitability: a poultry grower and Random House."⁵³ By 2001, Random House had been combined not only with Epstein's first employer, Doubleday, but also with Knopf, Bantam, Pantheon, Dell, Crown and Ballantine. The last was one of the major romance novel publishers when that industry first bloomed, and all of these houses had conflicting editorial priorities prior to merging. The companies that fused with Random House form only a single conglomerate, but the system is not a monopoly.

> General book publishing in the United States is currently dominated by five empires. Two are based in Germany—Bertelsmann, which owns the Random House group, and Holtzbrinck, which owns St. Martin's and Farrar, Straus & Giroux. Longmans, Pearson, based in London, owns the Viking, Penguin, Putnam, Dutton group, and Rupert Murdoch's News Corporation owns HarperCollins and William Morrow. Simon & Schuster and Pocket Books belong to Viacom, which owns Paramount Pictures and MTV among other media properties. By liquidating redundant overheads these corporate owners hope to improve the low profit margins typical of the industry.⁵⁴

This list includes nearly all major book publishers and makes up an overwhelming share of the worldwide publishing industry. Yet, because there are still five competitors, they are continuing the process of driving each other out of business, and in the next couple of decades the world might end up with just one publishing monopoly that has successfully eaten all of its competitors—at least, that is what Epstein foresees. Epstein points out that between 1986 and 1996, as the quantity of major publisher-holding companies shrank, the best-sellers gained a larger market share, until "sixty-three of the one hundred best-selling titles were written by a mere six writers, Tom Clancy, John Grisham, Stephen King, Dean Koontz, Michael Crichton, and Danielle

Steel."[55] The lack of significant competition for a "literary" marketplace and the overabundance of competition for unliterary best-sellers created this skewed system. The other future Epstein proposes is a world of pure self-publishing via print-on-demand by enterprising authors, such as King's 2000 sale of his *Riding the Bullet* ghost story via his own website and the Espresso single-book printing machines that sprang up around the country shortly after Epstein predicted their emergence.[56] If anything, he is certain that Random House has not been able to acquire the types of quality classical long-run authors that it was able to pick up between the start of the bloom in New York publishing in the 1920s (i.e., Liveright's Modern Library, which became Random House in 1927) and the beginning of its collapse at the end of the 1960s. Today, Random House does not have to acquire new decades-later-to-be-classical writers because if it shuts down, it can continue to make a profit from its "backlist" titles, including works by "Kafka, Proust, Camus, Faulkner, O'Neill, Dr. Seuss."[57] However, these companies have not shut down, and instead overextended their reach while failing to find equivalent new titles, and they have been forced into mergers to satisfy the bankers.

One of the reasons these older entities, like Random House, have not been able to find new great authors is because authors currently use agents who have publishers bidding on the best-selling authors and driving the price of good authors out of the reach of good publishers, and good authors can wither if they work with publishers that are only profit-driven, rather than artistically inclined.[58] "Name-brand authors need publishers only to print and advertise their books and distribute them to the chains."[59] Epstein writes in frustration that while authors previously needed his editorial advice to make great literature, modern authors only need a printer and marketer, unless they opt for using ghostwriters and editors who reformulate their plot and simplify their language, rather than increasing the work's literary value. Stephen King explained that he left Doubleday because the "fifty-fifty paperback split" was "an awful lot to pay for what is essentially an agent's fee."[60] King was receiving 50 percent of all profits from paperback sales, and thought this was too low, which is that problem the Epstein is lamenting—when a publisher has to pay a brand author more than 50 percent, it is cutting so far into its profits that it can hardly afford to pay its editors. King has also frequently joked in interviews that he is "such a brand name" that he could sell his "laundry list."[61] "Name-brand authors" pull publishers into buying their worst work, while writers who do not have recognizable names have trouble selling their best work; thus, the entire publishing industry is diluted.

While the situation was bleak for Lewis in 1961 at Oxford and Cambridge in Britain, illiteracy in America was even worse back then, and it has slid downward over the following decades:

> A study prepared in 1978 indicated that 54 percent of American men and 46 percent of American women do not read books.... Today, twenty-five million adult Americans cannot read or write, period. Forty-five million are functionally illiterate, cannot read a help wanted ad or recipe, write a check or address an envelope. It is estimated that sixty million adult Americans can't read or write beyond an eighth grade level. This number is said to be increasing by 800,000 to one million each year. A 1993 survey released by the Department of Education found that ninety million Americans over the age of sixteen do not have the most basic reading and writing skills required for employment.... Every year, 700,000 students graduate without the ability to read their diplomas.... Literate reading has been declining among young adults during the last two decades ... [and] more than half of all college seniors flunked a basic history and literature test.... Illiteracy gets all

the press, but just as sad a problem is aliteracy, which has been defined as the ability to read without the desire to do so. This affliction, even among high school and college graduates, is rampant.[62]

While these numbers are from more than a decade ago, the fact that America is near bankruptcy, crime is still on the rise, and the publishing industry remains in financial distress are all indicators that these statistics have only slid further since 1999. Across the nineteenth century, intellectuals fought in print, in courts and in legislatures across the world to help the poor by creating a free public education system. In contrast, in the twentieth century American anti-intellectuals have fought against the education system and for their freedom to refrain from learning. The battle has not yet been lost, but publishers are aware that the "barbarians," or the unliterary, are an overwhelming majority, and therefore they also adapt an anti-intellectual and an anti-literary stand in their publishing decisions. The chicken-and-the-egg problem is that if children read more enjoyable, current, literary literature, they would be less likely to become unliterary and anti-intellectual. Publishers do not account for the sales success of classical writers over the centuries, nor the potential gains from radically changing their publishing choices; instead, the oligopoly follows a stringent set of formulaic rules that are doggedly anti-literary. Thus, even the publishers are helping to make "book reading" into "an imperiled, disappearing activity."[63]

Aware of the publishers' anti-literary preferences, authors who strive to create best-sellers, like Stephen King, argue that "what has to come first is total accessibility to the reader,"[64] or the plainest possible language and style that will be legible to the unliterary and the barely literate. In another interview, King made an even more direct statement, when he called movies "a medium that any illiterate with $4 can experience ... what [critics are] doing is taking a movie that's made, at the basic level, for illiterates, and criticizing this as if it were the work of Immanuel Kant. In that sense, the novel of *The Shining* is certainly better than the film."[65] King is arguing that critics should not evaluate his generic horror novels with the same yardstick they use for literature because his novels are made "for illiterates." If King put this blurb on his back covers, I would count it as fair advertising.

For literary authors who manage to break through the initial hurdle of acquisition, the next major challenge is that the big publishing houses are likely to refrain from funding a sales campaign with an unknown or literary author at its head. An "advertising and promotion budget is set for each book, based on the size of the author's advance, the author's track record, any good things that have so far happened to the book (the receipt of blurbs, a sale to a magazine or book club, or a television or movie production deal)."[66] Those at the top of this scale receive millions for a sales campaign, which might include sending chocolates with review copies and throwing attention-grabbing launch parties, like Random House's "book party at a topless bar for its mystery novel *Topless*."[67] While some small publishers can also afford the drive to the topless bar, a literary author would be less likely to think that his appearance at the bar would help his career. Big publishers create best-sellers by inundating the public with advertisements, news appearances, and various other types of costly promotion. A new author, literary or unliterary, cannot create equivalent sales with their first novel without investing their own capital into the campaign to create a proven track record. As a result, few "new" authors break into the top best-sellers list, which has been populated by celebrity authors, such as Stephen King and Danielle Steel, for many decades. While in the first half of the twentieth century Oxford professors, like Lewis and Tolkien, could break into the mainstream by "writing down" to the populace, more recently only secondary teachers like Dan Brown and Stephen King have managed to break in. Have you heard of a best-selling novel from a Harvard or Oxford professor in the last five decades? Impeccable literary technique is insignificant without a proven track record of extraordinary book sales.

Stephen King has explained several of his sales techniques in interviews, one of his top strategies for selling more books. King points out, "I *can* at least go on a talk show and talk. A lot of writers can't. Writers tend to be an inarticulate bunch, taken as a whole. And of course, talk shows, TV, and radio don't really want writers to discuss anything. They want you to entertain. You've got to get out there and tap dance your balls off. And a lot of writers can't, or if they can, they won't, because they feel it intrudes on their dignity. I guess I felt I didn't have much dignity anyway, so what the hell."[68] Harvard professors would not put their names on a formulaic horror novel because it would indeed interfere with their "dignity." But it costs both "dignity" and money to succeed in advertising a best-seller, as King stresses: "That's the nature of that beast ... you have to prime the pump with so much money before you get anywhere."[69] Among the various ways in which King pumped money into his advertising campaigns was buying WACZ, his local radio station in his hometown in Maine. He explained this move as a "chance to plow money into the community where I live." At the same time King confesses that those who work for the station make "slave wages" and that he wants to do "radio drama" with the help of the station with "theater-of-the-mind programming" in which he would participate, selling his own stories.[70] King has fully utilized this radio channel to advertise himself and his work. A writer who can buy the media channels that might review or criticize his work and life is one who is more likely to run a successful promotion campaign than one working on "slave wages" and trying to make art.

Another interesting way in which brand-name authors and filmmakers can make additional money from their books is by running advertisements for "name-brand products." If you are watching a blockbuster film and you see a star drinking Coke or Pepsi, you can logically conclude that the name-brand company paid between a few hundred thousand and a few million dollars for this advertisement. Stephen King has replied to critics who noticed the use of name-brand products in his works by saying that they create an "environment that the reader can identify with totally." Thus, he argues that he might use "Triscuit or Colgate in every book" if these are "something that everybody knows about.... Anywhere in New York, anywhere in the country, somewhere there's going to be a Coke sign. People identify with Coke."[71] While it might be true that there is a Coke sign "somewhere," it's more likely that King profits from these ads than that readers feel comforted by reading repetitions of brand names that they are also saturated with in TV and other repetitive commercials.

One of these hurdles, in theory, should apply to hack new writers rather than to literary writers, but frequently it trips up the latter as well. The *New York Times* book review section can "break" a book's sales, and inclusion and a positive review mean an enormous jump upward in sales. Vanderbilt argues that the *New York Times* should refrain from running negative reviews, and should only review the books that the reviewers liked. This is one point on which I disagree with Vanderbilt. He quotes many hostile and negative reviews that destroyed books and writers' careers, but most of the quotes accurately match the problems in the formulaic hack novels under review. A much bigger problem is that frequently best-selling authors, like Stephen King, receive positive reviews of their new books even if their literary value is far less than the value of the worst negative review offered by the same publication. If *New York Times* book reviews were more vigilant and much more negative, they would be likely to single-handedly drag the whole publishing industry upward. As things stand, new authors and poorly advertised literary fiction infrequently make it into the *New York Times*' review columns, and it stands as yet another barking guardian of best-sellerdom. Vanderbilt compares critics to the Food and Drug Administration, but without a "structured screening process."[72] I think the two are much further apart, and the current review system would be closer to the FDA if the federal agency only approved drugs that are poisonous and currently outlawed (ecstasy, heroine, etc.) and refused to allow drugs that cure cancer, tuberculosis and other debilitating diseases.

Critics are biased toward the major publishing houses that treat books like household products in part because they buy costly advertisements that keep the newspapers and magazines alive in an age when readership of printed newspapers and magazines is sharply declining. "Although publishers have never stated publicly that they run ads to foster good relations with a particular publication, many publishers have conceded that their advertising is sometimes run"[73] to encourage a publication like the *New York Times* to release positive reviews of its titles. Literary writers and independent publishers that cannot afford to run daily page-sized ads for weeks or months in these publications are much less likely to be selected for reviews.

The last and the biggest hurdle to quality literary production is the formulaic writing and editing process and its formulaic novel output. This is the key subject of this book: How and why do most of the books that become best-sellers shortly after their release have repetitious, generic formulas? Vanderbilt explains this phenomenon as the process of agents, ghostwriters and editors building "consciously crafted" "best-sellers." He brings up an interesting example of how an agent hired a ghostwriter to write his future best-seller novel, and "two attractive stewardesses" to sell the book on "a cross-country publicity tour."[74] Since few writers are good at public appearances, the stellar performance most best-selling writers make when appearing on national television shows suggests that the practice of hiring doubles and ghostwriters is common, rather than exceptional. If a ghostwriter or an overzealous editor is hired for a project, they are typically asked to create a book that uses a specific formula from a prior best-seller; in other words, "a publisher's idea of a good book is a book very much like another book that has sold well."[75] This process creates what even Stephen King calls a "big Mac," as the best-selling formulas chosen are always simplistic (so as to speed up the delivery of a sellable manuscript). Literary writers have the choice of either agreeing to this process and making their works unliterary or privately funding or finding funders for their literary work. As a result, many literary fiction writers today rely on government grants and fellowships to create and publish their masterpieces, rather than on the publishing business. Literary writers are much less likely to agree to turn their opus into a big Mac than unliterary hack writers who just want to make a buck from the venture. For example, Scott Fitzgerald thought that he was "writing down" when he wrote *The Great Gatsby*;[76] try as they might to make a big Mac, literary giants frequently end up making a classic (in other words, a postmortem best-seller).

The triumph of big Mac fiction over literary fiction is mystifying until one looks at these clear hurdles that prevent literary writers, without the capital to promote themselves, from competing with oligopoly publishers and their army of ghostwriters, "golden" doctor editors, aggressive sales tacticians and various other assistants.

Booker's Basic Plots and Other Perspectives

My approach to literary formulas is similar to the categorization model used by Christopher Booker in his recently released *Seven Basic Plots*.[77] He demonstrates that there is a similar pattern that most genres of fiction are based on, and that this pattern has some basic variations that break down into seven plot patterns (with two additional minor variations). Like many of his predecessors, he breaks down novel-time into five basic stages and explains the changes in mood (suffering vs. joy, success vs. failure, or constriction vs. freedom) that typically occur during each of these five stages.[78]

Booker explains that a "properly constructed" story goes through five major stages in its plot. In the first stage, the hero (H) (this can be a heroine, but she would

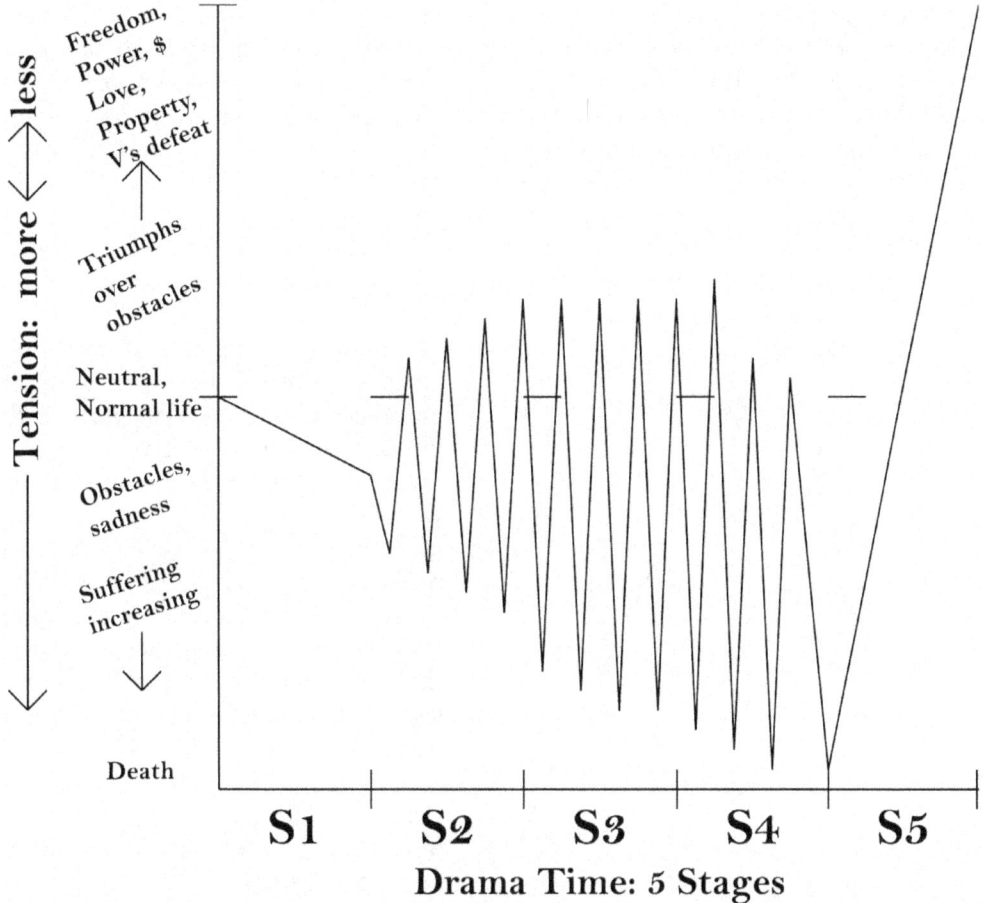

Figure 1. Tension and Happiness versus Suffering through the 5 Stages of Drama Time.

be taking the masculine or dominant role) is frustrated, incomplete, and constricted, which means there is tension that needs to be resolved, and the hero begins taking action. One or more obstacles are typically presented at this stage to inspire the hero with a need for action. The obstacles across the drama are created by the villain or a group of villains (V). The villain can also be a hero-villain (HV), meaning the hero himself. The second stage begins with the hero setting out on a voyage, a quest or some other attempt to achieve his goal. Beginning on this course is difficult. The hero starts to see dramatic action—in other words, the movement and change in his successes and failures to overcome the presented obstacles. Tension and suspense are created when a new threat to the hero's life or well-being is presented, as the reader sympathizes with the hero and waits with suspense and fear for the hero's triumph or potential death. Changes of setting are common in the middle three stages. The hero overcomes the initial small conflicts or obstacles presented by the villain, but barely so, without seeing significant overall success. In the third stage, the hero overcomes more severe constrictions (or limitations on his freedom, life, success, etc.). The hero receives a clarification of the true power of evil and realizes his own injurious weaknesses. In the fourth stage, the hero sees potential for success, but the villain's power becomes overwhelming (this is both extremely confusing and threatening for the hero). The hero manages to barely overcome the new obstacles, but each new threat is more and more life-threatening, and typically the hero nears death; this lowest point is the "Nightmare Climax," when the hero's victory seems impossible. In the final fifth stage, tension is resolved via a reversal, which is always extremely sudden and therefore surprising. The hero kills or overpowers the villain (or is himself overthrown if he is HV), and the various supporting plot lines are also resolved positively and unknotted, decreasing confusion and removing all of the previously presented threats to the dramatic world's happiness and life. The hero and all the other "good" characters experience an increasing sense of liberation and an "opening to life" leading up to a complete "happily ever after."

Booker spends most of the book giving examples of how this common plot line and the 7–9 basic plots work in classical and popular world literature. The seven main plots present variations in the basic plot formula, including the different form plots take when a hero-villain replaces the hero as the main character. For example, HVs only exist in tragedies, in which they die or become completely powerless in the end; the HV's final death means a positive ending for the other characters that were negatively affected by HV across the drama. I translated this universal plot summary into Figure 1 because it does not fit the curve-shaped plot structure that most composition students see in high

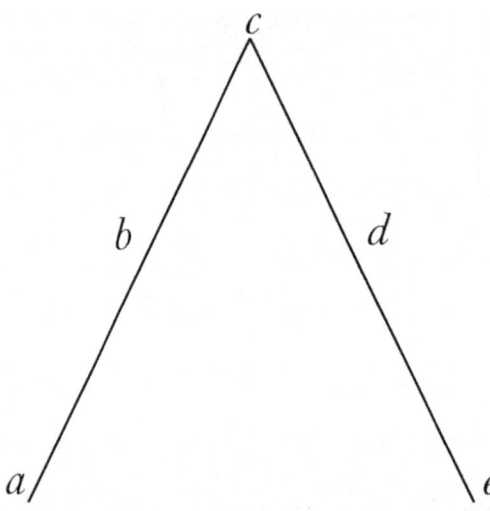

Figure 2. Gustav Freytag's Dramatic Structure Pyramid.

school or college. In fact, Gustav Freytag's plot diagram is frequently misrepresented. On page 115 of an early English translation of Freytag's *Technique of the Drama*, the diagram in Figure 2 appears.[79]

Freytag's pyramid has been translated into the term "dramatic arc" by modern critics, who have misinterpreted the points on his diagram and transformed it into a bell curve, like the one used to demonstrate visually where the grades on an exam fall. In a bell curve there is the highest point, similar to Freytag's pyramid. Both are also symmetrical. In a bell curve around 68 percent of the space under the curve is near the middle, or within one standard deviation, and there are two tails that spread out, getting lower and lower in both directions. A search online returns several images of this bell curve arc, but most of them are from blogs or other informal websites, so I have created my own version of this diagram in Figure 3.

I have to take you back to my youth to explain what bothers me about the bell curve dramatic arc. When I first saw this curve in high school as a demonstration of the dramatic arc, it troubled me enormously. I tried asking the teacher questions about how it can possibly be representative of a dramatic plot, but she moved on to other topics. Here is approximately what I was pondering: If the Y axis represents "Narrative Tension," or suspense and action, and the x axis represents "Narrative Time," which actual dramatic story can possibly match this curve? I imagined a drama in which the first quarter is at near flat-line, with nothing much happening, and later there is a steady snail-speed acceleration in tension, which then gains in speed in slight degrees, reaches top excitement at the middle of the book, and then gradually gets more and more boring and less tense across the entire second half of the book. The students in my introductory literature and composition classes over the last four years have also struggled to understand this diagram. Clearly a slightly more mathematical or logical approach is needed for understanding dramatic tension across dramatic time.

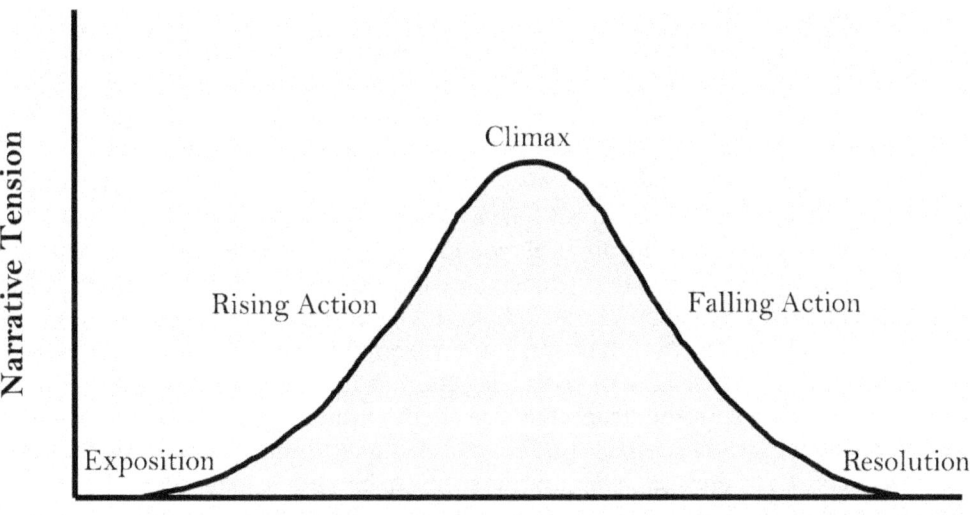

Figure 3. Dramatic Arc: The Bell Curve.

Gustav Freytag explained his original pyramid in section II, "Five Parts and Three Crises of the Drama," of "Chapter II: The Construction of the Drama" as follows:

> Through the two halves of the action which come closely together at one point, the drama possesses—if one may symbolize its arrangement by lines—a pyramidal structure. It rises from the *introduction* with the entrance of the exciting forces to the *climax*, and falls from here to the *catastrophe*. Between these three parts lie (the parts of) the *rise* and the *fall*. Each of these five parts may consist of a single scene, or a succession of connected scenes, but the climax is usually composed of one chief scene. These parts of the drama, (*a*) introduction, (*b*) rise, (*c*) climax, (*d*) return or fall, (*e*) catastrophe, have each what is peculiar in purpose and in construction. Between them stand three important scenic effects, through which the parts are separated as well as bound together. Of these three dramatic moments, or crises, one, which indicates the beginning of the stirring action, stands between the introduction and the rise; the second, the beginning of the counter action, between the climax and the return; the third, which must rise once more before the catastrophe, between the return and the catastrophe. They are called here the exciting moment or force, the tragic moment or force, and the moment or force of the last suspense. The operation of the first is necessary to every play; the second and third are good but not indispensable accessories.[80]

Freytag realizes in the last sentence that the terms he is using cannot apply to all forms of drama. The middle and the end of some dramas end up differently than a fall and a catastrophe. In comparison, Booker's recent description of the common plot pattern uses more neutral terms to allow for both tragedies and comedies. The term "catastrophe" hints at a death or a negative ending, unlike the terms "resolution" or "conclusion," which imply an untangling of the events and a final victory of the hero or the catastrophe of the hero-villain (depending on the particular plot structure employed in a given drama). Booker explains how Freytag uses this term: in "tragic stories ... the hero or heroine's fortunes usually begin by rising, but eventually 'turn down' to disaster (the Greek word *catastrophe* means literally a 'down stroke,' the downturn in the hero's fortunes at the end of a tragedy)." In a comedy there is "*peripeteia* or 'reversal of fortune.'"[81] This distinction was the reason Freytag expressed hesitation about the exactness of his pyramid shape for other genres, including comedies.

Besides Freytag and Booker, there are many other diagrams that are used to represent dramatic tension in the main movements of the plot. One other alternative I should mention is Victoria Lynn Schmidt's eight diagrams for possible curves of the plot. Most of her lines are curved, but I have used straight, simplified lines and placed all of these lines one under the other, so you can see them comparatively in Figure 4.

Each of the peaks represents a tension peak. If the peak touches the top of the designated space for tension in the structure, it is a climax. According to these structures, there can be up to five climaxes in a story, exemplified by the episodic structure. If the peak and fall of the climax takes a longer period of time, it is designated as a major climax; in the episodic structure there are five minor climaxes, without a major climax. The majority of examples used to give examples of these structures are films like *Jurassic Park* and *Forrest Gump*, so this seems to be a guide focused on screenplay writers trying to figure out what film producers mean by a three-act structure in film scripts. Another interesting aspect about these diagrams is that some of the hills do not align with the next hill in the structure (especially in the episodic structure). This represents "a series of chapters or stories linked together by the same place or theme

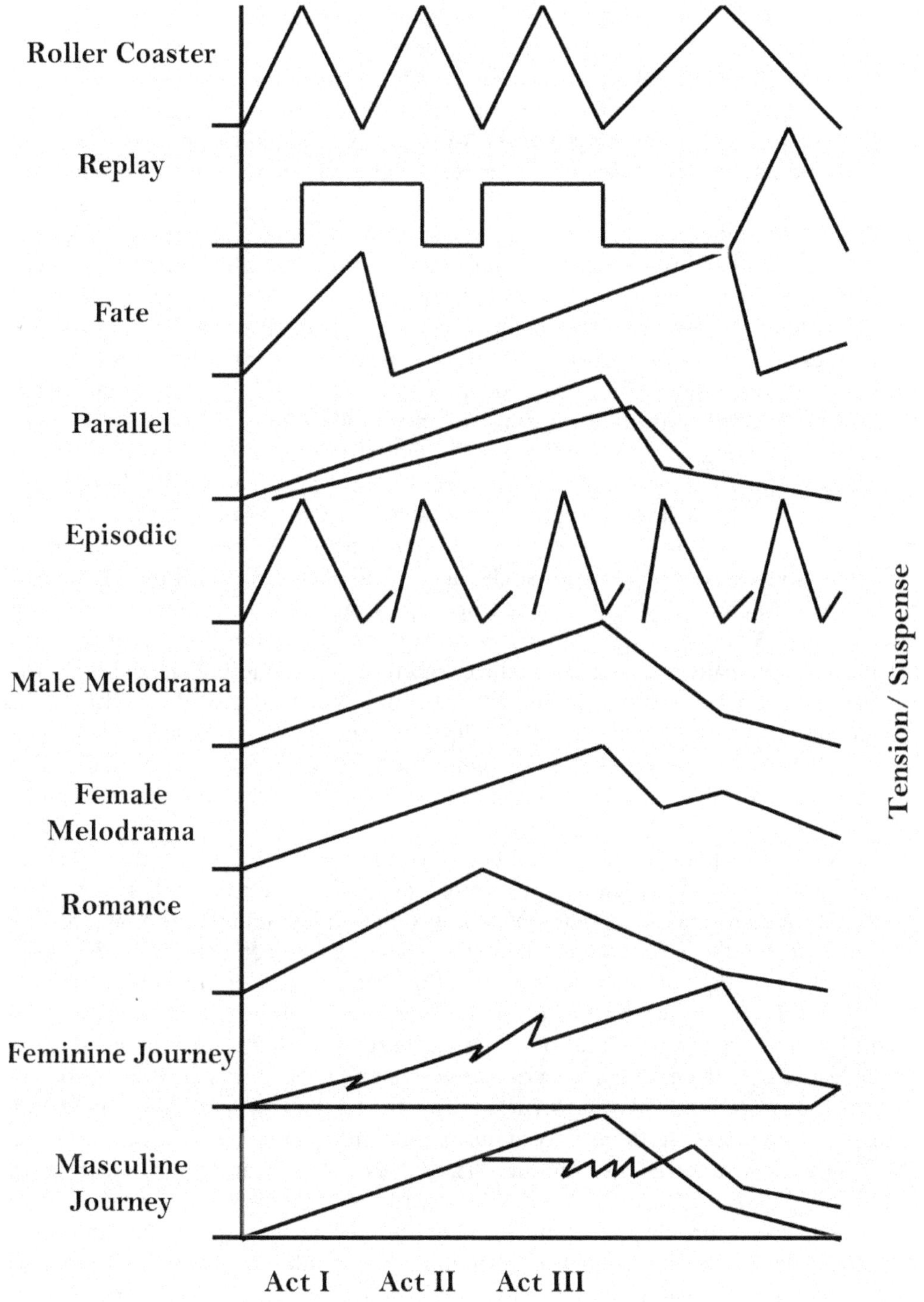

Figure 4. Schmidt's Story Structures.

but held apart by their individual plot, purpose, and subtext."[82] Why these hills go back up after the end of their resolutions is uncertain.

Another diagram that mystifies me is the replay structure: "The Replay is defined as having two to three versions of events in one story."[83] *Groundhog Day* is an example that Schmidt uses, commenting that the story can be told from one or several characters' perspectives, but it has to be repeated several times (specifically, three times, as the diagram suggests), with the last repetition climbing higher in tension than the previous ones, but all of them reaching the same resolution. The concept of a story having three similar-in-tension build-ups and then three identical repetitive conclusions is extremely puzzling. In *Groundhog Day*, while the day is repeated (perhaps hundreds of times), the main character constantly approaches the day in a new way and brings each repetition to very different ends, but none of these ends conclude the story in a resolution—they just end a plot spike, at least until the very end, when the plot reaches the bottom of the diagram and resolves fully.

It is interesting to consider the parallel plot structure in this mix, as there are some stories that include two plots from two different perspectives that basically go through the same background and reach a single shared resolution. Booker does not count the two-plot structure as one of his master plots because it is, by definition, two plots rather than one. Most classical authors use a mix of different types of plots when they mix plots, as one can be a quest and another can be a rebellion. Schmidt uses *Seinfeld* as one of her key examples, but even in this "simple" series, the plots are typically nonparallel, as the characters pursue individual goals and only occasionally come to work together toward a single unified goal. In addition, it is troubling that one of the two parallel plot lines does not arrive at the same conclusion as the other one. I've never seen a *Seinfeld* episode in which we never find out what happened at the end of the conflict one of the four lead characters experienced earlier.

Another unexplained point about these diagrams is why there is a different shape between the male and the female melodrama. Schmidt explains that this means that the female melodrama has an "ending" that is "open-ended or ambiguous and follows a Final Obstacle,"[84] whereas the masculine one doesn't. I object. Schmidt defends this separation by saying that male heroes can follow a feminine plot line and the reverse, but that would mean that she is calling some men girly, and some women manly. This seems like a pretty sexist separation. There is no reason a writer cannot write a final obstacle and a closed ending into a drama with a female lead. In addition, according to Christopher Booker and other structuralists, the final obstacle is present in all dramatic structures. Clearly, the variety of misunderstandings that can arise from a writer studying these structures is too numerous, and there is a clear need to create more exact graphic representations of dramatic situations, structures and plots.

Despite these problems, Schmidt's categories are interesting because they show the distinctions between "dramatic throughlines," "conflicts," "genres," story "structures" and "dramatic situations." The throughlines are the initial ideas for a plot; conflicts are the set-up sides in a dramatic tension; genres are the big groups that fiction falls into, like the ones in each of the following four chapters; story structures are the ten plot lines that I represented in Figure 4; and dramatic situations are more detailed versions of the six basic "conflicts," adding up to fifty-four different situations. I do not spend too much time on these because a typical complex plot for a novel includes two or more of these situations. I will name them here so that the reader can evaluate how they can affect the construction of fictional stories. The fifty-four dramatic situations are as follows: Supplication & Benefaction, Deliverance & Sojourn, Vengeance for a Crime & Rehabilitation, Vengeance Taken for Kindred Upon Kindred & Appearance of a New Kinsman, Flight & Pursuit, Disaster & Miracle, Falling Prey to Cruelty or Misfortune & Becoming Fortunate, Revolt & Support, Daring Enterprise & Healing Journey, Abduction & Reunion, Enigma & Invention, Obtaining & Letting Go, Enmity of Kinsman & Hero to Kinsman, Competition & Concession, Adultery & Fidelity, Madness & Genius, Imprudence & Caution, Crimes of Love & Sacrifice for Love, Slaying of Loved One & Conviction, Self-Sacrifice & Self-Preservation, Discovery of Dishonor of Loved One & Discovery of Honor of Loved One, Obstacles to Love & Unconditional Love, Conflicts with God & Supernatural Occurrence, Mistaken Judgment & Intuitive Judgment, Remorse & Empathy, Loss of Loved One & Rescue of a Loved One, and finally Odd Couple & Fish Out of Water.

Schmidt actually promises 55 dramatic situations, and delivers the last one in the form of a "Blank Situation Template." She recommends that those who want to create their own situation should begin by answering a list of questions. These questions are of interest to this study because most writers who start a new genre ask at least some of these questions as they form the shape of their structure and dramatic situations. In addition, the plot elements even for formulaically established structures or situations are not set in stone and have many possible variations, which these questions help writers to evaluate. Finally, they can help a critic to compare common plot structures and dramatic situations by comparing the elementary questions that shaped them.

- What is your reasoning for creating this situation?
- Are you absolutely sure you can't use one of the situations already outlined?
- Will this situation be a plot, subplot, or incident?
- What is at stake for the hero? Or what is the hero's dilemma at the beginning of the situation? What needs to be solved? Or is this a Slice of Life situation? If so, what is the point of this situation? What do you want to convey?
- Can you piece together a beginning, middle, and end? ...
- Find the beginning: What does the hero want? What is his objective?
- Find the middle: What does the hero do to get it?
- Find the end: How does the hero get it?
- What do other characters think about this situation and what the hero wants? Will anyone try to stop the hero?
- Is there a clear-cut antagonist? What does the antagonist want? Is the antagonist human? Or something intangible?
- What type of obstacles can you put in the hero's way? How many? Will they escalate as he gets closer to the goal?
- How does the hero change during this situation? Does this situation cause another situation to happen?
- Does the hero or reader learn from this situation? Or is it just a fun ride?
- Will you have a theme?
- Will a smaller character become the heroic character during this situation? Will characters switch places?

- Will a sidekick character come onto the scene to help the hero?
- Will the hero want to share the spotlight with someone else? ...
- Could you use an antihero?[85]

I created Figure 1 in order to visualize a universal plot structure that is more exact graphically than either the bell curve or Freytag's diagrams of dramatic construction. The universal plot structure fits most skeleton popular formulaic genres because its shape represents the tension changes seen in "a good ride on the roller coaster"[86] (which Stephen King used to explain his plot structure). The roller coaster is the basic principle for modern storytelling. Have you ever been on a roller coaster ride in which you go up once and then down to the ground and it is all over? What about a roller coaster where the machine immediately speeds up to 200 miles per hour and roars up to the top of the highest peak in the first second of the ride? The principles that go into the design of a roller coaster are nearly identical to the principles in the construction of a formulaic novel. I will create diagrams similar to the basic plot diagram in each of the main chapters besides tables that show the common plot patterns to illustrate the patterns visually. The repetitions in the formula are more apparent when they are put on a visual plot line, as opposed to just comparing paragraphs or table plot summaries. The universal plot diagram might fit most standardized and "perfectly" constructed novels, but there are still some variations in each of the major genres discussed in this book. The variations make up a small percentage, so it is fair to generalize plots with the simplified diagrams.

How does a writer choose which genre they are going to work in for their next project? Probably the same way that readers choose the genres that best appeal to their temperaments: "A child chooses one book over others on the basis of two things: the desire to experience one fantasy as opposed to another and the ease with which she can identify with the voices of the narrator and characters…. A romance and a mystery, for example, differ widely in voice, language, structure, images, and heroic values."[87]

Booker's plot model is the best fit for this analysis because it provides four plot lines that correspond with the key formulas of the four genres under study. Formulaic fiction is written with the roller coaster Booker plot in mind because it builds tension in waves of stress and relaxation. Other concepts from Booker also help to explain formulaic writing, as the "nightmare climax" and "reversal" are constant in all formulaic genres. In contrast, Freytag's pyramid and the bell curve dramatic arc do not logically fit the movements of any of the key formulaic genres, but the concept of building tension and release that these simplified diagrams represent is one that is present (albeit in a highly mutated form) in Booker's and my own plot constructs. Meanwhile, Schmidt's plot lines serve as a great example of overcomplicating plot structure. There are certain limitations in standard storytelling that forbid the use of several equivalent climaxes, or rectangular drops from tense to zero in the middle of a story. There are some experimental stories that have attempted everything from nonsense to absurdity, to plot structures that definitely do not fit the four key plot lines for the best-selling genres. But these exceptions are by definition anti-formulaic and fall outside the four genres that are the focus of this study, so they will not be examined. However, Schmidt's questions for writers who are considering designing their own plot line are a unique way to look at how genres and formulas are created.

Basic Plot Line Terms Dissected

In the summary of Christopher Booker's basic plot line, there were several terms that are frequently discussed in books about the process of writing fiction, and which need to be defined here, so that it is clear what they signify when they are used later in the book.

There are several traits and characteristics that protagonists have in common: "Your hero must have at least one weakness" because it "lends humanity."[88] For example, they can be "physically handicapped" or "have a mental hang-up," "ignorance," "inexperience," or "callowness," or they may be "sad," "little," self-deceived, or temperamental.[89] While in the Aristotelian tragedy this is called the fatal flaw or Achilles' heel, in suspense novels, the weakness is a formulaic characteristic that creates "empathy" in readers for the "vulnerable" character, who is taken advantage of by the villains, who poke at this weakness. However, adding some flaws into your hero's character can be problematic, according to the classical model, because the hero is supposed to be "beautiful," rather than monstrous and ugly. If a writer inserts one of the above qualities in abundance, it is likely the character will become ugly in the reader's eyes, and psychologically readers are not likely to empathize with an ugly or otherwise seriously flawed character, as the "hero" would become anti-heroic. The flaw in the protagonist instead has to be "normal" enough so that "readers will recognize aspects of themselves" in the hero. Another important rule that is frequently problematic in popular fiction is that the characters have to be "consistent" (they cannot change their innate character traits),[90] but this is difficult to achieve in a series written by multiple authors or when the writer is writing the whole book at a gallop in a couple of months.

The hero also has to "emotionally relate to the other people in your story."[91] The key ingredient of a popular novel hero's character is that they must be "compassionate," and this frequently becomes the most formulaic and repetitive ingredient in the formula. The rule is "Your protagonist must care about others." The classical model states that the hero must not care only for "self-survival" and should not be selfish, and he also should be rescuing somebody in distress or helping others in order to gain the status of a "hero." The "call" that begins the action in most fantasy, science fiction, detective, and other types of plots is to "preserve the lives of any person (or any creature) he or she feels responsible for."[92] In the Judeo-Christian religions being proud and selfish is a sin, while being selfless and serving others is the mark of a hero.

Frequently, popular writers make the heroes anti-heroic by giving them flaws such as demonic, vampiric, and otherwise inhuman or destructive characteristics. The insertion of a violent temper or an evil element in the hero's character satisfies the current popularity of deviant behavior and a general decline of religious dominance. However, authors then attempt to insert "compassion" or loving feelings into these anti-heroes. In the *Twilight*, Bella repeats that she loves Edward and keeps crying over this love as he beats and violates her and repeatedly puts her life in mortal danger. The expressed feelings fail to match the actions or descriptions in the story, and both the characters and their "compassion" become merely a repetition, failing to evoke a sense of real feeling in the readers, and therefore this technique fails to inspire empathy.

Mixed moral standards mean that typically best-selling heroes are initially "selfish" and eventually become "caring" by finding "love" and then feeling responsible for the person they love and those who are connected with him or her. This is problematic because the nature of this "love" is frequently explained by stares, followed by kissing and then sex, leading rational readers to conclude that sex is the motivating selfish "call" that springs the hero into action. Somehow the modern audience empathizes with this call and buys these books. But the writers refrain from changing the formula and keep repeating that the characters care about each other and feel a love connection, when in their actions it is clearly a purely sexual connection. Here is an example that William Nolan gives to demonstrate his point about compassion: "In my novel *Logan's Run*, the protagonist initially makes his run for a selfish purpose.... But during his run, Logan learns how to love, as his relationship to Jessica, *sister of a man he's killed* [my italics], deepens and expands. Thus love alters him."[93] This is a very common technique in modern fiction. The hero frequently hurts somebody the heroine loves or causes misery in her life and then the two develop love for each other. In Logan's case, did the sister want her brother murdered? Did she order a hit on him and fall in love with the hit man? No. While those are logical outcomes, they would not be very sentimental or caring responses, now would they?

Edgar Allan Poe captured the relationship between murder and love realistically in his short story "The Black Cat," in which the narrator describes how he cut out one of his cat's eyes, and then hanged the animal, but afterward started to miss the cat and got a new, similar cat. But the similarity between the two quickly started to annoy and then terrify the narrator, and he felt extreme hatred toward the new cat, until he swung an axe at it, but when his wife stopped his hand he split her head with the axe. He then buried her in a wall in the cellar, but when police came they discovered the body because he buried the cat with the wife by accident and it shrieked. The narrator calls the cat the "monster" and feels like a "freeman"[94] when he thinks the cat has run away. The narrator sees himself as a hero in a standard Overcoming the Monster plot scheme, in which the cats and his wife are the monsters, and he feels the plot formula required liberation at the semi-ending, when he is about to escape retribution. The audience perceives that he is the villain, and feels a sense of resolution when he is caught by the police upon their discovery that he is monstrous. Despite the fact that the main character is anti-heroic and purely selfish, readers have enjoyed this story for over a century because it depicts the realistic feelings and reactions that lead up to and follow the murders, instead of a sentimental repetition of loving feelings despite gruesome and anti-heroic actions. While great writers know how to manipulate formulaic rules to fit their characters and plot lines, the power of formulaic rules overwhelms modern popular writers, and they trust the required formulas that lead them into falsely sentimental and unbelievably absurd situations and emotional responses.

Another element of the standard popular formula is that the character has to "change" before the end of the novel. The curve of happiness and life satisfaction in most stories typically ends with the hero being happier than he or she was at the beginning in order to satisfy readers who have invested in the character's triumphs over his obstacles. Resolution of a conflict in a classic comedy typically happens through a change in either the power that was keeping the lovers apart or in one or both of the lovers that was preventing them from being happy together. The notion that a hero's character has to "change" from the beginning to the end frequently creates inconsistency and make the character unbelievable, as his or her traits appear to mutate suddenly. Nolan's rule is this: "The events of your story *must* cause your protagonist to change.... Lessons must have been learned. Emotions must have been deepened. The character's basic approach to life must have been altered because of the trials and dangers encountered en route."[95] A murderer falls in love with the sister of a man he murdered, and so he kills numerous "evil" people in order to protect her and to enter into a sexual relationship with her (an action novel infrequently ends in marriage). He has changed because he has learned that he must kill evil people, rather than good people, or he has decided to retire to a distant island on the money he made so far from killing people. What is the formulaic point of this forced change? And is this a change of character or of circumstances due to new decisions by a character that keeps their same core values and beliefs (or lack thereof)? Forcing on your readers the notion that a killing villain has become a hero because he has fallen in "love" can only create the "cardboard heroes" that Nolan insists "no longer make the grade in today's popular fiction market." He goes on to say, "Your readers want to follow a protagonist who demonstrates strength, intelligence, and compassions—and who matures into a better person because of the events of your story."[96] If the main character has to become a "better person," this logically means that he or she must be a hero-villain who manages to overcome their dark flaws and evil inclinations. This is not the only possible plot line that is likely to appeal to readers. A hero who is initially good, remains good, and rescues the world from evil is another equally satisfying outcome. A hero-villain who is evil and dies for his sins is also likely to be satisfying for readers. So, writers should think through the laws of formulaic fiction and should understand how these formulas function in order to create the appropriate change in the appropriate characters.

An element that is essential to most classical and popular stories is the death threat necessary to create suspense. The hero must actively fight for and against something because it is threatening his life and the lives of those whom he feels obligated to protect. The "removal of the threat," or reaching the point in a story when the outcome is no longer "uncertain," "ends" the reader's suspense. Anticipation of love or marriage is just that—"anticipation"—but the terror that comes with threats to the hero's well-being and life creates an empathetic clinging attachment of the reader to the hero's fate, as if their own life is in danger. At the same time, Nolan and other writing coaches recognize that "you must avoid overloading your narrative with too many consecutive scenes of shock and terror, one directly after another in an unbroken sequence."[97] This need for positive upswings and small victories over small and then larger obstacles across the drama is necessary in the standard dramatic plot diagram. The hero's fortune swings up and down in a tension rhythm that fuels the plot with "constrictions" and releases of emotional tension. Nolan is primarily talking about the horror genre, in which these swings must be more extreme and the threat to the hero's life must be constant in order to make it into a true horror story where the standard *fear* for the hero's well-being turns into hair-clutching *horror.* While Nolan warns against overdoing the frequency of death threats against the hero's life, they appear with a greater frequency in horror novel than in other genres. Still, even in horror, if the monster is running down a city street and eating a new victim on every page of the book, it is likely that the readers will start to see the actions as satiric and ridiculous, as extreme horror can easily slip into extremely funny absurdity. Inserting moments of rest and peaceful existence between the violent acts allows readers to compare the states of relaxation and fear and to hope for a positive ending, as opposed to dark comedies, in which the reader might hope that the main and supporting characters will all be slaughtered by the hungry monster.

There is a central problem with the currently popular formula for dramatic horror: for the death threat to be "real" and to produce the most horror, there has to be a tragic conclusion in which the hero-villain dies at the end. Edgar Allan Poe, considered the founder of modern murder mysteries, and a leading writer in gothic horror, relates a truly horrific story in "Ligeia," when he depicts an extremely beautiful and intelligent wife dying at her peak. She leaves a poem that claims people are only "puppets," and that the "threat" that befell her is a "natural" death, or the "Invisible Woe," and that the surviving "hero" is "the Conqueror Worm."[98] Poe creates suspense despite the fact that he confesses to his readers at the beginning of his story that his wife will die. The threat of her impending death drives the plot onward as he describes her life and her death. Poe is skillful enough to carry the suspense to the end even after the biggest threat of the wife's death is realized mid-story. As a literary critic himself, who made a living by writing reviews in addition to the fiction and poetry that he published, Poe summarizes the anti-formulaic nature of his plot at the point in the story when the main "threat" is about to be realized "too soon." It might be a personal preference, but I would rather read a poem about the victory of the hero "Worm," followed by an anti-climactic ending, than keep reading about a threat of death to the hero's life that always ends with the hero's triumphant victory. There are many other things that Poe's readers can anticipate after the narrator's wife dies, such as whether he will have a violent or otherwise dramatic reaction to this death, which is suggested by the trauma he expresses across the narrative. While there are many possible alternative variations for creating suspense, mortal danger or the life threat to the hero's or his beloved's life is a standard formulaic element in most popular novels.

In an "introduction" to an anthology of horror stories, Stephen King explains the elements that make up the horror genre: "The best tales in the genre make one point over and over again—that the rational world both within us and without us is small, that our understanding is smaller yet, and that much of the universe in which we exist is so far as we are able to tell, chaotic. So the horror story makes us appreciate our own well-lighted corner of that chaotic universe, and perhaps allows a moment of warm and grateful wonder that we should be allowed to exist in that fragile space of light at all."[99] This is among the most honest and direct statements about the nature of horror fiction and suspense from a best-selling author, because it points to the basic nature of fear and to the threat that moves the tension of the plot up and down in all of the formulaic genres discussed in this book. An extremely horrific death threat, according to this theory, makes readers feel comparatively safe, regardless of the horrors that they are facing in their real lives. On the other hand, horror might be popular because this death threat might make readers feel extremely horrified about the world around them, but anxious to read more about other potential threats.

Anne Rice explains that the death threat and sexual suspense are linked because "there's something about the excitement of ghost stories that's like sexual excitement. The victim in these stories is always forced into submission. The vampire story in particular involves a kind of seduction, a taking of the victim."[100] Horror writers work to link sex to fear with their writing. They also explain to critics that their formulas of using the death threat and sexual tension successfully bring in and keep readers. If readers feel relieved and sexually gratified by horror or by seeing death and destruction, they are rewarded and will want to return to the horror genre that stimulated them.

There are several other popularly used techniques for creating suspense that Nolan discusses. First, there is the "Don't Open that Door!" principle,[101] which means that the writer should give clues to the reader that will make the reader want to stop the hero from opening a presented door or following a certain route because readers have been informed by the narrator of a danger that the hero has missed. Thus, the reader is anticipating a problem befalling the hero that he or she is ignorant of, and therefore empathy and suspense are created.

Second, the "Isolation" principle is the process of leaving the hero alone to fight at the most dangerous points of the story, so as to make them more "vulnerable."[102] In theory, readers are more likely to empathize with vulnerable characters. However, this isolation makes for loner-heroes, without close companions or friends to help them on their journey, quest, or monster hunt.

Third, naked heroes are more vulnerable and therefore more sympathetic, and thus make for more suspenseful stories. Nolan even gives this formula: "Nakedness = vulnerability = suspense."[103] Have you have recently watched a Hollywood movie and wondered why the heroes are naked either once or most of the time? This is because naked people are vulnerable and suspenseful. But are male naked heroes really vulnerable if they are engaging in sexual intercourse with the heroine? This principle does not work as well for heroes as it does for female victims. Nolan gives several examples of showering female victims being slaughtered to demonstrate the impact of nude vulnerability on suspense. In the few sentences or scenes between the naked woman entering the shower and the psychotic monster killing her, the readers' suspense should be at its peak. I just do not understand why more writers have not utilized the naked-young-man-in-the-shower-being-brutally-murdered trick. In romance novels this nudity frequently creates anticipation of the sex act, or a sexual suspense.

A fourth device for creating formulaic suspense is bad weather. For example, it rains dozens of times in the course of the last book in the *Twilight* series. In theory the howling storms "help isolate the characters,"[104] as their mobility is supposed to be restricted, making them more vulnerable. Instead, what happens in *Twilight* is that the author keeps repeating that it is raining without any symbolic, emotional or restricting affect, just because there is supposed to be bad weather in a popular novel. Only in horror stories about natural disasters that threaten the fate of the earth, or when the storms are described as having unusual powers, is the use of "bad weather" meaningful and successfully increases suspense. Repetitive occurrences of mild rain are likelier to inspire a sense of lulling sleepiness in the readers.

A fifth possibly horrific element of formulaic suspense is darkness. To use Nolan's cliché, "Things That Go Bump in the Night" are potentially frightening or are likely to create a sense of impending doom and suspense in readers. Authors who properly utilize the device of darkness realize that if it is "pitch black" and the character cannot see anything, there can be no clear description of the threat. H. G. Wells used the element of darkness to make his monsters more mysterious, as he depicted only their outlines or key features, saying that there was not enough light for the main character to distinguish the details. Monsters that are somewhat mysterious in their appearance are likely to keep a reader in suspense regarding their nature longer than monsters that are specifically detailed in the light of day. The darkness allows some of the potential victims of the monster to remain ignorant of its true nature until they are in the monster's grasp. Nolan proclaims, "Never allow *all* of the characters in your story to believe in the monster." In theory, the narrative becomes more "credible" if the characters are only gradually convinced of the monster's reality.[105]

Finally, formulaic novels have to end with the hero's victory. Victory and a happy ending are required because "readers ... invested so much time and sympathy in the characters and story that anything less than victory at the end is emotionally unacceptable—a letdown, a disappointment."[106] Happy endings are more standard in the American market than in the European one, although there are a few exceptions even among American formulaic fiction with tragic endings. Still, the repeated advice even for writers in the horror genre is that the hero should ultimately win.

The Y axis of the plot diagram represents both tension and mood. The term "mood" in this context refers not only to the happiness or sadness of the protagonist but also to their life-status—in other words, if the protagonist is dead, their "mood" is at the lowest possible point, while if the protagonist is extremely rich, has a positive lover and otherwise is full of youthful joy, the "mood" meter is at the highest possible point. Mood and tension move in the opposite directions from each other. If the protagonist's mood is glum, tension is high, and vice versa. Unless there is a major structural problem in the story or it is an absurd dark comedy, at the points when a sidekick, supporting heroes, or the protagonist are hurt or killed, the reader should feel apprehensive, concerned and tense, hoping that the protagonist will make it out of this predicament. In formulaic generic novels, mood and tension move on a similar path when tension is inverted.

Formulaic novels are built on a few principles of construction, which must be precisely followed or the final result becomes anti-formulaic or lopsided. Classical, literary writers use these ideas as general literary theory that they apply if the original formula they devise requires them. Formulaic writers who mimic the plot lines, characters and settings from a novel or a set of generic novels that preceded them must follow each of these prescriptions to avoid obvious mistakes. Most formulaic writers fail to execute at least one of these elements properly, and I will discuss these glitches in the sections assigned to individual authors.

To sum up, a purely formulaic unliterary novel has a protagonist with a major problem, who is at least occasionally naked and alone, and is frequently in the dark and experiences bad weather episodes. The protagonist is compassionate and selfless (unless his major problem is that he is psychotic, in which case he can be selfish and homicidal). The protagonist's life and ability to have good sex are constantly under threat throughout the story, until the end when he or she survives, grows rich, and has a positive sexual experience.

Chapter 2

Fantasy, Science Fiction and Horror

"I think I can really scare people to the point where they will say, 'I'm really sorry I bought this.'"—Stephen King[1]

The terms "science fiction," "fantasy" and "horror" include a range of different subgenres, which are all part of speculative fiction. While the genre of horror is the equivalent of superhero fiction in the eyes of the category-makers, and also does not have its own categories in the Simba Information statistics, because the number one best-selling author in America is Stephen King and he practices in this genre, it has to be included in my classification. In addition, structurally horror is the most representative genre among speculative fiction types because the principles that govern horror represent an exaggerated version of the principles behind all speculative fiction. As was discussed in the "Basic Plot Line Terms" section of the previous chapter, horror employs an exaggerated roller coaster plot line, with super-intensified death threat and sexual suspense elements that drive the steeper climbs and falls in dramatic tension. Thus, examining the horror genre helps to clarify the same principles when they are offered in altered combinations in the other genres. For example, science fiction is frequently based on a horrific event that threatens to destroy the world, thus creating an enormous death threat at the beginning and additional death threats later, and frequently deaths of minor characters. Fantasy also often has a monster threat that has to be overcome and conquered by the hero before the end of the story. In theory, fantasy is the other side of horror, similar to the distinction between utopia and dystopia. Utopia is supposed to be an idealized imagined society, while dystopia should be a frightening or an "undesirable" speculative world. In practice, all of the works I am examining that are typically placed in the "fantasy" category represent horrific, rather than idealized, worlds that desperately need their respective heroes to overcome the problems they are facing to relieve the built-up tension.

Typically, fiction that has children and young adults as its primary market is labeled fantasy, and fiction intended for adults is labeled horror, because it is difficult for publishers to penetrate moral censors if they attempt selling popular "horror" to the young. The line between science fiction and horror is similarly blurry. However, the line between science fiction and fantasy is clear cut, as the first focuses on science, and the latter does not have a central scientific component. H. G. Wells is commonly credited with founding the science fiction genre with *The War of the Worlds* (1898), about an alien invasion, which was innovative, in comparison with prior fantastic fiction, because it featured alien technology and explained the invasion and its failure in scientific terms. On the other hand, here is a definition for the word "fantasy" from the online Oxford Dictionary: "The faculty or activity of imagining things, especially things that are impossible or improbable." The origin of the word is given as "late Middle English ... from Greek, 'imagination, appearance,' later 'phantom,' from *phantazein* 'make visible.'" Since all of fiction is imaginative, and the earliest fiction was mythology, which imagined gods with faculties that were "impossible or improbable," fantastic fiction is the most ancient form of fiction. Religious texts, epic poetry, all forms of drama, medieval romance, some forms of juvenile fiction, all forms of religious and inspirational fiction, and some romance novels all have fantastic elements or fantastic subgenres.

Modern fantasy fiction, or the formula for fantasy fiction that is currently popular, started with George MacDonald's *The Princess and the Goblin* and *Phantastes* (1858), William Morris' *The Well at the World's End* (1896), C. S. Lewis' *The Chronicles of Narnia* (1950–1956), and J. R. R. Tolkien's *The Lord of the Rings* (1954–1955). The genre became a best-selling success with *The Gods of Pegana* (1905) by Lord Dunsany (1878–1957), about a group of invented deities that live in a place called Pegana. It is likely that a work like *Pegana* was not possible until 1905 because previously it would have been called blasphemous banned from publication. It also helped that Lord Dunsany was a baron, and it was more difficult to sue him on blasphemy and sedition charges. Starting in 1905, similar fantasies about imagined gods and magicians have provided welcome escapist literature for both the young and the old.

One of the key authors in this field who will not be discussed in this study is George Orwell, unknown by his birth name, Eric Arthur Blair (1903–1950). Orwell's first novel was *Animal Farm* (1945), which he published right after the end of World War II. Orwell stands out for an obvious reason among the works that will be covered: he picked up the tradition of political and culturally critical moralist science fiction and fantasy, which otherwise withered after Wells, and has not been at the top of the best-seller lists since Orwell's time. The field that Orwell joined with *Animal Farm* was one with roots as far back as Jonathan Swift's *Gulliver's Travels,* in which British society was satirized in the tiny people, giants and horses in the fantastic worlds that Gulliver travels to. This branch of fantasy was one of satire and anti-establishment myth-making. Authors like Swift and Orwell realized that while the establishment popularized religious and totalitarian fantasies, they could reply with fantasies of their own, ones that were rebellious and created fantastic worlds that served as metaphors or allegories for the problems they saw in the real world that surrounded them. This satiric tradition has been lost in modern popular publishing because of the dominance of the publishing oligopoly, which is the establishment, and is not likely to start publishing satirical fantasies about itself in the upcoming decades.

Orwell first became recognized for *Down and Out in Paris and London* (1933), an autobiographical account of his life as a casual laborer and then a tramp in these great cities. The success he got from this project won him reporting jobs in the 1940s, and these allowed him some time to write the two novels that made him one of the best-selling writers of the 1930–1956 period,[2] although most of the success came after his death from tuberculosis in 1950. The two novels that he is best known for are *Animal Farm* (1945) and *1984* (1949). The first of these two leans on the satiric, while the second is pessimistic and tragic, as Orwell was contemplating his own forthcoming early death, and the fact that he was not going to live into his eighties to see what the world would be like in 1984. "These two books, with their mixture of narrative and of social and political commentary represent probably the most famous two fiction titles produced by an English author in the twentieth century." This fame is measured, in part, by the quantity of words from them that have entered the English language: "Big Brother," "mini" and "Newspeak" among them.[3] After World War II ended with two nuclear explosions in Japan, the world had a demand to read about this horrific new world that was taking shape around them. As the memory of World War II faded, readers returned to having a taste for escapist fantasies, horrors and science fiction stories, and not those that represented the problems in the "real" world.

The in-depth background for the foundation and structure of the science fiction genre will be studied in depth in the section on H. G. Wells. The key works and writers that established what we know of today as the horror genre will be examined in the section on Stephen King. The section on J. R. R. Tolkien is the best source for information on the founding members and principles of the fantasy genre. The rest of the writers examined are all in the fantasy genre: J. K. Rowling, Rick Riordan and Stephenie Meyer. Fantasy dominates the best-seller lists in this field, while horror and science fiction hold occasional top positions. Because horror and science fiction only developed in the last century, they have undergone significant changes since their creation. However, recent decades have moved all three of these genres toward homogeneity and formulaic minimalism, which has blurred the distinctions between these categories and between individual works within subgenres.

Structural Elements of Fantasy and Science Fiction: Characters, Setting, and Plot

While the founder of science fiction, H. G. Wells, wrote against generic norms, and only partially conformed to realist generic standards in the second half of his life, most best-selling science fiction today is extremely formulaic. By studying examples of these publications, one can clearly see the patterns they share in everything from plot to character types, character descriptions, setting descriptions and a long list that includes almost all components of a typical science fiction or fantasy popular generic novel. The relationship between fantasy, horror, science fiction and their related subgenres can best be visualized in the diagram in Figure 5.

Fantasy and Science Fiction Plots

Many critics and fiction writers have summarized the fundamental plot that fantasy, horror and science fiction have in common. All three of these novel-types nearly always center on what Christopher Booker calls the "Overcoming the Monster" plot. A summary of the plot reads like a fairy tale because when the plot is simplified to its core elements it retains those elementary blocks that were built into it during the time of oral fairy tales and myths. A hero or heroine faces a

> superhuman embodiment of evil power. This monster may take human form (e.g., a giant or a witch); the form of an animal (a wolf, a dragon, a shark); or a combination of both (the Minotaur, the Sphinx). It is always deadly, threatening destruction to those who cross its path or fall into its clutches. Often it is threatening an entire community or

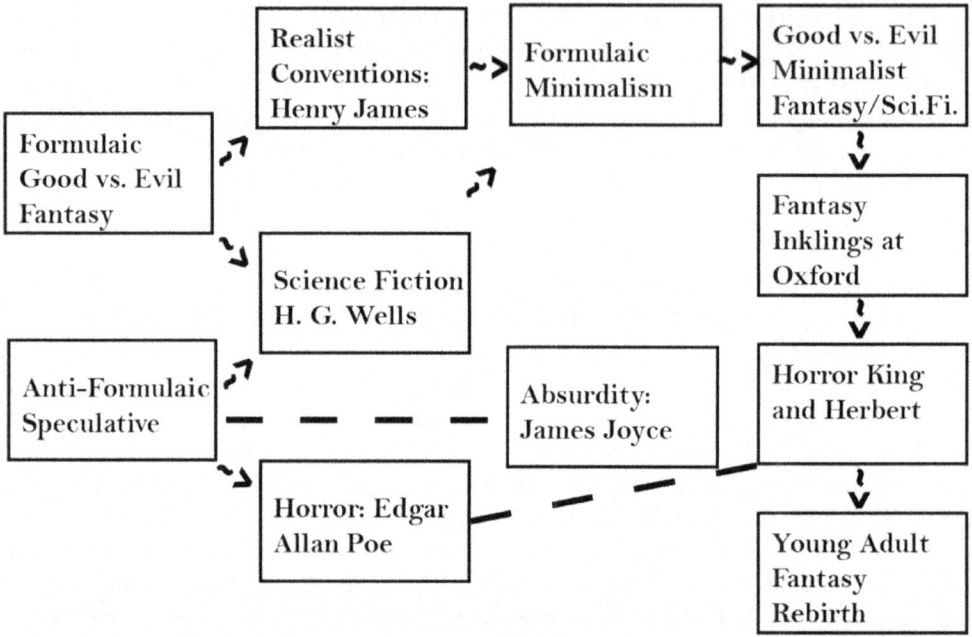

Figure 5. Speculative Genres Diagram.

kingdom, even mankind and the world in general. But the monster often has in its clutches some great prize, a priceless treasure or a beautiful "Princess."

So powerful is the presence of this figure, so great the sense of threat which emanates from it, that the only thing which matters to us as we follow the story is that it should be killed and its dark power overthrown. Eventually the hero must confront the monster, often armed with some kind of "magic weapons," and usually in or near its lair, which is likely to be in a cave, a forest, a castle, a lake, the sea, or some other deep and enclosed place. Battle is joined and it seems that, against such terrifying odds, the hero cannot possibly win. Indeed there is a moment when his destruction seems all but inevitable. But at the last moment, as the story reaches its climax, there is a dramatic reversal. The hero makes a "thrilling escape from death" and the monster is slain.[4]

In addition to killing the monster, the hero is also rewarded for this victory with a prize, such as a treasure, a princess (or possibly a prince), a kingdom or a group of people offering to be ruled by him or her. You can insert almost any character names and place settings into this formula and it would fit the plots of nearly all popular horror, science fiction and fantasy stories, including *Harry Potter, Percy Jackson,* and *Twilight.*

However, the full formula used in these genres is not only the basic Overcoming the Monster plot line, but also repetitions in formulaic details like character descriptions, chapter endings, and numerous other ingredients, which can all be counted and quantified down to pure formulas, with nearly no spontaneous anti-formulaic occurrences in mainstream, popular, unliterary fiction. What might appear to be variations are typically only slightly different settings and characters that engage in very similar dramas. In addition, another illusion of dissimilarity is slightly different themes or story types that, when repeated enough times, split a genre into subgenres. In science fiction, the "deadly invasions of the earth by monsters from outer space," and

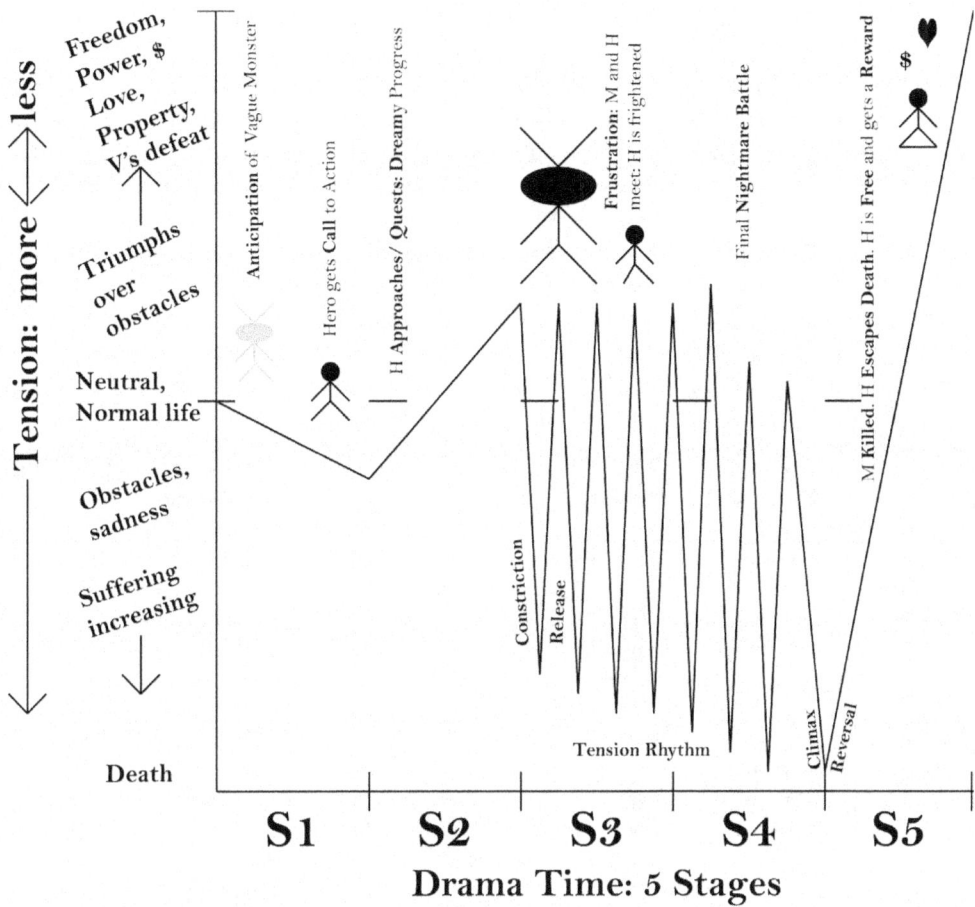

Figure 6. Overcoming the Monster Plot Diagram.

the "world threatening catastrophe"[5] are extremely common and might be called the alien invasion and the world catastrophe subgenres of science fiction.

A graphic depiction of the Overcoming the Monster plot will help to explain its pattern. This plot has a positive, unknotting resolution and meets the generic curves of a standard formulaic story for all genres, unlike some other generic plots that offer more distinct variations.

The monster is represented as a character with horns to simplify the distinction between good and evil. The monster is gray at the beginning of the plot because he, she or it is typically indistinct and hazy at the beginning, and only later becomes defined and grows in its comparative power, while the hero keeps the same powers he had when the plot started. The five stages of the plot do not necessarily represent specific quantities of pages out of the novel. The next stage begins when a major change in tension and mood speed or rhythm occurs. Thus, at the end of Stage 1, the Hero begins seeing some successes during the "dream" stage, or Stage 2. Stage 3 is typically taken up with a roller coaster rhythm, which intensifies in Stage 4. Stage 4 ends when the hero is closest to a potential death, but manages to escape and begins winning over the villain. The higher on the "happiness" meter the hero goes, the more likely it is that the villain and his assistants are being slain, wounded or otherwise overpowered. While some best-selling novels might have elements that diverge from this pattern, such as a tragic ending, most follow this exact scheme.

The psychological principles behind this structure are as follows: (1) If readers care about the hero, they will become more invested in finishing the story if the hero's life is put under greater and greater threat. (2) Constant horror or a constant fear for the life of the hero would lead to mental exhaustion and a dulling of emotions; emotions can be kept on edge if the hero resolves small difficulties and then falls into new problems that need to be resolved. (3) If readers are taken on an emotional roller coaster and encouraged to sympathize with the hero, they would feel personally hurt if the hero dies tragically or loses the battle at the end. (4) The hero cannot win the conflict before the beginning of the final act or part of the plot, and frequently the

Plot Movement	*Doctor Moreau*	*The Hobbit*	*Black House*	*Half-Blood Prince*	*Jackson: Labyrinth*	*Breaking Dawn*
S1: Threat Appears	Prendick shipwrecked, suspects beastliness	Bilbo told of treasure kept by dragon	Fisherman killer (child eater) revealed	Voldemort makes several attacks	Luke plans invasion of Camp Half-Blood	Edward sexually beats Bella
S2: Initial Victories	P realizes Moreau is turning beasts into people	Gandalf saves dwarfs from trolls; B solves riddles	Jack successfully investigates salesman murders.	Wizard hurts Dursleys to help Harry, H travels to school	Percy and friends find and enter Labyrinth to find Daedalus	B enjoys violent sex and married life
S3: Minor Roller Coaster	M and his assistant die; puma and beasts wild	B wins over spiders & elves	J recalls suppressed memories, resigns from LAPD	H fights with Malfoy, succeeds in Potions	P fights Kampe, Briares, gets lost and separated	Baby nearly kills B, becomes vampiric
S4: Steep Roller Coaster	P tries to live with beast-people, the de-evolve	B finds door, steals treasure, dragon attacks	J agrees to investigate Fish and finds magic cause	H stalks Malfoy, dumps Ginny, D poisoned	P fights sea demons, volcano erupts, battle prep	Volturi attack, B & E gather troops
S5: Resolution	P rescued, loses his mind	Battle won after deaths, B gets rich	J stops end of the world	D and others die in battle, H wins	Many die in Camp battle, P survives	Cullens win, B & E happy forever

Figure 7. Overcoming the Monster Plot Table.

hero only wins in the last chapter or two in a novel. If the protagonist wins too soon, the formulaic nature of the roller coaster plot does not leave any events that can occupy the remainder of the time, unless new villains or new obstacles are presented for the hero to overcome.

The movements between these six horror, science fiction and fantasy novels from six different writers all have very similar elements happening at the same points in their respective plot. In Stage 1, a threat is identified and beefed up to explain why the hero is motivated to react to it and to set out on a quest to overcome the monster (or the villain) in the story. In Stage 2, the hero sees some victories. These victories can be over minor enemies, overcoming the unknown, finding allies, or over one's self and one's partner. In all six works, in Stages 3 and 4 their enemies grow more powerful and the heroes have to struggle more and more to overcome each new problem. The last stage has one exception, as Wells founded the science fiction genre at the end of the nineteenth century, long before modern horror and fantasy were solidified fields. Wells created a formula for science fiction that makes a moral point against a concept like animal experimentation by including a tragic ending that leaves readers with a sense that something is wrong in the world. Wells' formula was corrupted by his imitators, who quickly came up with the happy ending plot structure that you can see in the other five works on this list. These other five works all end with a few deaths of minor characters and the triumph of the hero, who is rewarded with money, a happy marriage, and the like.

The plot pattern in modern formulaic horror, science fiction and fantasy is something that best-selling writers in these genres are hyper-aware of and use regularly as they plan a new novel. Looking at some quotes from two of the currently best-known American writers in this field, Stephen King and Anne Rice, will help to explain the use of this pattern from their perspective. Stephen King has written and said more about formulaic writing within the horror and fantasy genres than his competitors, perhaps because his popularity has allowed him to publish nonfiction books about the writing process, and also in part because, as a prior high school English teacher, he has confessed that he has an urge to lecture about writing or to give lengthy interview replies. King has reported that "the only books of mine that I consider pure unadulterated horror are" those that "offer no rational explanation at all for the supernatural events that occur."[6] He also explained that some of his stories lean toward fantasy and others toward science fiction, with "horror" as the overall generic background. So, it's interesting to look at how King saw the plot line for "horror fiction," which he believed was "always the same in terms of its development."

> There's an incursion into taboo lands, there's a place where you shouldn't go, but you do.... And the same thing happens inside: you look at the guy with three eyes, or you look at the fat lady, or you look at the skeleton man or Mr. Electrical or whatever it happens to be. And when you come out, well, you say, "Hey, I'm not so bad. I'm all right. A lot better than I thought."[7]

In another interview, King explained the plot of *The Shining* in different terms, writing that he began by choosing the "form," "framework," or plot of "a Shakespearean tragedy ... in five acts, which finally translated themselves into parts: Job Interview and Preparatory Matters, Closing Day, Wasp's Nest, Snowbound, and Matters of Life and Death."[8] Both plots have a tragic, cathartic ending. Both plots are brief summaries of the Overcoming the Monster plot, with the twist that the monster might potentially win over the hero.

In horror, the monster is especially terrifying, but basically achieves the same goal of setting up a death threat and tension between the hero and something out to get him or her. The need to exaggerate the death threat was best explained by King when, in an interview with *Playboy*, he said, "I suppose the ultimate triumph would be to have somebody drop dead of a heart attack [after reading one of his horror novels] literally scared to death ... part of me would be thinking, Jesus, that really *worked!*"[9] While there has to be a threat of death in most formulaic popular genres, this threat has to be heightened to an extreme in horror for readers to feel "horrified," instead of simply suspenseful. King has offered contradictory reasons in interviews for his need to terrify horror readers. Typically he explains horror as fulfilling a purging "catharsis," but on at least one occasion he offered a more frank answer: "Despite all the talk you'll hear from writers in this genre about horror's providing a socially and psychologically useful catharsis for people's fears and aggressions, the brutal fact of the matter is that we're still in the business of selling public executions."[10] There might be public executions in fantasy and science fiction as well, but in horror writers can freely admit that watching the executions is why readers enter the genre.

Anne Rice's death threat and sexual tension theories can be seen in all of her fictional works, including *The Mummy or Ramses the Damned.* With only a few exceptions, as in her first novel *Interview with the Vampire,* Rice typically begins her books with a very long stalling introduction to the key characters, settings and concepts before the werewolf or the mummy begins its killing spree or sexual seduction. In *Ramses,* the story begins with the slow uncovering of an Egyptian tomb, or rather a library and body of Ramses the Damned. On the first pages repeated threats are seen in hieroglyphs that the archeologist, Lawrence, uncovers around and inside the burial place. A "slab of stone" in a passage says, "'Robbers of the Dead, Look away from this tomb lest you wake its occupant, whose wrath cannot be contained.'"[11] Lawrence and his assistant Samir do not stop and Lawrence translates another warning: "Beware, all those who would let the rays of the sun pass through this door."[12] The archeological dig continues, as Lawrence tries to figure out why Ramses was buried a thousand years after the time when he was supposed to have been buried, historically speaking. Then the story jumps to family and friend difficulties that Lawrence is having with his daughter Julie (who has just refused a marriage proposal from Alex), his prior homosexual lover from Oxford, Elliot (who at first walks with a cane, but will be restored to immortality at the end, after taking magical poisons), and his friend Randolph, who has a gambling-addict son, Henry Stratford. Meanwhile, Lawrence develops an attraction for the mummy and starts imagining that the mummy is still alive, as he can hear it breathing occasionally, and then sees it stir. The fact that the mummy is not in a sarcophagus suggests to him that it might miraculously still be alive. Lawrence touches the mummy, as if trying to seduce it to wake up. After Lawrence touches the mummy, the author cuts him off in mid-sentence with an ellipsis: "if only you could see..."[13] This ending for the section suggests to the reader that the mummy might awaken and vampirically drink Lawrence's blood, but this doesn't happen. Having built up suspense with this suggestion, the narrator goes on to describe the lives of the rich and glamorous. The narrative frequently mentions sleep or the characters being "drowsy" from the soft classical music,[14] and speculates that the mummy has "merely slept."[15] Then, suddenly, Henry comes to speak with Lawrence about his need for money for his family's shipping business, and the mummy's curse strikes and Henry is maddened into putting poison into Lawrence's cup and watching him die. There is a suggestion that Henry has been possessed by the mummy and forced to commit this murder, but later Henry himself turns up dead in the mummy's wrappings, after the mummy, or Ramses, returns to life. The story is built on "old clichés," such as "I shall love you till my dying day."[16] It is extremely melodramatic and the narrative is watered down, but the initial threat of death to all who come near the mummy, the deaths that follow as a result of this curse, and the sexual unions that "resolve" the tensions in the novel at the very end are the formulaic links that hold the story together.

King and Rice are at the top of the formulaic unliterary establishment, but studying lesser-known formulaic writers shows that those below them follow the same techniques, although other writers hide them less and are left with bare plots and clichés.

Fantasy and Science Fiction Characters

The fantasy, science fiction and horror formula insists on a few constants regarding the nature of the key characters. The hero has to be beautiful and good; the villain has to be ugly and evil. In earlier science fiction, Wells could create a hero who was a smart and not particularly young scientist. And Tolkien could use a hairy dwarf as his hero in *The Hobbit*. However, in an age when books sell millions of copies only after the film version succeeds, stories that have young and beautiful heroes are over-

Character Type	*Doctor Moreau*	*The Hobbit*	*Black House*	*Half-Blood Prince*	*Jackson: Labyrinth*	*Breaking Dawn*
Hero	Prendick	Bilbo, Gandalf	Jack	Potter	Percy	Edward, Bella
Villain	Moreau, beasts	Trolls, dragon, spiders	Fisherman, salesman, King	Voldemort, Death Eaters	Luke, demons, Titans	Volturi
Sidekick(s)	Montgomery, M'ling	Dwarves	Police: city/town	Hermoine, Ron	Annabeth, Grover, etc	Cullens
Victim(s)	Puma, other beasts, Prendick, Moreau	Dwarves	Eaten boys	Weasleys, Muggles, good wizards	Demigods at Camp	Jacob, Bella
Community	Beast-People and scientists	Varied mythic creatures	Landing, Wisconsin: small town	Wizards, witches	Olympian gods and half-gods	Vampires, shape shifters

Figure 8. Overcoming the Monster Characters Table.

whelming the marketplace and returning it to chivalry tale conventions. Harry Potter, Percy Jackson, Bella and Edward all look like they are in their teens. On the other hand, villains have been ugly in this genre of fiction since the first demons were created in ancient mythology. Modern filmmaking is mutating some villains into handsome and young Volturi or rebellious Olympian gods. But even the Volturi are, on average, older than the heroic Cullens clan. The villains all have animal or demonic features, which are occasionally also shared by the heroic vampires, witches and other magical creatures. The victims that the heroes have to rescue are occasionally their sidekicks or themselves, and frequently include their community at large or even the whole world.

Christopher Booker, after studying hundreds of stories, concluded that "through the world's storytelling, we find the monster being described in strikingly similar language." The descriptive character repetitions that Booker notices get at the heart of formulaic writing. There are several personality-trait adjectives that the "monsters" have in common, which are described with a limited variety of synonyms: (1)"Alarming": "horrible, terrible, grim, misshapen, hate-filled, ruthless, menacing, terrifying"; (2) "Mortally dangerous": "deadly, bloodthirsty, ravening, murderous, venomous, poisonous"; (3) "Deeply deceitful and tricky": "cunning, treacherous, vicious, twisted, slippery, depraved, vile"; (4) "Mysterious and hard to define": "strange, shapeless, sinister, weird, nightmarish, ghastly, hellish, fiendish, demonic, dark." The reason the Overcoming the Monster plot is the best fit for science fiction and fantasy is because "the monster will always have some human characteristics, but will never be represented as wholly human. By definition, the one thing the monster in stories can never be is an ideal, perfect, whole human being."[17] Many, and possibly all, of these descriptive terms appear in typical science fiction and fantasy novels.

Early Greek, Indian, Native American, and European "Overcoming the Monster" stories were told in a world where animals were threatening to humans and hunters actively hunted animals for food. Therefore, monsters still frequently have animal characteristics. In addition, to enforce law and order, rulers endorsed religions that explained what was good and bad behavior. Many early religions used metaphors to describe evil, or personified human sins in mythically evil characters with exaggerated flaws. Gods and demons that represented theft, murder and other sins that rulers wanted to forbid were presented as inhuman monsters to frighten the populace into good behavior. Executions of evildoers were regular occurrences in those eras, but today capital punishment is much rarer and reserved for only the worst crimes. But the formula for Overcoming the Monster stories has remained the same across the millennia. So, the same descriptive terms that were used in Homer's *Odyssey* and in the Jewish Torah are still used today to describe evil vampires, Titans, and wizards.

Formulaically, evil characters are "at odds with the world, behaving selfishly or anti-socially, they are either 'after something,' as Predators; wanting grimly to 'hold onto something,' as Holdfasts; or, as avengers, resentfully trying 'to get their own back.'"[18] Similar to the Devil in the Christian Bible, evil characters are rebellious against the established authority. They fight against society; for example, Lord Voldemort wants to overthrow the ruling magical order and place his allies in the former rulers' place. There are some classical anti-formulaic examples, such as Swift's *Gulliver's Travels* and other works that have used fantastical or science fiction characters to make satirical statements about the problems that exist in society, but in standard formulaic plots satirists and others who see problems in society are the ugly monsters.

The science fiction and fantasy character formula uses the same elements today as were used in knight-errantry tales, such as the Spanish *Amadis de Gaula* by Garci Rodríguez de Montalvo (1508),[19] which was written a century before the first modern novel, *Don Quixote* (1605, 1615) by Miguel de Cervantes, who consciously parodied Amadis' "madness" over unfulfilled love in his own book. *Don Quixote* broke all of the character formulas used in prior knight-errantry tales. Amadis fights against a monster in the form of the wizard Arcalaus, and overcomes the evil giant, Endriago, to win the love of his childhood sweetheart, Oriana. Amadis is described as "fearing death." Oriana, the beautiful princess, as well as other good female characters, is described as "fair." In contrast to these vague descriptions, *Don Quixote* is filled with multi-sensory descriptions, which are typically extremely negative and depict obscene content such as bodily functions and grotesque smells. One example is particularly memorable. It occurs in "Chapter X: Wherein Is Related the Crafty Device Sancho Adopted to Enchant the Lady Dulcinea, and Other Incidents as Ludicrous as They Are True." During an interaction that Don Quixote and Sancho had with Dulcinea, Quixote imagined that evil "enchanters," his "adversaries," had "transformed and changed her into a shape as mean and ill-favoured as that of the village girl yonder; and at the same time they robbed her of that which is such a peculiar property of ladies of distinction, that is to say, the sweet fragrance that comes of being always among perfumes and flowers. For I must tell thee, Sancho, that when I approached to put Dulcinea upon her hackney (as thou sayest it was, though to me it appeared a she-ass), she gave me a whiff of raw garlic that made my head reel, and poisoned my very heart." To this Sancho replies with agony,

> O miserable, spiteful enchanters! O that I could see you all strung by the gills, like sardines on a twig! Ye know a great deal, ye can do a great deal, and ye do a great deal more. It ought to have been enough for you, ye scoundrels, to have changed the pearls of my lady's eyes into oak galls, and her hair of purest gold into the bristles of a red ox's tail, and in short, all her features from fair to foul, without meddling with her smell; for by that we might somehow have found out what was hidden underneath that ugly rind; though, to tell the truth, I never perceived her ugliness, but only her beauty, which was raised to the highest pitch of perfection by a mole she had on her right lip, like a moustache, with seven or eight red hairs like threads of gold, and more than a palm long.[20]

Four hundred years after *Don Quixote*, while the book is still recognized as a genre-founding world classic, popular writers have not followed the model that Cervantes offers here. Cervantes proved that a novel can be even more popularly read if the main hero and his love interest are ugly or have severe physical and mental deformities. Basically the philosophical question that Cervantes raised and answered was this: Can good characters be ugly? It is clear to any reader of *Don Quixote* that this ugliness is hilarious and keeps their interest. The foul smell, the mole, and the moustache on Dulcinea's upper lip are unforgettable, striking and unique, even among the millions of books that have been written since *Don Quixote*. Modern storytellers have disregarded the possibilities for ugly good characters and evil beautiful characters and continue to re-create archaic ugly monster villains.

Christopher Booker also noticed this odd beautiful-hero and ugly-monster connection and proposed that occasionally stories have a "monster hero." I think this term is pretty misleading, as it can refer to either an ugly hero or a hero who is also the villain of the drama. The animated corpse is called a "monster" in Mary Shelley's *Frankenstein*. The professor who creates the monster, Dr. Frankenstein, is guilty of conducting an immoral experiment that endangers those he loves, and of several other egotistic and negative characteristics that typically belong to villains. The monster is also villainous, as he kills Elizabeth and Clerval in revenge. At the same time, both Dr. Frankenstein and the monster are heroic, as Dr. Frankenstein is attempting a heroic reanimation of the dead, and the monster is engaged in an attempt to be paired with a mate, an attempt that, when rejected, forces him into murder. Booker explains that *Frankenstein* turns the Overcoming the Monster plot "upside down," because at the beginning the "hero" is "dark" and the "monster" is "light," and in the end the hero is "overcome by the monster."[21] Another option that Booker does not consider is that while the monster is called the "monster," he might just be the ugly hero-villain in the story who overcomes the fully evil villain personified in Dr. Frankenstein. Darwinism and scientific experimentation on people (living or dead) were concepts that were greatly feared by writers as late as Wells, who at the end of the nineteenth century wrote *The Island of Doctor Moreau*. Mary Shelley saw the monster as the hero in comparison to the sins against God and nature committed by Dr. Frankenstein. In *How to Write Horror Fiction*, William Nolan defines the "monster" as a creature that "may or may not be supernatural," or "any type of weird menace, not just the more familiar monsters we all know and love: vampires, ghosts, demons, werewolves, and zombies."[22] Making a hero ugly confuses critics and possibly also the author of the plot line.

While typically formulaic writers admit that they are writing fiction according to a recipe, some modern writers refuse to acknowledge this about their fiction. In an interview in the *Pennsylvania Literary Journal*, Cinda Williams Chima, a bestselling author of the young adult Heir series, comments, "I've been a fan of high fantasy for years, and I began writing stories in the world of the Seven Realms after reading George R.R. Martin's *Song of Fire and Ice*—the Game of Thrones series. I loved what he did with character—there were no archetypes, no heroes, no villains, just layered, complex, realistic people in a fantasy world."[23] The key terms here are "high fantasy" and "no archetypes, no heroes, no villains." High fantasy is associated with anti-formulaic characters that go against the typical Overcoming the Monster plot structure and character types.

Chima points to one particular character in her series that presented a difficult challenge: "Han is street-smart from the outset, but he needs to develop the social and political skills he needs to navigate the Gray Wolf Court—and to successfully interact with the people he calls 'blue bloods.' His language changes over the four books, gradually morphing from street slang to court speech. I found it helpful to read straight through all of the scenes in one character's POV, to make sure that the voice is distinct and consistently evolving."[24] Han's speech changes because characters have to "change" and develop for the better throughout a modern formulaic popular story. Few writers use dialects and speech variations because to show a change, as in this case, one potentially has to alter the way the character speaks as he or she grows from rags to riches, especially if the character joins a royal court. A story can be pulled together faster if the writer refrains from complicating his or her formula's linguistics. The structural formula with standard character types, a standard generic plot and standard settings is time-consuming enough.

While character types are the most crucial for a formulaic writer to settle during the outlining and plotting stage of pre-production, the next problem a formulaic writer has to solve is a set of questions about character quantity. How many characters should be presented? How quickly should they be gotten rid of or killed? How many characters should survive to see the climax? Stephen King introduces an interesting concept when he discusses the relationship between characters and plot structure in *The Stand* and a few novels with a similar "theme" and "style" that followed it, explaining that when he first conceived the story, he "built" the book "like a pyramid" by starting "with the one character," and then adding a new character in each of the following chapters. But King realized that he had "something that was becoming very, very cumbersome, and I ended up doing something that was like a diamond instead of a pyramid. That is, it got fat to a certain point and then it began to shrink to a point again, which was the climax." (The difference between what King terms the "pyramid" and the "diamond" character structures can be explained with the chart in Figure 9.)

Looking back at the plot table, you can observe that most popular novels in this genre follow the diamond character numbers structure. There is a sharp increase in character quantity during Stage 1 and characters are frequently added all the way up through Stage 4. For example, Prendick meets Doctor Moreau and the other residents of the island. Bilbo meets Gandalf and a large group of dwarves. Readers meet various inhabitants of the small town in the *Black House*. Readers are introduced to the Muggle Prime Minister, Professor Slughorn and other new characters in the first chapters of *Half-Blood Prince*. Percy Jackson likewise meets several new friends and enemies. And Bella and Edward travel to an island where they meet the new help-staff. (Fewer new characters are introduced in *Breaking Dawn* than in the other five books on this

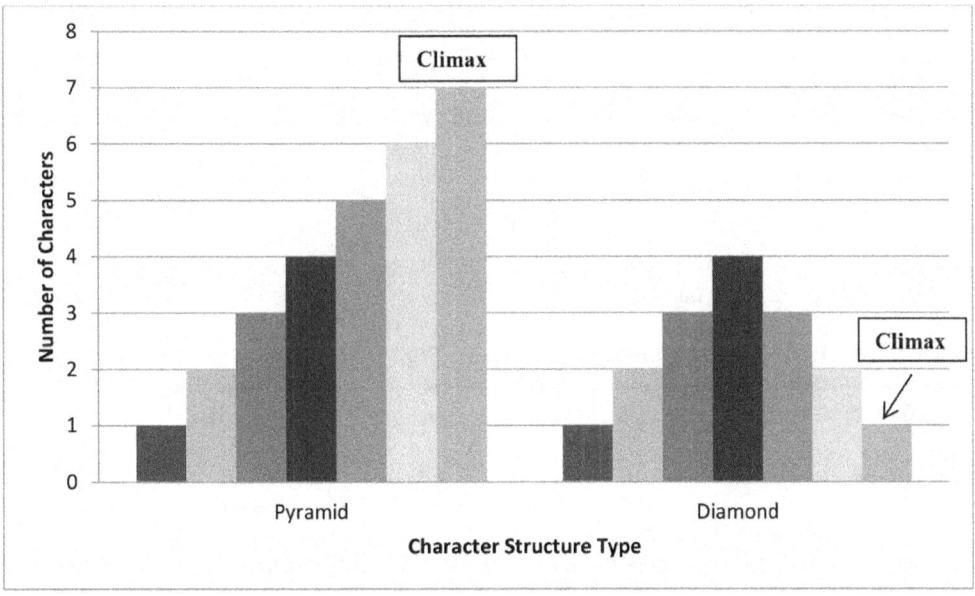

Figure 9. King's Changes in Character Number over Novel Time in Pyramid and Diamond Novel Structures.

list because it is the last book in a series, and serves as the last act of the series in some formulaic ways.) The time when characters start to die differs between these books and also depends on where a book is within a series, if it is not a stand-alone book. We find out about the first deaths of minor, barely known characters on the first pages of *Half-Blood Prince*. Prendick's shipmates also die in a shipwreck and then from a cannibalism attempt in the opening pages. In fact, the only work on this list in which somebody does not die on the first pages is *Breaking Dawn*, but this is because instead Bella suffers a violent sexual beating instead. Deaths frequently continue alongside new character introductions, with new villains and heroes frequently killed some time after they are introduced. Doing a precise death and new character introduction count between these six works would be difficult, because frequently hundreds or thousands of characters die in incidents when bridges collapse or mass battles slay whole armies, and the death tolls are almost never given with precision. Still, the principle behind character numbers is that most of the new characters introduced on the sides of good and evil have to be killed off before the end of the book, or the writer risks having to "resolve" what happened to each of these characters after the hero's triumphant final victory. If a hundred new characters survived to the end, it would make for a very long and tedious fifth act.

FANTASY AND SCIENCE FICTION SETTINGS

At first, it might appear that at least the settings of fantasy, science fiction and horror stories change with each particular story. From the six stories in Figure 10,

Setting Type	*Doctor Moreau*	*The Hobbit*	*Black House*	*Half-Blood Prince*	*Jackson: Labyrinth*	*Breaking Dawn*
Hero's Home	London	Hobbit hole	Landing, Wisconsin	London, Hogwarts	New York City	Forks, Washington
Villain's Lair	The Island of Dr. Moreau	Dragon's cave	Other dimension, black house	Varied dark or abandoned houses	Labyrinth, prison, wrestling ring	Castle in Italy
Time	Present	Alternate Timeline	Present	Present	Present	Present
Darkness and Bad Weather	Hides Beasts' features	Dark in hole/ cave/ underground	Jack has inner darkness	Night scenes, storms	Dark underground, volcanoes	Frequent rain, nights
Speculative World	Island of Mutated Beast-People	Fantastic world of magical creatures	Dark Tower and real world collide	Magical world within the real world	Olympic gods and offspring in real world	Vegetarian & human-drinking vampires

Figure 10. Overcoming the Monster Settings Table.

three take place in different states in America: Washington, Wisconsin and New York. Two stories bring the characters occasionally into London. Only one story has a setting that is entirely fantastic and out of this world. But then similarities become apparent: Five of these six stories are set in the present day (whichever year they were written in). All have a gothic location where the characters go when they enter the magical world, such as the castle of Hogwarts or the romantic island of Doctor Moreau. In addition, all of these stories allow for a creepy villain's lair, which usually has gothic castle or dark and scary horror house characteristics. And bad weather and darkness beset the heroes in all six stories. Can you imagine if Harry Potter and his friends practiced magic in an average suburban home in broad daylight? Such an ordinary location would be an unthinkable setting for a gothic tale of fantastic horror.

The principles and rules that formulaic settings in this genre have to follow are similar in structure to the rules governing horror film settings. Stephen King described the settings of his novels in terms of their similarity to screenplay setting foundations: "Each chapter" in *The Shining* "was a limited scene in one place—and each scene was in a different place, until near the very end, where it really becomes a movie, and you go outside for the part where Hallorann is coming across the country on his snowmobile. Then you can almost see the camera traveling along beside him."[25] King is referring to the standard screenplay format, in which each new scene begins with a line like this: "EXT. SNOWY COUNTRY MOUNTAIN—DAY." In film screenplays, a change of location means a new scene because the cinematographer has to cut the take to move to the new location. Because King's early and later success was tied to films (for example, the film version of *Carrie* was a hit before the book sold a million copies), and he wrote many of the screenplays for his own books, he got into the habit he describes here of writing novel settings, anticipating the translation to film and following some film standards to make this transition easier for the anticipated script adaptation. Film screenplays have never made the best-seller list, so this strategy is hardly likely to appeal to readers, but it is a convenient one for King.

In the same interview, King elaborated further on setting, saying that the horror field's "movements are as stylized as the movements of a dance. You've got your gothic story somewhere in the gothic castle with a clank of chains in the night. In *The Shining*, instead of a gothic castle, you have a gothic hotel, and instead of chains rattling in the basement, the elevator goes up and down—which is another kind of rattling chain."[26] Horror stories are confined to classical gothic settings, and many rules that apply to gothic settings also apply to fantastic and science fiction settings. One of these rules is that the setting should not be plain or realistically normal—the setting has to intensify the story and be a cause of fear, dread and amazement in all three of these story types. Of course, King has also confessed that most of his settings are small towns in Maine and that he has "never written a book using the city as a setting," perhaps because he does not know the city "well enough yet,"[27] or perhaps because writing descriptions with the same type of setting in all of his novels was a formulaic trick and an easier approach than setting changes. Among the stories reviewed in this chapter, there are some visits to London and New York City, but typically no significant magical activity takes place in the open in these cities, as unleashing gothic horror in broad daylight in a city would stop readers from being able to suspend their disbelief.

Best-Selling Writers in Fantasy and Science Fiction from Wells to Meyer

H. G. WELLS AND THE FOUNDING OF THE SCIENCE FICTION NOVEL (1866–1946; FIRST NOVEL, *THE TIME MACHINE*, 1895)

H. G. Wells was acutely aware that he was not following the popular formulaic or generic norms of his time. From his perspective, his fiction did not fit into any specific single category, but rather was a set of literary experiments with different formulas and types. Even his autobiography is called an *Experiment in Autobiography*. It was written near the end of his life and is a lengthy volume of personal philosophy and reflections rather than a chronological recitation of biographical facts, an approach that is intentionally anti-formulaic when contrasted with other autobiographies of his time.

His lifelong quest for new formulas stemmed from his "failure as a student," which led him to failing to acquire a "proper scientific career." He had failed to fit in with the formulaic scientific writing and research style. He decided to switch careers and began creative writing. As a scientist, he dissected the fiction that was popularly consumed and created "copious rubbish, imitative of the worst stuff in the contemporary cheap magazine." Even now publishers typically ask writers to read the things they publish and match the style of these publications. Thus, copying the style of the cheap magazines in which he hoped to be published to begin his career was a strategic move for Wells. He attempted what most popular generic writers do today: "I made not the slightest use of the very considerable reservoir of scientific and general knowledge already accumulated in my brain. I don't know why. Perhaps I was then so vain that I believed I could write *down* to the public. Or so modest that I thought the better I imitated the better I should succeed. The fact remains that I scribbled vacuous trash." Wells stresses the word "down" in this passage. He was acutely aware that the Education Acts, and especially the Education Act of 1871, had "enlarged the reading public,"[28] which led to an increased demand for new writers in the 1890s, but he was painfully aware that most of this demand was from readers with very rudimentary reading skills. So during his first attempts he tried to meet this demand by writing very simple prose that matched the reading level in the cheap magazines. However, unlike some hack writers who must put bread on the table with their scribbles, Wells soon found a position as "an assistant in a school deep in the country."[29] Having an income from teaching meant that Wells did not have to write "down" to anybody and had some leisure time to develop intellectual fiction for a much smaller, but more resilient reading public. A circumstance that made success in fiction more urgent for Wells was that the living conditions (i.e., sharing a room with two ministers and intellectually un-stimulating students) at his new school were poor. These problems gnawed at him and made him desperate to make a success in fiction, but not desperate enough to write down to the people or conform to the established formulas that he was closely familiar with.

In the middle of the 700-page *Experiment in Autobiography*, Wells includes a chapter called "Dissection" that contains sections with philosophic titles, unlike the summary and date section titles that dominate the rest of the book. At the end of this chapter is a section called "Digression about Novels," which is structured as a defense of an anti-formulaic novel-writing method against the classical novel formula that Wells' friend, Henry James, attempted to sway him into. Wells separates novels into three main categories: the low trashy novels written for the people, his unique writing style, and the high novel that was popular across the nineteenth century with the upper class. The category of low novels includes several different popular genres from the nineteenth and early twentieth centuries: gothic, historic, and Bildungsroman. But the category is not referring to the founding fathers of the genres like Sir Walter Scott or Mary Shelley, but rather to their hack great-grand-children, who began mimicking only the outlines of these formulas and wrote fiction as if they were printing money. A majority of classical writers from the middle to end of the nineteenth century in Britain knew each other or had similar circles of friends who attended the same salons and gatherings. Henry James, Oscar Wilde, Charles Dickens, Robert Louis Stevenson and a long list of other authors mention meeting each other in their autobiographical writings and refer to the discussions they had about the novel. While Wells was young when most of these authors were nearing the end of their lives, he still benefited from their conversational lectures on proper novelistic method. Each of these writers made significant innovations and methodological progress that further elevated the status of the high novel. The most influential figure for Wells was Henry James, who was "a shrewd and penetrating critic of the technique by which he lived." Today few popular fiction writers also write literary criticism of technique because the technique they use is primarily that of the low novels, or work watered "down" for a public that allows repetition and cheap suspense tricks to rule the craft. A hack can hardly criticize another hack on their technique.

However, James and Wells had a good deal to discuss, especially because their strongly developed and complex methods, techniques, and formulaic ideas differed. The key disagreement between them regarded the dense realistic and briefer fantastic descriptions that these two writers specialized in. "He liked me and he found my work respectable enough to be greatly distressed about it. I bothered him and he bothered me."[30] While Wells disliked low novels, he also did not like the grandly formulaic "Art Form" of "The Novel." The disagreement was over whether novels were a part of a literary "market place" or if they had to "do and be" something that fit with the classical formula of the novel's dimensions. In a critical opinion on Wells' *Marriage*, James wrote that it failed to comply with the novel's rules: (1) Wells "cut out an essential" conversation that bloomed into love, "after a feast of irrelevant particulars"; (2) the length of the couple's conversation was "improbable"; (3) the man in the conversation talked "at the reader instead of to the girl" and conveyed key points about his life through this conversation instead of disguising the facts in the flow of the story; (4) most importantly for James, the characters "did not behave unconsciously and naturally." These key criticisms are also essential building blocks of the realistic novel's formula, which James excelled in and founded. In realism, events, conversations and characters have to be probable and realistic, as if the novel mimics a slice of real life: "If the Novel was properly a presentation of real people as real people, in absolutely natural reaction in a story, then my characters were not simply sketchy, they were eked out of wires and pads of non-living matter and they stood condemned."

Thirty years after receiving this criticism, Wells finally formulated an objection to it: "the Novel was not necessarily, as he assumed, this real through and through and absolutely true treatment of people more living than life. It might be more and less than that and still be a novel." Most modern critics can extrapolate that Wells could have instead explained that his science fiction and fantasy novels were a different genre from James' realistic novel, as this is what Wells' reply hints at, but James was not referring only to the use of scientific fiction in Wells' novels, but also to their general noncompliance with James' rules of realistic descriptions and characters. Wells' characters are caricatures because he enjoyed drawing, reading and writing caricatures, and he found that in the literary marketplace there were readers from all classes who also fancied these light sketches with heavy metaphorical significance, rather than exact realistic details. Without Wells being able to formulate this rebuttal, James explained,

> I have read you ... as I always read you, and as I read no one else, with a complete abdication of all those "principles of criticism," canons of form, preconceptions of felicity, references to the idea of method or the sacred laws of composition ... which I shake off, as I advance under your spell, with the most cynical inconsistency. For under your spell I do advance—save when I pull myself up stock still in order not to break it even with so much as the breath of appreciation; I live with you and in you and (almost cannibal-like) on you, *on* you H. G. W.[31]

While James notices deviations from the novel's central formula, he forgives these divergences in Wells because the stories are spell-binding and allow the reader to flow through them briskly, as only great fiction can. The successful execution of these divergences from the high novel's formula is what helped Wells to create the new science fiction genre, as other writers also wanted to live "on" Wells' story, structure and technique.

Wells' style was to write as if he were sketching, rather than making a detailed oil painting: "I sketch out scenes and individuals, often quite crudely, and resort even to conventional types and symbols." Wells explains in his "critical papers" "that realism and exhaustive presentation were not [the novel's] only objectives" or even "its proper objectives," because the portrayal of reality was better fitted for the realm of "biography," whereas the novel should be based on "super-reality with 'created' persons."[32] Wells concluded that in a literary marketplace where the majority of the readers were interested in diluted rather than dense prose, he had to give them light sketches of his intense philosophical ideas, as this was a form his publishers and readers wanted to buy.

Aside from Wells' objection that fiction should not be a portrait of reality, Wells also believed that the subject matters of the nineteenth-century novel were outdated within the twentieth century: "The Novel in English was produced in an atmosphere of security for the entertainment of secure people who like to feel established and safe for good. Its standards were established within that apparently permanent frame and the criticism of it began to be irritated and perplexed when, through a new instability, the splintering frame began to get into the picture."[33] World War I, the Russian Revolution, the spread of Communism, and various other violent and socially insecure events and movements turned the ideas in the nineteenth-century novels on their heads. For example, the rebellion novels that Dickens and Scott wrote about the French Revolution turned into the terrorist novels that Stevenson wrote about Irish nationalists with bombs at the end of the nineteenth century. Were rebels fighting for human rights or were they violently disrupting human rights of safety and security?

The women's and civil rights movements also disrupted the accepted ideas about marriage and social relations. A portrayal of a woman who wanted to be married as her chief life-goal suddenly became unrealistic, shattering one of the core principles of the nineteenth-century realist novel. The conditions of poverty and work also mutated and were no longer as graphic as the naturalist novels had depicted, as the standard of living rose, but poverty spread. The technological, industrial and scientific revolutions overwhelmed people with continuous changes across the twentieth century.

The clash between morality and science was one that Wells felt most acutely as somebody who had attempted to make it in the sciences. Wells is known as a novelist whose future predictions frequently came true, perhaps because scientists took his ideas as inspirations and experimented within the areas that Wells explored at a rapid pace in his science fiction. The science fiction Wells established was his generic response to the overwhelming force of the scientific revolution that amazed, frightened and inspired his writing. His formula fit his time restraints and the nature of his scientific inquiry. Without running chemical, biological, or physical experiments to determine if his hypotheses were correct, he depicted his hypothetical outcomes in fiction. Therefore, he could not paint realistic scientific portraits of the beast-people in *The Island of Doctor Moreau*, among other tales, because he had to be vague enough in his predictions to leave room for scientific facts if in the future somebody did attempt a similar experiment of turning beasts into people. This scientific curiosity, philosophical details and the engaging stream of the plots is what attracted James to Wells' novels, despite his dogged refusal to comply with the realist formula that James believed was the ideal novel.

Wells' perspective on formulas in the novel mutated as his own writing changed. He wrote his best-known science fiction books, *The Time Machine*, *The Island of Doctor Moreau* and *The War of the Worlds*, in the 1890s. By 1912 he was both financially secure (moving into the Easton Glebe house) and respected in the literary circles. The ability to maintain a significant library and to have a pleasant place to write is a significant component for writers, and one can tell how much Wells cared about his work environment from a complex picture he did back in 1892, a detailed contrast to most of his other sketches. This was the year when Wells published *Marriage* (the work that James so closely scrutinized) and gave his lecture to the Times Book Club on "The Contemporary Novel."

"The Contemporary Novel" was a "pronouncement against the 'character' obsession and the refusal to discuss values"[34] and for "enlarging the scope of the novel" into "political ... religious ... and social questions."[35] Sedition laws prior to 1912 made in-depth, honest and dissenting discussions of these three realms life-threatening (i.e., Oscar Wilde's imprisonment and death over a decade earlier). When Dickens and Scott wrote "Novels with a Purpose," they frequently disguised radicalism with subversive tactics, making the purpose less threatening to the establishment. Wells complains that the early nineteenth-century "Novel with a Purpose" "examined no essential ideas; its values were established values, it merely assailed some particular evil, exposed some little known-abuse."[36] Wells' science fiction "Dialogue Novel" makes the moral conflicts and abuses grander by choosing well-known and feared abuses and simplifying them into striking metaphors to "present a thesis upon contemporary life and social development."[37]

Wells' lecture on "The Contemporary Novel" is really a diatribe against the "Weary Giant" theory of novel reading. Wells' argument is very similar to Lewis' criticism of the unliterary that I discussed in the previous chapter. Putting aside the need for subversion when writing radical literature, writers at the turn of the twentieth century faced a greater foe: the Weary Giant. As the reading public expanded, publishers and writers split into two camps (which are still in place today). One camp concluded that the majority of novel readers are in the middle class and work regularly for a living, and that they read between dinner and bed-time and need a novel they can doze off to and finish reading in less than three hours. In other words, Weary Giants read for "entertainment, relaxation, fantasy, and escape."[38] According to Wells, the Weary Giant

> wants to forget the troublesome realities of life. He wants to be taken out of himself, to be cheered, consoled, amused—above all, amused. He doesn't want ideas, he doesn't want facts; above all, he doesn't want—*Problems.* He wants to dream of the bright, thin, gay excitements of a phantom world—in which he can be hero—of horses ridden and lace worn and princesses rescued and won. He wants pictures of funny slums, and entertaining paupers, and laughable longshoremen, and kindly impulses making life sweet. He wants romance without its defiance, and humour without its sting; and the business of the novelist, he holds, is to supply this cooling refreshment.[39]

The second camp concluded that even if their middle- to upper-class readers were tired, they still wanted to be challenged, educated, and surprised by the novels they read. Wells' analysis leaves little doubt of his optimism that this second camp was winning in 1912: "Both fiction and criticism to-day are in revolt against that tired giant, the prosperous Englishman. I cannot think of a single writer of any distinction to-day ... who is content merely to serve the purpose of those slippered hours." Of course, modern readers might have noticed that the "old predominance" of Weary Giants in literature has recently resurfaced with a vengeance, as the pendulum of popularity and repute is swinging back toward the first camp.

Wells spends the bulk of the lecture explaining his distinction between weary and wakeful readers and writing techniques. The wakeful writer engages in "earnest and aggressive writing." However, as mentioned earlier, Wells did not fully support the wakeful writers' strict "classifications and exact measurements of a science" or their propensity to "set up ideals and rules as data for such classification and measurements." Wells questioned whether the definitions of a novel, a play, or a sonnet should be adaptable to new variations in length, content, and other dimensions. Wells argues for "a return towards a laxer, more spacious form of novel-writing," or for a "revolt against those more exacting and cramping conceptions of artistic perfection," and a "return to the lax freedom of form, the rambling discursiveness, the right to roam, of the earlier English novel, of 'Tristram Shandy' and of 'Tom Jones.'" The anti-classification and anti-scientific view of the literary art that Wells expresses is what has led to literature's current divide between hyper-formulaic popular fiction and anti-formulaic academic or artsy fiction that occasionally becomes even more formless than James Joyce's *Ulysses*, first serialized in 1918, half a decade after the "Contemporary" lecture.

Here an aside is necessary to demonstrate the roots of the nonsense or densely absurdist literature that stemmed from an interaction between two genre-setting writers: Joyce and Wells. The connection between Wells' Weary Giant theory and

James Joyce is not an accidental one. It began as early as 1917, when Wells was among a small group of critics that highly praised Joyce's first novel, *A Portrait of the Artist as a Young Man*. This publication followed Wells' lecture from 1912 on the necessity to experiment in novel-form, and so it is likely that if Joyce was familiar with either Wells' influential literature or these theories, any criticism that Wells made regarding his first novel would have been taken to heart by Joyce. In the 1917 review in *The Republic*, Wells finds the "memorable novel" to have many commendable qualities, and that Joyce is "a bold experimentalist with paragraph and punctuation." For anybody who has read Joyce's *Ulysses* and *Finnegans Wake*, the errors that Wells finds are extremely mild: he objects that there are no changes in "time and place" between scenes, that there are sudden jumps from "third person to the first," and that "he uses no inverted commas to mark off his speeches." Wells applauds some and criticizes other such innovations, concluding, "I think Mr. Joyce has failed to discredit the inverted comma."[40] Upon reading this review, Joyce must have felt compelled to reply, and their correspondence continued until 1928, when, instead of writing another review, Wells wrote a letter to Joyce directly because his criticisms were peaked and he could no longer call Joyce's new works "memorable" and could not recommend them to the general public. Wells' previous criticism found Joyce's mistakes to be charming, and it's possible that Joyce took this as a commendation and encouragement and decided to take these experimental elements and push them to their limits. In 1928, after the publication of *Ulysses*, as the first short pieces of *Finnegans Wake* were coming out, Wells wrote in a letter that he had been "studying" Joyce "a lot." Among other things, Wells seriously considered using curses similar to Joyce's in his own works, but he concludes that it would not work for him because he does not believe in God (i.e., hell, Jesus, and so on do not have the same effect), and bodily organs and functions have never "shocked" him. The fact that Wells kept up with the absurdist and modernist movements, and especially Joyce, is apparent in the style he later chose for his 1934 *Experiment in Autobiography*, but, like any other trend-setter, he only took some discursive elements from Joyce and other absurdists without slipping into nonsense. The key objections that Wells finds in *Finnegans Wake* are some of the elements that he commended in his "Contemporary Novel" lecture decades earlier. The "literary" "extraordinary experiment" or "vast riddles" have "escaped discipline," and he has "turned" his "back on common men," specifically "on their elementary needs and their restricted time and intelligence." *Ulysses* and *Wake* are "more amusing and exciting to write than they will ever be to read." Wells objects that he received neither "pleasure" nor "something new and illuminating," and therefore for him it is a "dead end." Wells ultimately concluded that he could not "follow" Joyce's "banner" of the absurdity genre, and had to follow the elements that he established with his own "science fiction" genre.[41]

This digression into Joyce is not meant as a symbolic rambling, but really shows the conflict in Wells that he struggled with from his days as a youth studying Henry James and Charles Dickens to the critical correspondence he had with Joyce. This same dualism was what most literary giants have struggled with across the modern, postmodern and current literary periods. This is a dualism between experimentation and tradition, between logic and absurdity, between discursive and formulaic novel writing styles. The duality is also between the weary and the wakeful giants. As you might have noticed, Wells finds fault with Joyce for the reasons that he commended in "The Contemporary Novel." Wells complains that *Finnegans* is too taxing on the reader's and his time and intelligence, but in "The Contemporary Novel" he ridiculed writers who wrote for the Weary Giant, who lacks time and intelligence. The apparent contradiction stems from the fact that most classical writers who founded a "new genre" were experts at merging and mutating previous formulas for the novel. Wells would never have created the science fiction genre if he had not constantly revised and questioned the established writing method and popular formulaic norms. So, Wells applauds Joyce's experiments in *A Portrait*, but finds that Joyce veered too far into the gutter in *Ulysses* and *Finnegans Wake*. The spectrum between absurdist, science fiction and realist novels is defined by degrees of extremity and several varying elements. James Joyce, H. G. Wells and Henry James each grabbed one of these extremes and took them to their limits. Naturally, they found the work of the others interesting, but could not imitate the alternative techniques or genres without losing some of their personal style and preferences.

Wells' style was to write "lightly and with a certain haste," creating "caricature-portraits."[42] This creative style is especially vivid in his sketches, which he drew throughout his life and frequently used to simplify his ideas to their rudimentary symbolic and pictorial outlines. The formulation and development stage for a science fiction writer must involve some form of visualization in order to create supernatural, superhuman, or simply nonexistent beings, situations and settings to populate their stories. H. G. Wells' "picshuas" are a great example of the relationship between art and writing for a science fiction writer. During the peak of his writing career, he created hundreds of ink drawings that he called picshuas. Many of them were of the people he loved, or included political commentary, but a few were visual plans, interpretations or comical portrayals of his science fiction novels. For example, in 1905, Wells included the note "Queer Tale, H. G.!" to his second wife (Amy Catherine Robbins, with whom he eloped in 1894, referred to here as "Jane") on her copy of *The Island of Doctor Moreau*, published in 1896; this note appeared beneath a sketch of a cartoonish figure sporting a bushy tail. In the book Wells keeps saying that the beast-people are indescribable and that the author cannot create a drawing to do them justice. If Wells had included this drawing in the book, the genre of the piece would switch from tragedy to comedy, as the play on the words "tale" and "tail" and the actual cartoonish mixture of human and animal parts is hardly as horrifying as the vagueness of the confused descriptions of a frightened narrator makes them out to be. It is likely that Wells doodled as he composed *The Island*, and that this helped him to create vivid descriptions, a step that few science fiction writers take today.

Another interesting pischua, for the purposes of this project, is taken from the cover of Wells' *The War of the Worlds*, dated around 1898, the year this book was published. Gene K. Rinkel and Margaret E. Rinkel explain that it visualizes Wells' wife, Bits, as a Martian invader, or a "little 'Dictator,'" because Bits had expanded her role in those years from "helper and critic" to "business manager and handler of his foreign publishers and translators," and this move was both positively surprising and threatening for Wells, portrayed in the picshua as a little man in a hat yelling "Oo'er!" (an exclamation similar to *Ah!*).[43] It's likely that this was drawn when Wells was doing the final edits on *The War of the Worlds*, and that it helped him to think through the symbolic and visual dimensions of his book.

In another picshua, a scene from *The War of the Worlds* is depicted, this one drawn later. The "Alien tripod illustration," by Alvim Corréa from the 1906 French edition of *War of the Worlds*, is an artist's interpretation of Wells' cartoonish picture. The visual representation of a chase by the Martian after Wells and his wife once again makes the symbols in the story personal for Wells' life, and shows that he projected his own impressions and feelings onto his fictional characters.

In the 1890s publishers had very different criteria for selecting novels than they do today, but there were also some clear similarities. They "wanted us [writers, including Wells] to be new but did not want us to be *strange*," and gave "secondhand tickets to literary distinction," but it wasn't wise for writers to permanently occupy vacant chairs of classical writers, or else they would be pigeonholed into the slot and wouldn't be able to ever write something in a different style or genre.[44] Nineteenth-century publishers wanted novels with new original stories, but that fell clearly into established formulas, and especially one of the formulas popularized by best-selling predecessors from a few decades earlier, such as Scott or Dickens. However, writers felt pressure to try a few different formulas over their literary careers to avoid becoming repetitive. Most popular novelists today specialize in one of their predecessors' formulas, sticking so close to generic rules that the works become extremely repetitive in their formulaic elements. Dickens, Scott and Wells created new chairs to sit in by refusing to follow just one earlier formula, instead merging several different formulas and adding components to create new genres. Wells exclaims that he would not "write as other writers wrote" because his "exceptional origins and training gave me an almost unavoidable freshness of approach"; thus, Wells "was being original in spite of my sedulous efforts to justify my discursive secondariness."[45]

Similar to Kathleen Woodiwiss, Wells also started a movement that has led the novel down its current path: he is credited as the founder of the science fiction novel genre. In his autobiography he explains that one of his good friends, Henry James, the founder and leader of the realist novel movement, wrote long letters to him with both criticism and adoration of his fiction. As recounted earlier, James did not think that Wells was following the established novelistic formulaic rules because Wells did not include detailed descriptions of his characters and actions that might have allowed the readers to feel as if they were stepping into his stories. Still, James was mesmerized by the "spell" that Wells created with the plot and dramatic narratives of his novels. Wells thought this spell lay in the philosophical dialogues and cartoonish satirical character studies that he executed. I mention this history because it will help me to explain why I particularly like Wells' *The Island of Doctor Moreau*.[46]

Like *Percy Jackson* and *Twilight*, *Island* is written with a first-person narrator, and while Percy is dyslexic, and Bella and Jacob are sentimentally love-obsessed, this narrator is a bit hazy in his descriptions because he is suffering from paranoia or is horrified by the experience he had on the "island." The difference is that Edward Prendick's psychology is realistic; as we learn about his school experiences, and the exact events that led him to the "island," readers feel horrified because the narrator specifies the precise causes of his paranoia, rather than just repeating that he is frightened (as Bella and Percy tend to do). Despite the fantastic descriptions, the reader is able to simultaneously learn, be horrified and amazed, and flow with the grand adventure that is unraveling in the plot.

Edward Prendick's ship is capsized. He escapes on a small boat with two other men, but they run out of food and draw straws to decide who among them they are

Figure 11. "H.G. Wells" (Bain News Service, George Grantham Bain Collection: Library of Congress Prints and Photographs Division, Washington, D.C.).

going to eat. The lot falls on one of the other men, but he resists and, after a struggle, the assailant and him fall into the sea and die. Edward is left alone, drifting in the boat, until he is picked up by a passing ship. The ship arrives at the "island" and the captain asks Edward to leave with the other passengers, but the islanders do not allow him to come with them. Finally, the ship puts him in a small boat adrift near the island and leaves him there. The islanders then take pity and allow him to set foot on shore, and he does so. Upon his arrival, he starts noticing that many of the people on the island have animal characteristics, and assumes that the Doctor is running experiments to turn humans into animals. This drives him mad, and he attempts to flee, but then he finds out that the Doctor is actually attempting to turn animals into humans through vivisection, or by cutting off parts of the animals' bodies and replacing these with parts from other animals or performing something like plastic surgery to correct features of the dogs and other beasts to make them appear as if they are people. Edward stays and studies this process and its outcomes. One night he is awoken by louder-than-usual screams from the puma that the Doctor is attempting to vivisect; the puma manages to run away and the Doctor follows, but the puma is too strong and kills the lone Doctor. Many of the beast-people drink and eat some of the Doctor's blood and meat, and this drives many of them blood-crazy, so that they revert to their animal instincts. Soon Edward is the only human left on the island; at first he lives with the beast-people in their forest huts, and then lives on his own once they have become beasts again, and is finally rescued by another ship.

The central concept is both simple and complex. Even today the ideas in this story are topical and relevant for our daily concerns. Plastic surgery, human beastly behavior, and genetically merging species are topics that are now at the forefront of philosophical and scientific discussions. Wells was known for forecasting scientific discoveries, partially because he must have inspired many scientists with his science fiction. At its best science fiction is supposed to do exactly what it achieves in *The Island*. Dramatic narrative science fiction was meant by its creator, Wells, to describe a scientific idea that is morally, philosophically or scientifically troubling and exciting in order to both educate and entertain readers. However, most recent science fiction writers borrow Wells' plot formulas and central stories, such as time travel or vivisection, and repeat them with only minor changes, typically stripping the meat from the stories instead of adding additional content.

The Structure of Wells' Science Fiction

H. G. Wells designed a structural formula for his science fiction stories and novels that fit his philosophy, sarcastic pessimism, political opinions, and writing preferences. In *The Logic of Fantasy*, John Huntington describes some of these key structural elements.[47]

Wells' stories have a "two-world structure" at their core, in contrast to the good versus evil structure that is common in most current science fiction, as well as in the fiction that preceded Wells, as far back as the first bibles or mythical stories in India, China, and Greece. Huntington explains the elements that play significant roles in this "two-world" structural formula:

> First, the structure itself is free from moral suggestions; the oppositions it sets up are purely physical and we cannot apply to them the moral terminology of good and bad. Thus, it is not a matter of showing that one world is to be preferred to the other. Second,

the principle behind the opposition is narrative. The point of such stories is not to describe a change, but to set up a static antithesis and then to fill in the relation between the two elements. Third, in such a structure neither world in itself holds our interest; what is important is that two of them together and the linked opposition they establish.... [Even Wells' narrator in "The Plattner Story" points out the clear] absence of plot.[48]

Huntington does not believe Wells' narrator, and he concludes that there is a clear "two-world" plot pattern in Wells' early novels, including *The Time Machine*, *The War of the Worlds* and *The Island of Doctor Moreau*. This is the two-world static opposition model, which is a form of "aesthetic antithesis" with a "systematic balance,"[49] which he describes in the passage above.

Huntington argues that Wells' early two-world novels are especially critically and popularly acclaimed because, unlike his later plots (with resolutions to the set-up conflicts), the two-world novels create a "static nightmare which has the virtue of forcing us to reconsider our own world," one that runs on "intellectual tension." This split in Wells' plot structures is also visible in the two main types of science fiction written in recent decades. Larry Niven builds the plots in *Draco's Tavern* on "intellectual tension" of the unraveling debates, instead of doing what modern filmmakers have done with Wells' own two-world stories, or ending them with the destruction of the "evil" force and the triumph of "good" in their resolved conclusions. There are many parallels between Niven's and Wells' structures because Niven has consciously imitated some of the techniques he liked in Wells. For example, in "Five Years to Infinity,"[50] Niven also tried to predict future events, as Wells did in some of his later (and pretty successful) attempts at prognostication. When asked about the similarity, Niven replied, "I never quite forget Wells."[51] He also explains that "in another age" "immortal poets" wrote in both "active sciences" and "science fiction," hinting at Wells.[52] In an interview regarding this point, Niven replied that, like Wells, "I was the clumsiest man in my chemistry lab class at Cal Tech. I don't have the patience or the temperament for scientific research."[53] While both Wells and Niven did not do much hard scientific research, both approach their science fiction by asking hypothetical scientific questions that cannot be answered by the scientists of their time and coming up with a scenario in their stories that represents the conclusions and assumptions drawn during their research stages.

The two-world intellectual tension model is very rare today, as most publishers and producers evaluate projects based on "melodramatic conventions that inspire unreflective affirmation."[54] The "neat" ending in which the dramatic conflict has been resolved gives readers a sense of rightness in the world; a "static" ending leaves them with a sense that something is still wrong in the world, and serves as a call to action after the film or novel is over: "Though no 'answer' is finally produced, the act of such mediation makes the author and his audience alive to the complex dynamics of the problems."[55] Huntington clarifies this point toward the end of his book:

> If the logical interest of Wells's early work lies in his willingness to tolerate and explore contradiction without restlessly seeking to simplify and resolve its tension, what marks [the] later mode and sets it importantly apart from the earlier imaginative style is a tendency to seek single answers and solutions, to see contradiction, not as the expression of the complexity of human desire and the contradictory seeking and interests that have so far prevented any easy settlement of social problems, but simply as muddle, a confusion that some clear, directed thinking will resolve. In this new mode, contradiction, which

formerly was essential to the understanding, marks a crisis that must be resolved by attaining some kind of unity, usually by disproving or discarding one of the opposing elements of the contradiction.[56]

In *An Experiment in Autobiography,* Wells wrote that he was learning from the advice that his mentor Henry James and other literary giants gave him, and that he was constantly attempting to improve his method for it to comply with the rules of proper fictional formulation that they used in their realistic novels. Wells wanted to keep the science fiction, unreal elements that distinguished him as the originator of a new genre, even during his own lifetime, but he also wanted to elevate the genre to fit the conventions that were necessary ingredients in realistic novels. The realist novel's formula includes in its core the melodramatic solution with a "single answer" to the novel's problem. Aristotle talked about the three unities of action, time and place, but also about the resolution or catharsis that has to happen once the tragedy is over and we feel a release of the negative emotions that the tragic actions in the play evoked in us. More recently, more specific formulas for all dramatic fiction (novels, plays and various other modes of literature) have arisen that have prescribed to authors how to go about constructing their fiction. In 1863, with the publication of *Technique of the Drama: An Exposition of Dramatic Composition and Art,* Dr. Gustav Freytag[57] created a pyramid that is commonly used in composition classes today to explain the dramatic arc structure. It is likely that Wells and James both read this book and the related literary theory on the proper structure of the novel.

As writers in the late nineteenth century competed in a tight literary market both in America and in Britain, they frequently published sarcastic or bitingly negative reviews of each other's work, and the criticism was typically that the newly published literature failed to fully meet the requirements of the great novel, or the formulaic rules of great dramatic fiction that were being critically discussed in these literary circles. It is likely that Wells felt this pressure and changed his formula from the static two-world structure to the dramatic tension and resolution model in his later works. For example, Huntington comments that within *In the Days of the Comet,* Wells fails to employ the "ironic thought" and "logical fantasy" that characterized his "authentic scientific romance,"[58] a break that occurs due to the addition of the "realistic part" of the novel. The realistic dramatic school was pulling Wells away from his scientific romance model, and he made a few flawed steps to oblige them. In addition to making his stories more realistic, Wells also moved from an "anti-utopian" system to a "utopian prophetic" one.[59] In other words, Wells went from a world that is neither ideal nor a nightmare, but exists in stasis, to the predictions about the future and conclusions about human nature that he draws in his later stories.

There would not be a static confrontation if there were two different sides to engage in the unresolved conflict. In Wells, the sides are typically humans versus nonhumans, or occasionally two nonhuman species against each other. With possibly all of his science fiction stories, Wells creates a "strange, new, nonhuman being," such as the "Eloi, Morlocks, Beast People, Martians, Selenites," in order to demonstrate different "possibilities of human confrontation with other forms of (conscious) life."[60]

An interesting pattern in the three central Wells novels that I examined for this project is that all of them involve some form of cannibalism or attempted or suggested cannibalism. In *The Time Machine,* the Morlocks eat the Eloi. In *The Island of Doctor Moreau,* three humans draw straws in a boat to determine whom they are going to eat. In *The War of the Worlds*, Martians drink human blood for its nutritional value. Huntington concludes that in Wells' "early works cannibalism is a test of difference: if cannibalism or the fear of cannibalism is involved (as with the Morlocks and the Eloi), then the two species are really one, but if it is not involved, then they are separate ... if the other species is different from ours, murder is not involved."[61] The Martians are not committing murder when they drink human blood because the species are different. If there is a distinction in hierarchy, or if one species is superior to another, then they are different and "the evolutionary 'doctrine' of survival of the fittest justifies killing them."[62]

In *The Seven Basic Plots*, Christopher Booker explains that there is a "fundamental rhythm" to stories, in which the happiness or chances of survival of the hero swing up and down, at first gently and then more and more extremely between the poles, until the hero is down to his lowest point, when death is imminent, and then, with the help of a miracle, he achieves a complete victory over his monstrous enemy and recovers ultimate happiness, success and liveliness.[63] In Wells' *The Island of Doctor Moreau*, and his other early two-world static structures, the degree of danger of death, and the cycle of happy versus depressed all the way to the point of being suicidal, plays out in a pattern similar to Booker's "Overcoming the Monster" plot, with the exception that the "monster," even if overcome or killed, fails to bring with his demise joy or satisfaction to the hero, who frequently declines further into misery at the very end of the novel without bringing his, or the reader's, emotions back up. By showing the reader the hopeless misery in this fictional world and leaving him with a sense of doom, Wells is sending his readers off to effect change on their own, instead of showing a successful victory of the monster in his constructions. In addition, the two-world novels are tragedies in the Aristotelian sense because there is no catharsis or purging of emotions; they remain at the surface of the reader's mind.

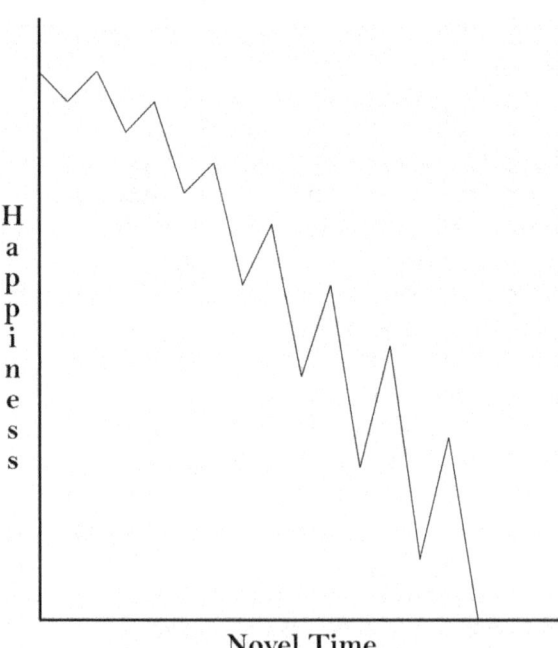

Figure 12. Wells' Two-World Novel Time and Happiness.

J. R. R. TOLKIEN
(1892–1973; FIRST NOVEL, *THE HOBBIT*, 1937)

While Wells was the key founder of science fiction, due to his popularity, J. R. R. Tolkien can be credited with founding the modern fantasy novel genre. Tolkien is not the only Oxford professor who made it into Bloom's "bestsellers of the twentieth century" list (he was teaching at Oxford when he wrote both *The Hobbit* and the *Lord of the Rings* trilogy). Oxford is unique in its hiring of popular novelists. For example, it currently offers classes with Davis Bunn, who has sold over 6 million copies in the spiritual novel genre. Other Oxford affiliates include the bestselling academic, Joseph Heller (1925–2000; *Catch–22*), who studied, after earning a masters degree from Columbia University, on a Fulbright scholarship at Oxford University between 1949 and 1950. At the time when Tolkien taught at Oxford, there were two other major fiction writers on the staff: Charles Williams and C. S. Lewis, with whom Tolkien formed the "Inklings," a conservative religious club, but one that also worked on creating fantastic spiritual fiction. Despite this interest, Tolkien's novels fit much better into the fantasy category than into spiritual and religious genres. The fantasy genre formed from the Inklings' anti-modern stand: "[Tolkien's] preference for a lost and heroic age before" World War I "and before electricity was shared by many contemporaries." Because of Tolkien's popularity, many imitators sprang up, which together "formed the basis for a whole fictional industry of fantasy novels and mythic lost worlds."[64]

The style and structural elements of his stories reflect some of the worst habits of the present-day fantasy genre. *The Hobbit* was Tolkien's first major fantasy for children, and was later followed by *The Lord of the Rings*. *The Hobbit* is representative of many of Tolkien's marketing strategies and technical problems. The book begins with what appears to be an explanation of a nonexistent ancient English language, in which, for example, T is replaced by an upward arrow. In addition, the narrator explains that instead of "dwarfs" the story uses the plural form "dwarves" (a "reason" for this is apparently offered in *The Lord of the Rings*). While this gives the appearance of linguistic sophistication, the narrative does not include enough linguistic abnormalities to have included these explanations. While the invention of ancient, alien and other foreign languages is an engaging technique, used in some of the best science fiction and fantasy, here it is simply used to lend the appearance of sophistication to a narrative that is watered down to monosyllabic words, repetitive dialogue and a lack of both description and engaging action. Maps and pictures serve a similar purpose of distracting readers from the narrative itself and giving it the appearance of style, while style is lacking in the language.

The second major problem is that, as with most popular forms of entertainment, the first few pages are a lot cleaner than the remainder. The initial pages introduce a hobbit, Bilbo Baggins, and describe his lineage and living accommodations with enough detail to create sympathy and interest in this hero. On page 3, the narrative becomes repetitive and diluted, as if assuming that a reader has either bought the book before arriving on this page or put it back on the shelf.

The third problem that stands out is that the dialogue in the story fails to convey important information that might move the story forward, or add density to the characters. For example, on page 3 and 4, Bilbo and the wizard Gandalf have a conversation about saying "Good morning!" and the various things this phrase might mean. If you had a similar conversation on your way to work, you would probably be extremely frustrated and annoyed, and readers must have a sense that the story is taking a dive as they paddle through it.

The fourth troubling element is the constant repetition of action and character pile-up. After the slow and somewhat interesting introduction of the two main heroes, Bilbo and Gandalf, the following four pages are spent on the introduction of dozens of dwarves, who are barely described in appearance or manner other than to say that they all look like dwarves with hoods and beards, and act similarly rudely as they push Bilbo out of the way to step over him and into his hobbit hole. Stephen King, as discussed previously, once explained that he had difficulty in his stories with gradually introducing characters, so that there would be too many characters and he would have to kill them off gradually to build up to the climax; if there are too many surviving characters at the end of a story, then their lives all have to be "resolved" in the conclusion. Instead of introducing characters gradually across the narrative and allowing them each to have significance, or perhaps just introducing them all together as a single nameless crowd, Tolkien introduces them one by one or in small groups, but fails to explain any significant distinctions between them. Many fantasies have this problem of crowds of supporting characters that take up story-time as they enter, but fail to serve a narrative purpose.

The fifth frustrating problem here is that instead of using description to tightly summarize something like what the dwarves ate, Tolkien has them call out their varied requests in many voices in a dialogue: "And raspberry jam and apple-tart." "And mince-pies and cheese." "And pork-pie and salad." "And more cakes—and ale—and coffee."[65] These types of dialogue lines cannot be found in any classical novel from the nineteenth century, as it is a common mistake of wasting dialogue on meaningless repetitions, instead of using it to build characters or to progress the action.

The sixth problem is making threats that are later explained as jokes or bluffs. Anton Chekhov's "gun" principle explains why this is a grave mistake. In an 1889 letter to Alexander Lazarev, Chekhov included a frequently quoted line: "Do not put a loaded rifle on the stage, if no one is going to fire it." In *The Hobbit*, the dwarves sing a song in which they threaten to "Chip the glasses and crack the plates! … That's what Bilbo Baggins hates."[66] But in the next sentence after this song ends, the omnipotent narrator declares, "And of course they did none of these dreadful things, and everything was cleaned and put away safe as quick as lightning." Considering that they entered Bilbo's hole without asking for permission and the narrator stressed that they had no manners, and keeping their direct threat in the song in mind, their speedy cleaning is a contradiction of the various foreshadowings the author inserted earlier. Tolkien has placed several loaded "guns" on his stage to create fake suspense, without any intent to fire them, in a children's story about cute dwarves. The dwarves later wage battle, but they do not break the plates they actually threaten to break.

The seventh and perhaps most serious problem is the fact that the writer appears to be consciously trying to put his readers into deep slumber. This is a technique that many formulaic writers engage in, and it is especially prevalent in fantasy novels. Perhaps the thinking goes that if the reader falls asleep, they might see some exciting fantasies that will keep them off the scent that something is amiss in the fantasy they are trying to read. The repetitions of the entering dwarves and the parallel dialogues contribute to the sagging eyelids syndrome. In addition, the writer frequently refers to "sleep" and explains that the hero (and perhaps the rest of the supporting cast) is tired. Thus, in *The Hobbit*, Tolkien adds the following line to one of the dwarves' songs: "In places deep, where dark things sleep."[67] The monosyllabic, nonsensical, sing-songy and iambic song itself also contributes to the sleep induction.

The eighth difficulty appears to be a contradiction to the seventh, but is actually problematic because it exists right next to it. As the dwarves finally get around to discussing what the "adventure" they are planning is all about, and when Bilbo hears the words "*may never return,*" he falls down to the floor shaking and screaming "struck by lightning, struck by lightning!"[68] This is a case of formulaic, manufactured horror that has no grounding in any actual foreshadowing or supporting details from the narrative. Frequently these types of horrified shrieks are inserted right after parts of the narrative in which the main character has fallen asleep, or in which there is a song or a dialogue that makes the character sleepy. It is likely that after being half-asleep themselves, the readers will feel a sense of illogical alarm at these shrieks, similar to how anybody feels when they are suddenly awakened out of a daydream. I am certain that this list would get very long indeed, if I did not fall asleep at this point in the narrative.

LARRY NIVEN (1938–; FIRST NOVEL, *WORLD OF PTAVVS*, 1966)

In Larry Niven's *Draco Tavern*,[69] each chapter is an individual short story on the same theme of aliens coming to visit or live on Earth and visiting a station tavern in Antarctica. Many of these stories do not have fully resolved endings, but they also do not begin a new story's climb at the end. Larry Niven summarizes the endings in *The Draco Tavern* as follows: "Sometimes I surprise. Sometimes I teach. Sometimes I write puzzles. Sometimes the ending is inevitable. I think you'll find all of that in the *Draco Tavern*."[70] When asked in a follow-up interview question if *Draco Tavern*'s anti-formulaic elements made it less marketable with publishers, and whether it might have found a publisher if he initially wrote it as a novel rather than gradually as short stories, Niven replied, "These stories cover about forty years. I certainly wouldn't have had the patience to write them as a novel. But I think it would have earned more money and maybe an award."[71] This shows the importance of revision and reflection for the development of a story—a set of stories that took Niven the longest time to complete is perhaps his best-constructed literary work.

While *The Draco Tavern* came out in 2006, most of these stories were written in the 1970s and 1980s, and by the time he published his more recent stories, Niven was already an incredibly prolific writer with a brilliant ability to create realistic science fiction. The short stories in this collection read more like a patchy novel because they all center on one setting, the Draco Tavern, after which the book is named. Aliens have come to Earth, but most of them stay in Siberia at the tavern, where their spaceport is, with only a few alien species venturing out to explore or utilize Earth. The tavern owner, Rick Schumann, is the central character, and the first-person narrator. He frequently mediates alien disputes, both among themselves and with humans, or spends his time trying and failing to become extremely rich by using alien technologies. The aliens have unique cultural and physical quirks, and they engage in outrageous and hilarious misbehaviors, which are a pleasure to read.

There are several elements that separate this book from the work of hack, formulaic science fiction writers today. First, the conversations are not purely yes-no dialogues, in which one character doggedly disagrees with some simple point or, more frequently, desire that the other is expressing. Instead, the conversations are typically about larger themes, such as priesthood, religion, spirituality, and suicide. The last is surprisingly frequent and typically caused by sexual frustration. The suspense in the story is created not only by the ticking-bomb threat of the characters' potential death but also by the intense philosophical discussions the characters have about significant past, present or future actions. The question of whether the aliens believe in God suddenly also becomes a potential threat to humans (ticking bomb), but the threat is almost secondary to the threat of the hero losing an argument he is having with one of the aliens on the topic. To defend an atheist position, the author presents an example of extreme religiosity, and if the example succeeds in convincing the reader, this becomes a conclusion or resolution, even if no eventual resolution actually takes place. Also, the ideas might be engaging when the narrator disproves a previously considered theory with a joke that turns it on its head and gives the reader a new and entertaining perspective. Second, the invention of alien "grammar," linguistics, languages, and cultures is a trick that has defined the best science fiction since H. G. Wells, and it is well crafted in these stories. Third, the stories frequently have surprising endings, such as the reader realizing at the very end that the narrator was engaging in an interactive space-travel fantasy game, rather than actually going on an expensive space expedition in the final paragraphs of a story. And the fourth, and most noticeable, positive element in these stories is the scientific lectures that are scattered between the jokes, the horror, the philosophy and the action. For example, in "The Missing Mass," Teng, an astrophysicist, gives Rick a lecture on the Hubble constant, missing mass, the Casimir effect, the expanding and collapsing universe, supernova explosions, gas giant stars, and a string of other technical terms. Some of the conclusions drawn are fictional, but still scientifically sound, and would be of interest to any casual or serious science student.

There are a few clouds, however, in this book's otherwise thought-through structure and style. Some of the introductions are repetitive, citing points that were brought up in earlier stories (a consequence of their short-story origins). But this is also the reason the stories are denser with ideas and details. The reading public does not tolerate formulaic and repetitive short stories in major magazines, while for some reason it consumes repetitive novels in large quantities. Would this book have found a publisher if Niven had presented it as a completed novel today without the stories' initial success?

In "One Night at the Draco Tavern," the author digresses into a play, complete with dialogue and stage directions. The stripping of descriptive details leaves the dialogue bare and flat and reveals the problem some of the less philosophical dialogues in these stories have: *Larry*: "Would you be the bartender?" *Rick*: "I own the Draco Tavern."[72] Here the characters are filling in back-story with a dialogue instead of letting it emerge as a minor detail in the first-person narration. This "telling" rather than "showing," and the repetitive nature of some of the recurring conversational themes, topics, and background information, is a recurring stylistic flaw.

In summary, while Niven occasionally stumbles, these stories are finely crafted and an entertaining read that I would recommend to science fiction fans.

STEPHEN KING (1947–; FIRST NOVEL, *CARRIE*, 1974)

The horror genre underwent a major transformation in 1974 with the publication of Stephen King's *Carrie* and James Herbert's *The Rats*. The first is about a high school girl being overcome by supernatural powers and going on a murderous rampage; the latter describes "a plague of mutant black rats." James Herbert is also listed among the top best-selling authors from the end of the twentieth century, as his "sales neared forty million books by the late 1990s, but unlike the books of Stephen King few have been filmed," so his name is not as popularly recognizable.[73] The two authors joked that they invented "splatterpunk" with their best-selling 1974 works, but both later moved into supernatural horror and thrillers, as well as some related "serious" or more formulaic genres with their later novels.[74] King recognized "Richard Matheson and Robert Bloch" as the two key writers who taught him "how to write" and "made it possible for [him] to make a living. They created the genre."[75]

King and Herbert's direct predecessor in horror is H. P. Lovecraft (1890–1937), whose Cthulhu Mythos stories were particularly "influential" on King and Herbert, but his work has not reached anywhere near an equivalent best-selling status. In turn influenced by Wells' science fiction and Poe's gothic horror, Lovecraft's stories are formulaically closest to Poe because they are also highbrow fiction, typically utilizing first-person, intellectual (as well as mad and horrified) narrators and "shock endings," which suggest a meaning, instead of fully resolving the conflict in the story.[76]

The major innovations that Lovecraft made to the horror genre can be better understood when one looks at the step in horror fiction between Lovecraft and Poe in the form of one of the least "secret" of all secret societies—the Order of the Golden Dawn. Modern equivalents of this order are the Discordians and Scientology. The Golden Dawn initiated the rise of magical religious writings and beliefs (which we know today as branches like Wicca paganism, which still uses as its key foundation the set of tarot cards that one of Golden Dawn's chief members, A. E. White, designed at the end of the nineteenth century). The Order is typically seen as being at the roots of the horror and fantastic genres because its founders and best-known members were artists and writers. The Golden Dawn was composed of three orders. The First was based on Hermetic Qabalah, or the mystical book of the key Jewish religious foundations, and focused on the study of the four elements and the tarot. The Second was the "Inner" and moved from the study to the teaching of magic and alchemy. And the Third was the "Secret Chiefs," who ruled over the lower two orders.

The Order took shape around 1886, when the key founders passed around the Cipher Manuscripts, which described the basic nature and rules of the Order. The Order's best-known members, including William Butler Yeats, joined in the 1890s, when it was at the peak of its popularity. The last of the original founders, Samuel Liddell MacGregor Mathers, was kicked out of the Order in a "revolt" in 1900. Mathers had added MacGregor to his name because of his obsession with Scotland (and perhaps Sir Walter Scott). The order split apart and gradually disintegrated after Mathers left, but still continued in various forms until the present day, though the last official temple of the Order was abandoned in 1978. The only widely recognizable horror genre name from this organization, besides Yeats, was Bram Stoker (*Dracula*), though his membership has not been definitively proven. The Order influenced the general public's perception of the occult, magical and horrific. Thus, even if Lovecraft, Wells, Wilde and Stoker were not direct members of the Order, they had an appreciative view of horror in part because of the Order's influence. Atheism and alternative religious practices only started to be accepted by the establishment as nonpunishable offenses at the end of the nineteenth century, around the time of the Order's founding. While horrific Judeo-Christian morality tales have existed since the Old Testament, the century following 1886 saw the rise of all major classical horror writers: Lovecraft, Wells, Wilde and Stoker. After 1886, even writers who wrote about Christian morality, like Marie Corelli, used many spiritual and magical elements because they were exposed to these ideas in high society and intellectual company.

The period between Lovecraft's death in 1937 and 1974 saw the growth and popular distribution of horror films and horrific pulp fiction cartoon strips, both of which shaped the very different brand of horror that emerged in the work of King and Herbert in 1974. They show the development of a more repetitive formulaic pattern that these authors built for their brand of the horror genre.

Bloom credits Stephen King with being "the best-selling American author of all time," growing into extreme success in the 1980s.[77] This idea seems a bit suspect until one realizes that many of the top best-selling authors of all time (Barbara Cartland and J. K. Rowling, for example) were British, and so cannot compete with King as the best-selling Americans.

In what Douglas E. Winter called "the first book-length study of King's fiction,"[78] he published an interview reply from May 3–4, 1982, in which King said, "I think I can really scare people to the point where they will say, 'I'm really sorry I bought this.' It's as if I'm the dentist, and I'm uncovering a nerve not to fix it but to drill on it."[79] The idea that a writer wants readers to feel "sorry" they bought his book is an interesting concept, and it would be interesting to do a study on how many King readers return to read a second book by him. Maybe this is why most popular novels are extremely formulaic: the writers are trying to make readers feel sorry they bought them.

Another explanation for King's abrupt replies (the above is certainly not an isolated incident) is that, according to his own confessions, at some points of his life he used large quantities (his own numbers vary) of drugs. When asked in a *Playboy* interview if he had smoked "grass," King replied, "No, I prefer hard drugs ... I did a lot of LSD and peyote and mescaline, more than sixty trips in all.... I've got to say that for me, the results were generally beneficial. I never had a trip that I didn't come out of feeling as though I'd had a brain purgative; it was sort of like a psychic dump truck emptying all the accumulated garbage out of my head." This was troubling to the *Playboy* representative, who asked whether the "experience with hallucinogens [had] any effect on [his] writing later on." "None at all," King insisted.[80] Either way, King's interview replies are much more honest than those of most of the other popular genre writers, most of whom have not confessed to using "hard drugs."

In an interview with *Penthouse* in 1982, King says about *IT* that he "got everything in this book ... Frankenstein, Jaws, the Creature from the Black Lagoon—f**king King Kong is in this book, I mean, it's like the monster rally.... Called *It*. I should call it *Shit*."[81] This mix reveals King's derivative inspirations for the mix of characters he placed into *IT*. In another interview, when responding to a line of questions on the formulaic nature of his writing, King erupted with a quote from God: "'So where were you when I made the world?' In other words, 'Shut up, f**k face, and take what I give you.'"[82] King equates his work as *the* writer with God in several interviews, insisting that critics who find fault with his "creations" should "Shut up."

I will not follow Stephen King's advice, as reading a few of his recent novels disconcerted and frightened my sense of style, logic, and overall polite writing habits. I had previously read *Carrie* and thought it was pretty well written, as was his book *On Writing: A Memoir of the Craft* (2000), which had some inspirational advice when I read it for the first time around six years ago. Sadly, King's novels from this past decade are a mixture of the hyper-formulaic and illogically absurd that makes them unreadable, at least for a literary critic. For this study, I looked at two of King's recent novels. The first is the fifth book in the Dark Tower series, *Wolves of the Calla* (2003). The second is a book that King wrote with Peter Straub, as co-writing with Straub represents a significant part of King's literary career; this one is called *Black House* (2001), a name very similar to Charles Dickens' *Bleak House*.

The style in several parts of *Black House* is a mixture of Dada absurdity and *Bleak House* realism. While detail typically enriches a story with texture and helps readers to enter the fictional world, here details jump between unrelated elements, complete with grammatical errors and changes in voice, person and tense that disorient readers. For example, the novel begins with the statement, "Right here and now ... we are in the fluid present."[83] Most of the novel remains in the present tense, but newspaper articles and flashbacks cause disorientation as one returns to the present-tense account. In addition, the narrator explains that the "present" is "a few years into both a new century and a new millennium,"[84] but the current present is a decade later than that time, so it's pretty confusing as to which "present" the narrator is in, and how we can be there with him. The second trouble is the use of "we" in the passage above; across the narrative, the narrator writes as if the reader and him are "floating" from place to place in present time while watching the events unfold. The constant interruptions of the narrator that comment on what "we" are seeing further compromises the reader's ability to follow the root of the story. In addition, a lot of the details that fill the introductory pages are of names of counties, railroads, streets and shops. For example, here is a list of "shops" in this town that "we" are in: "Benton's Rexall drugstore, Reliable Hardware, Saturday Night Video, Regal Clothing, Schmitt's Allsorts Emporium."[85] All of these details do not make any difference for the story, and readers must either skim through them or read them at the peril of these names melting into a line of jumping sheep. Still, it is likely that some readers might stop and read these descriptions, and they might even become interested when they start reading about a police station, and might assume that now the action will begin, or that it will be explained what this story is all about. No such luck.

"We" float out of the police station after a couple of paragraphs and end up in the radio studio of "KDCU-AM, Your Talk Voice in the Coulee Country," where George Rathbun is in the middle of his "popular morning broadcast" of *Badger Barrage*,[86] which is a sports show that features the host insulting his listeners while making obscure references to a game the reader has not seen and is not given a summary of. Even if somebody is a sports fanatic, this description is a complete change from the Dickensian descriptions that preceded it and loses both readers who want a close description and those who enjoy reading about sports. There are only two things that the dialogue between Rathbun and his listeners achieves: (1) it allows King to use a string of insults, and (2) it allows him to insert an advertisement for the radio station that he bought decades ago and apparently still owns. The insults include the following: "'How did that scrawny pasty-face creep get a radio show in the first place? ... Oh, I forgot, you like that s**t." Also, "He hasn't been to the dentist in six, seven years. His teeth look like s**t." After this discussion about feces, the broadcaster moves on to "love": "I love you *dearly*, that is the honest truth, I love you like my momma loved her *turnip patch*, but sometimes you people DRIVE ME CRAZY!"[87]

From there the story jumps to the giant Mouse, who, "in a cloud of beer and marijuana," asks Bobby if he has ever read Jacques Derrida, and when Bobby confesses he hasn't Mouse exclaims, "'No s**t, Sherlock!" Just as the reader is totally flabbergasted, trying to figure out how on earth all this stuff is connected, Tom Lund reads a newspaper article about "the Fisherman" murderer, who is suspected of having committed a string of gruesome crimes.[88] But the story jumps from there to the Maxton Elder Care Facility and introduces an unrelated character, Chipper, who is apparently a married crook and the operator of the facility, and who proceeds to have sexual intercourse with his secretary, Rebecca Vilas (who briefly tries using a "stage-Irish accent," but then gives up on it), on the sofa. As King has said in many interviews, he does not like describing sexual intercourse, so before the sex begins, he cuts out of the scene, writing, "and before Chipper obliges her, we do the sensible thing and float out into the lobby, which is still empty."[89] Yes, the lobby is empty, just as this narrative is empty of meaning. The jumps in the narrative are in fact more of a deconstruction of a story, as opposed to the logical elements of a coherent fictional narrative. If King was designing a house, he would have just thrown a bunch of bricks around the yard, squirted some cement over the bricks, and perhaps defecated on top of it all to complete the work of art.

Later on in *Black House*, the narrative disintegrates into something closer to the more standard popular formulas. The heroines regain "blue" "eyes,"[90] and "fuller-breasts."[91] Dialogue becomes choppy and ellipses regain dominance: "'In heaven, there is no beer ... that's why we drink it here ... and when ... we're gone ... from here.'"[92] Chapter endings start to include death threats: "'Speedy, I'd like to wring your neck.'"[93] Or chapter endings include questions left unanswered that serve as cliff-hangers, as in the "Drudge Report" at the end of Chapter 28: "The first answers may come tomorrow.... Developing."[94] The writing on the wall becomes monosyllabic, poorly spelled, and repetitive, as when Jack discovers a greeting on a wall in red:

CUM GET MEE
CUM GET MEE

The characters start getting sleepy, and they start making readers sleepy: "Above all, he needs rest. Sleep, if sleep is possible ... fall asleep it does...." This is followed by a description of Jack's breathing slowly stopping, and the body disappearing, only for us to be told at the beginning of the next chapter, "Oh, forget about that." Jack has in fact disappeared from the cornfield, but not in the way "you" apparently think.[95] Either way, the use of sleep as a horror element is about as effective as using it as a climatic episode in an odyssey adventure. In fact, the final chapter before the epilogue ends with these words: "In the dark behind the chapter in which Jack Sawyer sleeps, Parkus answers her question with a single world: *Ka.*"[96] So, sleep is significant enough to include in the grand finale, as is the illogical and nonsensical answer, which seems to allude back to feces. Before it all ends, repetitions overwhelm the dialogue: At one point Jack thinks about "the boy" that he "*Pushed me. Pushed me with his mind.*" And then Jack commands the boy to "*Break it.*" To which Tyler echoes, "Break it?"[97] Finally, characters express melodramatic "love" for each other in the end: "'I love him...' 'And he loves you.'"[98]

The Dark Tower V: Wolves of the Calla is troubling for a critic for other reasons. In the foreword, which is called "The Final Argument," King offers a summary of the first four books of the series. Quoting this entire seven-page summary and dissecting the plot of the series might offer an interesting study in a formulaic and yet absurd and illogical plot line. King explains, "The Dark Tower is Roland's obsession, his grail," thus summarizing the story plot line as that of the Quest. This makes it unique in contrast to most other fantasy and science fiction stories, which often have an Overcoming the Monster story structure. But there are plenty of monsters in this story to be overcome, including the Wolves that the title of this fifth book is referring to. The story has a lot of similarities, as King confesses in this introduction, to *The Wizard of Oz*, as the heroes walk along something like a yellow-brick road, or, in this case, the Path of the Beam, toward the quest-goal, the Tower.[99] However, the story is an anti–fairy tale and does not fit into any clear category because it jumps between too many different genres without a coherent order. The elements of the story include time travel, gunslingers, resurrection, pagan tarot cards, future predictions, heroine junkies, abductions, some love, robots, and gigantic bears. Some of the above elements belong in fantasy, others in science fiction, yet others in realistic urban crime stories, and still others in fairy tales for young kids. While there might be some logical and formulaically pleasing way to combine all of these elements, Stephen King does not attempt to create a logical union and instead makes an absurd combination, with the intention of presenting disorder and nonsense.

In *Wolves of the Calla* King clearly inserts an unbelievable quantity of insults and profanities to sell more books by shocking readers. In the course of this study, I have not seen this many profanities per page in the work of any other writer I looked at. The number is multiplied in the prologue because King calls one of the "patches" that Tian's family owns "Son of a Bitch." This phrase appears more frequently in the subsequent pages than the word "breasts" appears in Woodiwiss, or at least once on every page. The other profanities include "bitch"[100] or "idiot's face" with a "donkey laugh"[101] (when referring several times to his sister Tia), as well as "s**t,"[102] a few cases of "f**k you,"[103] and "bawling c**t."[104] And I'm not counting more casual insults like "bugger" and "ass." I'm not sure what these insults do for unliterary Americans, but for me they are so stunning that the narrative disintegrates into a shouting match between rude farmers, which conveys nothing more than the simplicity and baseness of the characters. The story is more linear in these first chapters than *Black House*, so it is readable, and not entirely absurd, but it does not invite readers into the narrative, but rather seems to shoo them away with a yardstick of insults. The descriptions are certainly anti-formulaic, as the robot's arms are "silvery" rather than white, and he is "impossibly tall" rather than just tall or short.[105] Of course, a robot has to have a metallic color, and fairy tale and science fiction characters have to have exaggerated and unusual features, according to the standard formulas, but King clearly goes a few extra steps to make his characters especially unique. In addition, King breaks with fantasy and fairy tale formulas by creating ugly key characters, as Tian has a "stink-smell,"[106] in addition to exploding with profanities when he talks, and his sister Tia is repeatedly said to look and act "like a horse."[107]

It is interesting to note that the last word in *Black House* reappears here as a character, Ka, who "had come to Calla Bryn Sturgis."[108] Why Ka? If it is indeed a reference to feces, the symbolism eludes me. Another similarity between these two novels is that repetitious dialogue appears in *Wolves* as well. The repetitions are most frequent at the end of chapters and sections—at the end of the prologue, Pere Callahan gathers the troops by saying, "Time to be men.... Time to stand up, gentlemen. Time to stand up and be true."[109] These repetitions appear to be attempting to put emphasis on flat language and suggest strong emotion on the part of the speaker, but they typically just hurt the ear, without adding meaning to these key lines of dialogue, which are supposed to move the story forward into the next section. Yet another similarity with *Black House* is the allusion to the writer, or the strong presence of the writer in the narrative of the story. In *Wolves,* Stephen King breaks out most clearly in the ending, where Callahan sees the cover of a book that Jake is reading and it is *Salem's Lot* by Stephen King. Suddenly, Callahan "felt false to himself, not real.... *It's a joke,* part of his mind assured him. *It must be a joke, the cover of this book says it's a novel, so—* ... 'Damn it, I'm a REAL PERSON! ... I *can't* be in a book ... I'm *not* a fiction ... am I?'" He concludes that to find "reality" he has to find his "wife."[110] Is this an attempt to frighten readers by telling them that the story they have been reading is true? Or is the goal of this ending to show how absurd and fantastic the story has been, and to completely forbid readers from suspending their disbelief? The similarities between *Wolves* and *Black House* point to a formula, but this is not a formula for horror fiction—it is a formula for selling more books than any other American writer, and having the freedom to make fun of the writing craft and the formulaic writing process itself as King's writing career comes closer to its end.

JOANNA KATHLEEN ROWLING (1966–; FIRST NOVEL, *HARRY POTTER AND THE PHILOSOPHER'S STONE,* 1997)

J. K. Rowling holds the record for being the "first billion-dollar author" (male or female) with the *Harry Potter* children's fantasy series selling over "400 million copies."[111] Because of the extreme sales from the first books, *Harry Potter and the Deathly Hallows,* the seventh and last book in the series, had "the highest initial print-run for a fiction book" at 12 million copies.[112]

The *Harry Potter* series has more formulaic repetitions in it than possibly all of the other books on this list, or perhaps they are more obvious to me because I read all seven books in the series from beginning to end, whereas I could not do the same with the other authors on this list simply because there is only so much a critic can handle before reading further is unbearable. It is likely that few literary critics have ventured into these waters because it is so painful to not only read but also study closely the repetitions in an unliterary fictional series. Reading through Alexandre Dumas or some of the more literary series, like Anne Rice's *Vampire Chronicles,* has some entertainment value and offers insight into both the human condition and affective writing technique. On the other hand, reading a full series like *Harry Potter* is extremely demoralizing for a writer and mindboggling for a critic. Rereading one of these *Harry Potter* books for a second time proved to be downright nauseating. I wish I could avoid this introduction, but giving the formulaic details without this overall impression would not do justice to my account.

The overall structure of the series follows the Overcoming the Monster plot line point for point. After living with his abusive aunt and uncle, Harry finds out that he is a wizard and is taken to the magical school, Hogwarts, with the help of the half-giant Hagrid. Before he makes it to Hogwarts, Harry is warned by Hagrid of why he was placed with his aunt and uncle, and how his parents died at the hands of Lord Voldemort; at first Lord Voldemort is a vague monstrous threat, but at the standard point of the story (that is, midway through the series) he materializes into a physical form and then gains strength and begins a direct war with Harry and his supporters, including the Order of the Phoenix (mostly professors and Aurors, or professional evil fighters) and Dumbledore's Army (students). Upon Harry's initial arrival at the school, a duality is set up between the "good" Gryffindor and the "evil" Slytherin, with two more houses in this system that are associated with a lack of power and generally refrain from participating in the battle between good and evil (unless they absolutely have to). Harry quickly runs into various setbacks when he first comes to Hogwarts, but then finds Quidditch and makes friends with Ron and Hermoine, so he starts to adjust to the magical world. For the rest of the series, Harry experiences constant challenges, victories and losses, as he goes up and down on the tension roller coaster. This plot summary matches the Overcoming the Monster plot exactly, with all of its standard movements, including the ending in which the monster and his army are overcome and the hero obtains a wife, riches and other rewards.

The formula is not only in the overall plot structure, but also in the repeating movements and elements across the story. The sixth book in the series, *Harry Potter and the Half-Blood Prince,* is particularly interesting for a close study of these patterns because it builds up to the most melodramatic death in the series—that of Headmaster Dumbledore—and sees the beginning of the climb in tension up to the climax, while at the same time retaining some of the repeating elements from the first five books, in which the three friends go through the motions of taking wizarding classes and worrying about school and sports. The last book in the series breaks with this pattern, as the three heroic friends spend it looking for the Horcruxes (which hold parts of Lord Voldemort's soul), instead of going through the standard motions of their schooling.

Following a typical pattern in formulaic stories, the first chapter or two in each of the books in the series are much more polished and developed than the rest, including the last, concluding chapter in each book. For example, the first chapter of *The Half-Blood Prince* examines the relationship between the Prime Minister of Muggles, the outgoing ex-minister Fudge, and the newly appointed Minister of Magic, Rufus Scrimgeour. The conversations that they have catch up readers who are just joining the series on key events in the battle between good and evil, with several colorful incidents detailed, such as the splitting in two of a bridge and several unexplained deaths. All three ministers are panicked and terrified, which sets up tension right away in the first pages of the book. They also touch on a few "philosophical" topics, such as political opposition, blame-throwing in politics, and the best ways to deal with blackmail, before and while slowly disintegrating into the formulaic movements that make the remainder of the book unbearable for literary readers. The first chapter ends with Fudge making the "deep" observation that while they are "*wizards,*" "the other side can do magic too" (as an explanation for why the wizards have not been able to prevent Lord Voldemort and his Death Eaters from breaking the bridge or committing their long list of other crimes).[113]

Since this is a book near the end of the series, it begins and ends during the segment of extreme roller coaster spikes and crashes of the Overcoming the Monster plot. To achieve these swings, the narrator and characters have to frequently explain the mood that the community or the heroes are in.

Descriptions of characters are very similar to the formulas used in *Twilight* and

Percy Jackson, but here there is a bit more variance, perhaps because the latter two copied only parts of it. The character descriptions in *Harry Potter* come in one of these two basic structures: (1) A character is compared with an animal ("froglike,"[114] "old lion"[115]), with one to three adjectives (color, shape, type) and a noun that details up to five of the standard descriptive elements ("hair," "eyebrows," "eyes," "spectacles," and bodily peculiarities, such as "limp,"[116] as well as the shape of the "face" and skin tone or color,[117] and the shape of the "nose" and "hand" type or movements,[118] in addition to the "cloak," "hat," "gown," or other types of clothing).[119] (2) A character is described as having changed from the last time he was seen by the other character(s) in the scene, such as being suddenly "thinner, balder, and grayer."[120]

Sympathy for the hero is created by stressing a few sad characteristics about his upbringing. First, at the beginning of the story, we find out about the child abuse that Harry Potter has suffered at the hands of his uncle, aunt and their son. One proof of this is that Harry stays "out of arm's reach of his uncle" because "long experience had taught him" that coming closer might end up with his uncle committing violence against him.[121] Despite knowing of this abuse, Dumbledore and the rest of his "friends" and family in the magical community do not report the situation to the child welfare system and otherwise do not take action to save Harry permanently from this abusive situation before he turns seventeen because, without these abuses, there would be no logical motivation for Harry to return to a magical world where numerous characters die and Harry himself suffers from various injuries every year.

The second most common background element that is utilized to create sympathy for Harry Potter is the fact that both of his parents died when he was a baby. This detail is typically brought in when supporting or new characters tell Harry that he looks very much like his father, "except for [his] eyes," which are his "mother's." Harry typically thinks after each of these comments that he "had heard it so often he found it a bit wearing," if not extremely annoying and troubling.[122] But these repetitions of how various professors previously taught his parents, or their fellow students' impressions of them, keep pointing out to readers that there is something sympathetic about the "Boy Who Lived," whose parents died a horrifying death at the hands of the evil Lord Voldemort.

Characters are frequently scared by surprise appearances so as to raise suspense and the threat level with the arrival of each new character in a scene, rather than just piling characters on and having them talk about stuff. The scary entrance allows for an emotionally charged incident, or for "something to happen," without a major death or injury. For example, "a soft cough behind him"[123] freezes and scares the Muggle Prime Minister; the cough is coming from a moving portrait that announces ex-minister Fudge's upcoming arrival in the his office.

Muggles (non-magical people) are portrayed as being ignorant in order to pique readers' interest in the magical world and to make it appear superior to the normal world, full of Muggles who are constantly insulted (those with non-magical parents are derogatively called Mudbloods) not only by villains (i.e., Draco Malfoy and Lord Voldemort) but also by some neutral or "good" characters. For example, the Muggle Prime Minister feels "like an ignorant schoolboy"[124] because he failed to realize that wizards were involved in the splitting of the Brockdale Bridge and other otherwise unexplained events. While a more realistic Prime Minister might have brainstormed strategies he could take to restore order and help apprehend the escaped magical convicts, or otherwise might have responded logically, this Prime Minister is merely shocked and basically speechless. Readers who are suspending their disbelief are likely to form a closer emotional link with the in-the-know magical folk, and to feel disdain for the foolish politician. Typically Muggles only echo statements made by magical folk, like the Prime Minister repeating, with emphasis on the scarier (for him) word, "A *mass* breakout?"[125]

The characters' names are stressed to make them more memorable to readers, so that they will keep the books in their minds and be more likely to return to read the next book in the series. One example of this is how Lord Voldemort is called He-Who-Must-Not-Be-Named; this change uses reverse psychology to recall Lord Voldemort's name to the reader's mind, and to remember it better when the actual name is used (typically in a whisper, or with the dismay or flinching of some of the listeners, who are frightened or superstitious of using the Dark Lord's actual name). Another memorable name is Dumbledore, who is called "Dumby" by a "lopsided man" shortly before his death,[126] and in other parts of the series a play is made on his name that stresses "dumb" and "bore." A string of insults in the name certainly makes it more memorable. And while marijuana is not a key term in the *Harry Potter* series, the name of the main character is very similar to the insult "hairy potter," which might have referred to a marijuana-smoking guy who neglects his facial appearance; in addition, the word "harry" also means "to harass; to annoy"—between these two associated meanings, certainly readers are not likely to forget the name.

Surprise and minor resolutions are frequently created by using some of the elements from bad mystery novels. One of these is the device of creating a surprise by introducing new information, and making it appear as if the reader and the other characters in the scene have been fooled because they failed to notice something. For example, while the first chapter is misleadingly called "The Other Minister" and the Muggle Prime Minister spends around fifteen pages speaking with Fudge, under the assumption that he is still the Minister of Magic, it is suddenly revealed by Fudge that he was "sacked three days ago!" and that the new Minister of Magic is about to arrive.[127] Thus, the reader and the character of the Muggle Minister are surprised by this news, and readers likely feel as if they should be reading the narrative more closely to catch these types of inconsistencies, but, no matter how closely they read it, no genuine clues are offered in the narrative. Mysteries are also awkwardly solved with the help of "sheer luck and more talented friends,"[128] like Dumbledore or the other teachers who intervene and give the answers the three key young heroes typically fail to see. In another forced resolution to a mystery, after Dumbledore and Harry view a memory together of a request made by Tom Riddle (a.k.a. Lord Voldemort) for the Defense Against the Dark Arts job at Hogwarts and Dumbledore's refusal to grant him this post, Dumbledore explains that the outcome was that "we have never been able to keep a Defense Against the Dark Arts teacher for longer than a year since I refused the post to Lord Voldemort."[129] The idea that this job was jinxed came up as early as the second book in the series, so this is a significant resolution, but the answer is only discovered because Dumbledore chooses to explain this to Harry at this particular point, shortly before his death.

Occasionally repetitions of the same elements are hidden by absurd or ridiculous actions. For example, when attention is drawn to "the portrait of the ugly little man" in the Muggle Prime Minister's office for the tenth time or so, the narrator adds that on this occasion the man in the portrait "was digging in his ear with the point of a quill."[130] The detail is not significant to the narrative, but it is so absurd that the reader might laugh instead of feeling the weight of the repetition.

Transitions between events are typically forced by the need for things to constantly be happening, or for those in a dialogue to be in constant conflict with each other to keep tension high. Thus, for example, when the Muggle Prime Minister and the Fudge run out of things to say to each other and sit in "aggrieved silence"[131] for a few moments, they are immediately interrupted by the announcement that the new Minister of Magic is about to join them. On the other hand, interesting statements or events are frequently interrupted in order to keep readers in suspense and guessing what is about to happen. For example, when Narcissa Malfoy begins begging Snape, "Help me—" she is interrupted by Snape's hand, as he shoots at the staircase with his wand because Wormtail was listening on the stairs.[132] Even Snape calls this, as well as the pages of back-and-forth dialogue that follow it (before the actual request is finally made by Narcissa), "tedious interruptions."[133] Narcissa only returns to her initial request for help seven pages later, explaining that she wants Snape to make an Unbreakable Vow that he will protect Draco, and will kill Dumbledore himself if Draco fails, which Snape finally agrees to another five pages later, at the very end of the chapter.

Conversations typically follow a pattern in which a new problem or a problematic character is raised and gossiped about in detail before the dialogue moves on to the next problem. For example, the Muggle Prime Minister and the new Minister of Magic first discuss the Muggle's "security," personified by Kingsley Shacklebolt, a new secretary the Ministry of Magic has placed in his office; then they move on to talking about the second problem, Herbert Chorley, who is quacking like a duck because he is under the Imperius Curse.[134] This discussion does not disguise the fact that the points of conversation are not significant to the key plot of the story, and it runs through these items quickly and with a feeling that all of the speakers want to get the talk over with as fast as possible, having inserted as many threatening problems and stressful character hurdles for the Muggle Prime Minister as possible. Piling on one problem after another creates a feeling of "speed," as if something is happening, even if these events or discussions are not significant in the large scheme of things. Because nothing important happens during an average conversation in *Harry Potter*, they typically end with one of the parties suddenly announcing something like "Well, that's really all I had to say."[135]

In order to create the illusion that the repetitions are less repetitive, the first seven (or so) chapters in each of the books have different, and frequently new, settings and introduce some new characters that will play the biggest roles in the main roller coaster plot for the current book in the series. Here are the settings and key characters for the first eight chapters of *The Half-Blood Prince*: *Chapter One:* Setting—Muggle Prime Minister's office, featuring the Muggle Prime Minister and the Minister of Magic. *Chapter Two:* Setting—Snape's house, featuring Snape's meeting with Bellatrix and Narcissa (with the minor reappearance of Wormtail). *Chapter Three:* Setting—Dursleys' home, featuring Dumbledore taking Harry away from the Dursleys. *Chapter Four:* Setting—Horace Slughorn's new home, featuring an introduction to Slughorn's elitist personality (as he is recruited to teach at Hogwarts). *Chapter Five:* Setting—the Weasley's Burrow home, featuring the Weasleys, and the reunion of the key heroes. *Chapter Six:* Setting—Diagon Alley, in which the heroic friends run into Draco in a clothing shop. *Chapter Seven:* Setting—the Hogwarts Express, on which the young magicians travel to Hogwarts and encounter Slytherin enemies. *Chapter Eight:* Setting—Hogwarts, where the characters that were introduced earlier interact. Starting with Chapter Eight, the heroes remain in Hogwarts for the remainder of the novel, only making occasional trips to the local magical village and going to the Burrow for Christmas. The above is the standard travel-and-hold pattern common to the first six books of the *Harry Potter* series, as the characters run around the United Kingdom's map and new characters are brought into the plot; after that, the characters are limited to those already introduced and actions are limited to the one key location, Hogwarts. The running around in the beginning chapters creates the illusion that the repetition of the same plot pattern of the school year's movements across each of the first six books in the series is actually variant.

Violent events happen at least a couple of times in each of the chapters, as without these violent incidents the narrative mostly consists of argumentative dialogues. These episodes of violence can be against an object, an animal, a magical creature, one's self, furniture, or other magicians, with a few other "imaginative" possibilities. Typically, inanimate objects, animals and the like are hurt or die at the beginning of a book, and minor characters (and possibly even one or more of the major characters) die near the end of the book. This structure slowly builds the death threat up and keeps adding tension and suspense to the narrative. The death threat is frequently extremely obvious: for example, "Every single one of [the magical clock's] hands was now pointing at 'mortal peril,'" which implies that every member of the Weasley family is in danger of losing their lives at this point of Book Six.[136] The death threat frequently is more of an actual death, as when the two sisters, Narcissa and Bellatrix, arrive on Snape's street, and Bellatrix kills a fox because she thinks it is an Auror, spying on them.[137] On the next page, her sister and Draco's mother, Narcissa, burns Bellatrix's arm when Bellatrix tries to stop her from pleading for Draco's life with Snape.[138] Another minor threat of violence is when Mrs. Weasley puts a bowl under her steaming onion soup, just a moment before it nearly pours all over Harry, and then Harry can "feel his throat blistering" on the onion soup as he tries to reply to one of Mrs. Weasley's questions.[139] In addition, there are references to violent incidents that take place outside of the main action—for example, Mr. Weasley reports on the cases he's handling in his new managerial job for the Office for Detection and Confiscation of Counterfeit Defensive Spells and Protective Objects, helping those who buy defective products that are supposed to protect users from You-Know-Who, but end up making their "ears fall off," and the like.[140] Beatings among friends are pretty common, as when Ron wakes Harry up with "a sharp blow to the top of the head" on discovering that Harry is sleeping at his house, but hasn't informed him that he had moved in a few hours earlier than he was supposed to.[141] The Weasley twins even manage to severely injure a guest staying at their house while they are away at their joke shop when a "tiny fist" device of theirs punches Hermione in the face and gives her a "purple black eye," which Mrs. Weasley cannot get off with her standard magical remedies.[142]

The repetition of violence is especially blatant in the scene at the Dursleys' home. Dumbledore begins harassing the Dursleys by rudely entering without Vernon's permission. Uncle Vernon fails to correct Dumbledore because, the narrator explains, Dumbledore appears "very difficult to bully." Then, when Vernon speaks "in a tone that threatened rudeness in every syllable,"[143] Dumbledore begins to slide from rudeness to outright and then extreme violence. Poor Aunt Petunia emerges from "her usual pre-bedtime wipe-down of all the kitchen surfaces" to be reminded by Dumbledore of the "exploding letter" he sent her earlier.[144] Then, as the Dursleys are basically speechless, Dumbledore invites himself into their sitting room, and, after sitting himself, zooms the sofa over, knocking the three Dursleys "knees out" with it and forcing them to sit down.[145] Then Dumbledore points out that the Dursleys have committed an error of manners by failing to provide refreshments for him. He corrects this by offering them a bottle of "Madam Rosmerta's finest oak-matured mead," which the Dursleys attempt to ignore as three glasses of mead approach them. Dumbledore then continues his attack against the Dursleys by first "nudging them gently on the side of their heads" with the glasses,[146] then "knocking quite insistently on the side of Vernon's head," which Uncle Vernon finally begins attempting to "beat" "away"[147]; finally, the glasses "rapped smartly over the head[s]" of the Dursleys,[148] until the "glasses bounced up and down on their skulls, their contents flying everywhere,"[149] which forces Uncle Vernon to shout a protest and finally stop this harassing incident. It is not the violence against this family that is troubling here, but rather the repetition with intensification of the same violent element across all of these pages; the writer isn't inventing new, shocking violent events, but keeps having the glasses knock against the Dursleys' heads; this repetition is more likely to evoke annoyance in readers rather than shock, which is the typical intent for including a lot of violence in a scene.

Violence and pain are ingredients even in elements that are typically peaceful and beautiful in fantastic magical worlds; for example, Apparition is extremely painful: "[Harry] was being pressed very hard from all directions; he could not breathe, there were iron bands tightening around his chest; his eyeballs were being forced back into his head; his eardrums were being pushed deeper into his skull."[150] This extreme pain that comes with Apparition means that the characters have an added death threat or the chance that they might die every time they attempt Apparition.

The death threat is frequently realized in an actual death in the *Harry Potter* series: Slughorn points out that there is a high "mortality rate" among the members of the Order of the Phoenix, who frequently end up dying in the line of duty, as Sirius Black did at the end of Book Five.[151] Sirius dies soon after Harry discovers that he is one of the good guys and that Sirius is his godfather; this "cruel" and "brutal ending"[152] adds sympathy for Harry Potter's sad and lonely background, introduces a melodramatic violent event, and adds suspense and tension to the narrative. The only way to have made the plot more forced and absurd would have been to have added a few more potentially great parents for Harry, and killing each of them with each new book. Instead, Rowling settles for having Harry stare at a spider climbing along Dumbledore's hat as he's explaining his sympathy for Harry regarding Sirius' death, to which Harry replies by thinking about some grieving time he spent "staring at the misted window" (before falling asleep leaning on the window in chapter three), and then concludes that expressing grief makes him feel "stupid."[153] A couple of paragraphs later, Harry snaps out of this stupidity by telling himself "life's too short," and dramatically proclaiming, "I'll make sure I take as many Death Eaters with me as I can, and Voldemort too if I can manage it." The exclamations about life being too short and the vows of revenge are standard formulaic elements in genre fiction where characters die frequently and the hero has to find motivation in their deaths to seek revenge and proceed on a homicidal rampage against the evil monster. The formulaic nature of this exchange aside, this is the most uninspired, anticlimatic, melodramatic and yet anti-dramatic depiction of "grief" imaginable; yet, in theory, it helps to create sympathy for Harry.

An example of violence against the self in *Harry Potter* includes Dobby trying to run "at the fire" because he does not want to say bad things about the Malfoys out of habit; Harry catches him and forces him to explain what Draco Malfoy has been doing that has been "bad" despite Dobby's severe reluctance.[154]

The other common element that serves to balance the violent events are the repeated scenes of groveling, begging, kneeling, pleading, and other forms of sado-masochism, or a role playing with ultra-dominant and ultra-submissive characters. This groveling is always extremely melodramatic and would even look forced in a high-satire staged play, in which actors have to shout so that somebody in the back row can hear them, and have to drop down and hit the floor with their falling bodies to create a dramatic visual effect. For example, when begging Snape to kill Dumbledore instead of leaving it to Draco, Narcissa "crumbled, falling at his feet, sobbing and moaning on the floor."[155] Snape's decision to succumb to this psychotic begging is a bit more believable as a result, but the Unbreakable Vow he subsequently makes seriously impedes the reader's ability to suspend disbelief. Snape and Narcissa get on their knees in a ceremony that is close to a marriage ceremony, in which their hands are tied with a magical snake, like a marital ring. Narcissa is married to Lucius at this time, who is imprisoned in Azkaban, and the ceremony is intended to bind them in a pact of murder, rather than marriage, but creating the melodramatically extreme scene makes it more surprising, shocking and thus tense and suspenseful.

There are around three ways that new information is introduced into the plot line: (1) an event happens chronologically as part of the story; (2) one of the characters summarizes how the event happened to the other characters that weren't there; (3) a character reads about an event or key news from a newspaper or a magazine article, offered in full text.[156] Each of the *Harry Potter* books includes at least a couple of newspaper articles, which provide scandalous, unique or shocking news or opinions. The details of these articles are always later discussed in dialogues between characters, the news stories being used as primary evidence that the discussion's points are based on. The most frequent element in each book is dialogue, followed by descriptions of scenes in second place, with descriptions of actions a distant last. The story is saturated in dialogue, but the dialogue is so choppy it gives the illusion of moving the story quickly.

The plot of *The Half-Blood Prince* is supported by the antagonism between Harry, Hermoine, Ron and Dumbledore and their enemies, Lord Voldemort, Draco, Snape, and Bellatrix, as well as the supporting characters on both sides. The conflicts are both verbal and physically violent in nature. In one of the key scenes Harry attempts to spy on Draco, and instead ends up watching him have his hair stroked by Pansy, as he reports that he is basically planning to quit school and join the Death Eaters in the following school year, and then, spotting Harry, stuns him and breaks his nose.[157] Malfoy becomes a key figure in the narrative because clues lead Harry to believe that he is a Death Eater and out to harm somebody at Hogwarts, an idea that is confirmed by the confession at the beginning of the book that Draco was ordered by Lord Voldemort, under the threat of death for him and his entire family, to carry out a mission of some kind. So, Harry spends the book trying to stalk and follow Draco around, using the Marauder's Map, his invisibility cloak and all other tricks at his disposal, and yet fails to figure out what Draco is up to before the end, at which point Dumbledore ends up being murdered. At the same time, Rowling starts building sympathy for Malfoy, instead of building him up as a ruthless villain. Harry notices that Malfoy looks "ill" and "grayish," as he's even forced to call in sick and miss Quidditch.[158] It turns out that Malfoy is using the Room of Requirement that Harry and Dumbledore's Army kept using to practice Defense Against the Dark Arts spells in the previous year, and Harry cannot enter this room while Malfoy is using it because the room can only be found by the person or group currently in charge of it. As a result, Harry knows that Malfoy is constantly "disappearing" somewhere, but does not know where he is going, so Harry becomes "obsessed with Draco Malfoy"[159] and nearly gives up on his lessons and sports activities trying to solve the mystery or track Draco down. There appears to be a much stronger homosexual attraction or "obsession" between Harry and Draco across this series, than any serious attraction between Harry and Ginny, whom Harry eventually ends up marrying, despite initially dumping her after two weeks because "It's been like ... like something out of someone else's life."[160] While this is a common cliché, it is illogical in this situation unless Harry has been living the lie that he's straight. At one point Malfoy sneeringly calls Harry "the Boy Who Scored"[161]—a pretty suggestive phrase (scored with whom—certainly not with Ginny).

Sympathy is also built up for the entire Malfoy family when Dumbledore explains that He-Who-Must-Not-Be-Named is extremely angry with Lucius for unwittingly allowing the capture and destruction of a piece of his soul in one of the Horcruxes, as well as his failure to recapture the prophecy in Book Five.[162] If the Dark Lord sees Lucius as an enemy and sent in Draco hoping Draco would die trying to kill Dumbledore, then there is hope for the Malfoys' redemption and admittance back into wizarding society without a permanent imprisonment in Azkaban once the "good" side wins in the end. Because the crimes that the Malfoys have committed across the series are extremely severe, Rowling goes further to create sympathy by having Draco cry to Moaning Myrtle, "No one can help me ... unless I do it soon ... he says he'll kill me." If this was not enough, Harry overhears this soppy story, and Malfoy reacts by shooting a hex at him, and then they block and shoot back a few more hexes, until Malfoy nearly puts Harry under the excruciating pain spell. Hearing this, Harry blocks it with a "SECTUMSEMPRA" spell that cuts Draco's "face and chest" as if it was "slashed with an invisible sword," and Snape has to come in to heal and rescue Draco and take him to the hospital ward to recover.[163] This forces Harry to feel guilty and shifts more sympathy toward the injured Draco.

The fact that Draco helps the Death Eaters to enter and attack Hogwarts and then assists in the murder of Dumbledore is an extreme wrong, even if all his family's lives are on the line, as Dumbledore explains that they all could be protected if they switched sides. The final scene of the murder is extremely stretched out, as Malfoy keeps repeating that he has to kill Dumbledore and Dumbledore at one point closes his eyes, as if "about to fall asleep,"[164] and at another praises Draco for his ingenuity in allowing Death Eaters in, as if complimenting him on "an ambitious homework project."[165] This conversation is improbable in the extreme and does not reflect any realistic replies to a similar predicament by either of these two parties. So, despite all of the attempts to build sympathy for Draco as one of the victims of the story, the happy ending in a great family life and riches awarded to Draco at the end of Book Seven is ultra-forced and fails to fulfill both the standard loss and death of the villain and the reward of the hero formulaic fantasy plot lines. Morals are warped in the *Harry Potter* story, without being obviously backward. Both the good and the bad characters are violent bullies. It is disturbing, from a moral perspective, that so many kids bought this "fairy tale."

RICK RIORDAN (1964–; FIRST NOVEL, *BIG RED TEQUILA*, 1997)

In the *Percy Jackson* series, Percy Jackson is a half-god Olympian who battles demons, competes for godly distinction, and leads a charge against the rebelling archenemies, the Titans. This premise is very similar to that of *Harry Potter*. Percy is also young at the start and goes through school, accumulating magical and godly knowledge that helps him to overcome deadly challenges, with the help of his sidekick friends. Magic with Christian North European (i.e., Merlin) symbolism is replaced by magic with Greek mythological symbols and personalities. But the formulaic translation is illogical. Gods are by definition all-powerful and all-knowing, while magicians can be flawed and can die. Aware of this problem, the author has brought in the only enemy that was ever a serious threat to the Olympian gods—the Titans. But the Olympians defeated the Titans in epic battles that were led by Zeus; not even a major demi-god like Hercules could've conceivably challenged the Titans' strength. The idea that Poseidon's illegitimate demi-god offspring, Percy, could defeat the Titans with the help of a couple of other incompetent demi-gods is ridiculous. While the formulaic elements are similar, the author is assuming either that readers are ignorant of Greek mythology or that they will suspend disbelief to the point of blindness just because they are obsessed with the formula of watching a tiny, silly, and fumbling student rise up and beat extremely powerful enemies.

The quotes on the back cover from the major reviewers are indeed true, but what are they saying? "Next Harry Potter" from *Kirkus Reviews*; "breakneck pace" from *Publishers Weekly*; and "the cliff-hanger ending will leave readers breathless." from the *School Library Journal*. Here's a sentence that integrates all of these ideas in a new light: "A formulaic replica of *Harry Potter* that runs forward at a breakneck pace with barely any descriptive details, relying for speed on extreme cliff-hangers at the end of every chapter and book that repeatedly threaten the untimely demise of the young hero." Why didn't any of these top three reviewers write a harsh critique like what I am proposing, instead of basically saying the same thing, but strongly recommending this book? Either the publishing scene is so bleak that this book is the best fiction out there or the editors of these publications feel pressure to go with the critical "flow" and praise best-sellers from major publishers, even if they are enormous literary flops. The quantity of money that these publishers spend to promote these titles is probably related to this phenomenon.

The main formulaic separation from *Harry Potter* is the use of the first-person voice, or Percy's voice. But the writer uses it to lower the reading level and to occasionally insert grammatical mistakes, typos and other errors, possibly attributed to the age of the half-god narrator. The errors are there not only because Percy is young but also because he has "dyslexia." It takes him "a few minutes to decipher: TRIPLE G

RANCH/ FRAGILE/ THIS END UP."[166] How can somebody with dyslexia narrate five volumes of a young adult book? That explains the frequency of clichés, spelling and grammatical errors, the illogical switches from anywhere to somewhere and everybody to somebody, and the Brooklyn ghetto slang speech of the flying horses.

A formulaic repetition that is present in science fiction and fantasy books from *Harry Potter* to *Twilight* to *Percy Jackson* is the simple formula used in character descriptions. The long version of the character description formula is as follows: mood + age + hair + shape + clothing + armor, special markings, jewelry + mysterious element (which is typically one of the prior elements with a slant). Here's an example from *Percy*: "The swordsman smiled dryly. He was in his *fifties, I guess*, with short gray *hair* and a clipped gray *beard*. He was in good *shape* for an older guy. He wore black mountain-climbing *pants* and a bronze *breastplate* strapped over an orange camp *T-shirt* [my italics]."[167] The description of a god, a semi-god, or a cheerleader uses this same formula. Minor characters just get fewer details, such as only hair + shape. While there are numerous ways to describe a human character, and even more to detail supernatural elements of divinity, the writers of these popular books just use this stale formula to save typing and editing time. The above description is one of the longest character descriptions in the book; in other words, it uses two adjectives to describe a couple of the elements.

The funniest part of the book for me was the fight formula, repeated for every one of the two dozen or so fights in the book. Here are the chronological steps in the *Percy Jackson* fight formula: (1) Conversation between heroes is interrupted by a "surprise" attack. (2) The attack is described with a few sketchy details. (3) The heroes discuss possible plans for winning the battle, arguing back and forth in a yes/no pattern. (4) Meanwhile, the attacker is reinforced or somehow becomes even stronger than originally judged. (5) The hero (with only occasional help from sidekicks) makes a few defensive strikes. (6) Despite the failure of the discussed plan, the heroes manage to escape with the help of a lucky coincidence, a lucky hit, or the lucky appearance of a powerful assistant. While the first couple of times I read this formula, I was pretty sad at how repetitive, illogical and anti-heroic it was, by the third or so occurrence I started laughing and still cannot stop. Perhaps this book is a satire on the best-sellers' formulaic writing process for those who understand its elements.

STEPHENIE MEYER (1973–; FIRST NOVEL, *TWILIGHT*, 2005)

The repetitions begin on page 1 of *Breaking Dawn* with Bella, the first-person narrator, explaining that she had already had her "share of near-death experiences" and is now "facing death again." Maybe this is an encouraging start for a fanatical *Twilight* fan, but having studied the repetition of the death threat in the typical formula of a best-selling novel, it was a very discouraging beginning for me. In *Percy Jackson* as well as in the *Twilight* series, every chapter ends with a direct reminder that the hero is likely to die on the first page of the next chapter. Now, readers know that, according to the formula, the hero always wins in the end, and they usually know that they are on book 1 or 2 of a 5- or 7-book series, so if there is any chance of a death, it has to happen at the end of the series. Even then, however, the hero cannot die because it would be tragic and therefore unfit for children or young adult readers. What is appropriate for these youths is the repetition of the threat of looming death at least once per chapter, and possibly on every page of the book. This phenomenon is the ticking-bomb device running wild and without restraint. The publisher knows that they have to lower the reading comprehension level as much as possible, using the most limited vocabulary to attract the widest possible audience, but that this final watered-down hyper-readable text will be devoid of any meaning or beauty, and so they fill it with constant threats of death and pain, inserting these liberally across the narrative to keep readers at the edges of their seats. The narrator summarizes the impending death device, calling it "that part of the horror movie when the victim realizes she's forgotten to lock her deadbolt."[168]

Several other elements are extremely annoying for adult, critical readers. It rains at least thirty times during the course of this novel, and the narrator always mentions the fact that it is raining. The quantity of crying in the book might be approximately equal in frequency to the number of references to rain. Both rain and crying are part of the general overly sentimental mood of the book. Sentimentality hits fantastic peaks: "he loved me," "deep joy," and the like.[169] The repetition of a single event, incident, or occurrence, like the repetition of rain and crying in *Twilight*, is a problem that creeps up in most other types of formulaic writing. For example, in an interview with *Penthouse Magazine*, Stephen King summarizes a review from the *New York Times* about *The Stand*, which the reviewer called "*Rosemary's Baby Goes to the Devil* and slammed it off in five paragraphs. One of the things he said was that too many people pee in their pants in this book. Well, when something happens to someone that's really scary and is very startling—that kind of 'boo' ... most people piss in their pants. I'm sorry if that becomes tiresome after a while. That doesn't change the fact that it happens."[170] While it's an interesting thought that if defecation happens a lot, it might as well happen repeatedly in formulaic novels, King is clearly making a joke about a formulaic repetition that is more obvious than most of his other repetitions. King is "sorry" that he was caught by the critic and tries to make a joke out of the problem. Meanwhile, literary readers who have to keep reading about the thirtieth time the hero peed in his pants are likely to be pretty "sorry" they bought the book.

The love that Edward, Bella, Jacob and the various supporting characters who join their triangle feel for each other is the most repeated cliché, without much evidence to support this first-person narrated sentimental presumption. There is no poetry to it and no substantial or believable reality to the word "love" when it is used so repeatedly, at inappropriate moments, and usually tied to a sexual urge, rather than romance or artistically explained attraction. There is little love in modern reality, but why would somebody want to read such an unromantic, dead romance novel?

The character descriptions here are even duller than in *Percy*: "He had the most beautiful soul, more beautiful than his brilliant mind or his incomparable face or his glorious body."[171] While it is good to know that, unlike Percy, Edward was not dyslexic, he cannot have a beautiful soul and still be a vampire that abuses Bella and puts her under a constant death threat. Even more importantly, while other readers might fill in the image of the actor who portrays Edward under the description "glorious body," I really cannot fall under beauty's spell unless a sincere effort is made by the author to give specific details that support this claim of the character's "glorious body." What exactly is a glorious body for a man today? Is it Michelangelo's "David?" What is the ideal weight: 100 pounds with zero-fat, 140 pounds with some abs, or 200 pounds and tall with giant muscles and a mustache? These vague descriptions are designed to fit whatever body type the reader prefers, but for someone who is reading in order to see an invented world, they instead see generalizations and foggy outlines.

Why did the author choose to write a vampire saga? Is it symbolically reflecting modern life? If so, it seems to be making a statement about youth gangs and warfare between the more and less violent gang sects. A young girl becomes a queen by joining a gang to gain power, beauty, and prest°ige that she could not obtain on her own as a pawn because of her limited mental and physical abilities. As part of the initiation, the gang puts her through various life-threatening situations, until she is violently sexually abused during her honeymoon, and then gives birth to a blood-sucking baby when her husband rips the babe out of her womb with his teeth. There have been a couple of feminist reviews online that note this anti-woman plot line, but I have not seen any reviews that question the message in the vampire genre in general, which has occupied the top spots on the best-selling films, TV series, and novels over the last couple of decades (though I cannot say that I dislike watching *Vampire Dairies* or reading Anne Rice's *Vampire Chronicles*). Here is a thought—maybe women just like watching guys and girls sucking each other? It is a pretty shallow thought, but the only other idea that comes to mind is that most people are psychotic and enjoy watching vampires kill or torture people.

Chapter 3

Romance

> "I won't claim every romance written is wonderful.... With the illiteracy rate in the country an embarrassment, a sin, every book picked up and read for pleasure is a celebration, its own triumph." —Nora Roberts[1]

In her 1984 critical book, Kay Mussell made a statement similar to Nora Roberts' but from a slightly different angle: "romances remain misunderstood because they are read by a largely inarticulate audience that lacks access to outlets of opinion and expression."[2] As a fan of the romance formula and of popular romance fiction, Mussell is not being critical when she calls the romance-reading public "inarticulate," but is rather taking the anti-intellectual position that the unliterary is the best market for writers to grab and uses the word "inarticulate" as a compliment. Similarly, Nora Roberts recognizes that most of her readers are borderline illiterate and feels elated that she has been able to meet their needs.

Besides the reading level of the predominantly female reading market that buys romances, the next most obvious characteristic of a romance novel is that its central topic is a romantic relationship between two people. While there are some novels that focus on romances between members of the same gender, I have not read any about loving relationships between more than two people or about only one person loving him- or herself. Karen Hubert summarizes the romance genre as "the movements people make toward one another. A romance depicts rhythms of human contact and interaction; how people meet, come together, move closer, move apart, separate, reunite, separate again, meet and so on. Every moving apart (due to distrust, jealousy, physical separations) is a test that love can overcome only if it is 'true.'"[3] I will dissect these movements of the romance plot later in this chapter.

The top commercial publishers have a "don't-rock-the-boat-when-you're-making-money" mentality.[4] "Hackneyed stories" are made when there is a "gold rush" in series fiction, and this phenomenon is still at its peak. Nancy Coffey, who started her career editing at Avon and first picked out Kathleen Woodiwiss, then later worked for St. Martin's Press, and is still active in her independent agency, Nancy Coffey Literary & Media Representation, commented, "When you are on a treadmill you don't have time to reject manuscripts or ask for rewrites. [But] if women read six mediocre novels in a row, they will hesitate to pick up a seventh."[5]

If a bad formulaic book makes it past the publisher, readers frequently notice the mistake of formulaic redundancy: "Awareness of repetitiousness is proportional to both the number and length of time readers have been exposed to the series stories;

not surprisingly, dissatisfaction with sameness or redundancy is highest among heavy and widely experienced readers." Readers also frequently notice other mistakes that can become "personally insulting, [which] include the grammatical (nonexistent words such as indignance, and the confusion of 'lie' and 'lay' in a genre in which a lot of it occurs); cover illustrations that do not match settings or character descriptions; and superficial, inaccurate, or unbelievable career descriptions."[6] More editing might fix some of these grammatical and spelling errors, but "heavy-handed copyediting" can also insert additional repetitions and stylistic problems, "resulting in one 'wanton' heroine after another who is plagued with 'melting bones' during love scenes."[7] While one editor might delete the reappearance of "nipples," another might add "breasts" on every other page, or insert "wanton" whenever a heroine is sexually aroused. Between 1972 and 1982, a "revolutionary decade," the "American Romance" formed, and it is indeed different from the "rigid British formula," which still continues to be one of America's top exports[8] (along with other forms of entertainment), but the continuing depression that America is in points to market problems with this as well as with other exports. Regardless of consumer dissatisfaction, the continuing equilibrium among the small group of best-selling romance publishers means that today, like back in the 1987, it is "even more unlikely that anything very interesting will happen in the series romance business in the near future."[9]

To study hack writing as a profession, one need look no further than some of the names of the romance novel authors who remained popular for several decades; this list includes Woodiwiss (who kept writing romances steadily between 1972's *The Flame and the Flower* and 2007's *Everlasting*, published in the year of her death), Nora Roberts, Georgette Heyer and Barbara Cartland. Comparing the work of these four authors confirms that the popular romantic novel genre has maintained the same basic formula from 1921 to the present, with a few significant changes in tastes and formulaic elements. In 1976, a couple of generations ago, Karen Hubert wrote, "Each generation probably adds its own brand of realistic detail, but the same basic melodramas and motifs remain, from the first blush of attraction to the world melting away, leaving only the two lovers, self-contained on a starry, moonlit beach."[10] What are the basic plots, characters, settings, and motifs of this romantic melodrama?

The History of the Romance Genre

Before discussing the structural elements of the romance genre, and looking closely at a few key formulaic writers, the term "romance" needs definition and some background information. More background must be offered regarding romance because it is a topic that possibly all works of art (cave drawings, statues of mother goddesses, and perhaps even the pyramids) are about. It is difficult to think of an ancient or a modern work of literature that does not touch on a romantic relationship, at least as a minor plot point. The abundance of romantic writing appears at first to cloud the distinctions that can be made about the modern romance novel. Fortunately, the modern romance is so formulaic in terms of characters, plot and setting that it is easier to separate formulaic romance novels from the crowd of general literature than the other focal genres in this study. But to understand the building blocks that comprise modern romance, we have to begin by looking at the genres that came before it, which are visualized in Figure 13.

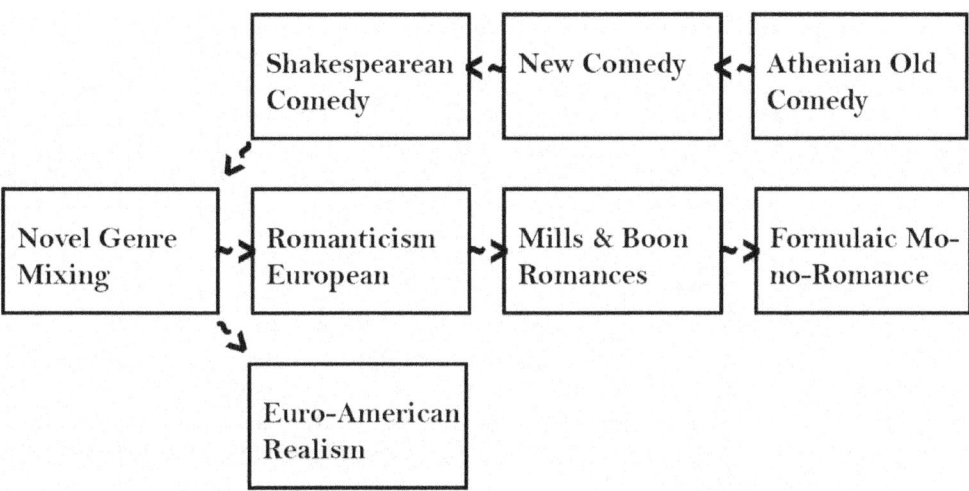

Figure 13. Romantic Genres Diagram.

Drama

Aristotle distinguished four genres in drama: comedy, tragedy, epic and parody. The epic retained most of the elements from epic poetry, simply being translated into the dramatic form. As for the other genres on Aristotle's list, Dionysian dithyrambs came first, then satiric plays or parodies, followed by tragedy and finally comedy.

> Satyric drama was the intermediate stage in the derivation of tragedy from the dithyramb.... The dithyramb was an improvisational song and dance in honor of Dionysus (Bacchus), the god of wine, and was performed by a band of men provided with goat-like horns, ears, hoofs, and tails and clad in a goatskin (or in a goat-hair loin-band) in imitation of Dionysus' attendant sprites, the satyrs.[11]

It is difficult to tell when the creation of dithyrambs started, as they were performed in semi-private religious ceremonies, and were not clearly recorded in writing until around 680–640 BCE. The first tragedies were developed by Aeschylus (525–456 BCE), Epigenes of Sicyon, and Thespis.[12] The generic distinction between tragedy and satire was important in the later theoretical writings of Aristotle because the dramatic festivals were divided into categories of tragedy and satire, and upcoming writers wanted to know the formulas for these distinct genres. According to Aristotle, tragedies caused catharsis or purging in their viewers, or a feeling of "pity" and "fear," as the main characters died or otherwise reached tragic ends. Aeschylus wrote *Prometheus Bound* about Prometheus giving fire to humans and being punished by Zeus for the act, and *Agamemnon* about the adventures of King Agamemnon. Epigenes of Sicyon preceded Aeschylus, but his tragedies, written in honor of Dionysus, were much closer to the traditional dithyrambs. Thespis played a crucial role in the development of theater into current dramatic arts like the cinema and the novel, for he invented the "actor":

> Thespis' innovations were partly borrowed from the Peloponnesus and partly his own. Included among the former would be the dropping of improvisation, the use of meter, the goat prize.... Most distinctive among the latter was his invention of the first actor. In

early choral performances it was customary for the poet himself to serve as coryphaeus, and in Bacchylides' dithyramb we have seen how the coryphaeus was set apart from the other choreutae, answering the questions which they propounded. It was inevitable that to someone should come the happy thought of developing this role still further and of promoting the coryphaeus to a position independent of the chorus. It is significant that the verb which was first used to designate the actor's function was ... "to answer," and that until the time of Sophocles all playwrights were actors in their own productions.[13]

Modern fiction would not be possible without the concept of an actor. If drama continued as a choral production, fictional drama would not include the vital element of "character." Epic poetry and religious texts had heroes, but the creation of an actor, who was playing the parts of various characters, with the help of masks, helped to develop fiction into a subject further distanced from religious truths.

After tragedy, comedy joined the Athenian festival circuit. The word "comedy" meant "comus-song," after the phallic *comus* masquerade celebrations that preceded it, which involved satiric verbal abuses of certain persons.[14] Verbal abuse or satiric derision was a crucial element in early comedies. The purpose of all comedies, of course, is to amuse the audience and to leave them with a joyous feeling. Athenian comedy was initially divided into Old, Middle, and New Comedy: "Old Comedy came to a close shortly after the beginning of the fourth century BC Politics and scurrilous attacks upon contemporaneous personages made up the bulk of its subject matter. Living men, such as Pericles, Socrates, Euripides, and Cleon were represented by actors on the stage and were lampooned with the utmost virulence." The genre of comedy was in rapid flux in these early stages of its development. Middle Comedy "renounced the political and personal themes of its forerunner and was largely given up to literary criticism, parodies, and mythological travesty. New Comedy, in turn, abandoned such subjects for the most part and devoted itself to motives drawn from everyday life."[15] These three types of comedy all have modern echoes because they have been mimicked by many generations of comedic writers. The first comic dramatists to win the Athenian Dionysia festival were Chionides (*Poor People* and *The Heroes*, around 460 BCE) and Magnes (*Battle of Cats and Mice* and *Frogs*, in the same period). Aristophanes (446–386 BCE) is one of the best-known early dramatists, especially because his play *The Clouds* lampooned Socrates and other Athenian intellectuals in such a harsh way that it led to Socrates' trial and execution.

THE EARLY NOVEL

A millennium went by between the invention of comedy and the invention of the first novel. The unusual element that distinguishes the novel from earlier fictional genres is that it's a very long prose, fictional narrative. Long prose made early appearances in works like the Japanese *Tale of Genji* by Murasaki Shikibu, a noblewoman, around 1021. Verse epics, like *Gilgamesh*, also led to the modern novelistic form. Other influences on the novel included medieval romances, like *Amadis of Guala* and the *Death of Arthur* (which were historical and focused on grand, royal characters), and novellas (short fictional stories). *Don Quixote* (1605–1615) is occasionally called the first modern novel because it focused on the mind and adventures of a troubled, non-noble character, and not only includes epic or heroic elements but also is a tragedy, a satire and a comedy. *Don Quixote* specifically ridiculed or satirized the medieval romances that came before it, as presenting an unattainable knightly code of honor and valor; thus, it included a generic critique that helped to define the dimensions of the modern novel as a separate entity from medieval romances, novellas and epic prose. The novels that followed *Don Quixote* were *Robinson Crusoe* (1719) and *Gulliver's Travels* (1726), and they also included a mixture of different genres and used diverse plots, characters and settings.

The novel was distinguished as a form that could include letters, poetry, prose, comedy, tragedy, satire, and various other generic forms inside its bounds. Thus, it was enormously diverse in form, unlike comedic drama, tragic drama, or metric poetry, which had highly formulaic boundaries. Still, the novel had several major periods in its development that set generic limits on its nature. The two major early movements in novelistic form have been Romanticism and realism. Romanticism was the "reproduction in modern [eighteenth- and nineteenth-century] art or literature of the life and thoughts of the Middle Ages."[16] Romanticism bloomed across Europe, and especially in England, France and Germany. It was an escapist movement, in which artists dreamed of escaping industrialization for a better earlier world. In its later stages Romanticism became more closely associated with nature and human emotions than with reproductions of medieval living. Alongside these pastoral and epic love-story elements, Romanticism also frequently returned to the theme of rebellion and revolution, or of human rights and liberty, as it bloomed around the time of the French and American Revolutions, the Industrial Revolution, the end of slavery, and various other rebellious social and violent movements.

Romanticism

During the Romantic period, the novel included some anti-romantic and anti-marriage works, such as those by the famous French author George Sand. Sand is known for *Lavinia* (1833), *The Devil's Pool* (1845) and several other novels, plays and short stories. While there were many conventions in the nineteenth century, both in France and in Britain, about what constituted literary and proper fiction writing and what was unliterary and poorly written, Sand rebelled against formulaic elements of these conventions. "Habitually she wrote what she wanted to write, without stopping to ask whether it conformed to any recognized literary genre."[17] Sand wrote to make a living after separating from her husband, but she was successful in selling her works regardless of whether she complied with conventions; in fact, she almost advertised herself as anti-conventional by wearing men's clothing in public and publicizing the fact that she did not let her editors correct her grammar. Sand had a "celebrated disregard for established conventions.... She won't dress her prose in the orthodox frills and flounces, any more than she will dress herself in such things. She won't submit to the literary rules laid down by the Académie Française, any more than she will submit to the social rules laid down by the French aristocracy."[18] Thus, Sand represents anti-romanticism, anti-formulaic and plain writing that focuses on relating stories and social and political messages without the inhibition of flowery literary conventions.

In contrast with Sand, one of the literary French contemporaries with whom she frequently appeared in the same magazines and anthologies was Alexandre Dumas. Unlike Sand, Dumas was highly formulaic in his novels. For example, he had a series of adventure romances that focused on four friends and their romantic and political battles in *The Three Musketeers* (1844), *Twenty Years After* (1845), and *The Vicomte of Bragelonne: Ten Years Later* (1847). These books have little in common with current romance novels, as they focus on male heroes and the love stories are only background goals behind the friendship and musketeering campaigns of d'Artagnan, Athos, Porthos and Aramis. But they were among the first popular novels in France, and they are written in a series and share similar formulaic elements, which make them distant relatives of the current romance novel. Most of this study focuses on British and American best-selling novelists, but at some points in literary history, popular literature from France and other countries heavily influenced the changes that occurred in British and American publishing. Both the early Romantic movement and absurdity spread across the world from its Parisian origins. American and British novelists have dominated the world best-seller lists over the twentieth century partially because of the widespread dominance of the English language, but many of these writers read foreign writers in translation or in the original languages, so it is important to consider these influences.

How did the radical transition from Romanticism to romance novels happen? While Shakespeare and other early writers described love affairs in tragedies and comedies like *Romeo and Juliet* and *A Midsummer Night's Dream*, in the works the romances motivate the heroes, but are not the all-engulfing issues. The family problems between Romeo and Juliet, and the social and cultural taboos and misunderstandings, account for the plot's core in *Romeo and Juliet.* Greek authors, like Sappho, depicted intimate homosexual relationships, but mostly in shorter poems, rather than in epics or novellas. In a period between the initial "invention" of the modern novel and the beginning of the Romantic period, the first "romance novel," *Pamela, or Virtue Rewarded,* was published in 1740 by Samuel Richardson, and it focused entirely on courtship from the perspective of Pamela, a formula that had not been previously attempted in print in Europe. While Jane Austen is viewed as a society prude today, she was actually one of the first nineteenth-century romance novelists, with books like *Pride and Prejudice*, which also focused on courtship and the female protagonist.

Realism

After a couple of centuries when Romanticism dominated literature, realism moved into prominence, and later several offshoots of realism developed, such as naturalism, represented by Émile Zola at the end of the nineteenth century. Realism is anti-idealistic and makes a claim that the fiction depicted is based on truth, rather than a lie. The idea that fiction is truthful goes back to religious texts that portrayed gods as "real," rather than as invented creations. But the realist authors do not claim that their narratives actually happened, but rather that the spirit and historical or cultural background behind the events is based on "reality." In general, realist works are concerned with "sordid and harsh aspects of human existence," and can look at the poor and disenfranchised members of humanity because realism "reached out to a much wider social range, in terms both of readership and of characters represented, than earlier more elite forms of literature." Pam Morris blames this class divergence on the notion that realism was developed by women, which she says led to it being "a form uninfluenced by classical conventions."[19] While Morris is correct in her definition of both realism and its public, I do not agree with her on the relationship between female authors and conventions. Simply because realist novels were frequently written by women hardly means that realism was anything but the next gradual step in the evolution of literature, in the taxonomy I am describing here. After all, what might be the first novel, *Tale of Genji*, was written by a noblewoman, but while she clearly broke with traditions in her form, she read prior literary works, and then felt that her story needed a different literary form to be fully expressed. Few of the major players in European realism were women. Literary realism in France was developed by writers such as Stendhal (1783–1842; *The Charterhouse of Parma*), Honoré de Balzac (1799–1850; *The Wild Ass's Skin*), and Gustave Flaubert (1821–1880; *Madame Bovary*). Thomas Hardy (1840–1928; *Far from the Madding Crowd*) was one of the leading British realists. Other countries participated in the realist movement, including Russia's Leo Tolstoy, author of works such as *Anna Karenina* (1875–1877), about a wife who has an affair and later commits suicide. After realism and naturalism, "high art" literature turned to modernism and then to the postmodern.

REVIVAL OF THE ROMANCE GENRE

In 1921, romantic ideas were picked up by Georgette Heyer with her historical romances, including *The Black Moth* (1921), which were highly formulaic and featured the "saturnine male lead, the marriage in danger, the extravagant wife, and the group of idle, entertaining young men."[20] Another contributor to this romantic rebirth was the British Edith M. Hull's *The Sheik*, about abduction, rape and the love that followed in an Arab desert. Perhaps it was unique because it was comedic, instead of tragic, in its structure and ending. It showed the female heroine becoming sexually aroused and falling in love despite the fact that she had been sexually violated, an act that typically ended with a suicide or homicide in most earlier popular fictions about equivalent circumstances.

More so than the historical and exotic romance novels that started appearing, Gerald Mills' death in 1928 caused a major catalyst in the romance market, as the remaining partner in Mills & Boon, Charles Boon, subsequently changed the company from publishing a wide array of fiction and nonfiction titles to focusing exclusively on the romance genre.

AMERICAN TRAGI-COMEDY: MARGARET MITCHELL

The next significant publication that altered the romantic genre was Margaret Mitchell's "anti-romance," *Gone with the Wind* (1936). Scarlett O'Hara is a strong female heroine who only falls in love with the man who has been pursuing her, Rhett, at the end, and shortly after this he leaves her; the unusual detail that makes the book anti-romantic is that Scarlett is hopeful about the future and decides to fight on with or without Rhett, going against the formula that the lovers have to end up either together (in a classic comedic romance ending) or with one or both of them dead or in extreme misery (in a tragic ending). While this ending was anti-romantic at the time, later novelists picked up on the character traits of this strong female heroine and built on her in the romance genre that continued adapting traits from popular successes throughout the century before taking the shape we are familiar with today. Margaret Mitchell is notable both because she was among the best-selling fiction writers in the period between 1930 and 1956[21] and because she won the Pulitzer Prize in 1937. She is only known for a single novel, unlike most of the other best-selling novelists, who typically publish dozens, if not hundreds, of novels to achieve equivalent sales rankings. Her reputation was greatly assisted by the success of the film adaptation of this novel. There are few other best-selling authors from the twentieth century who have also won the Pulitzer Prize, as this is a highbrow achievement, whereas film adaptation are a lowbrow popular achievement.

Graphic Sex, Obscenity and Romance: Vladimir Nabokov

The best-selling erotic romance novel of all time has actually been Vladimir Nabokov's *Lolita* (1955), a tragedy about a middle-aged literature professor seducing a pubescent stepdaughter and thereby destroying both of their lives. *Lolita* was written a couple of decades before *The Flame and the Flower*, and it was adapted in film by Stanley Kubrick in 1962, so it is likely that Kathleen Woodiwiss was thinking of this work when she decided to write a novel that did not conform to the previously established criteria in romance publishing. Both novels include sex, love, obsession, and pornography or erotica (depending on one's definitions of these terms). *Lolita* was released in the middle of the conservative 1950s, and while it was enormously popular, it did not immediately shift the conservative publishing market. But Woodiwiss' novel caused a stir possibly because of its simplistic, formulaic and yet popularly appealing ingredients. Publishers looked around and asked themselves why they could not do that too, and this brought about an eruption of extremely formulaic and repetitive novels that solidified romance formulas used to this day. The rape of stepdaughters did not stick; however, the rape or "seduction" of vulnerable young women is still with us. If Nabokov had tried to submit *Lolita* for the first time to Avon, instead of his initial Paris publisher, in 1980, or even today to Harlequin, it would have been rejected because it did not comply with the strict guidelines of the accepted generic norms. *Lolita* would have been thrown away at its first page by a romance editor because it is a first-person confession of a man who is about to die in prison of an illness; it starts with a literary self-criticism; and the narrator indicates that he has changed the names to spare those involved, as if it's really a true story.[22]

The book has been a success with readers over the last half-century because it's written in a realistic and detailed style for a reader who is interested in dissecting the reality and mystery of a man who would commit the depicted crimes. An example of this hyper-descriptive style is a short story from the same year when *Lolita* was published (1958), "First Love," in which Nabokov spends most of the narrative talking about details like a political cartoon he saw in *Punch,* Bolsheviks that were shooting aristocrats in Russia, Perry reaching the North Pole, "romantic, auburn cars," mineral water, a train ride, and numerous other minor narrative points and descriptive fine points before he finally introduces his "first love" in the third and final part of the story—a boyish, French girl called Colette, with whom he immediately falls in love, protects from a bully, kisses, and then is separated from after a final arranged meeting in Paris.[23] Similarly, *Lolita* does not describe just the sexual activities between the professor and the twelve-year-old American girl, but also numerous mundane and romantic details about their daily lives; thus, the obscenity is diluted in the everyday and also intensified by the textured reality of the situation. But this is not a formula that was grabbed by the marketplace as reproducible. Of course, *Lolita* cannot be packaged and reproduced like furniture because it is layered with several different generic formulas, and is the work of an English professor; basically, the formula is so complex that it cannot be recreated without the mimicker being immediately discovered and brought up on plagiarism charges. If *Lolita*'s formula is simplified to its basic ingredients, it is pure obscene pornography and is not printable by any press aware of its reputation. However, *The Flame and the Flower* is based on such a simple formula that includes so many repeating movements that the formula can be reproduced with new settings, plots, and characters without losing the emotional, sexual, and dramatic tension that attracted readers to the original.

UPLIFTING ROMANCE: CATHERINE COOKSON

While Catherine Cookson only sold 90 million copies of her novels, compared with Barbara Cartland's 1 billion sold books, she is perhaps just as popular because, in 1998, "a third of all popular fiction borrowed from local libraries was by Cookson," and "nine of the top ten most borrowed books were Cookson novels." Thus, Cookson might have been read by as many as a billion readers, most of whom borrowed her books for free instead of buying them. Cookson insisted that she was not a romance novelist, perhaps because only one of her books was published with Heinemann (which specialized in romance only), and most of her early books between 1950 and 1980 were published by Corgi Books, an imprint of Random House, which continues to distribute more heavily to libraries than romance publishers, which strived to put books into the readers' hands with mail-in orders, series, and flashy covers and shelving in bookstores. However, Cookson is still categorized as a woman's romance novelist on library and bookstore shelves, as despite their "socially realistic and regionally distinct" elements, they are "family saga" stories with "a blend of historical and generational romance."[24] The use of poor and struggling strong female characters is the primary element that separates Cookson's novels from the standard "uplifting" romance novel formula. Her heroines also win in the end, so the overall shape of the plot line can be called comedic, though the quest for a man might take second place in these works to the heroine's struggle with poverty.

SELF-PROMOTION: JACQUELINE SUSANN

There was yet another catalyst that created the modern romance formula and it was Jacqueline Susann. Her innovation was not in any element of the romance novel, but rather in the way she promoted herself to make it to the top of the best-sellers list. Two years after the D. H. Lawrence versus Penguin trial, in 1962, Susann was diagnosed with cancer and, as a result, decided to publish a fiction book. Perhaps drawing her inspiration from the legalized obscenity in *Lady Chatterley's Lover*, Susann wrote a story that was full of drugs, sex and scandal, *Valley of the Dolls*, which was greatly assisted in its production by a small publishing company, Bernard Geis Associates, and was raised into popular awareness by Susann's tireless efforts to promote it on all television, radio, newspaper and in-person means she inventively thought of. It became a best-seller in 1966, and was named the top American best-selling novel of the twentieth century by the *Guinness Book of World Records*. While the small publishing company was not able to change the book into something formulaic or to lift it above the critical category of "trash" fiction, it made the elements of sex, drugs and scandal into important formulaic ingredients for future best-sellers.

Romance Publishing Mergers and Monopoly

In 1957 romance novels entered the American popular market with Mills & Boon's help, which started using Harlequin as its American reprint distributor: "'From 1964 onward, Mills & Boon romances became the only titles published by Harlequin' (Harlequin 16)."[25] In 1971, Harlequin bought Mills & Boon, Boon having died a couple decades earlier and Harlequin growing rich from its enormous sales figures. This merger created what is still one of the top romance publishers; Harlequin is known for publishing best-selling authors, including Anne Rice's *Sleeping Beauty* series.

The genre was fluctuating into a rejuvenation of the gothic romance, and was swimming all over the place, when suddenly there came along a marketer who might have single-handedly created the basic outline of the formula that still defines the romance novel. Lawrence Heisey was hired in 1971 by Harlequin and intentionally gave birth across his career to the "brand name or series romance." He achieved this enormous task by initiating "consumer research, then had his editors 'help guide the creativity of authors' via editorial guidelines based on the results of that research." The formula that the marketers and editors came up with was "simplistic stories, cartoonlike covers, and simpering cover blurbs," at exactly 192 pages in length, which could comfortably fit into racks in "supermarkets and other mass merchandising outlets." After the Harlequin titles became thus recognizable, the company started a "reader service," or a "book club without a return option." Returns were eliminated and sales were now guaranteed, so quantity became a more significant challenge than quality. The fact that this approach saved 50 percent that would have gone to wholesale booksellers was extremely significant, for the profit margins exploded and suddenly authors and the publisher could grow rich at a rate far over the 50 percent difference, as all of this saved money was pure profit, whereas the bulk of the other 50 percent was mostly consumed in production costs. Suddenly, novels were an extremely profitable commodity that cost very little to print and distribute. The result was that Harlequin "published at least 144 romance novels per year from 1973 to 1980, the period of greatest growth for the company," as, for example, it sold "thirty million books in English in 1973," and then went up to 35 million copies in the United States alone by 1977, and kept growing.[26]

In the 1970s, Harlequin focused on publishing and paid Simon and Schuster a percentage for distributing their titles in the United States, but at the end of the decade, Harlequin realized that it could make substantially more by personally handling the distribution because by that point the company had an enormous share of the romance market in the United States and was confident that the libraries and consumers who were buying its books would continue to do so regardless of the name of the distributor. Simon and Schuster reacted to this sudden ending of their profitable business partnership, and the enormous market-share that Harlequin began to occupy, by launching Silhouette Books in 1981. Silhouette remained Harlequin's top competitor during the peak of the romance publishing wars between 1972 and 1984, in which year Harlequin bought Silhouette Books from Simon and Schuster, "ending the most intense competition in the market and leading to much more stability in the market."[27] In other words, after 1984, Harlequin lost any motivation to continue developing the romance genre because it had a monopoly over the romance marketplace.

The romance monopoly is held by an international conglomerate today, but it stemmed at the turn of the twentieth century from Britain. The fact that the largest North American publisher began by printing only United Kingdom titles means that there are British roots behind the American romance novel formula: "British romance conventions shaped almost all romance novels ... most of them used settings that resembled British models—landed estates, wealthy and powerful families, complicated plots involving issues of inheritance and family secrets," or, in general, "aristocratic romance conventions grafted onto American locales."[28] When American writers started to be included in the competition in the 1970s, some of these conventions began to change, as exemplified by the fact that, in the new romances, "sex before marriage did not invariably result in punishment of death."[29] In other words, a book could end with sex rather than marriage and still be a comedy rather than a tragedy.

The most recent and the most significant change in the formula for a popular romance novel occurred "between 1972 and 1982," with the rise of "the new paperback romance novel," which "radically changed earning expectations."[30] This period represents the spread of the "bodice-ripper" and "erotic historical romance." These new formulas opposed the less sexually explicit and more religiously conservative Heyer and Cartland historical romances and their formulaic relatives. The starting date is very exact because this shift occurred immediately after the publication of the 1972 *The Flame and the Flower* by Kathleen Woodiwiss with Avon. The shift in the genre is apparent in the wording used to summarize romance novels in a writing textbook from 1976, in which Karen Hubert explains that in the "final scene ... avowals of love are sealed by a kiss, a proposal, a wedding or, nowadays, by the sex act."[31] The inclusion of "nowadays" suggests that the graphic portrayal of sex was newly popular in 1976. While *Lolita* and other works that depicted sex were published much earlier, by 1976 the use of sex, especially in the ending, was widespread enough to mention it as a part of the basic formula in a textbook. A few years earlier, in 1972, Harlequin was already rapidly growing, but it was not yet obvious that the romance genre would explode as it did. So it was fortuitous for Avon to pick up on this trend and take on a book that quickly became a best-seller and added to the rapid expansion of the genre. By 1976 the romance genre was popular enough for how-to books on writing it to become popular in the market, and it would've been much more difficult for Avon (or any other competitor) to enter the established marketplace.

Karen Hubert describes one typical interaction between writers and the romance industry during this critical period. She explains that she read from a Harlequin romance in one of her creative writing classes, which she was teaching how to write a romance: "These books are sold in five-and-dimes [equivalent to a dollar store today] and are full of adolescent crushes and hand-holding idylls. I chose a story about a young girl who awakes blissfully happy on her wedding day only to receive a telegram from her betrothed breaking their engagement. I intended to ask the group to take the character's place and write the end of the story." To Hubert's surprise, she discovered that the female students in her class didn't think the story was "romantic enough," so she asked "them to write what *they* considered a good romance story."[32] This passage is telling because it shows that Harlequin romances were extremely cheap and readers partially considered them to be anti-romantic or anti-formulaic at this time. The students thought Harlequin romances were not "romantic enough" because between 1972 and 1980 Harlequin was breaking earlier formulaic conventions and readers who were used to earlier works felt that Harlequin wasn't meeting their romantic expectations. Because Harlequin and the other leaders in the romance marketplace stuck to this "new" formula, by now the standard plot line these modern romances depict is considered romantic, and the earlier version of the romance novel is out of style and feels unfamiliar.

From 1971 onward, there was a small group of leading publishers that fought a marketplace battle during this decade that created what we still know today as a paperback romance novel; they were Silhouette, Ballantine, Harlequin, Avon, Bantam, Dell Ecstasy, Pocket Books and Playboy Press. These eight publishers won billions of dollars across this decade, and while they experienced some mergers and turns of direction, most of them are still the major players in the romance and erotica marketplace today. Three decades later, in 2001, out of the 2,143 new romance titles released by all publishers, the top publishers in terms of number of titles produced were "Harlequin (1,067); Kenningston (204); Pearson (138); and Random House (107)."[33] This is a much shorter list because Random House consumed Ballantine and Bantam, while Harlequin ate Silhouette, and most of the others have also been swallowed up in the string of mergers over these three decades. Unlike literary formulaic shifts after the French Revolution, or during the Industrial Revolution, this shift was one purely driven by profits, sales, and assumed market demand. Charles Dickens would have been rejected in this competitive marketplace. Sir Walter Scott did not do "market research" in 1814 when he published *Waverley*, but by a bit of luck and good timing he ended up being one of the first best-selling writers in the world with what was then a new genre—the historical novel. One hundred fifty-eight years later Woodiwiss wrote a historical novel that included the type of sexual violence that the knighted Scott would surely have frowned upon. But it had an interesting historical backdrop and included a change of settings from the English country to London, to a ship, and then to a wealthy American plantation, and when it came across the slush pile on the desk of an editor at Avon, she thought it was pretty good and, after discussing it with the team, accepted the manuscript. *The Flame and the Flower* sold millions of copies, and it was the perhaps the biggest multiplication in sales volume since Scott. If Scott took the publishing industry from expecting 100 book sales to 100,000, Woodiwiss jumped from 100,000 to multiple millions. There was a gradual increase in average and best-selling sales across the book market between these two publications. Today the romance novel marketplace makes up the largest percentage of total book sales. In recent decades, single-title book sales have seen an extreme spike in the mystery generic categories, as represented by Dan Brown's *The Da Vinci Code* (80 million copies since 2003 and still climbing). Romance novelists who produce enormous quantities of novels across their lifetimes are more likely to gain enormous riches and are among the best-selling writers of all time in the *Guinness Book of World Records*. The degree of competition even among the top eight romance novel publishers is extreme, with most of them releasing hundreds of new titles every year.

Besides the formulaic differences between *Lolita* and *The Flame and the Flower*, several major demographic changes occurred by 1972 (which haven't changed that much since), which meant that America was ripe for a romance industry explosion. The protests for civil rights and against the Vietnam War, as well as the growth of the drug industry in the 1960s, both caused and were the results of these shifts. "By 1980, 54 percent of all women sixteen years of age or older were in the labor force," earning "fifty-nine cents for every dollar men took home. Four out of ten marriages were ending in divorce, double the rate of a decade before, and one and a half million unwed couples were living together, three times as many as in 1970."[34]

These trends continued steadily from 1980 to the present day. Today, the majority of Americans start their sexual lives at an early age, with the average age of first intercourse being between 16 and 17, or in the last year of high school. Sexual fantasies are an important part of the American sexual experience—for example, even as early as in 1953, 50–55 percent of both genders responded erotically to being bitten. Most Americans are sexually active well into their 50s, and some into their 70s, with 86–90 percent of men and women having had sex in the past year (single, married and partnered). Most Americans of both genders are monogamous, with 94 percent of both men and women only having one sexual partner in the past 12 months. Men obtain more sexual pleasure from intercourse than women, with 75 percent of men and 25 percent of women always having orgasms with their partner. As for relationships, young people under 24 are more likely to casually date, and then most marry at around 24; roughly half of these divorce shortly thereafter, and if this group remarries, they are likely to go through divorce again: "More than half the participants in the 2010 national sex survey ages 18–24 indicated that their most recent sexual partner was a casual or dating partner. For all other age groups, the majority of study participants indicated that their most recent sexual partner was a relationship partner (NSSHB, 2010).... Nearly all Americans marry during their lifetime, yet close to half of all first marriages are expected to end in separation or divorce, many within a few years (Bramlett, 2002) and subsequent marriages are even more likely to end (Karney, 1995)."[35] This is a pretty nightmarish reality. Young girls have to go through numerous bad dates and several sexual partners to find the "one" they want to marry, and then half of them divorce and have to go through the whole circus again. Keeping in mind the frequency of rape, and the fact that most men are statistically "selfish" in relationships, with a small percentage of women achieving orgasms (and fewer women having received oral sex than men), women on average are pretty dissatisfied in their sexual lives. The rate of women in the workforce has jumped up and down over the decades since 1985, but it is basically the same today, with only 58.1 percent of women in the labor force and earnings going up to 82 cents on the dollar of what men make. "Among married-couple families, 54 percent had earnings from both the wife and the husband in 2010, compared with 44 percent in 1967."[36] A large portion of women are still full-time homemakers, and those who work are still likely to be making less money than men, even if they are highly educated.

Clearly there is a practical need for women to "escape" in "fantasies" that romance and other forms of simple fiction provide. But if women read romance novels to "rebel against their domestic imprisonment," most find that this rebellion is bitter after having read enough of these novels to notice how repetitive they are. Afterward, it is likely that their romantic fantasy life will be negatively affected by this disappointing experience. In a statistical study that Carol Thurston conducted as part of her book in 1982 and 1985, she found that "a number of romance readers ... reported that their husbands often reacted to their reading at two levels: hostility to the activity itself ('Why don't you watch TV with me...') and then to what was being read ('...instead of reading that garbage'). Thus, the very act of reading at times is an assertion of independence."[37] The same evidence also shows that reading romance novels is seen as threatening and damaging to a married relationship by husbands, who might view this activity as a form of cheating, similar to catching a husband viewing pornography online. Despite inflated findings by the romance industry itself, it's likely that simple, mindless and extremely repetitive and formulaic romance novels might be doing more harm than good in terms of women being more satisfied in their sexual lives.

Obscenity Debate

The decades between the 1920s and 1972 changed the publishing industry because strict British and American censorship laws were put on trial. The trials from primarily the 1920s, 1950s and 1960s, which led to eventual changes, at first saw many publishers and booksellers imprisoned and new morality laws put in place, like the 1955 "Children's and Young Person's (Harmful Publications) Bill." The twentieth century began with Oscar Wilde's death after having served a labor-camp sentence for "gross indecency," or homosexual behavior. The debate in the 1950s "focused upon a number of seizures of titles, interdictions placed upon certain titles, and an increasing trickle of publishers and booksellers being prosecuted for indecency and immorality." In 1951 alone, there were "nineteen successful prosecutions" against the "industry" and "writers such as Stephen Francis" overseen by the Catholic Association.[38] Spiritual and religious novels were also popular between 1918 and 1951 (and later), so in a way these cases were a battle between three literary genres, as well as between Christian morality and librettist, pro-sex and drug proponents. On the one hand was Christian moralism, with its religious novels, and on the other "erotic content" and "gothic horror," which are better known today as the romance and fantasy genres. The Catholic Association and other groups are just as aggressive about arguing against romance and horror today (i.e., the debate about the promotion of magic in *Harry Potter*). The fault was placed on "indecency and immorality," and the romance genre frequently slipped into both when it touched on pornographically sexual relationships between lovers.

The debate regarding obscenity in fiction changed in the 1960s. In 1961, C. S. Lewis wrote, "The law about literary obscenity operates almost exclusively against particular words, that books were banned not for their tendency but for their vocabulary and a man could freely administer the strongest possible aphrodisiacs to his public provided he had the skill—and what competent writer has not?—to avoid the forbidden syllables."[39] It's very likely that Lewis was thinking of the 1960 trial, under the Obscene Publications Act of 1959, between the British Republic and Penguin Books over the "unexpurgated" version of D. H. Lawrence's *Lady Chatterley's Lover*, which had already been published in the abridged form by several different publishers since it came out in 1928, but which Penguin wanted to release in a cheap, popularly available edition. The British government objected to Lawrence's use of obscene words such as "f**k" and "c**t." Penguin won and sold millions of copies of the book, the trial providing extraordinary publicity. *Lady Chatterley's Lover* and another dozen novels that D. H. Lawrence (1885–1930) wrote over his short lifetime continued to sell extremely well, so that Lawrence has made it into a short list of best-selling authors from the 1957–1974 period according to Bloom's *Bestsellers*, despite achieving nearly no fame during his own lifetime. The Penguin trial was the best thing that could have happened to his posthumous literary career, as it became a "*cause celebre* for the 'Sixties generation.'"[40]

D. H. Lawrence's trouble with censorship started much earlier, during his lifetime, when he opposed World War I, in part because his wife was German, and this led to antagonism with the government that resulted in the branding of his *The Rainbow* (1915) novel as "obscene" because it explores a lesbian relationship between the heroine and her teacher, and other sexually explicit incidents. After this incident, Lawrence and his wife left Britain and traveled around the world, as Lawrence published half a dozen other "obscene" novels, including *Lady Chatterley's Lover*. The style that Lawrence used can be seen in miniature in one of his short stories, "The Horse Dealer's Daughter" (1922). The heroine, Mabel Pervin, is distraught over her family's poverty and misfortune; she goes to tend to her mother's grave, and then she jumps into a lake and nearly drowns. A young doctor, Fergusson, pulls her out of the smelly water and escorts her back to her house, where he undresses her. "The question the story addresses is whether intimacy has the power to frustrate grief and despair."[41] In other words, Fergusson and Mabel engage in fondling each other at the end and it cheers Mabel up a bit, but then it depresses her again. Several elements from this story are typical to formulaic romance novels. First, the heroine keeps repeating "Do you love me, then?" over a dozen times in the course of a few pages. Second, there is a repetition of the word "breasts," as they are "pressed," revealed, wetted, and otherwise keep reappearing as a key detail in the text; the references to "breasts" also become absurdly repetitive in such works as Woodiwiss's *The Flame and the Flower*. In fact, Lawrence also frequently repeats that a "flame" starts burning in the doctor, as his sexual desire and personal feelings for Mabel develop.

Of course, "The Horse Dealer's Daughter" was banned before it became popular, so there are several elements that distinguish it from politically acceptable romances. For one thing, the woman has "animal shoulders," which at first horrify the doctor and then attract him. Do you recall hairy shoulders in the last few romance novels that you read? In general, the two people who end up together in modern romances find each other attractive to begin with; the man or the woman are not typically described as ugly, revolting or deformed, as it would spoil the "romantic mood." The fact that Fergusson keeps recalling that Mabel and especially her "hair smells so horrible" hearkens back to Lady Dulcinea's garlic breath from *Don Quixote*, as opposed to a formulaic romance novel characterization. The story ends with the doctor insisting that he wants to marry Mabel "quickly, quickly—to-morrow if I can." And in the last line, the heroine is "frightened" of him wanting her, "almost more than her horror lest he should *not* want her."[42] She does not provide a final answer of whether she will marry the doctor, and the resolution to the sexual tension between them remains unresolved, which goes against the key element of all formulaic romance novels, in which the sexual and romantic tension between the lovers must end in their positive and relieved union. This anti-formulaic and anti-romantic view of animalistic sexuality offended the patriarchal establishment more than the isolated obscene words that Lewis assumed had to be avoided to meet the censorship requirements in Britain.

In reaction to Penguin's 1960 victory, "Labour MPs" and other groups started filing frivolous lawsuits and banning complaints, like the proposal to ban Harold Robbins's *The Carpetbaggers* simply because it was "literary rubbish."[43] Trials continued with some especially notable legal cases, like the 1971 case in which the editors of *OZ* magazine went to jail for obscenity, after "the longest" trial in "British history."[44] And then the 1980s saw seizures of "drug-related titles."[45] There are still lists of books banned by religious groups for their obscene, immoral or un–Christian (pagan, Muslim, fantastic) elements, though these bannings are not supported by prison sentences. Besides bans, the main source of litigation in publishing has been focused on financial losses since the 1980s.

Random House is more significant in terms of trend-setting than many other major publishing houses. This was the publisher that organized a topless bar book launch for *Topless*. It also published many of Catherine Cookson's novels, which she insisted were not romances, though they are still categorized as such. One of Random House's top editors, Jason Epstein, has even published a book about the details of Random House's publishing enterprise as he experienced it in *Book Business: Publishing Past Present and Future.* So, it's not surprising that one of the most heated cases in the 1990s returned to the concept of "literary rubbish" in a fresh new light, and this time not in a frivolous capacity. This was the 1994 Joan Collins versus Random House case, which went all the way to the Supreme Court. Joan Collins had a two-book deal with Random House for $4 million, "to be paid in stages as manuscripts arrived." Random House wanted to receive a refund of the "half a million dollars paid out on a worthless collection of disconnected pages ... delivered 'unfinished'" from Joan Collins, for *The Ruling Passion.* The lawyers debated the difference between *quantity* of words, pages and basic elements of a story delivered on time, according to the contract, and its literary *quality*. As in the 1960s, quantity won over quality and Random House had to pay Collins the remainder of the contracted sum for the delivered book.[46] In general, in the second half of the twentieth century courts seemed to favor immorality and hack writing, and these trends increased the production of both of these from the best-selling publishers. While there were several setbacks, Penguin's victory in 1960 shifted British and American censorship litigation and opened the floodgates for sexual, drug-related and other "immoral" content to enter the popular publishing industry.

THE WORKSHOP FOR READER-WRITERS SALES STRATEGY

One of the ways the romance publishing industry and its "parasite enterprises" made a profit was by holding workshops and creating an "outpouring of instructional manuals on 'how to write a romance.'"[47] These manuals are just as formulaic in structure as the romance novels themselves, and comparing the chapter titles and sections as well as the basic advice given in several of these would show that the content is extremely similar despite the different authors who produce them. Part of the publishing industry's strategy is to make the romances seem simple enough to write to attract readers who might be tempted to become writers and encourage their efforts, even if without a chance for success. Readers who want to earn enormous profits and acclaim from publishing a romance novel are extremely loyal and are likely to spend more on more books in the genre and on how-to books about the genre. There is a group among romance fans who only read romances because they intend to or are in the process of writing one. This grassroots do-it-yourself enterprise has been fueled in part by publisher-sponsored (Silhouette and Harlequin) seminars held in department stores all around the country, as well as Cinderella stories about high school graduates who achieved not only fame but fantastic fortune.... A number of romance authors have come from the ranks of readers who say they were moved by the belief that "I can do better than that!" These how-to seminars serve primarily to publicize and sell books, however, since herds of hopeful authors are instructed by editors to "read at least thirty of our books before even attempting an outline—and be sure they're new ones so you'll know what we're looking for today."[48]

Thurston describes one new grandmother, at 42, quit her great job after buying over 1,200 romance novels to start a "new career" as a romance writer.[49] These sales tactics to wannabe authors are still in place today.

A book published in 1999, *North American Romance Writers,* includes essays about writing and the romance genre in America from some of the best-selling and award-winning writers in the industry. Most of these authors bring up the point that their transition to best-selling writers began when they started reading large quantities of romances. Mary Balogh writes that she said to herself as she read one of her first formulaic romances, "'I can do this,' and that it seemed like it was "an easy road to riches. A few years later I spent a year's leave of absence from my teaching job after the birth of my third child." She read another romance, Georgette Heyer's *Frederica,* and then "devoured every other book she had written."[50] Keeping in mind the Cartland-Heyer plagiarism debacle, which will be discussed later, it is likely that many historical romance novelists who followed Heyer devoured most of what she had thoroughly researched and popularly published. Another writer in this same collection, Alison Hart, exclaims, "I studied the romance 'formula' [by] reading the books."[51] In an interview for the *Pennsylvania Literary Journal,* the interviewer instinctively asked about the best books to read in order to learn about the fantasy formula. To this Cinda Williams Chima replied, "First, read widely in the genre you would like to write. Read classic and contemporary examples. For instance, anyone writing high fantasy should read *The Lord of the Rings*—not to emulate Tolkien, but to join the fantasy conversation. Reading great fiction is like taking a private workshop from a master. Also, read outside your genre. Good books of whatever genre have more commonalities than differences. Great writing is great writing is great writing."[52] Chima does not truly answer the question regarding which books she emulated in her fantasy series, as Tolkien's book is written in a denser style that Chima doesn't emulate. Instead, she focuses her reply on the fact that those who want to write in a certain genre have to read a lot of books in that genre, equating this with taking a "workshop from a master." The word "workshop" clearly echoes the standard terminology that's used when encouraging writers to buy more books to become great writers, thus avoiding giving specific formulaic suggestions that might provide cheaper and simpler advice to aspiring writers.

The tendency to sell books by explaining to readers that the only way to become writers is to buy as many books as possible in that genre is not isolated to the romance genre. In the interviews Stephen King gave in the 1980s, he hid this suggestion better than most romance novelists and marketers, saying instead, "You have to read the market. You can't send a *True Romance* story to *Fantasy & Science Fiction* because they're not going to read it. You can't send a western to *Fantasy & Science Fiction* because they're not going to read it. You can't mention things such as childbirth or menstruation or the death of children in magazines like *McCalls* or *Good Housekeeping*, because they deny that those things exist."[53] Here King advises writers to buy books in numerous genres to sell in one of these genres, and to read an enormous quantity of books, because without a close reading, they might miss what sorts of things cannot be mentioned in each respective genre. Figuring out what should be done in a given genre would take reading just one book, whereas figuring out what shouldn't be done would require writing a dissertation on the subject and an enormous quantity of book purchases. In another interview, King touches on the second major justification for "reading" and buying books in a genre, since after reading the formulaic works typically published, a potential writer is likely to say, "'I do better stuff than that...' when they read it, they make that vital critical judgment and say, 'I'm better.'" King stresses that reading formulaic fiction will reassure potential writers that they are better, and thus encourage them to write to be "paid money for it."[54] Even if the market is closed to new writers, advertising that mimicking the formulas of the genre will potentially make readers into writers leads a significant number to buy these poorly written books.

King also included self-advertisements inside his books. In Book V of the *Dark Tower* series, he writes in the introduction, "If you have not read those [prior four] books before commencing this one, I urge you to do so or to put this one aside. These books are but parts of a single long tale, and you would do better to read them from beginning to end rather than starting in the middle."[55] The story of the quest for the Dark Tower is a disjointed one, so clearly King isn't concerned about readers starting in the "middle" and simply wants to sell seven books instead of just one by pitching the full series. Writing novels in a series of seven or more novels is a favorite format with popular publishers because there are more repeat readers who will want to finish the full series once they've read one of the books, but who would have been less likely to pick up six more books on other topics by the same author.

Another clue for when a romance novelist is trying to market herself while giving "advice" to writers is when she starts talking about the feminist qualities of romance novels; typically this includes repeating a line like "the genre ... written by women, for women, and to women.... We are 'sisters.'"[56] Or, as Nora Roberts echoes, the fact that romance novels "are written primarily by women, most usually for women, is one of the most positive of feminist statements."[57] What on earth does "feminism" mean in this context? Is feminism really all about women making more money from writing romance novels? The message that romance novels are not chauvinist, but rather feminist, is parroted by most female critics of romance literature, but the only way a quest for a man to discover one's self can be feminist is for the reader to ignore the story and focus on how much money the woman who wrote it made. At one point in her essay, Nora Roberts exclaims regarding the notion that women shouldn't be shown Cinderella endings because they aren't realistic, "Are we stupid? Are we so ridiculously impressionable that we must be protected because we can't separate fiction from reality?"[58] If a woman believes the hope portrayed in one of Nora Roberts' stories, she is "stupid" and crazy—this is a pretty negative view of the majority of her readers, most of whom are Weary Giants who read romances to hope and to escape into a fantasy world, where one has to suspend their disbelief or mistake fiction for reality. Nora makes this attack in order to defend the "feminist" foundation in her plot lines, or to explain that, despite the evidence to the contrary, her novels are pro-women and pro-feminist. If you start to suspect something is amiss, many writers introduce their advice with comments like "a good writer is a good liar."[59] How can you object to somebody who admits they are lying? If you catch them lying, they will tell you that they honestly confessed that they were lying to begin with. In the quote that introduced this chapter, Nora Roberts calls for people to buy her books because so many in America are sinfully illiterate. The task of reading Nora's romances becomes a "triumph" even the barely literate can achieve.

Structural Elements of Romance: Characters, Setting, and Plot

The repetitive nature of the plots is more apparent in the romance genre than in others because there is less going on with the characters and the setting. The suspense is sex-based, rather than death-based, as readers anticipate the consummation or positive development of a sexual relationship between the hero and the heroine. The goal is simple. The characters are typically clones. So, the repetitions stand out more than in science fiction or mystery novels.

Reading over the commonly published formulas in how-to-write-romance books and articles, one finds advice such as that, in a modern romance novel, "the relationship is always a main focus and integrated into the plot's incidents. If, say, you're writing romantic suspense, you're not writing a story about a woman in danger—who happens to have a boyfriend. The hero and heroine ... are falling in love against a background of danger and suspense." This seems to be a good starting point. But then frequently one finds advice like "Most beginning romance writers start off with too much background." This advice might leave most amateur writers a bit paralyzed. If they are attempting to write a suspenseful romance novel, the thing must be all about the love, but must also involve a suspenseful (i.e., violent) plot that begins on the first line of the story, and should never include anything as horrid as "background." Rebecca York continues her criticism (which is echoed by most other how-to writers in this field), and inevitably asks, "What's going to make her [the editor] pick your book?" She then suggests initial lines that would do the trick: "The first line of Julie Garwood's *Honor's Splendour* is 'They meant to kill him.'" York's own novel is called *Killing Moon*. The lovers face external and internal conflicts (i.e., extreme violence) and overcome them through the "healing power of love." York concludes her essay by saying, "If it doesn't end happily, then it's not a romance."[60] It is likely that the volume of repetitive how-to advice about writing romance has helped to restrict the formula of these novels to very rigid boundaries. Just as an Aristotelian tragedy must end in death, a modern romance has to begin with problems and must end happily with the consummation of the love relationship (if it hasn't been consummated a lot earlier in the work).

Carol Thurston did two surveys of romance readers, one in 1982 and then the next in 1985. While many of the readers in the first survey might have been new to the genre, by 1985 they had either been reading romances for at least 3 years or abandoned the genre: "By 1985 the dampening effect of the high level of redundancy associated with series romances was evident in the decreased number of titles being read per month.... One reader complained, 'They're all beginning to sound alike, just a different cover and background. I have a growing stack of half-finished paper-backs...' Nearly half said they were exploring more of other kinds of fiction."[61] Even among hard-core fans of romance, dissatisfaction with repetition turns into very strong negative feelings after the pattern becomes apparent. Readers of romance are not typically literary critics and they cannot see the formulas at first, allowing themselves to feel for the characters because the emotional formulas do tug at their heart-strings. A study should be conducted to research whether hard-core romance readers who suddenly start to see the obviously repetitive formulas ever read popular fiction again. While the publishing business was exponentially growing in the 1980s, when Thurston conducted her study, it is shrinking today, with Borders and other major booksellers, academic publishers and other established players going out of business. It is clear from the quality of recent best-sellers that buyers are leaving the market after repeated disappointments. "Readers want 'more story' and are tired of shallow characters who share nothing beyond a 'jolt of electricity' at first sight or touch, then are overwhelmed by a mindless, compulsive physical desire and immediately fall in love and into bed.... Unless a credible relationship between heroine and hero can be developed, the sex is gratuitous (often equated with male pornography) and the story fails as an erotic romance."[62]

An interesting objection to the formulaic nature of the romance plot line is offered by Mary Cadogan in the introduction of her critical book on the romance genre. She attempts to prove, with the story summaries discussed in the rest of her book, that the genre of the romantic novel is extremely varied rather than formulaic, but she achieves this by expanding the definition of a romance to include religious romances, gothic horror, most of the classical romantic novels from the eighteenth and nineteenth centuries, and too many other works and authors that are typically grouped in other categories. While she insists that things changed between 1973 and 1994, implying that Woodiwiss initiated an overwhelming shift in the genre, this "change" cannot be supported by a close study of the best-selling works that were created in these two decades, as romantic novels simply became more formulaic and repetitive. The only way they can be called distinct is if one merges all of the subgenres into one and then says there are differences within it. But when one looks at the subgenres separately, it is obvious that each one relies on a very narrow formula that overwhelmingly dominates all other dramatic possibilities.

> It is often argued that romantic novels are unreviewable because they stick to the same basic plot and because there is no development generally in the genre, but during the last two decades [1973–1994] its frontiers have been pushed out to provide intriguing variations on previously accepted formulae ... [in which] the hero and the heroine ... [are kept] at arm's length until the traditional clearing-up-of-misunderstandings clinch of the closing paragraphs.[63]

With the analyses in this chapter, I am attempting to disprove both of the above claims. I believe romance is both reviewable and continues to be hyper-formulaic.

ROMANCE PLOT

The structure of a romance novel has the comedy basic plot at its core. Romance novels are written with the motto "'Unbearable pessimism' does not sell books"— instead, only "uplifting reading" sells well.[64] Classic romances (i.e., Shakespeare) fell in both comedic and tragic categories, but the modern best-selling romance novel is never tragic, and while readers might not laugh once as they read over the novel, it still has a comedic structural shape. The definition of comedy that Christopher Booker uses is a story that exposes "as ridiculous the state of self-delusion which affects human beings who have become isolated from those around them by their egocentricity,"[65] a definition that includes both "funny" slapstick comedy and best-selling modern romance novels.

Booker explains that the "love story" entered the comedic plot line during the New Comedy period, which followed in the century after Old Comedy, led by Aristophanes, who wrote *Lysistrata* (411 BCE), about a group of women withholding sex to make their husbands stop fighting in wars: "The action became centered for the first time on a hero and a heroine: and the chief effect of the confusion or conflict in the story is to keep the two apart until they can be brought triumphantly together in the closing scenes." In New Comedies, the two could be kept apart by the following: (1) "Hero and heroine ... passionately desire to get married but are being prevented from doing so by a selfish and unrelenting father, until finally something comes to light which persuades him to withdraw his opposition to the match." (2) "A quarrel between the lovers themselves."[66] The first option can be simplified for modern romances to be "forces outside of the couple," as today parental objections are not typically serious barriers to a couple's joining. The plot line and formula behind a comedic love story has remained basically the same since this period, with perhaps the sole distinction that it has become more repetitive and formulaic in the last few decades. Booker blames this increase in formulaic complexity (which later became formulaic repetitions) on William Shakespeare. Shakespearean comedy "opened up to include all the possibilities for confusion which may arise before their final pairing off," including difficulties during wooing, inconsistency, unrequitedness, and love triangles.[67]

Besides the major obstacle that keeps the hero and heroine apart, there is also a group of recurring humorous (or occasionally humorless) misunderstandings, such as the ones listed in Christopher Booker's chapter on comedy:

- characters donning disguises or swapping identities
- men dressing up as women, or vice versa
- secret assignations when the "wrong person" turns up
- scenes in which characters are hastily concealed in cupboards or behind furniture, only for their presence to be inevitably and embarrassingly discovered[68]

In a romance, the action is moved not by the drive toward the goal of killing the monster, but by an attraction between two lovers, and their interaction is intensified and becomes more tense and suspenseful if they encounter challenges and misunderstandings that prevent their full mutual happiness until the end. A diagram and a table of the plot movements that Booker describes will help to explain these patterns, and are found in Figures 14 and 15.

Figure 15 focuses on Georgette Heyer's *These Old Shades*, Barbara Cartland's *Knave of Hearts*, Kathleen Woodiwiss' *The Flame and the Flower*, and Nora Roberts' *Last Boyfriend*. Two of these works were chosen not because they are the highest sellers or the best known by these prolific authors, but rather because Georgette Heyer named Barbara Cartland's *Knave of Hearts* as the most serious plagiarism of her work, explaining that it has too many similarities with a few other novels, but

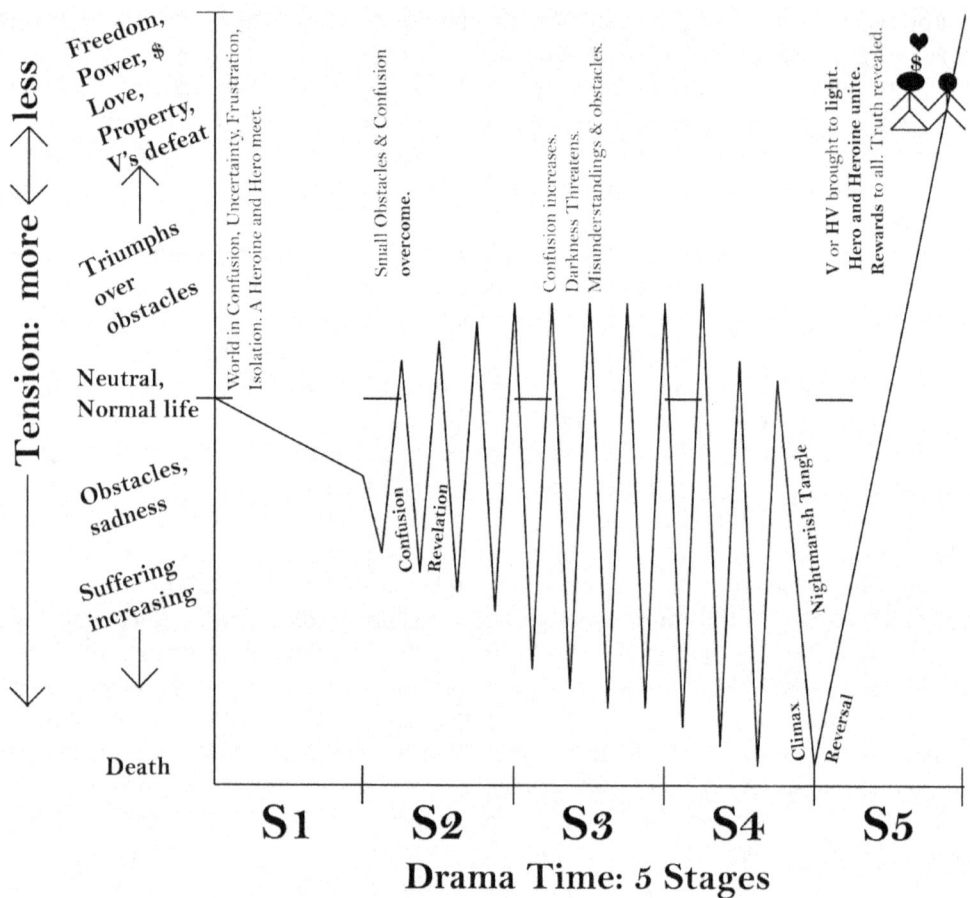

Figure 14. Comedic Plot Diagram.

especially with her *These Old Shades* Regency romance. In addition, Nora Roberts' *Last Boyfriend* was chosen because it is her latest best-seller, and Woodiwiss' *The Flame and the Flower* was chosen because it was her first and most well-known best-seller.

The roller coaster swings section is longer in the comedic plot than in the fantasy plot across novel time; three of the middle acts are spent on conquering ever-increasing obstacles. In all four novels, the two lovers who will be happy together in the end meet for the first time or see each other in a new light. Frequently, the heroine is undergoing hardships in the first act, such as being sold out as a laborer, extreme poverty, rape, or simply exhaustion from strenuous work. In three of these works, meeting the hero is a major initial obstacle or the reason for the downward slope of her life. The exception to this rule is *Last Boyfriend,* in which the setting is modern and the plot is anti-dramatic—in other words, it does not have the same dramatic tension as the other works. The middle three acts are filled with a typical variety of complications for comedic romantic plots: societal gossip and rejection, problematic parents, work complications, abductions and escapes, meeting dangerous villains, suicides and suicide threats, tightened entanglements, misunderstandings, and power

Plot Movement	*These Old Shades*	*Knave of Hearts*	*Flame and the Flower*	*Last Boyfriend*
S1: Meeting and Tangles	Avon meets and buys Leon (really Leonie)	Ravella meets guardian, Melcombe	Heather "kills" attempted-rapist uncle, meets and raped by Brandon	Owen is running construction business and re-meets Avery, in charge of pizza place
S2: Minor Obstacles	L introduced in court; Her father, Comte, recognizes and tries to buy her	R and M cause gossip and a stir in society	H is pregnant, B forced into marrying her: mutual hatred	Construction ends, Inn opens, A hesitates about O
S3: Mid-Roller Coaster	A teaches L to be a woman; C abducts L, who escapes with A	M takes R to gaming houses and the unsuitable places	Couple moves from London to an Charleston plantation, face jealous ex, etc.	O continues trying to make A let down her guard
S4: Steep Roller Coaster	L debuts in Paris; A tells society that L is C's daughter, hints she committed suicide, then C really does it	A revelation is made, further more serious entanglements are resolved	Mis-understandings, child born, have intercourse first time after rape, H blackmailed, B accused of murder	More of the same happens
S5: Joining/Resolution	A marries L, and she becomes rich	M and R marry, and she becomes rich	B clears name after second murder accusation, real rapist/murderer arrested, H and B live happily	A and O commit and O becomes her last boyfriend

Figure 15. Romantic Comedy Plot Table.

struggles. In the last stage, the lovers join fully in a happy, committed union, become rich or richer, untangle complications, and otherwise live "happily ever after."

The end to a romance novel comedy is a "cosmic happy ending," meaning a reversal from a negative state to a positive one at the point of the climax. Prior to the climax, the world in the novel is negative, which is characterized by the following:

1. the aggressive and oppressive use of power
2. disorder and things not being as they should be

3. things being obscured or hidden, so that no one can see clearly or whole
4. a lack of proper feeling, love or mutual affection

This state of things typically declines into extreme negativity until a sudden reversal, when the world's state moves upward and toward a positive or correct state, in which the following occur:

1. power is at last exercised wisely and justly, under proper authority
2. a true harmonious state of order has emerged out of chaos
3. things obscured, hidden or not recognized have come to light
4. human beings are joined together in a joyful community of reconciliation, friendship and love.[69]

Most modern romantic novels also have power plays and some other concerns that the lovers and those in their world worry about, besides whether the love affair will work out.

In a romance the love affair is the central component of the plot. Here is a description of what a Silhouette Books "plot" must be from a 1982 call from this publisher: "The book should open with [the hero and heroine's] meeting or the events leading up to it and end with their decision to make a lifetime commitment to one another. The tension and excitement in the book stem from the fact that neither protagonist is certain of the other's love until the end. Each scene must contribute to the process of discovery they're going through. The plot should not consist of a series of chance encounters, coincidences or filler scenes in which nothing substantial happens."[70]

When I first considered which of Booker's seven common plots romances are, I guessed that it was a quest. I assumed that the heroine was hunting for her man, or the prince was questing after the woman. Upon a closer inspection, this theory turned out to be inaccurate. Modern romances focus on the heroine, rather than on the hero, and she typically does not run heedlessly after the hero until she catches him. Still, the possibility that romance novels are not only happy-ending comedies, but also might be quests, is one that should be examined more closely. Alison Hart raises this possibility in "The Key Formula in Romance: A Woman's Quest." She embraces the "common criticism" that romances are "formulaic," saying that a "formula" relates "the structure of the book. I can think of no good book, in any genre, that does not require a strong, disciplined structure for a foundation."[71]

Hart summarizes the romance plot formula as "boy meets girl; some dreadful thing keeps them from getting together, then boy wins girl." One of the glitches with this summary is that in modern romances, the women typically are no longer victims "rescued" by a prince; this formula implies that the girl is the object of the hero's quest. Noticing this, Hart stresses that "romances are women's quest books." She goes on to explain the more complex formula that dominates the romances she's familiar with:

> In chapter one, something is established at risk for the heroine. The nature of this problem can have endless variations, but critical to the plot is that (1) this is a problem she believes that she cannot solve, and (2) the problem is huge enough to threaten her in some way—that is, she can neither ignore it nor move on with her life until this conflict is resolved.

The hero shows up at precisely this time in the story—and he has two possible roles. He can either *be* her problem—metaphorically, he can symbolize whatever her worst fear is—or he can exist to make her problem worse. Either way, he is the locked door in the heroine's life. Until she opens the door, she is blocked from fulfilling some critical need in her life.

As the story progresses, the action forces the heroine to confront her worst fear— whatever this conflict is. Her quest is always the same. Something is standing between her and the life goals she seeks. She must examine and define what matters to her as a woman, and then seek the inner strength to take the risk and reach out for what she really wants. She is not only "tested" on this quest, but through the book she will fail, several times, as she stumbles for the right answers that will help her overcome this problem.

The formula summarized here is a tragic plot, rather than a quest plot. Typically a hero is supposed to conquer some small obstacles as he or she progresses toward the goal of the quest. If the heroine repeatedly fails, the story is moving downward steeply without jumps back up, as in a tragedy. However, the idea that the man whom the heroine is after is both her "problem" and the object of her quest is likely to evoke laughter due to its extreme absurdity. If the hero is an extreme problem for the heroine, the story once again becomes a tragedy.

While this plot summary might reflect actual stories Alison Hart wrote, the explanation of the plot pattern is misleading. One of the reasons for the misunderstandings this plot explanation presents is that Hart has substituted the heroine for the hero in a typical quest plot, but instead of leaving the other elements in place, she has moved them all around until the formula is illogical. She writes that in "ancient romances," the quest hero rescued the heroine. But now "we are not selling those same values ... his primary job is to keep throwing the heroine off a cliff. He is a catalyst for trouble ... the hero functions to make sure those fears are tested. Sex is definitely part of that testing.... Love scenes ... add risk, tension, and further the heroine's conflict by making her more vulnerable." The awful nature of the sex the couple has at the beginning and middle of the story is blamed here on the fact that the hero is the problem that is plaguing the heroine in the plot. If a plot is based on nothing but a girl and a boy, and the author wrongly assumes that she is writing a quest story, it is very easy to create a heroine and hero who must hate each other until the final moment, because without constant antagonism (sexual, emotional and physical), there is no tension in the plot. At the end of a quest love story, the woman "wins" "her man" and conquers her "worst fear."

Because the plot clearly does not fit the realities of the romance genre, Hart concludes her theory by protesting, "Her quest is not him. Her quest is about becoming the kind of woman she wants to be." If the "man" was not the object of a romance heroine's quest, some romances would end with the woman discovering that she is happiest when she is pleasuring herself, or perhaps suddenly discovering that she is a lesbian. No, seriously, if the romance novel is written in the quest plot line, the man is definitely the goal of the heroine's quest. Trying to avoid facing these alternatives, Alison Hart finds another explanation: "A romance ... plugs into a woman's essential loneliness. The heroine is alone, facing this quest. No one can help her ... a romance is really an exploration of woman's 'coming of age.'"[72] According to Booker's study of the quest plot, the hero typically has one or more sidekicks, friends or assistants who help him or her during the quest. In most quests, heroes also receive guidance from helpful wise people along their way. A heroine being alone across the entire quest is some kind of a postmodern tragedy on the theme of alienation. And a "coming of age" story is a Bildungsroman genre, by definition. This is an example of how unhelpful best-selling novelists are when they give "advice" to potential competitors. If a writer attempts to seriously construct a plot according to these directions, he or she will end up with a tragedy about a loner woman who fights with a psychotic lover who keeps threatening her with terrible sex, until she comes of age (perhaps turning 16) and finally catches her man—perhaps finally having a single positive sexual experience with him. While one should not follow this advice, the advice should be dissected to understand some of the reasoning behind the elements that do make up typical romance plots.

Another way to summarize the romance plot is with Karen Hubert's romance plot skeleton, which was mentioned earlier on: "Boy meets girl. Boy and girl fall in love. Boy proposes, and girl accepts. Something happens to prevent their marriage. Boy and girl overcome the problem. Boy and girl marry."[73] To make a more detailed skeleton from this frame, Hubert includes several "Recipes for Romance," as she did with her "Recipes for Mystery," which are writing prompts and also questions and writing starting points that, when answered, would help a writer to fill in the gaps in the basic plot skeleton.

Here is an extensive list. You might have noticed the answer to each of these questions in the romance novels that you have read. Hubert's version is over 10 pages long, but I have simplified it to the bare bones of the romance skeleton, with a numbered list. The answers to these do not typically appear in this order in a romance novel.

1. "Where and how do lovers meet?" 2. "What is attraction?" 3. "What do lovers say to each other when they first meet?" 4. "What is unrequited love?" 5. "What are the blues?" 6. "Your date meets your parents." 7. "What is romance/love?" 8. "You keep changing your mind…" 9. "What is a romantic/unromantic spot?" 10. "Write a story describing a couple's first date." 11. "It's love at first sight!" 12. "What does a kiss feel like?" 13. "A boy asks a girl to go to a dance with him." 14. "You are a rejected lover…" 15. "Write a monologue of a jealous lover." 16. "Write a love letter." 17. "What are the kinds of promises lovers make to each other?" 18. "How do lovers betray or disappoint each other?" 19. "What qualities don't you like in a person?" 20. "Write a wedding ceremony." 21. "What is a honeymoon?" 22. "What do you do when you're feeling lonely—play records, read, lie on your bed, think, pet your cat, cry?" 23. "You run into a person on the street whom you once loved very much…" 24. "Write a lover's quarrel." 25. "Write a lover's apology." 26. "What does a person do to make someone like him?" 27. "What is your ideal boy/girl like?" 28. "You are being pursued by three men who want to marry you." 29. "Should women work after marriage?" 30. "Should a man do housework?" 31. "Does romance stop after people are married?" 32. "Do opposites attract? Why?"[74]

Nora Roberts provides a simpler summary of the romance plot: "The one man–one woman love story, the emotional commitment, the conflict, the sexual tension, and the happy ending."[75] This is the classic comedic plot line centered on a love story. The man is not necessarily the villain, but the problems the couple faces as they try to get together are the tension waves that propel the plot forward.

Romance Characters

The major difference between characters in the fantasy and the romance genres is that in a romance the hero and heroine need separate categories because there are always two central people in a love story, while the heroine or the hero might be only a minor supporting character in a fantasy that does not center on the love relationship. In addition, instead of being fantastic or terrifying, romance settings, by definition, have to be "romantic."

Figure 16 points to a few similarities and differences in romantic characters across these works. In all four examples, the hero is wealthy and comes from an established wealthy family, if not from the aristocracy. The status of the heroine's estate is typically questionable. She might have once belonged to a noble family, but is now impoverished and orphaned. She might not know her true aristocratic identity. Or, in Roberts' case, she might be a successful business owner and the fiscal equal of the man who is courting her. The villain is frequently the hero and a cast of supporting characters that cast obstacles in the way of the couple's happiness. At the same time, there is typically a separate (or the same) group of characters that are the couple's relatives, friends, and supporters, who that try to help them on their love journey. The hero and heroine travel between the poor, middle, upper and aristocratic classes

Character Type	*These Old Shades*	*Knave of Hearts*	*Flame and the Flower*	*Last Boyfriend*
Hero	Duke of Avon	Duke of Melcombe	Brandon Birmingham, owns plantation	Owen Montgomery, construction comp. owner
Villain	Comte de Saint-Vire, Duke of Avon	Duke of Melcombe	Thomas Hint, clothes-making assistant, Brandon Birmingham	Workaholics
Sidekick(s)	French Court	Gambling and other friends	Beau, child	Owen and Avery's friends
Heroine	Poor Léon Bonnard, later becomes Leonie Duchess of Avon	Poor Heiress Ravella Shane	Heather Simmons, poor, becomes rich, related to aristocracy	Avery MacTavish, owns pizza place
Community	French aristocracy and poor workers	French aristocracy and the poor	Charleston and London society, poor in England	Boonsboro town community

Figure 16. Comedic Romance Characters Table.

across these stories because the plot line typically leads them from rags to riches, or drops them down into poverty from riches and then lifts them back again. There are many corresponding character types and details between these novels.

Even in the first decade when the romance genre was forming, the stories started to feel like a "sea of redundancy ... rushing headlong towards market and reader saturation."[76] The qualities of romance characters are repetitive in part because they are dictated by tip sheets that publishers produce as a result of "marketing research" or their publishing preferences. Carol Thurston reproduced some of these "tip sheets" in her book. Silhouette Romance requires that the heroine be "always young (19 to 27). She is not beautiful in the high fashion sense, is basically an ingénue and wears modest make-up and clothes.... She never truly believes the hero loves her until the final chapter of the novel." And the hero is "hot-tempered, capable of violence, passion and tenderness. He is often mysteriously moody.... Always older than the heroine ... he is rich and successful.... He is never married." Unlike some other publishers, Silhouette expressed in this 1980 version of the sheet the notion that the couple could not "go to bed together ... before they are married. Bringing them to the brink of consummation and then forcing them to retreat either because of an interruption or because one or both of the lovers suffers from doubt or shame is an appropriate Silhouette device."[77] Other publishers had slightly different character formulas. Pocket Book's 1981 sheet states that the hero "should never physically abuse the heroine, and 'love at first rape' is expressly forbidden!" While Pocket Book forbids abuse, unlike Silhouette, sex scenes are required and should "occur with some frequency.... Sexual tension between characters should be immediate and powerful. When they consummate their passion, the reader should be more than ready for it. The sex should be pleasurable—not painful.... All sexual descriptions should be imaginative and lyrical—not graphic, clinical or mechanical."[78]

In *The Flame and the Flower,* the most common character description is the reappearance of the heroine's naked breasts. Vivien Stephens, an editor at Dell's Candlelight Romance line, complained, "The redundancy of erotic series romances became [too] intense ... 'I'm seeing too many nipples! Be more imaginative! There *are* other erogenous zones!'"[79]

The romantic heroine goes from "loneliness" to "love" and belonging over the course of the romantic plot. At the beginning she is typically "alone," and if she has "friends," they differ from her in "interests, temperament, and sensitivity. They are not really her equals, nor do they deserve to be her confidants. (That role is reserved for the reader.) Instead, they serve as foils or opposites who make her seem all the more alone and deserving of love. The reader identifies with her, of course; to make identification easier, her personality is, in a word, ordinary. She must never be so unusual that our interest in her search for love takes second place to our interest in her personality."[80] This passage includes several key formulaic elements that make the romance genre especially annoying for literary critics, with feminists at the head of this disgruntled group. The degree of individuality given to the hero or heroine in a romance has changed over the ages before settling at this current formula. In chivalry romances, the heroine was ideally beautiful and devoid of possibly all other character traits. In Cervantes' *Don Quixote,* the hero is anti-romantic and ugly. In Jane Austen's *Emma,* the heroine is selfish and extremely individualistic while she pursues her love interest. Since around the 1920s, however, the popular romance novel has focused on beautiful but very ordinary and barely defined heroines. Minimalism is partially to blame for the trend to only give the skeleton description of the heroine's personality. Marketing is the second major reason for this, as the marketing departments of publishing houses want to attract the greatest possible number of readers who might "identify" with the heroine and would allow the story to become about them rather than about two fictional characters. Without this suspension of disbelief and identification, the formula of the basic romance skeleton becomes too obvious and repelling. So, if the heroine is neutral in looks and personality traits, readers can see parts of themselves in her, as if they are looking at a horoscope or a fortune cookie.

ROMANCE SETTINGS

The setting of a romance novel is more set by the formula than the settings in mysteries, science fiction, or inspirational stories, as the places depicted have to convey a romantic mood. The "place" typically has to be "strange or new to the romantic protagonist" (typically a woman): "She may have come there to forget someone or something in her past. A Caribbean island, damp and foggy London, a house on a cliff overlooking the wild ocean: whatever the actual setting, it is less significant than the mood of loneliness and yearning for love it inspires in the central character."[81] Three out of the four novels in Figure 17 include what is described here as a romantic setting—in other words, a ship at sea, a gothic Southern plantation, or a London or Parisian court—whereas Roberts' *Last Boyfriend* has an anti-romantic setting in a modern-day suburb in a pizza shop and a construction business. All four stories con-

Setting Type	*These Old Shades*	*Knave of Hearts*	*Flame and the Flower*	*Last Boyfriend*
Hero's Home	Avon's mansion	Melcombe mansion	Brandon's plantation	Owen's middle-class house
Romantic Setting	French court in Regency era	French court in Regency era	London and Charleston mansions, sea ship, poor hut	Anti-romantic workplace
Time	Regency	Regency	Regency	Present
Bedrooms	Not focal in story	Not focal in story	Focal – London, Charleston, and sea bedrooms	Focal – at the new Inn and other locations
Romantic World	French aristocracy	French aristocracy	Charleston and London society, poor in England	Boonsboro town community

Figure 17. Comedic Romance Settings Table.

verge on the hero owning an expensive house, mansion, plantation or even a castle. However, *Last Boyfriend* breaks the pattern of the most common time period being that of the Regency (as Roberts' novel is the only one set in the present). These four works split into groups of two when it comes to the bedroom (and what goes on in the bedroom) being a key setting in the story: Heyer and Cartland began and spent most of their popular writing careers before detailed sexual scenes became legal, and certainly before they became a required norm in the romance genre. Therefore, Heyer and Cartland stay out of the bedroom, while Woodiwiss and Roberts enter the bedroom as frequently as possible.

Best-Selling Writers in Romance from Heyer to Roberts

The previous section already gave an overview of the key changes in the romance genre and the best-selling authors who shaped it, so I will not repeat this information here. The four writers that are examined closely in this section help to explain the romantic novel's formula from 1921 to the present day. They are among the top best-selling romance novelists from the last century, and a criticism of the problems in their formulaic romance novels points to many of the problems that can be discovered from studying other romance writers.

Georgette Heyer (1902–1974; First Novel, *The Black Moth*, 1921)

Georgette Heyer began her literary dabbling by creating the plots for plays she put on with her childhood friend Jane Aiken Hodge on Saturdays, which this friend saw echoed in Heyer's well-known novels, including *The Black Moth* (1921).[82] Heyer sold her first novel when she was seventeen to what is now Constable & Robinson, a company that was started in 1795 and published some of Sir Walter Scott's first poetic works as early as in 1805 and then what is known as the first historical novel, *Waverley*. In addition to printing *The Black Moth* in Britain, Constable made a deal with Houghton and Mifflin (Heinemann) for American distribution. Constable was an ideal choice for Heyer because it was a publisher that was interested in founding new genres (in this case, the historical romance novel), and it had one of the best popular distribution networks. *The Black Moth* has many formulaic elements in common with Sir Walter Scott's historical novels, which are typically set in the middle of the eighteenth century and include plot elements and characters like highwaymen, kidnappings, injuries, rescues, and interactions between the aristocratic and merchant classes. There is a slight transition from a focus on significant political and historical events to a focus on the love relationships of characters with the backdrop of history that changed historical novels (Scott) to historical romances (Heyer). Heyer "was always considered 'intelligent' if popular,"[83] thanks primarily to her thorough research and writing technique, similar to Sir Walter Scott and several other writers whom Constable published over the years.

In the 1930s, Heyer had published around thirteen novels with different publishers in the United States and Britain, and had formed a standard technique that she used for developing her novels across her literary career. Jennifer Kloester, Heyer's biographer, found evidence in her correspondences and notebooks of the elements of this process. Heyer typically began by writing a character description list (which she called "excerpts," as she later used some of these descriptions verbatim in the novels) because she wrote character-driven novels, led by "*dramatis personae.*" Here is a segment from one of these lists, made in the first weeks of writing *The Convenient Marriage* in 1933:

> *Marcus Drelincourt, Earl of Rule*. Hero of the best type. Very pansy, but full of guts under a lazy exterior. Age 35.
> *Elizabeth Winwood*, lady in the best XVIIIth cent. Tradition. Sweet & willowy. Age 20...
> *Horatia Winwood.* A stammering heroine, of the naïve & incorrigible variety. 17...
> *Pelham, Viscount Winwood.* Brother to above ladies. Young rake & spendthrift. Provides light relief...
> *Crosby Drelincourt.* Cousin & heir-presumptive to the Earl of Rule. A Macaroni, & a nasty piece of work, taken all round.
> *Robert, Baron Lethbridge.* Best type of villain. Fierce & hot-eyed & sardonic.

Kloester explains, "This sort of list was important, for her characters were often the starting points for her novels. She would first imagine an individual, then spend hours thinking about him or her ... devising a suitable name," then "a character's behavior and dialogue followed naturally."[84] When the brief character studies were completed, Heyer could visualize the interactions they were going to have: "All these people are naturally going to fall into a number of awkward situations, & I rather think Pelham has a duel with friend Crosby, while I am quite sure that Rule has one with Lethbridge. Lots of gambling. Horatia is a gambler, & I should imagine will get herself into a fairly sticky mess over it. But don't you fret—it will all End Happily." So, with the characters, time period and location selected, Heyer decided on the possible interactions between the characters, which turned into the major conflicts and turns in the plot line. Similar to most prolific writers, Heyer's "first drafts were so often the final drafts.... More than once in the first three decades of her career Georgette completed a manuscript in less than twelve weeks."[85] Once the plot and the characters were decided on, she followed these original plans closely, which meant there was no need for major character or plot revisions later on, which are the more time-consuming edits.

More than a decade later, Heyer developed a sarcastic view of her novel composition process. She wrote to Frere in 1949 with "a long, satirical advertisement for the book and appended a witty, self-mocking summation of her personal principles for successful novel-writing":

> 3. Brood for several weeks, achieving, if not a Plot, depression, despair, and hysteria in yourself, and a strong desire to leave home in your entourage....
> 4. While under ... [the delusion that you are a "Creative Artist"], jab a sheet of paper into your typewriter, and hurl on to it Chapter I. This may give you an idea, not perhaps for the whole book, but for Chapter II.
> 5. Introduce several characters who might conceivably be useful later on....
> 7. Think out a grand final scene, with the maximum number of incongruous characters massed together in some improbable place. Allow your sense of farce full play. This will, with any luck at all, make the reader forget what the rest of the book was like.
> 8. Try and work out how and why these characters got together remembering that it is

better to "gloss over," by technique (which if you haven't learnt in thirty years you ought to have learnt), than to put your head in the gas oven.[86]

Heyer clearly is pessimistic about her repetitive method and calls her works "unmitigated rubbish" done primarily for money or to "enrich the Inland Revenue."[87] But putting the sarcasm aside, these steps in the formulaic novel-writing process are very helpful with specifically explaining the technique most best-selling novelists at some point briefly mention, but not with this much detail. Heyer begins by creating character types, and deciding on their interactions and conflicts in the plot. Then she writes the first chapter, and while writing it she thinks of ideas for events and conflicts in the second chapter and beyond, and proceeds to write pretty quickly all the chapters between the first and the climax. Heyer subsequently creates the most melodramatic or high-intensity (which for the writer, at least, easily slips from tension into farce) climatic conflict possible. Once this major battle or another type of conflict is finished, she rereads the completed novel to recall the plot lines that she left dangling and to explain how all of the earlier tensions are resolved in the final chapter or chapters of the novel.

The most time- and creative-energy-consuming parts of this process are the initial plot and character formulation and then the editing and rereading that come during the writing of the climax and resolution. Besides writing the plot and characters in the first weeks (and in times of the year when she wasn't composing novels), Heyer also did extensive research into linguistics, manners, historical events and locations, and other elements that she recorded in her research notebooks and later used in all of her novels based on that particular period. This research was as intensive as what a historian might carry out in preparation for writing a history book. If she needed 12 weeks to complete a novel, she could have completed 4 per year, but usually wrote only one or two, and toward the end of her life she even went a few years without writing a novel. Because of the care she put into the research for her historical novels, Heyer was outraged, insulted and in a litigious frame of mind when she found out that a relatively new novelist (at that time), Barbara Cartland, was plagiarizing her research, plot lines, character details (including names), and an unbelievable string of other elements that she had labored for decades to develop.

Heyer had invested not only time into her research but also a substantial amount of capital when she built up a library of "some two thousand volumes" between her first Regency romance in 1935, the accusation of plagiarism against Barbara Cartland in 1950, and her later Regency romances. This library was composed of "general reference books and dictionaries of biography, phrase, slang, dialect, place-names, Latin, French, Spanish and English. She had collected a range of history books and texts about specific subjects such as snuff-boxes, coaching inns, the military, London, etiquette and clothing. For details of life in the period and its language she favoured primary sources over secondary, and owned works by most of the late eighteenth- and early nineteenth-century diarists."[88] It would cost a middle-class annual salary today to buy 2,000 thick reference and historical books, so this was an expensive undertaking. As she was describing the clothing of a gentleman in 1814, Heyer would check a book on fashion from the period, which she had probably read many times before. She also had connections through Constable and high-society noble families that allowed her access to private diaries from the period, which provided slang and conversational expressions she could not find in the dictionaries or even linguistic studies from the period.

A fate similar to Heyer's befell Sir Walter Scott, but to a lesser degree, when he started noticing imitations of his historical novels shortly after the release of *Waverley* in 1814. These imitations helped to establish the historical novel as one of the major genres and solidified Scott's popularity. Without imitators, a novelist cannot attain the distinction of being a classical or a great novelist. But while Heyer was recognized as the queen of Regency romances in her day, today she is not reprinted by Penguin or studied in literature classes as a classical author. The difference between Scott and Heyer is the density of political and historical philosophical reflection that strings together the plot and characters introduced into the story.

But there is yet another significant jump between Heyer and Cartland and other modern hack speed-writers: Cartland's romance novels strip away complex sentence structures, detailed character descriptions and explanations for the characters' actions. Cartland followed the standard advice publishers give, for she bought most of Heyer's novels and closely studied their formulas. However, she did not simply study some positive elements from Heyer, but borrowed an incredible quantity of them and used them nearly unchanged in her novels.

Cartland was attracted to Heyer's "burgeoning popularity" and overstepped "the boundary between inspiration and appropriation." Heyer was informed of "the possibility of plagiarism in May 1950" by a fan. After this warning, Heyer did a close structural and linguistic analysis of the three "Georgian trilogy" historical novels that Barbara Cartland had written up to that point: *A Hazard of Hearts*, *A Duel of Hearts* and *Knave of Hearts*. Heyer's study of Cartland began with a "cursory reading" of the first two novels, which she initially dismissed as the work of "'a petty thief' of names, characters and plot points. Among Cartland's more obvious 'borrowings' were several names from *Friday's Child*, including Sir Montagu Revesby, altered to 'Sir Montagu Reversby'; Hero Wantage, now 'Harriet Wantage'; Viscount Sheringham was 'Viscount Sherringham,' while Lord Wrotham remained 'Lord Wrotham.'" Heyer also noticed similarities with some of her other novels (among them *The Corinthian*, *The Reluctant Widow* and *The Foundling*), as well as "paraphrases of situations,"[89] a concept that is present in many of today's hack novels, but to such a large degree that they become an ocean of repetitions.

Heyer's annoyance changed from mocking ridicule to glum legal concern when, besides names and plots, she recognized the linguistic similarities. She noticed "a suspicious number of Regency cant words, or obsolete turns of speech, all of which I can pin-point in several of my books, and all of which I have acquired during fourteen years' study of the period. The facts that no word or phrase I have *not* yet used appears in Miss Cartland's works, and that she shows a strange ignorance of the meaning of some of those she does use also seem to me to be significant."[90]

Using period language similar to what an earlier popular novelist utilized was not a new concept, as, for example, Robert Louis Stevenson used some of the same Scottish phrases, words and spellings as Sir Walter Scott, and these also appear in many other works about Scotland, as well as in diaries and dictionaries from the eighteenth to nineteenth centuries. Typically writers like Stevenson, who relied too heavily on a prior novelist's linguistic elements, were criticized by reviewers for making mistakes in their grammar, phonetics, phrasing and other elements of the linguistics that they appropriated instead of acquiring through a careful decades-long study of the oral language. But Stevenson was also from Scotland and had a good grasp of the basic meaning and application of the Gaelic and Scottish words and sentences that he utilized. The Regency era lasted for a short period between 1811 and 1820, and this was the period in which that Heyer, Cartland and many other imitators of Heyer set their romance novels, over a century after the Regency ended. Scott, by contrast, set his historical novels 60 years before his time, which was 1814 onward, during a period between 1715 and 1752, in the Jacobite rebellions; Stevenson also focused on the Jacobite period, writing his novels at the end of the nineteenth century. Scottish linguistics had changed across the nineteenth century, but Stevenson was taught some of the same concepts by his relatives that Scott had been taught 80 years earlier. On the other hand, Heyer was writing about a period that had sharply different linguistic rules from her own time, and when Cartland mimicked the out-coming phrases of Heyer's extensive research, she took these words out of context. For Heyer, these misuses were extremely offensive. Heyer herself used as one of her Regency sources the "letters and novels" of Jane Austen, which she mined for "inspiration, vocabulary and phrases."[91] But instead of grabbing phrases and vocabulary out of context, Heyer carefully wrote down interesting words, phrases and other elements that she found in Austen and other works in her "(idiosyncratic) notebooks. These were then used as a ready reference for details on everything from costume to carriage, people, places, prices and postal system." Therefore, she was careful to avoid only using vocabulary and phrases from any one source, integrating Jane Austen's language into her own lexicon. Heyer even "compiled alphabetical lists of slang terms and popular expressions and gathered colloquial phrases."[92] In other words, Heyer completed several reference books that she used to write her novels, and this was the proprietary, academically researched information that she felt Cartland illegally violated in her close plagiarisms.

Heyer points out one of these significant errors: "'One slang phrase which appears in her book, *Hazard of Hearts*, I got from an unpublished source.' This, she explained, was 'a privately printed book, lent me by a descendant of Lieut. Gawler, because the owner had enjoyed *An Infamous Army*. I don't think I have met the expression elsewhere, and I am sure Miss Cartland has had no access to my sources.'"[93] Studying real people or hard-to-access primary sources during linguistic research was a technique that Heyer inherited from Scott (perhaps through editing suggestions that she received early on from Scott's publisher, Constable). The reappearance of an obscure slang phrase in Cartland's poorly researched novel pointed to thoughtless mimicry, rather than a logical linguistic reproduction.

Heyer contacted Cartland's publisher and her solicitor to complain about these plagiarisms, but did not file a formal lawsuit because she did not believe there was "copyright in names," which is still true today—hence writers creating fan art can, in theory, use names like Harry Potter, and an upcoming novelist can, in theory, call her main character Harry Potter and his best friend Ron Weasley, all without breaking a copyright law. However, this is a theoretical concept, and in reality Rowling has filed several lawsuits to prevent writers from writing fan fiction that uses her characters' names. This indicates one of two possibilities: "Harry Potter" is a brand name and not only a character name, and therefore it is more strictly protected, or only authors with a litigious purpose or enough money to prosecute several lawsuits at the same time can adequately defend against worldwide plagiarism of their characters' names.

Once Heyer concluded a study of Cartland's third Regency novel, *Knave of Hearts*, she noticed outrageous plagiarisms, which started to cross into illegal territory: "The conception of THE KNAVE OF HEARTS, the principal characters, and many of the incidents, derive directly from an early book of my own, entitled THESE OLD SHADES."[94] In an annotation that Heyer made in this book, she points out an erroneous paraphrasing. In Cartland's *Hazard of Hearts* (68–69) a short passage appears:

> He was in riding clothes, with **boots** of Hessian leather fitting perfectly over tight breeches of the latest shade of **yellow**, his **coat** of a rich shade of brown had been cut **by the great Stultz** himself.

Heyer explains the similarities between this passage and her own passage from *Friday's Child* (4).

> The long-tailed **coat** of blue cloth, made for him **by** no less a personage than **the great Stultz**, sat without a crease across his shoulders; his breeches were of the fashionable pale **yellow**; and his top-**boots** were exquisitely polished.

I am stressing in bold the significant words that are exactly identical between the two. The rest of the passage is a clear paraphrase, in which Cartland attempts to disguise her plagiarism by using synonyms or slightly different colors and descriptions to relay a similar fashionable image. Heyer uses irony in her explanation for the trouble with this passage, writing, "Strange that Miss Cartland, so well-informed on such details as the most fashionable colour for breeches, and one of the most fashionable tailors of the day, should fall down on the ABC of Regency dress. Hessians were worn with pantaloons, never with breeches."[95] Cartland has inserted the detail of the Hessians into her version, perhaps borrowing these from another one of Heyer's novels, without realizing that using the synonym "breeches" with the Hessians, instead of the "pantaloons" that she might have seen in this other work or might not have known of, was an obvious historical fashion mistake.

The plagiarisms are extremely blatant and abundant. After having to read through three novels full of these, Heyer broke into a string of literary insults. According to Heyer, Cartland had "no sense of period, not a vestige of wit, and no ability to make a character 'live.'... [The] whole thing makes me feel more than a little unwell ... I think I could have borne it better had Miss Cartland not been so common-minded, so salacious and so illiterate." Heyer goes on to say, "She is not only slightly illiterate: she displays an almost abysmal ignorance of her period ... Miss Cartland knows rather less about the period than an average schoolgirl." Heyer demanded an apology from the publisher; none came, but "the horrible copies of my books ceased abruptly."[96]

The example of how Heyer replied to Cartland's plagiarisms is a very unique one in this history of popular novel writing. It is perhaps the best-documented case study made by the author being plagiarized, and therefore one that found similarities where an eye new to these works might not have noticed them. While there are several other recorded legal cases and informal complaints of plagiarism among best-selling novelists, most are not this obvious. Being the founder of Regency romances put Heyer in the delicate position of being plagiarized verbatim at first, and only in general outlines later on; the latter was called imitation and admiring derivation. The later mimics took out most of the historic details, refrained from practicing complex linguistic tricks, and otherwise watered down the novels until a paraphrase of the predecessor was not noticeable because of its mirrored but dispersed paraphrasing in hundreds of other earlier works.

Barbara Cartland (1901–2000; First Novel, *Jigsaw*, 1922)

While Barbara Cartland was not a founder of a new genre, and clearly engaged in plagiarism and mimicry, she is known as one of the only billionaire authors, recently joined on this peak, after her death, by J. K. Rowling. When the production of novels makes the writer a billion dollars, we are really talking about an industrial and technological printing and publishing enterprise rather than a literary achievement. And since this is a study of formulaic writing, and of the technical as well as "creative" production of popular novels, Cartland is a key author to examine.

Even Thurston, who otherwise depicts the romance genre as vibrant and diverse, finds fault in Cartland's romance novels, explaining that Cartland has "honed the 'poor little Cinderella' plot line to a dull edge."[97] Thurston adds that by 1985, Cartland's "regency romances," as well as her appearance and behavior, "fueled the most tenaciously held stereotype of the popular romance novel, heroine, and author today." Cartland had completed barely half of her life's novel output by 1985, at only "370" novels. These were "tales of love, all of them based on a plotline that has changed little, if any, in fifty years: a delicate little ingénue with heart-shaped face ultimately is 'saved' from her depraved stepmother or the old lecher to whom her father has sold her or from freezing to death in the poorhouse by a worldly duke who has through extensive experience become disenchanted with women.... The heroine appeals to the hero's protective instincts and restores his faith in women, ultimately transforming him through her own goodness and purity."[98]

After 1985, Cartland kept writing and increased her record to over 1 billion sold books of her 723 published novels. Cartland had one of the longest literary careers in history, nowhere near rivaled by some prolific authors like Leo Tolstoy, who also started writing when he was young and kept writing until his death at 82, but barely finished a major novel like *War and Peace* in a year or two, and certainly could not compete with Cartland in quantity (unless perhaps one counts words rather than books). Tolstoy and Proust had the same problem—they started writing a novel and just could not stop until it was a masterpiece and in great proportions in length and quality. In contrast, Cartland had a disposition that wanted to move on to the next book as soon as possible; for example, she wrote 23 books in 1983, at a rate of one book every two weeks. This is a typing marvel, if nothing else. Cartland lived to be 98 and published her first novel, *Jigsaw*, in 1922. She primarily wrote historical and society novels until the romance industry picked up after 1972, at which point she started writing formulaic historical romance novels and became the best-selling novelist of all time.

Cartland repeated the poor Cinderella love and marriage plot in her novels, not only because it was a selling formula, but also because it fit with her political purpose; in fact, her political agenda helped her to sell more books to the conservative Christian marketplace. She makes this very clear in an essay called "Back to Basics and the Search for Love." She begins by advertising her romance novels and explaining that they have been mimicked by the rest of the romance industry: "In 1970 they said it was the beginning of the Romantic Era ... in America I sold a million copies of each novel I wrote. Then two years later the publishers woke up, and said to their authors: 'Write like Barbara Cartland but with pornography.' This was the beginning of the Permissive Era which produced Aids."[99] Cartland deflects any suspicion that she might be writing like Heyer by saying that everybody after her did not continue copying Heyer, but rather copied her. Either way, back in 1950, Cartland was accused of verbatim plagiarism of portions of Heyer's romance novels. It is likely that she imitated Heyer because her publisher told her to "write like Georgette Heyer." After Heyer complained, Cartland developed a poor Cinderella plot line that was based on Heyer's stories, but did not lift names or exact words from Heyer's books.

By 1970, Cartland's output was phenomenal and she was selling more books than Heyer, who died in 1974. In 1972, with the publication of Katherine Woodiwiss' *The Flame and the Flower*, the romance industry shifted into including more sexually explicit descriptions in their novels. From Cartland's perspective, Woodiwiss did not change the industry's formula; instead, the industry only borrowed repetitions of the words "breasts" and other sexual details from Woodiwiss and the rest of the formula from her. Cartland did not change her Cinderella formula and continued writing the same sort of novels up until and beyond the time she wrote her "Back to Basics" essay in 1997.

The last part of the above quote is perhaps the most outrageous. If one follows the logical implications of this argument, authors who brought sex into the romance novel also brought about the Promiscuous Era, and with it the AIDS epidemic. While in the past religious enthusiasts have said that evildoers and pornographers are going to hell, it is very different from accusing pornographers of the creation of a sexually transmitted disease. According to modern theories of AIDS development, it started to spread at the beginning of the twentieth century, and first began to explode in numbers during the massive vaccination period in Africa when millions were immunized with unsterile needles, which transmitted the disease from the bushmen (who hunted monkeys that carried the disease historically) to as many people as were injected with the same needle. Westerners trying to "save" Africans by selling or giving away immunizations are therefore more responsible for the initial spread of AIDS than sex of all types, and certainly the starving people of Africa did not read pornographic American novels between 1972 and 1997 that caused them to become sick with AIDS. However, Cartland runs a marketing campaign even in this "scholarly" essay that is helping to separate her novels as almost religious, and certainly more moral than those of competing romance novelists who began describing sex more graphically in order to attract readers.

But this is only the beginning of Cartland's argument. To focus the critique more sharply on the best-selling female writers competing with her, as well as on possibly all other female entrepreneurs from this period, Cartland exclaims that the "Women's Libbers" from the 1970s onward "were fighting even more violently to prove themselves, not the equal to men, but the superior." There are several issues with this segment. First, the past tense of "were" suggests that they had stopped "fighting." Second, the term "violently" suggests a violent feminist movement. The women's liberation movement didn't start in the 1970s, but rather in the early 1960s, and the first major conference of the movement happened in 1970, not in 1972. Besides its conferences, this movement was particularly known for its publication of a magazine called *Spare Rib*, an allusion to the rib that God took from Adam to make the first woman, Eve.

There was certainly no "violence" in this political and legal movement for women's liberation. The third and biggest problem with Cartland's argument is the hypocrisy at its closing. As the top best-selling author (prior to Rowling), selling a billion copies of her books before her death in 2000, she is accusing other women of fighting to be "superior" to men. Only if Barbara Cartland was a pseudonym for a male author, or a group of male ghostwriters, would this be a logical statement. If Cartland did not believe women should be equal or superior to men, she should have focused on cleaning up her mansion herself instead of wearing pink and spending most of her time beautifying and writing over 700 novels.

I have tried to stay away from feminist theory in this book, but I have never read a more insulting anti-female essay before, including sexist tirades in the work of Sigmund Freud on penis envy and everyday insults thrown at me by women-hating construction workers. It is extremely insulting to me because it is the equivalent of President Obama writing an essay saying that African Americans should not try be equal to or superior to white Americans. African American readers would be offended by reading this essay because Obama would be arguing either that he is not actually black or that he is superior to all of them. Perhaps Cartland plagiarized this essay from an earlier male writer, without looking very closely at the details?

In order to completely cover the absurdity and insults in her argument, Cartland relies on religious dogma to support her point, writing that the "Women's Libbers" were trying to get "rid of religion," and not just the Christian religion, but all religion, including "Witchdoctors," and "Buddhism." I do not know if any members of the woman's liberation movement were Wiccan, but I am pretty sure a few of them supported Buddhism (those were the 1970s, after all). Cartland points out that instead of teaching them some religion, modern women just instruct their children, "Don't get caught by the police—they are your enemy!"[100] Considering that Cartland was accused of major plagiarism by at least one of her competitors, what exactly does this anti-police statement mean? If she was "caught" for the plagiarism, her formulaic career would have ended in 1950, when she was just beginning to sell books, with the profits she had made up to that point being ordered by the court to be paid out to Heyer. So, why exactly is it a bad thing that children should be afraid of the police, instead of God? Do all religious children truly believe and fear that they will burn in hell if they commit a crime? The police are a more concrete entity to fear when committing a crime than any God one might believe in, as the death penalty or life imprisonment are more significant threats than potential hell-fire after death. Can it be that Cartland disregards logic in order to stress her own religiosity and to promote her non-sexual romantic novels?

Here is an additional clue: "[A]ll through the ages, the aristocrats were always supposed to be immoral and so were the peasants. The great middle class was strictly moral and never, in any way, discussed or talked about 'sex.'"[101] The middle class makes up the majority of England and America's populations, especially when one takes into consideration that some members of the lower class think of themselves as middle class. Cartland is arguing that the upper and the lower classes are, and have always been, "immoral" and that they frequently engage in immoral sexual behavior and "talk about" sex. But, for some reason (which she does not explain), the middle class does not. She capitalizes the first letters of "Middle Class" to further stress its importance. Once again, according to her, the greater sin is what her competitors are doing—writing about sex in their romance novels.

Cartland goes on to say that the feminists are trying to take religion out of public schools, and describes how they succeeded in this and how, with her help, this movement was reversed, bringing religious and Christian prayer back into schools. This is apparently an extremely grave situation. A year after writing this essay, with Cartland's help, the United Kingdom became one of the only countries in the world that still require school prayer in all public schools. In the same year as the passage of the School Standards and Framework Act of 1998, however, the Human Rights Act outlawed mandatory school prayer. Thus, England and Wales are currently in violation of this major human rights legislation. Cartland invested her money and her propagandistic arguments into this campaign, and this essay is a key example.

Most of the advice Cartland gives in her essay seems absurd and ridiculous at first. For example, she argues to ban divorce (or at least pro-wife settlements), stop women from arguing against marriage, allow the man control over "His Home and His Family," force women to put their careers on hold to "take care" of their husbands, stop women from taking men's jobs and watching men's sports programs, and offer "wages for wives" for those women who choose to marry. Instead of helping women who are struggling to find jobs of their own, she proposes to help women who have found financial support in a spouse. Cartland also capitalizes "His," as if men are equivalent to God, typically the only type of "His" that can be capitalized in the middle of a sentence. She tosses in the suggestion that women should not watch men's sports to make it all seem more ridiculous or light. However, she was very gravely serious on each of these points, and actively and successfully campaigned for these changes. While British writers have used their novels and critical essays to campaign for political causes since the first massively printed public books, the phenomenon of writers campaigning against their own interests, and for reversing prior human rights laws, is certainly unique. It is especially dangerous because Barbara Cartland was effective in selling both her backward political ideas and the novels that idealized these theories.

A look at three of her historical romance novels reveals the standard formula she reused in the hundreds of novels she wrote in this genre. These three novels are *Diane de Poitiers* (1962), *Desire of the Heart* (1974), and *The Cruel Count* (1974). In a biography of Cartland, Henry Cloud described one of these novels as follows: "*Desire of the Heart* was set in the reign of Edward VII, a period that had always fascinated her. The historical background was precise, the characters romantic and full-blooded, and the story followed the adventures of the rakish Duke of Roehampton and his arranged marriage with his ingénue bride Cornelia, as an escape from the scandal of a torrid love-affair with an unscrupulous vamp, Lady Bedlington." This praise is certainly not deserved. Yet, while he is blind to the weaknesses of the book, even this biographer admits that "Cornelia is a classic Cartland heroine, a Cinderella figure, who finally finds happiness and takes her wayward Duke by the power of her simple femininity." Unhappy with leaving readers with the implication that this is yet another one of Cartland's Cinderella stories, the writer goes on to say, "But what makes *Desire of the Heart* something of a landmark among all her books, is that it forms the pattern for all her subsequent 'virgin and Duke' historical romances. It remains one of her own firm favourites, and was so successful that it persuaded her to leave the field of the contemporary romantic novel for ever." Apparently, the book made so much money that Cartland even invested her time in writing actual historical biographies, such as *Private Life of Elizabeth of Austria* and *Metternich the Passionate Diplomat*, a very unusual digression for her.[102] However, the first 1974 "Barbara Cartland Bookclub" edition copy of *Desire of the Heart* that I received from my local library has both *Cruel Count* and *Desire of the Heart* in a single volume, so it seems unlikely that the second of these two works could have done much better than the first, which Cloud doesn't mention in his biography. There is, moreover, not much of a recognizable stylistic difference between the two. On the other hand, the library only had a couple titles by Cartland and this 1974 book was one of them. This aside, the key detail in Cloud's explanation is that *Desire of the Heart* served as a formulaic frame for Cartland's many later "virgin and Duke" historical romances—thus the basic plot line for these later romances is the "virgin Cinderella rescued by the Duke" comedic scheme (with some melodramatically tragic elements). Cartland's novels are written in a fairy tale style, as if the characters live "in a fairy-tale world."[103] The skeleton plot is a fairy tale, romantic comedy, which Cartland summarizes herself in one of her novels when she has an old crone or witch read the fortune of the heroine: "Diane shall cause tears to fall and joys to be known. And those who weep and those who rejoice."[104] These fairy tale Cinderella stories have melodramatic swings upward and downward in the heroine's fortune with, typically, eventual happy endings.

A few key elements separate Cartland's formula and style from those of other writers. First, she writes shorter paragraphs than most of her romance novel competitors. Her novels are truly written for the unliterary, with a conscious attempt to use the most commonplace, cliché and repetitious language possible. Almost all paragraphs are between one and three lines long. Second, Cartland has more blue-eyed women in her stories than other writers. Vesta in *The Cruel Count* and Lady Bedlington in *Desire of the Heart* both have blue eyes (the latter's eyes are also "surprisingly vacant," which seems to be a repetition). Another way to phrase this point is that when it comes to descriptions, Cartland prefers to use simple colors and shapes to describe things. For example, Vesta, in *The Cruel Count*, has "blue eyes" and a "small heart-shaped face."[105] And in *Desire of the Heart*, Lily has "pink and white … skin," "gold … hair," and "blue … eyes."[106] Cartland also uses the standard formulaic character descriptions, in which she says a couple of words about a characters' face, eyes, eyebrows, chin, mouth,[107] and perhaps a few other basic parts of the human anatomy. In some extreme cases, the descriptions of each of these features are longer than a couple of words: "Never had he seen such hair—red-gold glowing beneath an embroidered headdress."[108] The key points of attraction between lovers are always centered on the color of the hair or eyes or the shape of the breasts or the waist.

One of the most horrifying (at least for a critic) problems is the unbelievable quantity of repetitions within each of the novels. For example, in *The Cruel Count*, upon arriving at the port within the first two pages, there are numerous occurrences of words like "indeed" and phrases like "Thank you, Mr. Barnes," which appears at least twice.[109] The narrator also keeps repeating that Vesta was surprised that the Count failed "to send a representative to greet her on arrival."[110] She barely changes this phrase and keeps repeating variations of it for many pages without the story moving forward. In *Desire of the Heart*, there are a lot of repetitions in the ending, but in at least one of these, the speaker drastically and suddenly changes tone: "'Look at me!' It was a command now, masterful and sure. Then as she trembled, unable to obey him, he repeated 'Please look at me, Desiree.'"[111] Thus, Cartland has the hero repeat the same thing, but the change of tone from command to a plea changes Desiree's mind about the meaning of the phrase and she surrenders into doing whatever he wants.

The most common theme and description in these novels is age—specifically, the comparison between young and old people. These descriptions are applied in detail to the main characters, but also in passing to poor and rich people who happen to be around the main heroine. For example, Lady Vesta Cressington-Font notices that the men "carrying" her "trunks ... were so old ... they were almost bent double by their burden."[112] This is one of the most colorful descriptions of age, as characters are usually just divided into the "old" and the "young." Age frequently comes into play when there is an age difference between two lovers; most often the man is older, but sometimes the woman is. The seductress in *Desire of the Heart*, Lady Bedlington, claims that "never in her whole life had she known such ecstasy, such a wild glory of love as this young man, ten years younger than she was, had brought her."[113] However, when a man in his fifties proposes marriage to a teenage girl, Diane, her reaction is that "Louis de Breze in old age was ugly, a hunchback." Diane keeps thinking over his age, and remains extremely depressed about it. She even has a screaming fit, yelling, "'Old! Old!' The word seemed to echo all around her.... 'Old ... he's old ... old!'" Even Diane realizes that she repeats the word "old" over six times in a single page. Still, she decides to do her "duty" and marries him despite her strong reservations.[114]

Another physical feature that pops up almost as frequently as in the work of Woodiwiss is breasts, though here they are a bit more varied. Women at the port where Lady Vesta lands are "full-bosomed"[115]; meanwhile, Diane in *Diane de Poitiers* has "tiny pointed breasts, hinting at a budding maturity."[116] In contrast to these descriptions of women mostly only in terms of their breast and waist size, the descriptions of food are very detailed and carefully crafted; for example, at one point Vesta eats "fresh fish covered with the egg and oil and lemon sauce," followed by "lamb, young and tender, cooked on a long skewer with tomatoes and a green vegetable."[117] A bit later, Vesta fears that if the Count does not come to fetch her, soon she might supposedly run out of money to "pay for her food," which brings her much melodramatic grief.[118] There is a more romantic relationship with the food in these descriptions than with any of the characters in these novels, including the key heroines.

Yet another mandatory description is pointing out that the heroine is "well read," which typically comes through as a short summary of languages or subjects that she has attempted to learn, but frequently has failed to fully comprehend or remember. Many romance publishers required that the heroines be intelligent, or at least average, throughout the second half of the twentieth century, and certainly after the success of Woodiwiss' novel in 1973, a year before *The Cruel Count* and *Desire of the Heart* were published.

No Cartland novel is complete without a man threatening to lock the heroine up and have his way with her. "If you look at me like that, I shall carry you away to that lonely cave and then there will be no decision for you to make now or ever," says the Count to Vesta.[119] The couple returns to this proposition regarding the cave in the book's conclusion, when Vesta says that she only regrets "the cave where we were going to be ... alone." The Count is overjoyed by this news and reports that after they are married, for their honeymoon he will take her not to the "Palace," but "somewhere very quiet where we shall be together." Sadly, he refuses to take her to the cave for which she longs, but will instead take her to the "villa by the sea." The dominant-submissive fantasy is explained as "I want to teach you, my adorable perfect sweetheart, about love now that my Sleeping Beauty is awake."[120] (This concept of a woman needing to be disciplined and abused to learn about sexual love was later picked up by Anne Rice in her *Sleeping Beauty* sexual romance series.) Sleeping Beauty allusions are also made in *Desire of the Heart,* in the description of how Lady Bedlington's "beauty" was the type that had to "wait for the kiss of a Prince Charming before it came to the zenith of perfection."[121] The concept of the man "teaching" the foolish woman about love also repeats across Cartland's stories: "I shall teach you what love means, you sweet, ridiculous child ... I shall punish you for my desperate anxiety, for the dreadful times which I have spent without you ... by making you ... feel wild and wicked, until you cry for mercy. But I shall not be merciful! And you will not be able to escape me." This extremely threatening and domineering statement is followed by Desiree exclaiming, "I love you ... I love you ... and I am ... yours."[122] Basically, Cartland's women are submissive and the men are dominating. In *Diane de Poitiers,* Louis de Breze exemplifies this view when it is explained that he "thought it better 'to love a woman as a woman' than, after the fashion of some, 'to make an idol of her' ... Diane found little pleasure in his quick and spasmodic passions ... but she submitted to his demands with a docility and a sweetness."[123] While, in theory, Diane later finds a better lover in her "beloved" Henri II, the man continues to dominate and the woman to submit to his will, as exemplified by the fact that Diane dies with two of her illegitimate children by Henri II in her grave with her.

As in most formulaic novels, Cartland frequently confesses when she is sleepy or when her characters cannot stand the story anymore by having them express exhaustion and then retire to sleep. After sitting around, thinking about how "she had been awakened by a kiss" to "reality," and wondering what it would be like to be poor (but then dismissing this horrid notion), Vesta "suddenly felt very tired and she wondered apprehensively if the Count felt as tired as she did." Apparently, she committed the error of sleeping "against his shoulder" and was wondering if he failed to slumber well. She starts mumbling to herself, "I love you ... I love you," until she knocks herself out with the repetition: "Finally from sheer exhaustion she fell asleep." And thus the chapter ends. The next chapter begins with these words: "Because she was so tired, Vesta slept dreamlessly."[124] The urge to stress that all of the characters are just as sleepy as the readers, and perhaps the writer, is an essential element of formulaic novels. Most of the novels end with repetitions of "I love you," which are pretty sleep-inducing, as on the last page of *The Cruel Count*: "I love you ... I love you ... I love ... you."[125]

KATHLEEN E. WOODIWISS
(1939–2007; FIRST NOVEL, *THE FLAME AND THE FLOWER*, 1972)

The Flame and the Flower[126] is said to have founded the modern romance novel genre. Unlike some of the filtered romances that preceded it, this novel is shocking in its brutal portrayal of sex and of how a woman can be overpowered into love after she is sexually assaulted. Heather Simmons loses her aristocratic parents when she is in her early teens and moves in with her country aunt, who forces her to clean her hut, cook, and perform various other forms of hard labor. Heather endures this life for a couple of years, but when an uncle comes to visit and proposes that he will take her to London to get her a teaching job and a husband, Heather jumps at the chance and goes with him. Upon arriving, the uncle explains that he plans to ravish and use her and then to become her pimp and sell her to a whorehouse. Heather does not hesitate and beats him to what she assumes is his death (but we later find out that he only passed out and was murdered later that night by his assistant in the clothing shop that he ran). Thinking that she's now a wanted murderer, Heather runs out on to the London streets; she hears a pursuit behind her and assumes that she's being arrested, so she allows them to take her. A group of sea-hands take her onto a ship, and she thinks she is being transported to a labor camp in America. Instead, she is brought into a cabin, where Captain Brandon Birmingham proceeds to take her virginity and make love to her several times during the night, as she resists these attempts (more or less). In the morning, the captain leaves to buy her some new dresses and she uses his absence to escape and catch a ride back to her aunt's farm. She begins working there again, but in a couple of months discovers that her belly is rounding and that she is pregnant. With the help of her wealthy aristocratic Lord Uncle in London, Heather forces Brandon to marry her due to her condition, and he takes her with him to his plantation in America. During the journey and as she adjusts to wealthy life in America, Heather becomes more and more attracted to her old enemy and falls in love with him, and he feels such a strong attraction for her that he is unable to have sex with any other woman (including the prostitutes he is used to frequenting and his old lovers). The main tension from the first 50 pages until page 400 is whether the married couple will ever have sex again, as they both find ways out of this exercise. So, both of them keep thinking about sex, and each other's bodies, and both feel increasing frustration over not being able to find a way to do it, and, more importantly, to succeed in having good sex (rather than the pretty bad, foggy sex they had when he knocked her up).

This plot is complex enough for the reader to be in constant suspense across the saga. There is even a surprise in the end when the dressmaker's assistant is found to have raped and murdered the five or so women who had been killed in their city and reveals that he is guilty of killing the old dressmaker, and then is finally killed by Brandon with the help of a fallen tree and a few bullets.

This novel also features all of the repetitive elements that are the bane of popular modern romances (historical, fantastic, and otherwise). As in other books, many conversations degenerate into yes/no disagreements about nothing of significance. The funniest glitch, though, is the repetition of the word "breasts," both clothed and (much more frequently) naked. On some pages the word appears as many as three times, and it is rare for two pages to go by without this word appearing.

This book was written at an odd literary time when writers were still looking back to nineteenth-century and early twentieth-century literary examples, such as Dickens and Wells. Both Woodiwiss and Larry Niven show a generic mingling between two popular philosophies. The old popular fiction formula was to create fiction with the college-educated, middle-aged, middle class in mind. Readers did not want to read the same description of a character, or a scene, or an action twice. This preference for realism in description stems from the first modern novel *Don Quixote*, with its descriptions of insanity, sickness, poverty and even bodily functions, using exact details that put readers on the same donkey with Sancho. From 1605 until 1990 the novel was defined as a detailed study of a character and his or her environment, culture, manners, traditions, progression in life, and personal characteristics of appearance and behavior. In contrast, before 1605 and after 1990, the novel was and has returned to being a classical, highly formulaic, and repetitive romance. There have, however, been a few modifications. Before 1605, a princess would end up in distress and a prince would have to slaughter monsters, dragons, and evil princes to rescue her and win her hand in marriage. Since 1990, the novel has split into a few slightly divergent plot lines: (1) A silly, average boy or girl goes to school and there learns various magical tricks that help him to slaughter the evil monsters, demons, magicians, and so on that are trying to destroy the world. (2) An investigator, who is occasionally trying to have sex with women, goes on a quest to catch or murder the evil murderer, rapist, drug seller, and so on who has been terrifying the neighborhood; he succeeds and typically finds a girl willing to have sex with him at the end. (3) A woman or man tries to find good sex, and typically they find it in the end. (4) The hero goes on a religious or spiritual quest, typically finding a marriage or saving a foreign village from Judaism in the end. Basically, most novels today are about as stylistically complex as a novel from the Middle Ages. The major difference is that in the Middle Ages novels could not mention sex, and today novels must mention sex.

So, in this context, *The Flame and the Flower* is an interesting historical artifact. Woodiwiss portrays dialects accurately and gives detailed descriptions of illnesses and physical chores, but she also integrates repetitions of elements that are supposed to help a novel to sell more copies. And, if her sales figures are accurate, these elements did indeed help her to sell millions of copies.

NORA ROBERTS (1950–; FIRST NOVEL, *IRISH THOROUGHBRED*, 1981)

Roberts' first book to make the *New York Times* Best Seller List was *Genuine Lies* in 1991. Since then, she's had 115 *New York Times best* sellers. In fact, according to *Publisher's Weekly,* Nora Roberts has written more best-sellers than anyone else in the world. There are more than 280 million of her more than 160 titles in print all over the globe. During the last 22 years, an average of 21 books written by Roberts were sold every minute. Roberts has won an amazing 16 RITA awards from the Romance Writers of America, and she is the only author who has twice been inducted into RWA's Hall of Fame.[127]

These statistics indicate that Roberts is better at manipulating the *New York Times* best-seller list than the authors she has been competing against. "Roberts is known for her family sagas, each exhibiting different, richly detailed cultural traits. These include the Ukrainian Stanislaskis, the Irish Donovans, and the Scottish MacGregors."[128] The reason Roberts chooses family sagas is that they come with a small set of characters that can keep reappearing in future novels. In addition, a family saga can be set in a single small town.

I did not find any major plagiarism cases against Roberts, but there was one highly publicized recent case in which another romance writer confessed to plagiarizing several of Roberts' novels, for some reason adding that she did it because she was crazy: "Scandal found its way into Roberts's world when popular author Janet Dailey admitted to plagiarizing much of Roberts's work over a fairly long period of time. Dailey claimed that stress and psychological disorder caused her to do it, and she ended up paying a settlement and making a public apology."[129] Which "psychological disorder" could have caused a popular novelist to plagiarize the top best-selling novelist: psychotic greed, the uncontrollable need to ape everything Roberts said, or something else?

Even if Roberts has not plagiarized any other popular writers, there is something very strange about her fiction. As I discussed in the plot, character and setting sections of this chapter, *Last Boyfriend* differs from the other three works I studied closely because it has an anti-dramatic structure and an anti-romantic setting. While the other romance novelists attempt to cram in outrageous hyper-dramatic incidents across the plot, Roberts instead just has Owen working on finishing the construction of an inn (occasionally actually watching paint dry), while Avery's only action is flipping pizzas in her shop across the street. Fifty pages into the novel, they have a sexual encounter that is less romantic than sitting on a hotdog, and there is less emotional motivation for this merger than between two strangers catching each other's eye on a crowded street.

While the reader might hold out hope that something is about to happen, all hope is lost around the time these words are uttered: "Why? Why am I a moron?"[130] The description of the plot online was interesting enough, and the back cover declared that Nora Roberts was "America's favorite writer," according to the *New Yorker*, so what went wrong? Perhaps I once again misunderstood the blurb. It did not state that the *New Yorker* likes Nora Roberts, but only that "America" likes her. By America, it clearly meant that she has appeared on the list of American best-selling novels more frequently than any other contemporary writer, and that she has written hundreds of these best-selling novels.

Why would Americans like Roberts? Romance is America's "favorite" genre. It is bought more frequently than any other genre. Why? Theories about buying behavior are insufficient, but statistics on American sexual behavior explain the attraction better. In America, by age 24, 89 percent of men and 92 percent of women have had sex for the first time. 25–26 percent of both genders had sex before they turned 15. The average age of first intercourse is 16–17.[131] These statistics and those discussed earlier in this chapter indicate that the majority of Americans are having sex, but 94 percent of them are only having sex with one partner, and a good deal of them are married to that partner and so are likely to continue to just have sex with that one partner for many years to come. Only 25 percent of women orgasm during sex with their partners, however, so few women are sexually satisfied in their relationships. Women need to read fiction that might give them positive fantasies to think about as they continue having unfulfilling sex with their one partner. Some of the men are also unfulfilled and frequently escape into watching pornography or reading romance. The fantasies both genders are looking for clearly include being bitten (likely indicating vampires) and dominant-submissive role-playing for some, as well as multiple partners for men, and a superhuman or extremely romantic partner for women. Modern romance novelists have calculated the frequency of these fantasies and depict these in their stories repeatedly.

The trouble is that while a book like *The Flame and the Flower* might constantly mention breasts and continually depict a sexual and romantic flirtation between the main characters, in Nora Roberts' *The Last Boyfriend*, there are almost no sexual references or romantic attempts in the first 50 pages, at which point two of the characters suddenly have rushed and interrupted bad sex, and then go their separate ways with dim confusion. So, why would Americans feel that Nora Roberts is their "favorite" writer?

There are a few problems not even related to the lack of a positive romance that troubled and repelled me as I read this book. First, the plot is about a group of people who are constructing a new small motel. They are discussing where to put each of the chairs; organizing and rearranging stuff is the main theme in the book. These daily tasks are anti-romantic. Karen Hubert writes, "Romance is a social ideal, a state of being in which nothing ever has to be worked out. There are no arguments over who does the dishes or who drives the car. It is a state toward which we all, subliminally, aspire in our relationships."[132] Nora Roberts presents a world to which none of us can aspire, and one that is realistic because it depicts the daily grind, and yet it is minimalist in its descriptions. Second, the words "moron," "dumbass," and a string of other insults regarding the characters' stupidity make frequent appearances; knowing that the main characters are moronic just does not do it for me, but perhaps Roberts' average American reader is pretty happy to find moronic characters. Third, most of the conversations are casual chats about cooking, construction, and other boring and insignificant sketchy topics, which one might tune out even if engaging in a similar conversation with a close friend. Having no meaningful content to communicate clearly breaks every classical dramatic law in the critical books. Fourth, as mentioned earlier, most of the chapters in this and many other hack novels end with characters going to sleep, or else sleep frequently interrupts the storyline, making readers even drowsier as they read the rest.[133] Fifth, the characters constantly physically abuse each other: "she jerked up and nearly bashed his face with her shoulder,"[134] "she punched him lightly in the stomach,"[135] and the like. The punches and pulls are clearly attempting to awaken the reader from the extremely boring situations and conversations, but are cancelled out when the characters themselves fall asleep shortly after these incidents. I hardly think this is a technique that Chekhov or Dumas considered: "Hey, why don't I end each section with the characters becoming tired of their boring conversations, and then passing out into sleep?"

To summarize, the problem is that this book rushes forward without any plan or plot, as if the hack writer set a goal to type at least 10,000 words per day on any subject just to meet the deadline of writing 300,000 words in 30 days and move on to the five other novels she had to finish that year, and then on to the six months she had to take off on an island beach. The result is a product much worse than reality TV or a soap opera, or even any of the other formulaic novels on this review list.

Chapter 4

Religious and Inspirational

"The recurrent theme in [Douglas'] work is that of the conversion of the atheist hero to a practicing Christian."—Clive Bloom[1]

Thousands of years ago, the first texts around the world were inspired by either religious or financial motives. Cave men started drawing sticks on the walls to record how many animals they had slain, or how many days were left until the winter months. As they grouped together into communities, religious symbols started to enter their art and early writing. The dead were buried with monuments, and elders or holy people in clans started to be honored as religious figures. The generic history that led to the twentieth-century religious novel is visualized in Figure 18.

The first fully fleshed religious texts in the world were the Egyptian *Pyramid Texts* of around 2030 BCE.[2] These ritual spells had only one intended reader—the next pharaoh, after his predecessor died—and they guided the new ruler in preserving his predecessor's remains after death so as to lead him into heaven with the help of Osiris and the Sun, a process that included building intricate tombs, like the great Egyptian pyramids, on the walls of which the *Texts* were written.[3]

The earliest written and currently widely practiced religion was Hinduism, which took shape with the writing of the first in a series of four *Vedas*, *The Rig Veda* (1200–900 BCE), which is a collection of metric Sanskrit hymns about the Hindu gods, rituals and beliefs.[4] *The Rig Veda* is also the first known text to have a constant meter. However, the metric system in the *Vedas* is different from the common meters used today. The major difference is that instead of two or three syllables in an iambic or dactylic foot, the vedic meter has eight, eleven or twelve syllables per foot. And instead of counting all of the syllables, only the last four syllables in a foot have a repeating pattern of stressed and unstressed syllables, such as iambic or trochaic. Thus, the *Vedas* mark an important merger of religious literary style with poetic form.

The Jewish Torah was written relatively late, around the time of the events described in its history (722–444 BCE). The Torah includes 39 books that were written over a couple of centuries, and differ widely in style and genre. The 5 books that are typically published at the beginning of the Torah, the Pentateuch, are on the creation myth and describe the roots of the Jewish religion. These are followed by 12 historical books (history of the Jewish people and rulers from before 722 to after 444 BCE), 5 poetic books, and at the end the 17 prophetic books. Thus, the included genres are rhetoric, poetry, and religious mythology. The poetry books include the Psalms or hymns, as well as Proverbs and the Song of Solomon.

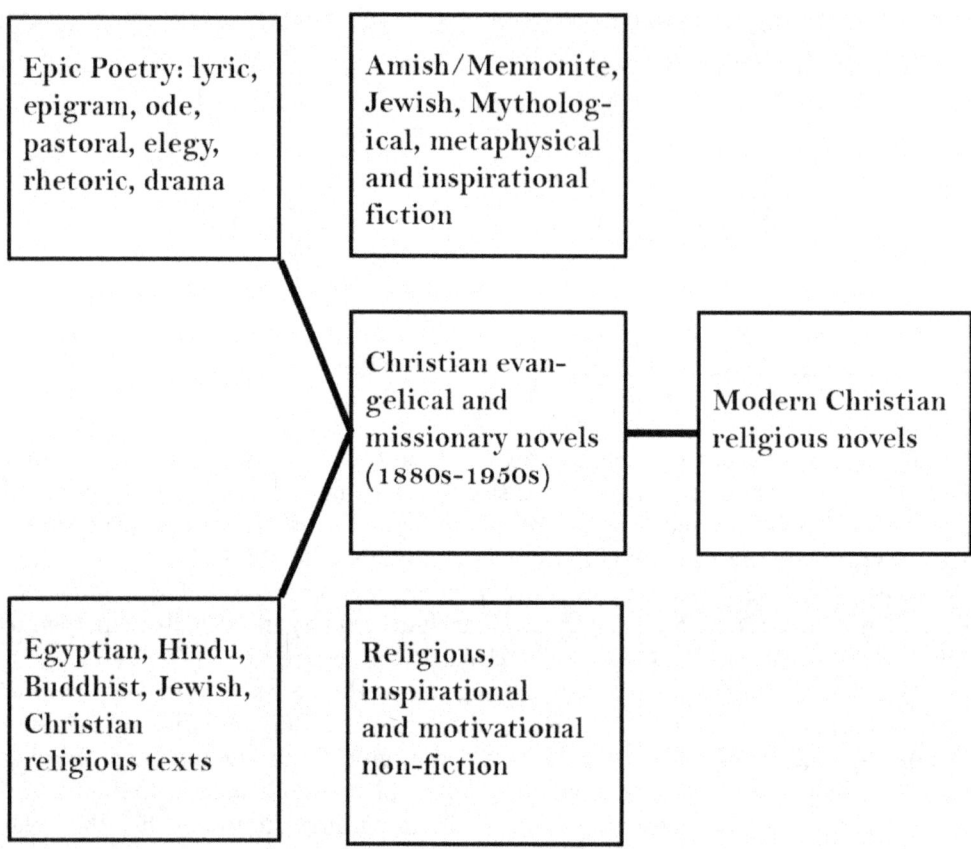

Figure 18. Inspirational and Religious Genres Diagram.

While there were clearly many religious books being written between 1200 and 444 BCE, there is a difference between "writing" a text and "publishing" it. The *Pyramid Texts* were not "published" or "distributed," and at first the *Rig Veda* sat on a shelf designed for scholars and religious leaders, and was not printed with the goal of converting the masses. The Buddhist *Diamond-Cutter Sutra* was the first to receive wide circulation, in around 868 BCE, primarily because the Buddha, or Siddhartha Gautama, was a sixth-century BCE Indian teacher, by adopted profession, and had disciples who helped him to record his chanted teachings and then spent their lives spreading his message to the people. *Diamond Sutra* was about *emptiness* and *compassion,* and was written in chanted, rhyming stanzas.[5]

The similarities between the *Pyramid Texts* and various other religious texts before and after the Torah are discussed in recent studies, including *Zeitgeist: The Movie,* in which Peter Joseph points out near plagiaristic similarities between earlier pagan religious symbols for constellation and lunar patterns and the equivalent numeric and figurative symbolisms in both the Old and the New Testaments. For example, the Age of Pisces, or the two fishes, symbolizes Christ because he was said to have been born during this period, but this symbolism was developed by earlier religions. In addition, the Garden of Eden and Noah's Ark have symbolic equivalents in the earlier *Epic of Gilgamesh.*[6] Religious texts were among the first works that were written with a specific purpose and literary formula, which occasionally borders on plagiarism of predecessors. Simultaneously, most religious texts are, on the whole, widely divergent from each other, and they contain very different philosophic foundations and structural elements.

Religious texts, especially the *Pyramid Texts*, briefly preceded epic poetry, and were at times more popularly read. Religious texts included chants, hymns, and ritual songs, which had a repeating rhythm, primarily because they were danced to or accompanied by a repeating drum in rituals, and because it was easier to remember any kind of orally recited text if it had repeating elements. Thus, some epic poems, such as Ovid's *Metamorphoses*, were religious texts themselves, as they described the acts or histories of the gods. One of the first surviving works to combine religious text and epic poetry is the *Epic of Gilgamesh*. Overall, there are many generic overlaps between religious texts as a genre and epic poetry.

Epic poetry had varied meters, rhythmic and rhyming styles, but it all had an epic or grand scope and subjects. The Babylonian *Epic of Gilgamesh* was written prior to 2000 BCE, which places it shortly after, or perhaps even before, the *Pyramid Texts*. This epic focuses on the legendary adventures of King Gilgamesh of Uruk, and royalty and gods continued to be the central figures in later poetic epics. Another example of an early epic poem about a king, from 1700 BCE, is *Altrahasis*,[7] which tells of a man who built an ark, similar to the *Gilgamesh* and the Torah arks, to save humanity from destruction. The early epics were also religious texts, and are now referred to as mythologies. The cultures that produced these epics were Greek, Hindu, Babylonian, Mesopotamian, and Roman. As written tablets started to be used in educational institutions and to pass on concrete knowledge, epics focused more on current historical figures and their epic achievements. Most of the early epics are called mythology, rather than fiction, because people worshipped the gods, demi-gods and divine kings presented in these works, rather than perceiving them as fictional stories. Gradually the lines between history, religion and truth blurred and writers started creating fictional epics, instead of aiming to put the works on a religious pedestal. Epics frequently had moral or religious undertones or references by the time the Old English *Beowulf* was written (8–11th century CE), but this epic did not lead to the populace worshipping heroes like Beowulf as religious icons. One of the leading epics from the eighteenth century is *Joan of Arc* by Robert Southey (1796), a tale about a woman who fights in warfare, and though she is a saint and sees visions, she is far from a typical king or male divinity main character (which was primarily used in earlier poetic epics).

By the time Homer wrote the *Odyssey* and Ovid wrote *Metamorphoses*, Greek and Latin epic poetry was mostly written in hexameter, which had shorter repeating foot lengths than the *Vedas*. The term "hexa-" means that there were six feet in a line. There were two different foot-types used in each of these lines—spondees (two long feet, primarily at the end of a line) and dactyls (a long syllable and then two short ones, usually used for the remainder of the line).

Over the centuries of the development of epic poetry, several related genres sprang out of this formulaic think-tank, and they gradually developed into independent genres. The genres that had epic poetry roots were lyric poetry, epigrams, odes, pastorals, elegies, rhetoric, and drama. Lyric poetry began as epic poetry that was sung, and then evolved into performances of poetry to the music of the lyre, which gradually became shorter and looser in nature than the long epic accounts of royal deeds. An epigram is just a brief, meaningful statement. The ode is a set of stanzas set to music in praise of a royal personage or subject, and has to be sung by the choir (as such, it is a branch of lyric poetry). The pastoral was a significant change in literature, as it was concerned with the pasture and with the lives of farmers and laborers, rather than solely with the grand deeds of the rich and powerful. The first major pastoral poem was Hesiod's *Works and Days,* which praises the Muses (while also addressing a major agrarian crisis occurring in Greece at the time the work was written) and gives practical advice on the almanac and technique to farmers. An elegy is a mournful song, such as a lament for the dead. Rhetoric is a non-rhyming and non-metric form of scholarly, pedagogic argumentative communication of ideas in essays or speeches. Religious and inspirational novels today are distant generic relatives of these early religious or inspired fictional works.

The religious novel movement had actually started in the first half of the nineteenth century, when pastors started reading religious serial novels to their congregations, but only really sold to a large percentage of Americans and Brits from the late 1890s to the World War I period. These novels continued to be popular after World War I, but saw a significant decline after World War II. While there are some best-selling religious novels today, they frequently do not keep selling past the initial year of their publication. It was around the time when Marie Corelli published *The Sorrows of Satan* that "Christian evangelical and missionary groups soon realized the power of fiction to disguise their religious, moral and social agenda—temperance, fidelity, family, loyalty, manliness, femininity, stalwartness in adversity, and the defense of the spiritual and moral status quo. It is extraordinary how many vicars and vicars' wives took up fiction before World War I and how many became best-selling authors."[8] Naturally, most (highbrow and lowbrow) fiction written prior to the twentieth century reinforced religious (Greco-Roman, Jewish, Christian) beliefs with moral "points," but as morality laws loosened, religious and spiritual novels became the antecedent and a conscious agenda, rather than a standard component in all novels.

The category of religious and inspirational literature clearly makes up a large percentage of the world and American literary market. First, the majority of the world still follows a religious faith of some kind. In the United States in 2008, 49.3 percent were Protestant, 25.4 percent were Catholic, and only 16.3 percent were atheists.[9] In the world at large in 2005, 59.4 percent were Christians, 27.4 percent were Muslims, and only 4.6 percent were "Other," which can potentially mean that far less than 4.6 percent of the world is atheist.[10] If nearly all of the world's population believes in a deity, it is only logical that they must purchase a great deal of religious literature.

The term "inspirational" is used in the general sense of the term, or, according to the *Oxford Dictionary,* as "providing or showing creative or spiritual inspiration," with inspiration meaning "the process of being mentally stimulated to do or feel something, especially to do something creative." The word's origin is in "Middle English (in the sense 'divine guidance')," but the current definition includes not only "religious" messages but also "creative" imaginings, as well as anything that stimulates any kind of "feeling." Clearly, this broad definition can include all of speculative fiction, all religious texts, all of romanticism, and just about all other types of literature, as there is hardly a fictional work out there that fails to make readers "feel" something.

The subgenres in the religious and inspirational fiction category are Amish and

Mennonite, Christian, Jewish, mythological, metaphysical and generally inspirational fiction. All of these have subgenres, themes, or literary features that include allegory, fantasy and history. All three of the top best-selling authors from across the twentieth century whom I am examining here fall into the Christian category. While there might have been some year-to-year best-sellers in the other categories, they do not occupy a significant enough overall share of the religious and inspirational fiction marketplace. New Age nonfiction and nonfiction in all of these categories performs very well, but there seem to be fewer Muslims or Jews interested in reading pastoral fiction. Bibles and other religious devotional texts are classified as nonfiction in standard listings.

In *Story Structure Architect*, Victoria Lynn Schmidt gives the definitions that distinguish the three main types of stories within the inspirational genre umbrella. "Religious" fiction "supports a particular faith and the teachings of that faith when inspiring others" (*A Course in Miracles*). Spiritual fiction offers a "neutral support of a person's spirituality without the use of religious elements. Spirituality is an individual way of being and living without dogma" (*Chicken Soup for the Soul*). Finally, the third category is not one of the key terms in this chapter's title because it is not included in genre classifications for this larger field. "Motivational" fiction "motivates a reader without religious or spiritual elements; it just uses facts" (*Personal Power*).[11] According to this definition, all three of the writers I examine closely wrote religious fiction.

Structural Elements of Religious Fiction: Characters, Setting, and Plot

While there are many similarities between the three works I examine closely under the religious novel umbrella, these works are not as similar to each other in plot, characters and setting as the novels in the other three genres discussed in this book. This distinction is present because these three works were written at a pre-formulaic (or semi-formulaic) time in British and American popular publishing. 1895, 1909, and 1920 are the publication dates of these three works. This choice is not accidental. First, the period between 1895 and 1920 saw a peak in the sales records of the religious Christian novels, so I chose works that fell into this period. Second, even though a few of these overall best-selling novelists published books after 1920, as all three lived for at least a year beyond 1920, the works that they published after the mid–1920s are still under copyright. Therefore, it was easier for me to pull up these three pre–1921 novels on Google Books. Finding religious novels in even a large library like the one at the University of Arizona is problematic, perhaps because of the religious content, or because they have steadily declined in popularity since World War II. Therefore, the works that are examined here were all written in a period when a shift was taking place in publishing between highbrow, literary standards and lowbrow, unliterary hack romance, horror, and mystery writing. Therefore, some of the generic elements repeat, while others diverge. In addition, while the plot line typically leads the hero from atheism or religious doubts to true belief, the route the hero takes to arrive at that conclusion is more diverse than the possible scenarios in the other genres. An artist losing sight, a Faustian deal, and attempting to market church-going are three very different story types. I will discuss some of the similarities and distinctions between them in this chapter.

The Formulas of Popular Fiction

Religious Plot

Spiritual and religious stories are typically quest plots because the hero is after a spiritual ideal, even if there is no Golden Fleece at the end of the journey. On a quest, the hero aims for a "distant, all-important goal" that he or she always reaches in the resolution.[12] The basic plot of a quest is summarized in Figures 19 and 20.

In the first movement, the heroes of all three stories learn some extremely distressing or misleadingly wonderful news. Geoffrey learns of an inheritance; Jane loses her sight; and the Reverend Blue is invited to a fortieth birthday party with old school friends. It is clear that Blue and Jane are terrified by these new developments, and while Geoffrey appears to be excited, readers are aware from the title (*The Sorrows of Satan*) that he has made a Faustian bargain. In all three stories, after this initial push that sets them off on a quest, the characters go through a building roller coaster of resulting problems in movements two through four. Because these are conversion stories, the heroes realize in the fourth movement that there might be something wrong with the route they have taken and search for the right answer, finding out that the goal of their quest is not what they initially imagined (money, fame), but

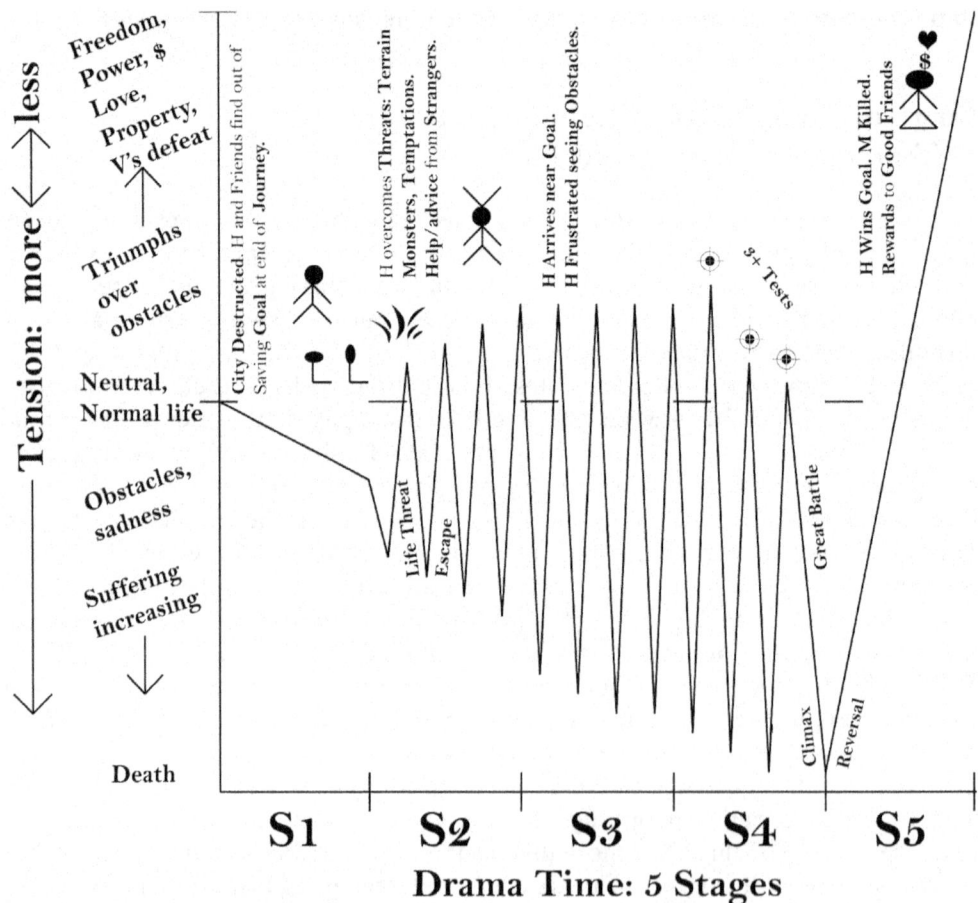

Figure 19. Religious Quest Plot Diagram.

rather faith in God and the Church. In the fifth and final movement, the hero actively seeks the goal of his quest and becomes a strong Christian believer. While I inserted the money sign as the goal at the top of this plot line in Figure 19, as I did in the other genres, money is not a simple goal in religious novels. Love is also an inconsistent reward. For example, Geoffrey gives up money (instead of finding riches) at the end and he refuses to visit the woman he loves (Mavis). However, in *The Rosary*, Jane and Garth marry. Stranger still, in *Wanted*, Blue was already married at the beginning of the work, and he does not gain or lose money or fame between the beginning and the end; instead, he gains a religious reawakening and a new understanding of his own sins and pride, rather than earthly rewards. What the hero receives as a reward for turning to God varies according to the sin that the hero or heroine committed that led to their downfall in movements two through four. If the hero is too greedy

Plot Movement	*Sorrows of Satan* (Corelli)	*Rosary* (Barclay)	*Wanted— A Congregation* (Douglas)
S1: Saving Goal Found, Quest Begins	Geoffrey, poor author, learns of inheritance, meets Lucio (Satan)	Jane, artist in love with beauty but lonely, suddenly blinded, and feels despair	Rev. D. Preston Blue is invited to a 40th birthday party, feels that his career as a preacher has been a failure
S2: Minor Obstacles	G's new wealth causes him to court Jane, who dies because he buys her in marriage	Blindness prevents J from doing art, and she is lost	B travels to the party and has many aggressive religious debates
S3: Mid-Roller Coaster	G commits greater sins due to wealth (causing a man to commit suicide) with S's prompting	J meets again with Garth and starts to be re-introduced to religion	After talking with MacGregor returns home with new energy to write better sermons
S4: Steep Roller Coaster: The Three+ Tests	G starts realizing his sins (and returning to God) when Mavis, courted as a potential lover, explains his fault to him	J and G undergo a roller coaster relationship and hurts G, and J is still hesitant about fully accepting religion	B attempts various schemes to increase his congregation
S5: Religious goal attained/ Resolution	G gives up money, S sorrowfully loses G's soul, which is saved (Faustian plot line)	J and G marry, and J fully accepts a renewed faith in the Christian religion	All of B's plans fail, as he is shown to be the lamb, and too prideful

Figure 20. Religious Plot Table.

and wants money, he is deprived of his money in the end. If the hero is too proud, he is deprived of fame and pride. And if the heroine is too conceited and focuses on herself instead of looking for a good husband, she is married before the novel closes. The endings are predictable by the event that sets the plot in motion, but are not formulaically identical to each other in any way other than being the religiously appropriate punishments or rewards for good or bad behavior in the eyes of the Christian Church. As a final note, I did not notice the repetition of the three tests that Booker noticed in the quest plot in these stories, but perhaps the tests are minor events that happen to the heroes in the last segment of the roller coaster, and do not stand out as obviously as they do in the *Odyssey* or other works of Greek mythology.

Religious Characters

There are a few clear similarities between the character types in these religious novels. All three of the heroes are from the upper classes, and all are highly educated, with one having gone to Oxford, another educated in a great school for girls in England, and the third also having studied in a respectable college (which a future top businessman and editor also attended) and then proceeding to a great seminary

Character Types	*Sorrows of Satan* (Corelli)	*Rosary* (Barclay)	*Wanted— A Congregation* (Douglas)
Hero	Geoffrey Tempest	Honourable Jane Champion, the duchess' niece (30)	Rev. D. Preston Blue
Villain	Prince Lucio Rimanez (Satan), a friend of Oxford friend, John Carrington, gold-mining in Australia	Blindness/ Evil	Jimmie Bardell (businessman)
Sidekick(s)/ Partner	Mavis Clare	Garth Dalmain (young, respected artist), Dr. Rob, Lady Ingleby, Duchess	Miss Brown (secretary), Tom MacGregor (editor), Mrs. Blue, Dr. Tracy
Victim(s)	Geoffrey	Jane	Blue
Community	London society	Religious community in a place similar to Hertfordshire, England	Religious and semi-religious people from middle and upper classes in a town similar to Ann Arbor, Michigan

Figure 21. Religious Characters Table.

that landed him a high post in the church relatively early in life. Their intellect is essential because the books are conversational and the characters regularly have to reply to complex philosophical, political and religious questions. These books would not be sustainable with lower-class heroes who could not put a sentence together to express either their doubts or confirmation about religion.

The villains all have money in common, and are typically wealthier or more connected than the hero. They seduce the hero into making morally erroneous decisions through their confidence, success, and other personal qualities that separate them from other men. At least in two of the cases, the "good" sidekicks or romantic interests are artists or writers; the artist is viewed as good at his or her core. In all three works, the hero is also the victim of the circumstances that set the plot in motion in the first movement, as sympathy is set up for them and their struggles. The world that the characters in religious novels operate in is divided into three camps: believers in God, doubters, and atheists or agnostics. Most of the supporting characters are in the upper-middle to upper class, but the church congregation can usually be from diverse classes.

In religious fiction, the story typically is mostly a set of conversations about religious topics or on general morals, ethics, and good versus evil. The characters are built up through these conversations. There are fewer incidents and the roller coaster has fewer spikes than in the other types of popular fiction. Half a book might be spent on the conversations that take place at a single party, without anybody being hurt, and with nobody placed in mortal danger. However, the danger often comes from having Satan or the Devil's representative nearby (*Sorrows of Satan*), or from a physical (blindness in *Rosary*) or mental (depression in *Wanted*) illness. Frequently, one or two people involved in a dialogue are lecturing or delivering a speech, which is only occasionally interrupted by the skeptical "student"; for example, *Wanted* has an entire chapter called "A Course in Psychology." Lloyd Douglas explains in his introduction that the book is primarily written for preachers, and possibly for a few intellectuals who are interested in church dogma. The language in the book is lighter and more conversational than most church sermons or religious nonfiction books, so it is likely that a wider public was able to appreciate this and other works by Douglas, while some other religious fiction novels were indeed only read by a few clergy.

Character descriptions in religious novels are frequently moral judgments, instead of specific descriptions of the common facial and bodily parts. For example, Geoffrey in *The Sorrows of Satan* describes Lucio, or Satan, with these words: "Lucio! The same as ever,—the perfect impersonation of perfect manhood! ... His countenance, pale, proud, sorrowful yet scornful, flashed upon me like a star! He looked full at me, and a questioning smile rested on his lips."[13] The term "sorrowful" refers back to the title of the novel, and the other adjectives describe Lucio's grand appearance, rather than just his personal dimensions. And the description of the person is given to point out that Lucio would still be interested in renewing the Faustian deal with Geoffrey, as his smile suggests.

Religious Settings

The setting is a hazier concept in religious Christian novels than in the other genre types. It is likely that if I chose three works by American pastors, the setting

Setting Type	*Sorrows of Satan* (Corelli)	*Rosary* (Barclay)	*Wanted—A Congregation* (Douglas)
Hero's Home	Back street London apartment, then mansion	Town home	Broad Street Church at Middlepoint, US
Religious Setting	Personal worship	Personal worship	Broad Street Church
Time	Present	Present	Present
Villain's Lair or Presence of Evil	House chamber, Church, all other wealthy places where evil people are	Aristocratic mansion	Editor's Office and Factory's Office
Religious World	London aristocracy	London and its suburbs' aristocratic class	American towns with religious congregations and those who are skeptical

Figure 22. Religious Settings Table.

would be closer to the items in the *Wanted* column, with many scenes in a specific church, and a few scenes in which the pastor ventures out into the "community." But these three works represent divergent ideas about organized religion. Both Jane and Geoffrey have a personal relationship with God, as they might speak to God in the moonlight or think about God at night. On the other hand, Blue might think about God privately, but the change that he undergoes centers on his relationship to the organization of his church services, rather than merely an internal conflict of faith. The fact that two of these works are set in London, while the third is set in rural American cities, probably also contributes to the divergence. While Satan makes a joke that the clergy are in league with him in *Sorrows of Satan*, Blue's religious revelation in *Wanted* is that the church is just and that he has to be more humble.

Best-Selling Writers in Religious and Inspirational Fiction from Corelli to Douglas

The religious and spiritual genre has fewer examples of well-known best-sellers between the end of the nineteenth century and the present day than any of the other genres considered in this book. Marie Corelli called herself (and was called by many critics) a spiritualist, though she is considered a religious novelist according to modern definitions. Moving beyond her and a few other notable writers, one faces several obstacles. While most of the other authors in this study specialized entirely in one genre, spiritual and religious works are frequently one-time generic experiments for writers. For example, Anne Rice wrote a few religious and spiritual novels in between her erotic romances, vampire and witch series, and her current werewolf series.

Another difficulty in fitting works into this category is that many spiritual works are also fantastic and typically slip into the other category. Among lists of the most significant fiction writers of the twentieth century, religious writers infrequently appear, while D. H. Lawrence, Nabokov and Wells are near the top of the list. Not that there are no best-sellers in the religious and spiritual category—they just typically do not enter the lexicon like the more outrageous and rebellious writers. For example, the three focal "best-sellers" in John Ferre's *The Religious Bestsellers of Charles Sheldon, Charles Gordon, and Harold Bell Wright* do not appear in Clive Bloom's list of *Bestsellers* from the entire twentieth century, which signifies that while they hit the American best-seller lists, they only stayed on the lists for a short period of time and did not continue selling for many decades. In addition, their sales are between 1 and 6 million copies per title, with not more than 10 million copies per author,[14] in comparison to the billion books sold by Barbara Cartland in romance. These sales figures have not changed much for the best-selling authors in spiritual and religious fiction today—for instance, Davis Bunn has sold over 6 million copies (mostly in major retail stores). The spiritual and religious genre has fewer extreme best-sellers, but it is still one of the top four overall best-selling markets. The separation between church and state might be one of the reasons few religious books enter major literature anthologies, and why these works are not typically taught in undergraduate or graduate literature programs, unless one takes specialized religious or spiritual literature classes. Without entering the anthologies and classrooms, an author's immortality beyond his or her lifetime is unlikely. Required books, like Mao's *Red Book* or the Bible, reach billion-copy sales. Meanwhile, books read for enjoyment need a time-tied marketing push to make them visible to public consciousness, but this awareness declines as soon as the marketing campaign cools down.

Ferre explained that he focused on the best-selling religious writers from the end of the nineteenth century and the beginning of the twentieth because this period was the "Third Great Awakening in the United States," when there was a renewed fervor about the social gospel.[15] Ferre groups his chosen authors into the subgenre of social gospel novels, which he describes as "melodramas, complex narratives that depict a world that appears to be violent and tragic, but which turns out to be governed by a benevolent morality.... Melodramas sustain readers' interest by their rapid episodic intensity in which a character is dangled above a moral abyss; then they satisfy readers emotionally by ending happily."[16] This is a description of the general quest plot, though it also partly fits the Overcoming the Monster plot. The quest here is an attempt to rid the world of evil and to discover true goodness, or "what Jesus would do." The plot comes closer to the Overcoming the Monster plot when one sees these stories as a battle between good and evil. Ferre explains John Wiley Nelson's view that in Christian America "evil is what prevents meaningful social relations or the maintenance of a desirable social institution." The "source of evil" is "outside of the community," and the "source of good is always a self-sacrificing individual."[17] In other words, "Because good is defined in terms of what Jesus would do in particular circumstances, it can be inferred that evil is whatever Jesus would not do, either in particular circumstances or under any circumstances."[18] This is a dualistic worldview that is present in nearly all major popular genres, as "good" (social conventions and the self-sacrificing individual) typically triumphs over "evil" (outsiders, foreigners, those who oppose social or religious conventions of the majority). In all plot types there is a dramatic clash between heroes and villains, and a resulting positive resolution for good. In religious fiction, the victory of good characters is a sign of their righteousness and religious devotion.

The social gospel genre of religious novels was primarily written to be read by the pastor-author to a congregation "one chapter at a time during the Sunday evening service,"[19] primarily to attract a larger attendance and to entertain the congregation while also teaching religious lessons. "The problem still remains that the churches are in a bad way. In most of them—which means two-thirds the number registered ten years ago, for one-third of them have closed up for lack of leadership—only a small per cent of the membership ever thinks of attending religious services regularly."[20] The tradition of pastors reading serial novels during service went back to the second half of the nineteenth century, as it has been described by members of pastor families, including Harriet Beecher Stowe, whose father was a pastor. These roots are vivid in the work of Barclay and Douglas, the first married to a pastor, and the second a pastor himself. However, Corelli had a more secular family background, as she was the daughter of a musician and a maid in London. Still, all three had a strict religious education and delivered informed religious opinions in their religious novels.

MARIE CORELLI (1855–1924; FIRST NOVEL, *A ROMANCE OF TWO WORLDS*, 1886)

Marie Corelli, also known as Mary Mackay, is listed as the top best-selling female author between the years 1900 and 1918 in Clive Bloom's *Bestsellers.* She is best known for *A Romance of Two Worlds* (1886), *The Sorrows of Satan* (1895), and *The Secret Power* (1921). While her first book has the word "romance" in it, she used this term in the general sense, as most novels were called "romances" in the nineteenth century. She was a strong religious believer and wrote novels with spiritual and religious morals in them to spread the gospel to the world. Her "books mixed pious sentiment with sensation, theosophy and comments on marital relations."[21]

The Sorrows of Satan begins with a political message that echoes the political and moral novel conventions of the time. Geoffrey explains the extreme poverty that he experienced as a struggling writer:

Figure 24. "I would sell my soul for a thousand pounds"—"I'll accept!" (Theatrical Poster Collection: Library of Congress Prints and Photographs Division, Washington, D.C.; New York: H.C. Miner Litho. Co., 1898).

"Poverty that compels you to dress in your one suit of clothes till it is worn threadbare,—that denies you clean linen on account of the ruinous charges of washerwomen ... this is the moral cancer that eats into the heart of an otherwise well-intentioned human creature and makes him envious and malignant, and inclined to the use of dynamite."[22] The dynamite reference is likely to be to the Irish Republican Army campaigns that peaked at the turn of the century. This political cause had been supported by many of the great nineteenth-century literary novelists, and Corelli begins in this way hoping, correctly, to attract lower-class readers who were passionate about ending unjust poverty (and potentially IRA supporters).

Unlike the other two books I examined closely in this field, *Satan* is written in the first-person voice of Geoffrey, the protagonist who makes the Faustian deal. At the beginning of the narrative, Geoffrey is so poor and hungry that he experiences "the gnawing pain, the sick faintness, the deadly stupor, the insatiable animal craving for mere food."[23] Geoffrey's parents were better off, but he decided to use his

Figure 23. Marie Corelli (Library of Congress Prints and Photographs Division).

"University education" to write literature. He is unfortunately rejected from full-time employment at journals. Because Corelli was herself attempting to write literature professionally despite the odds, her voice merges with the narrators when he exclaims that "a man gifted with original thoughts and the power of expressing them, appears to be regarded by everyone in authority as much worse than the worst criminal, and all the 'jacks-in-office' unite to kick him to death if they can."[24] This is a powerful statement that is truer and more relevant for literary writers today. Therefore, the triumph at the end of the novel is not only over Satan and the easy money that Satan offers but also over corrupting influences that stand in the way of intelligent literature. The drudgery of working as a struggling professional writer is further detailed when Geoffrey is fired from doing review work because he positively reviewed a literary work by a personal enemy of the editor. After that experience, Geoffrey does "'hack work' for the dailies."[25]

In fact, Corelli is doing something in this introduction similar to what I intend in this study. Geoffrey goes on to explain that he tried to sell some of his novels to publishers but failed because the initial readers were novelists themselves and rejected him because they thought that his acceptance would diminish their own chances for future publications: "Common sense points out the fact that the novelist 'reader' who has a place to maintain for himself in literature would naturally rather encourage work that is likely to prove ephemeral, than that which might possibly take a higher footing than his own."[26] I have not seen clear evidence that today publishers still use their own authors to review new manuscripts, but if they do, clearly it would be a system biased toward mediocrities.

In addition, Corelli seems incredibly aware of the shifting tide, as early as 1895, away from literary fiction to hack, formulaic, obscene or nonpolitical fiction. One editor gives Geoffrey a more specific explanation for the rejections than the others, saying, "You have been too earnest. And also, rather sarcastic in certain strictures against society. My dear fellow, that won't do. Never blame society,—it buys books! Now if you could write a smart love-story, slightly risqué,—even a little more than risqué for that matter, that is the sort of thing that suits the present age."[27] The word "risqué" means "daringly close to indelicacy or impropriety," so the editor is suggesting that Geoffrey should use more obscenity and perhaps sexual content in the guise of a "love-story." Corelli was against these risqué love stories as a religious novelist and believed that they diluted the public's morals.

The editor does not stop there and adds a long speech on the relationship between public demand and the supply of unliterary risqué fiction:

> It is my business to know the public taste as thoroughly as I know my own pocket. Understand me,—I don't suggest that you should write a book on any positively indecent subject,—that can be safely left to the 'New' woman,"—and he laughed,—"but I assure you high-class fiction doesn't sell. The critics don't like it to begin with. What goes down with them and with the public is a bit of sensational realism told in terse newspaper English. Literary English,—Addisonian English,—is a mistake.[28]

Several curious points are made in this speech. First, the reference to the "new woman" points to the growth of professional female writers, who, unlike Corelli, wrote hack romance novels, which later mutated into what we know today as the romance novel genre. The second interesting point here is that even in 1895, "high-class fiction" stopped selling and was received negatively by critics. For example, Oscar Wilde received hundreds of negative reviews on his *A Picture of Dorian Gray*, which came out in the same publication as the first Sherlock Holmes story (the latter did not receive any negative reviews). The third key point is that the linguistics of novels started to change at this point; as yellow journalism started overtaking American (and later British) newspapers, novel writers picked up on this choppy, unliterary English. The "Addisonian" allusion here is to Joseph Addison, who was an eighteenth-century English politician who founded the *Spectator* magazine and became a symbol for the political literary writing and editing style. Geoffrey responds to this attack by saying that he will sooner give up literature than begin writing unliterary fiction.

After this politically charged introduction, the narrative shifts to the religious thesis in conversions and internal monologues that Corelli has in common with other religious novelists. Geoffrey confesses, "To speak frankly, I did not believe in any God—then ... I had intellectually realized the utter inefficiency of Christian ministers to deal with difficult life-problems."[29] Only after indulging in despair and in his atheism does Geoffrey find the three letters that change his life and set the Faustian plot in motion. The first of these letters is from his Oxford friend, John Carrington, nicknamed Boffles, who has struck it rich from gold-mining in Australia with the help of Satan, or Prince Lucio Rimanez, the friend he introduces to Geoffrey upon receiving his request for a loan. The second letter explains that Geoffrey has suddenly inherited an enormous estate worth "Five Millions of Pounds Sterling" from a dead relative. Geoffrey reacts with enormous glee, as Corelli must have when she suddenly saw enormous profits from her literature (she did not give up her money, unlike Geoffrey). While Geoffrey does not respond to Satan's initial invitation for a meeting, Lucio puts himself in his way and forces himself into his life, to which Geoffrey exclaims, "The devil is in it!"[30] and indeed the Devil is. From there, the story is based on societal conversations about politics, morality, religion and other topics, as Geoffrey joins the aristocracy with the help of his new millions and Lucio, a friend with a lot of "connections" in high society. Geoffrey spends a good deal of his time courting the "fair" Lady Sybil, and contemplates whether he should simply pay her father off or attempt to make her fall in love with him: "I felt and knew that my projected courtship of Lady Sibyl would of necessity resolve itself into something more or less of a market bargain, unless indeed I could win the girl's love."[31] Sybil has a nervous breakdown to the attempts to buy her body in a marriage, to which Geoffrey responds by kissing her. Sybil then gives a five-page lecture on the "new woman" and on how she deplores the mixing of love and money, but stresses that, knowing all that, she is willing to marry Geoffrey, if he completes the marriage bargain as soon as possible.

The marriage ceremony commences and Lucio philosophically jokes, as he serves as the "best man," ""Did you ever hear it reported, Geoffrey, that the devil is unable to enter a church, because of the cross upon it, or within it?' ... 'It is nonsense, for the makers of the legend forgot one thing,' he continued, dropping his voice to a whisper as we passed under the carved gothic portico,—'the cross may be present, but so is the clergyman! And wherever a clergyman goes the devil can follow!' This is an example of how Satan expresses thorough knowledge of the Gospel and exposes the sins of the church, as well as the sins of men across the story. The condemned are not only Geoffrey because he accepts, without being fully aware of it, a Faustian bargain, but also the other sinners who break moral and religious laws knowingly and willingly.

After the wedding and then Sybil's untimely death, Geoffrey refocuses his attention on an intelligent woman, Mavis Clare, as Satan urges him to become her "lover." In the last fourth of the novel, the story is overwhelmed by Geoffrey's long monologues, in which he is overcome with guilt for the sin of lust and other errors that he is making. "And yet ... to kneel down with clasped hands and tell an inactive, unsympathetic, selfish, paid community called a church, that I am going to kill myself for the sake of love and love's despair, and that therefore I humbly implore its forgiveness for the act, seems absurd,—as absurd as to tell the same thing to a non-existent Deity."[32] Geoffrey is still an atheist, and he is more disappointed and doubtful about the church than ever before. Mavis rejects his advances, saying that Lucio and him are responsible for Sybil's death. The religious tension of unrelenting atheism starts coming to a climax. Geoffrey is haunted by "Three dark Phantoms that had appeared to me in my room in London on the evening of Viscount Lynton's suicide."[33] Suicides, murders, improper sexual relations and other sins pile up around Geoffrey. When these become overwhelming, Geoffrey finally turns to God: "Round us the moonlit landscape was spread like a glittering dream of fairy land,—and still the unknown bird of God sang on with such entrancing tenderness as must have soothed hell's tortured souls."[34] Geoffrey gives up his property and stays away from societal influences, personified in Lord Elton, in order to keep a solid moral footing.

He continues to think of Mavis, but does not actively pursue her. The novel comes back to the thoughts that Geoffrey expressed at the beginning against the unliterary publishing establishment and the unliterary and elitist society: "I now took a humble room and set to work on a new literary enterprise, avoiding everyone I had hitherto known, for being now a poor man, I was aware that 'swagger society' wished to blot me from its visiting-list." At the end, after becoming famous and critically acclaimed for her novels, Mavis writes, inviting Geoffrey to visit her, but he decides not to until he has cleared himself of impurity. The novel concludes with Geoffrey watching a new Faustian deal take place as an established cabinet minister shakes hands with the man he knew as Lucio, and the two walk into the "House of England's Imperial Government,—Devil and Man,—together!"[35] The suggestion is that the government, like the church, is corrupt, and while one literary writer might have escaped the Devil's deal, the Devil is still at work, and there are many men who still need conversion. Geoffrey needs all of his self-possession and God's strength to resist renewing the Faustian deal with Lucio, as he once again finds himself in relative poverty and obscurity.

FLORENCE LOUISA BARCLAY (1862–1921; FIRST NOVEL, *GUY MERVYN*, 1891)

Barclay wrote "romance stories" on "semi-religious issues." While many other popular romance writers stressed family values and religious morals, Barclay stands out as leaning more toward the religious genre because she was married to the Rev. Charles W. Barclay; the couple even spent their honeymoon in the Holy Land, discovering the "mouth of Jacob's Well," instead of going away to a beautiful island. At the end of the nineteenth century, Israel was sparsely populated by the Bedouin, Muslims and British colonialists, as the giant wave of migration into Israel by Jews only began after World War II. So this trip suggests a religious fervor that was a predominant passion for the Barclays. Barclay's top best-selling novel was *The Rosary* (1909),[36] which "sold over a million copies by 1921," a decade after its publication, "continuing to appear on the bestseller lists for twenty years."[37] The story shows a clear connection to the romance genre, as it focuses on a love story, unlike the two other focal works, in which the hero does not win the girl in the end. The story is about Jane, a female artist obsessed with aesthetics, who is accidentally blinded and, as a result, finds both love for a man and religion. Clive Bloom explains that *The Rosary* was among the top best-sellers for forty years, until the Cold War knocked it off the best-seller list. Bloom argues that Barclay had a significant impact on all women's fiction, and particularly on the romance genre, as "harbingers of the new fiction, not only because we see in *The Rosary* a thousand Mills and Boon romances (Barclay overwhelmingly appealed to women) but because her work was inherently modern in its approach to writing fiction (and especially women's domestic fiction)."[38] This "modern" approach is the formulaic minimalism that dominates all four of the key genres in this study. And "women's" fiction refers to fiction written by women with a strong female lead, which later dominated the romance genre.

Sales figures for *The Rosary* are counted from 1909 to 1921 in the quote above because the year 1921 is particularly significant, for that was the year when Barclay's autobiography was published by Putnam's Sons, the same company that published her novels. Here is one famous quote that exemplifies the theory behind the religious and spiritual genre, frequently cited from this work: "There is enough sin in the world without an author's powers of imagination being used in order to add even fictitious sin to the amount. Too many bad, mean, morbid characters already, alas! Walk this earth. Why should writers add to their number and risk introducing them into beautiful homes where such people in actual life would never, for one moment, be tolerated?"[39] This theory of literature as something that should portray goodness and hide horrifying evil is in direct conflict with the premise made by Stephen King and other horror and dark science fiction and fantasy novelists, who strive to frighten readers with the unspeakable evils at work in this world as well as imagined supernatural evils. Of course, the story of an artist who is blinded and learns to be happy with a man and religion is extremely horrifying for me (more so than the story of a witch who kills a school full of hated classmates and her mother in *Carrie*), but this might be a matter of personal fear response and taste. Barclay would have probably replied that the artist is blinded by God, rather than a foreign evil person, so there is nobody in the work to stop from entering one's household.

Another example of religious novelists holding a position against portraying the evil in the world is when Charles Sheldon, a best-selling novelist (though to a smaller degree than the focal three writers in this chapter), in 1900 took over the editing of the Topeka *Capital* for a week, and he "omitted coverage of scandals, crimes, and brutal sports, and refused advertising for liquor, patent medicine, tobacco, and women's underwear."[40] The failure to cover major crimes and advertise life-saving medicines is definitely an extreme example of fixing the world's problems by erasing them from the minds of the readers, rather than tackling these in reality. If characters in religious novels drink, they typically die, as several characters do in Ralph Connor's *Black Rock*.

An advertisement of *The Rosary* in the back pages of the first edition proclaims, "'An ideal love story—one that justifies the publishing business, refreshes the heart of the reviewer, strengthens faith in the outcome of the great experiment of putting humanity on earth. *The Rosary* is a rare book, a source of genuine delight.' *Syracuse Post-Standard.*"[41] While most blurbs are typically inflated, *The Rosary* might deserve such high praise because of its literary style. The reviewer also believes that the religious message in the book "justifies the publishing business"; the perspective that a novel has to serve a social or a moral purpose was believed to be the chief goal of literature until approximately the 1970s, when unliterary, formulaic and promiscuous, rather than moralistic, fiction started to dominate the market.

The Rosary has many generic elements that diverge from most formulaic fiction from the last fifty years, but it also has some similarities. The story begins with a detailed, romantic description of a scene; this is very appropriate, as the story is about an artist losing sight, so this offers some of the visual details that Jane will no longer see after she is blinded. Toward the end of this description, however, a standard formulaic element appears, in a reference to sleep: "The one brilliant spot of colour in the landscape was a large scarlet macaw, asleep on his stand under the cedar."[42] The note that the "macaw" was "asleep" perhaps serves a purpose similar to the low notes in Beethoven's "Moonlight Sonata"—to stress the peaceful mood. This is an example of how more recent formulaic fiction takes an element like this soft humming suggestion and turns it into repetitive sleepiness on the part of the main characters.

Descriptions of people in *The Rosary* are equally unique and anti-formulaic. For example, the Duchess is introduced with these words "She wore an ancient straw hat, of the early–Victorian shape known as 'mushroom,' tied with black ribbons beneath her portly chin; a loose brown holland coat; a very short tweed skirt, and Engadine 'gouties.' She had on some very old gauntlet gloves, and carried a wooden basket and a huge pair of scissors."[43] Instead of typical features, like the nose and eyes, Barclay focuses on the hat, chin and skirt, and explains how these were unusual and distinctive, rather than just listing a few adjectives to describe them.

One of the details that this religious novel shares with romance novels is the power-play between Jane and Garth, the central couple. The other two works in this chapter focus on the power and religious struggles between men, but this book focuses on the love affair, which makes it formulaically closer to a romance novel. There are love affairs with women in *The Sorrows of Satan*, but Geoffrey does not end up with Mavis in the end, so it is not his ultimate goal. A few lines from the final resolution scene demonstrate the type of power-play that Jane and Garth have: "Then Garth sprang to his feet. The sense of manhood and mastery; the right of control, the joy of possession, arose within him. Even in his blindness, he was the stronger. Even in his helplessness,—for the great essentials, Jane must lean on him. He raised her gently, put his arms about her, and stood there, glorified by his great love."[44] While Garth lifts the blinded Jane "gently," he expresses the same urges for "mastery" and "control" as the heroes of formulaic romance novels.

LLOYD DOUGLAS (1877–1951; FIRST NOVEL, *MORE THAN A PROPHET*, 1905)

Lloyd Douglas is a key religious and spiritual best-selling writer from the middle of the twentieth century. He entered popular consciousness more than Barclay or Corelli because there were numerous films, and even a television series, based on his novels. Douglas published around a dozen books before he had his first best-seller; one of the later ones on this list is *Wanted—A Congregation* (1920). His popularity made major cultural shifts immediately after the publication of his first recognized novel, *Magnificent Obsession*, in 1929, as it "led to a huge increase in the sales of Bibles in America during the 1930s." He also became a household name when an adaptation of his best-known novel, *The Robe* (1942), won two Academy Awards in 1953, shortly after his death. Like most best-selling religious fiction novelists from the first half of the twentieth century, Douglas was an "ordained" "pastor"—in his case, of the "Lutheran Church." During his pre-literary career he served as the "director of religious work at the University of Illinois" and as a pastor in the United States and Canada until 1933, when he started to see a significant income from his best-selling books. Nobody called him a romantic writer, or anything other than a religious and an inspirational writer. He had a clear "purpose" in the presentation of a "Christian thesis in the form of a novel and to include human interest in the gospel stories. The recurrent theme in his work is that of the conversion of the atheist hero to a practicing Christian."[45] This is a clear quest plot, with spiritual and religious enlightenment as its goal.

In *Wanted—A Congregation*, characters are primarily revealed through their dialogue, which dominates the story. For example, in a debate with Jimmie, a wealthy businessman, Blue exclaims,

> We won't quarrel with the dictionary. Let's get back to cases. A moment ago, you were saying that The Church is a beggar—and mentioned rummage sales in the same breath. Now, I freely admit that a rummage sale is not the most dignified market on earth, and if I had my way there would be no such thing, forever and aye; but, strictly speaking, is The Church a beggar when it conducts a sale—even though it is a—a rummage-sale? There's value received, you know. I suppose many a poor family has considered the rummage-sale a great assistance.[46]

This is a discussion about giving money to the church, in which Jimmie objects to giving too much money, and the Reverend Blue is outraged by this anti-religious view.

Character descriptions have unexpected elements and are typically pretty short in *Wanted*. Here is one of the editor: "MacGregor, long, lank, near sighted, and homely in the extreme to any but the affectionate eyes of a sworn friend."[47] MacGregor is one of the main supporting characters, so this is brisk considering his significance in the plot. This description does mention MacGregor's "eyes," but other than this standard feature, general adjectives are used to qualify MacGregor's distinction.

Blue even explains Douglas' short and choppy style when he talks about a 500-word article he was once asked to write for his local newspaper. Blue failed in this attempt, which his editor friend, MacGregor, jokingly calls, "By-products of a Useful Career?"[48] As a result, the local editor never asked him for a contribution again.

> When confronted with the necessity of reducing this whole sermon to a scant nine inches of eight-point, instead of jumping into the very ruck of things, and hurling red-hot chunks of his address at the public, in the first paragraph, the only method his inexperience could suggest was to begin with the calf!
>
> Having squandered his precious five hundred words in riotous introduction, there was no space left to say what possible excuse he might have had for mentioning this ancient narrative.[49]

The editor then goes on to give Blue advice on how he should write his sermons, comparing them to the work done by his reporters. All of the conversations in this novel center on a single key religious thesis, which is summarized in the middle when Blue argues that preachers "are discouraged because they are unable to see satisfactory results from their preaching. They can't preach because they have nobody to preach to. The people make life wretched for them because it is evident that they are unsuccessful."[50] Blue argues here that preachers can only be successful if they have a full congregation that is open to hearing a helpful message.

In the conclusion, all of Blue's efforts to bring in a large congregation fail and he reverses his religious thesis: "He knew that this was the poorest service he ever rendered."[51] In part, it was problematic because he was too familiar when referring to God as He, and otherwise too prideful and conceited. The new thesis is that a pastor has to be humble and should not try to sell his sermons to the public if the public is not naturally inclined to attend.

Chapter 5

Mystery and Detective

"[M]urder mysteries aimed at the barely literate working class ... relied on formulaic plots, clichéd characters and cases being solved either by a combination of ludicrous coincidence or last-minute confessions, or by the stupidity of the criminal in making ridiculous mistakes."—Russell Miller[1]

    The history of the mystery and detective genre differs from those of the other genres in this book because it is defined by key authors who altered the genre's formula, instead of major literary movements and genres. The writers who mimicked Wilkie Collins could be viewed as a "literary movement," but only because the mystery formula was simplified and standardized during this period. Figure 25 shows the line of development that changed and developed the mystery genre between the 1820s, when formal police forces were put in place in London and Paris, and the resulting mysteries that are commonly written today. Each of the key authors along this line made some adjustments to the genre, even if they were steps into minimalism or less logical investigations. At the same time, some of the tricks that are popular today were invented as early as E.T.A. Hoffman, but then were forgotten for a century or more until they were revived. Aside from the procedure used to solve a mystery and its plot structure, the major change in the genre was its overall linguistic and structural disintegration into minimalism after Conan Doyle. Therefore, the key focal figures in this part of the study are Arthur Conan Doyle, Agatha Christie and Henning Mankell because a look at their works shows the disintegration of the genre from its peak with Sherlock Holmes to its current state.
    The detective story is a best-selling genre among popular fiction because it

> is the very paradigm of the "rattling good story"; the reader cannot put the book down ... because of the sheer compulsion to find the explanation of "whodunit." At quite another level, the detective story enshrines that perennial hermeneutic of the narrative mode which works with deep structures of change and stasis, of onward-moving events and retrospective reflection, of mystery and its resolution. Within the simple and/or profound terms of plot-driven interest and excitement, then, the detective story is a genre of surpassing durability.... What ... is at the heart of the genre's appeal? ... It is the dialectic inherent in a tale which, of its very nature, speaks of mayhem—of criminality, transgression, violence, carnage, and (most usually) death—but which at the same time houses this Dionysian tumult and chaos within parameters of Apolline order, of (social and literary) convention, of rational explanation. In consequence, the genre can be at one and the same time conservative and subversive.[2]

This source goes on to say that the detective story holds appeal on several levels: theological in reflecting a "sense of guilt," "cognitive-cum-philosophical" in the psycho-

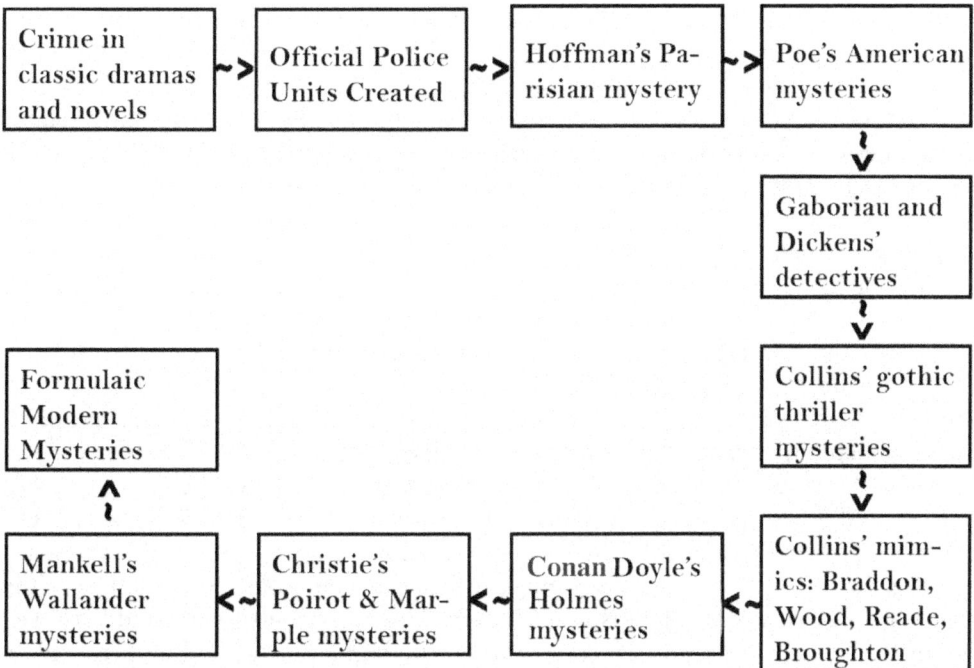

Figure 25. Mystery Genres Diagram.

logical battle between logic and irrationality or criminality, the level of its "sexual charge" intertwined with violence, and several other elements that make it stand out among other genres.[3] These are important psychological motivations that lead readers to buy mystery novels. However, frequently modern formulaic minimalist novels fail to meet these expectations as they cut the corners that are essential to achieve these effects on the reader.

For example, Agatha Christie strongly suggests the culprit in the first couple pages of *The Mysterious Affair at Styles,* or that it was the twenty-year-junior husband of the old heiress. In *The Troubled Man,* Mankell fails to tie up the clues he presents across the narrative in the end, which leaves readers feeling cheated of a proper resolution. Instead of moving ahead with speedy roller coaster ups and downs, the modern mystery crawls along, as its hero spends time sleeping, brooding, or running around like a "mad hatter." Even if there is some violence and chaos, they are typically left unresolved, without suggesting a deeper problem in these open endings. Unlike Wells, Mankell does not make a strong enough critique of the police force in order for the reader to walk away at least with a feeling that the law enforcement system has to change. A few negative comments against the police and against a few governments are made, but they are made by an Alzheimer's patient, who cannot adequately express his frustration and simply resigns. Having discovered who the spy was, Wallander lets the two naval officers kill each other, instead of taking heroic action to out Hakan's sinful spying past. The novel is formulaic, but with major illogical gaps in its fabric. But to understand how the generic conventions that Mankell is breaking were founded, we have to rewind to the roots of the mystery genre.

Early mysteries and detective stories were romantic novels, and to this day they have a cloud of romance around them, rather than a realistic look at how "true crime" is solved (or remains unsolved). Critics barely mentioned the words "crime," "mystery" and "detective" when discussing genres prior to the twentieth century. The concept of "mystery" and "detective" fiction as a major separate genre is a new one, even if the themes of mystery and detective work appeared long before 1915. This genre is especially difficult to classify and define because there are so many closely related terms for this genre, such as crime story, detective story, mystery, hardboiled, whodunit, legal thriller, and courtroom drama. Regardless of whether a story is a whodunit or hardboiled, there is always a central crime in the plot of a mystery or detective story.

When did crime enter literature? The theft of Helen in *The Iliad* is a crime, as are the murders in Shakespeare. Crime has been used as a dramatic plot device and as a theme in fiction across literary genres. Similar to an overriding focus on a romantic relationship in romance novels, crime and detective stories focus on the criminal act or on the investigation that follows it, instead of putting it in the background of larger moral or social issues. A few years after the success of Scott's Waverley novels, in 1819, E. T. A. Hoffmann published *Mademoiselle de Scuderi*, about the King's Guard investigating a gang of thieves rampaging through the streets of Paris, stealing wealthy lovers' jewelry, and also killing some of them. This sensational work sold very well and established Hoffmann's career, so novels with similar crime and detective plots became increasingly popular over the following decades. A few names that are popularly associated with crime and detective fiction are Edgar Allan Poe's "The Murders in the Rue Morgue" (1841), Wilkie Collins' *The Moonstone* (1860), Arthur Conan Doyle's Sherlock Holmes stories (the first of which was published in 1887), and Agatha Christie's *Murder on the Orient Express* (1934). The latter two authors further exploded the genre and brought it to its current best-selling popularity.

The turn of the nineteenth century appears to have seen an unprecedented spike in crime in the exponentially growing cities. Fiction writers replied to this trend with a spike in novels about criminal activity. In particular, E. T. A. Hoffmann's novella, *Mademoiselle de Scuderi*, stands out among these as having a significant impact on what later became the mystery and detective genre. Hoffmann echoes the alarm Parisians felt at the beginning of the nineteenth century in his historical mystery set in the seventeenth century: "Paris was the scene of the most abominable atrocities."[4] Hoffmann states that as early as in the seventeenth century, "the king appointed a special court of justice for the exclusive purpose of inquiring into and punishing" the "secret crimes" of several poisonings that were seen in Paris.[5] The troubles continued until Argenson, the Minister of Police, started ordering "the arrest of every person amongst the populace against whom there was the least suspicion."[6] This was the arduous process that top officials had to be involved in before a more structured police force was put in place in the 1820s. The story opens at night in 1680, when Madeleine de Scuderi, a writer of "pleasing verses" (including a "tedious" historical romance, *Clelie* [1656] and a favorite of Louis XIV, is awakened by a visitor that her ladymaid, La Martiniere, thinks is a thief, but turns out to be a man seeking Scuderi's help in fighting against the thieving and murdering gangs in the city of Paris.[7] Scuderi was a real French writer, and *Clelie* was her novel that included many characters who represented prior artists, including the ancient lesbian poetess, Sapho. The bulk of the story is comprised of long monologue-style dialogues and Scuderi's and other

Parisians' troubles with "valuable ornaments" that are being stolen by the gangs of thieves. In the conclusion, the mystery is solved, as a "public proclamation" appears that explains that "a penitent sinner had ... handed over to the Church a large and valuable store of jewels and gold ornaments which he had stolen,"[8] and these goods were then returned to the owners who claimed them.

Hoffmann's contribution is typically a minor note in the history of the detection genre because the work of the king's men counts as a separate function from the work done by modern police departments. "With the establishment of organized police forces around the world—London's Metropolitan force was set up in 1828—it was perhaps inevitable that the detective would emerge as a popular literary hero."[9] At first, "true crime" stories were popularized in the *Newgate Calendar*, and then interest shifted from the criminals to the police detectives who caught them. This initial interest was predominantly from the lower-class public, so publishers created "pulp fiction" (also known as "penny dreadfuls," "shilling shockers" and "dime novels") that fit their pocketbooks and their literacy level. The next wave in this genre came from the "autobiographical" accounts of "real-life detectives," including Eugéne François Vidocq's French best-selling book, *Les Vrais Mémoires de Vidocq* (1828–1829), and the British "imitations" that followed it: *Scenes in the Life of a Bow Street Runner*, *Recollections of a Detective Police Officer*, and *Experiences of a Real Detective*.[10]

The next leap in the detective genre happened precisely in 1841. Arthur Conan Doyle "always generously acknowledged the debt he owned" to Edgar Allan Poe for the creation of detective C. Auguste Dupin in his short 1841 story (which Conan Doyle discovered around 1875), "The Murders in the Rue Morgue," which served as the "prototype for many" fictional detectives that followed him, including Sherlock Holmes.[11] Poe had written several other gothic stories of horror prior to Dupin's mystery, but in these the focus was on describing horrific crimes and the motivations that led to them and not the process of solving such crimes. In Chapter II of *A Study in Scarlet*, Dr. Watson comments when discussing the "art" of detection, "You remind me of Edgar Allan Poe's Dupin." To which Holmes replies that the comparison is not a compliment for him because Dupin is "a very inferior fellow," as he failed to match Holmes' analytical genius.[12] Russell Miller, on the other hand, concludes that Dupin did indeed have, like Holmes, "peculiar analytical ability" and "academic brilliance," and that he was a "gentleman (amateur) detective," unlike the middle-class police detectives and the lower-class shock detectives that previously appealed to the mass public, but failed to grasp the imagination of the high literature establishment.

However, Holmes might have been more truthful in his summary than Miller. Here is how the narrator of "The Murders in the Rue Morgue" describes Monsieur C. Auguste Dupin: "This young gentleman was of an excellent, indeed of an illustrious family, but, by a variety of untoward events, had been reduced to such poverty that the energy of his character succumbed beneath it, and he ceased to bestir himself in the world, or to care for the retrieval of his fortune." He only had a small allowance remaining that afforded him the "necessities," and he indulged in buying books. The narrator and Dupin move in together due to Dupin's poverty, similar to Holmes moving in with his sidekick, Watson.[13] Dupin's eccentricities are perhaps more extreme than Holmes,' as, unlike Holmes (who invites too many detection customers in), Dupin does not admit "visitors." And the two characters are extreme loners until the murder springs them into action: "We existed within ourselves alone."[14] While both of these men are from aristocratic or wealthy families, they live in poverty and isolation, so it is hasty to say that Dupin truly represented an upper-class detective. Either way, it is clear that the eccentricities, detective logical abilities and other qualities that characterize Dupin did set a generic hero-type that has been echoed in many other mysteries. Besides establishing the standard detective hero-type, Poe also laid down

> the essential elements of classic detective fiction: a brilliant, charismatic leading character, a bumbling partner, a baffling crime, a client wrongly accused, a trail strewn with false leads and an unlikely perpetrator finally brought to justice. The plot of "The Murders in the Rue Morgue" became the template for hundreds of detective stories. First there was an account of the crime; then Dupin's visit to the scene and his musings on the clues that his admiring companion signally failed to observe; then police botch the investigation; and finally the mystery is solved and explained by Dupin, who accuses the authorities of falling into the "gross but common error of confounding the unusual with the abstruse."[15]

Poe was followed by generic innovators like Emile Gaboriau, who created the French version of the "gentleman detective" in Inspector LeCoq, and minor characters in the 1850s like Inspector Bucket in Charles Dickens' *Bleak House*.

The next key step in the development of the detective and mystery genre was popular "sensation fiction" that was established in 1860 by Wilkie Collins with *The Woman in White*. Collins achieved the formula for "sensation fiction" by mixing the "thrills of Gothic literature with the psychological realism of the domestic novel."[16] Like Poe, Collins' stories do not have all of the elements that characterize the modern detective mystery because of these unrelated roots. The "sensational" novel focused on three key topics ("murder, madness," and "bigamy") that are perpetrated in the home[17]; this is in contrast with the mystery genre, which focuses almost entirely on solving murders, regardless of whether they are committed in the household, the office or any other plain or exotic location. Initially, I decided to look more closely at Collins because, as Rob Warden has accurately concluded, he is "often, and erroneously, credited with inventing the mystery novel." Warden states that Collins really invented the "legal thriller,"[18] while Matthew Sweet argues that he invented "sensation fiction." Both agree that the formula behind Collins' novels does not match what we see today in popular detective or mystery novels. Warden also agreed that Collins' novels were "sensational," and that Collins' formula was to "make 'em laugh, make 'em cry, make 'em wait."[19] In other words, Collins helped to create the emotional roller coaster plot, with peaks of happiness and misery and periods of suspense in which the reader anticipates the next disaster.

Collins' "sensational" novels had the single setting of the home, and their chief mystery and gothic horror centered on the protagonist, who was in horrific danger of falling "ill" or risked "being murdered or driven insane" by the other members of his (or, more frequently, her) household.[20] While Sherlock Holmes' stories are related by his detective partner, Dr. Watson, Collins' *The Woman in White* is narrated by unreliable speakers who are the victims and perpetrators of the crimes and horrors thus related. The plot behind *The Woman in White* is based primarily on a real legal case of Adelaide-Marie-Rogres-Lusignan de Champignelles (1741–1787), who married the Marquis de Douhault in 1764. "By 1787 she was a widow. Her father had died in 1784," but her dead husband's brother managed to keep her father's "estate," leaving her in financial trouble. She attempted to negotiate the return of this estate to her, but the brother managed instead to drug her and put her into a mental institution, meanwhile announcing her death and keeping the entire estate for himself. Madame de Douhault eventually escaped from the asylum, but the courts favored the brother and she died in poverty without reclaiming her real name. *The Woman in White* relates a similar story, in which a woman is wrongfully accused of insanity for financial gain, and another woman takes her place among the aristocracy; these "two women in white" are "the madwoman Anne Catherick, imprisoned against her will in a private lunatic asylum, and Lady Glyde, with whom she is forced to exchange her identity."[21] Few modern detective mysteries focus on the struggles of a falsely accused madwoman. In addition, the problems in this plot are solved not by the police or private detectives (as is typical in modern mysteries), but instead through "violent independent action"—in other words, with the help of "Carbonari—a Mafia-like organization of Italian revolutionaries and assassins."[22] The speed of this novel is increased by narrated dramatic incidents and unique biased or falsifying perspectives, instead of through choppy dialogue or unrelated violent incidents. The various small and large troubles that the narrators describe are all related to the central story, as if the narrators are indeed acting like "witnesses" in court, but without the time constraints, and with an allowance for some descriptive digressions.

While *Woman in White* was Collins' first venture into sensational fiction, two of his later novels are closer to the formula of a modern detective novel: *The Dead Alive* (1874) and *The Moonstone* (1868). *The Dead Alive* is representative of the legal thriller because it "has many ... familiar elements of today's subgenre: a lawyer out of sorts with his profession, the legal process gone awry, and a touch of romance to tenderize the rigors of the law."[23] *The Moonstone* is closer formulaically to modern mysteries, though its focal plot is not a murder, but rather "the search for and recovery of a stolen jewel."[24]

Collins was lucky enough to be in a circle of critically acclaimed writers who "invented" most of the literary genres that were popular in the second half of the twentieth century, and (some of which are still popular today). Collins entered this group through his friendly and professional association with Charles Dickens, which led to the serialization of Collins' best-known novels in Dickens' popular magazines: *Household Words* and later *All the Year Round*. The Dickens and Collins families were even joined by the marriage in 1860 (the year when *The Woman in White* was published) of Charles Allston Collins and Kate Dickens. The "sensational" genre took off when Collins was joined by Mary Elizabeth Braddon, Ellen Wood, Charles Reade, and Rhoda Broughton, who, by mimicking Collins' "sensational" formula, created a "literary movement." The two women on this list are of special interest, for both either owned or edited significant literary magazines, similar to Dickens. Mary Braddon edited the *Temple Bar*, and also founded the less popular *Belgravia* magazine. She is best known for the "sensational" novel *Lady Audley's Secret* (1863), about a woman that commits unintentional bigamy, which is paralleled by the murders of her spouses. Ellen Wood, known for *The Channings* (1862), owned, wrote for and edited the *Argosy* journal. Both *Temple Bar* and *Argosy* published the work of Collins, themselves and other "sensational" writers in this "literary movement."

Sherlock Holmes called LeCoq a "miserable bungler" in *A Study in Scarlet*, but Conan Doyle clearly did not share this opinion and closely studied not only LeCoq and Dupin but also most prior examples of fictional detectives. After the blooming period in the genre between the 1820s and the 1860s, the genre was flooded with imitators that "corrupted" it with highly formulaic mimicries of the classics from the earlier period. This flood included

> "blood and thunder" murder mysteries aimed at the barely literate working class, mainly in London. They relied on formulaic plots, clichéd characters and cases being solved either by a combination of ludicrous coincidence or last-minute confessions, or by the stupidity of the criminal in making ridiculous mistakes. Sometimes suspense was maintained by withholding vital evidence from the reader; rarely was the reader made privy to a believable investigative process.[25]

The problems detailed above also dominate the current formulaic detective and mystery novels, which rely on these repeating elements more than on the complex logic and insight needed to develop a complex detective character like Holmes or Dupin.

Structural Elements of Mystery: Characters, Setting, and Plot

The most basic detective plot has to be "thicker" than some of the most complex formulaic romances because even the least original mystery writers have to insert some twists in the story, or else it will lack the key element in its name—"mystery." In a romance, the first movement might be taken up with biographies, the initial meeting, and perhaps some dramatic events. In a mystery, the first movement has to introduce the detective, the sidekick, and various other minor characters; it then has to present a dead body (or a theft, or some other crime), and begin the process of determining whodunit. Thus, there are longer lists of significant characters, more detailed plot lines, and frequently settings that play an active role in the plot.

Mysterious Plots

Because of this intricate complexity, the elements of the mystery plot are made clearer in a plot diagram and a table of three key works from the genre separated into the five movements of their respective plot lines.

> The essence of a story based on the Mystery [plot] is that it begins by posing a riddle, usually through the revelation that some baffling crime has been committed. Our interest then centers round the efforts of its central figure to unravel this riddle, as by tracking down the identity of the person responsible for the crime.[26]

There are a few unique elements in the mystery plot structure that I will now test against the three focal works. First, according to Booker, "the finger of suspicion is initially pointed at someone who is innocent, until the detective eventually reveals the true culprit."[27] Because Booker made this statement, I inserted the finger being pointed to an innocent man as a plot element in the second movement in Figure 27. All three works involve more than one potential suspect. In *Study in Scarlet*, the brother of the girl Drebber assaulted and Drebber's traveling companion are suspected before the actual murderer is found. In *Mysterious Affair*, while Alfred, the killer, is suspected first, this suspicion was based on false evidence, which Poirot rightly ignored, and later suspicion points to other characters, including John and Lawrence.

5. Mystery and Detective 167

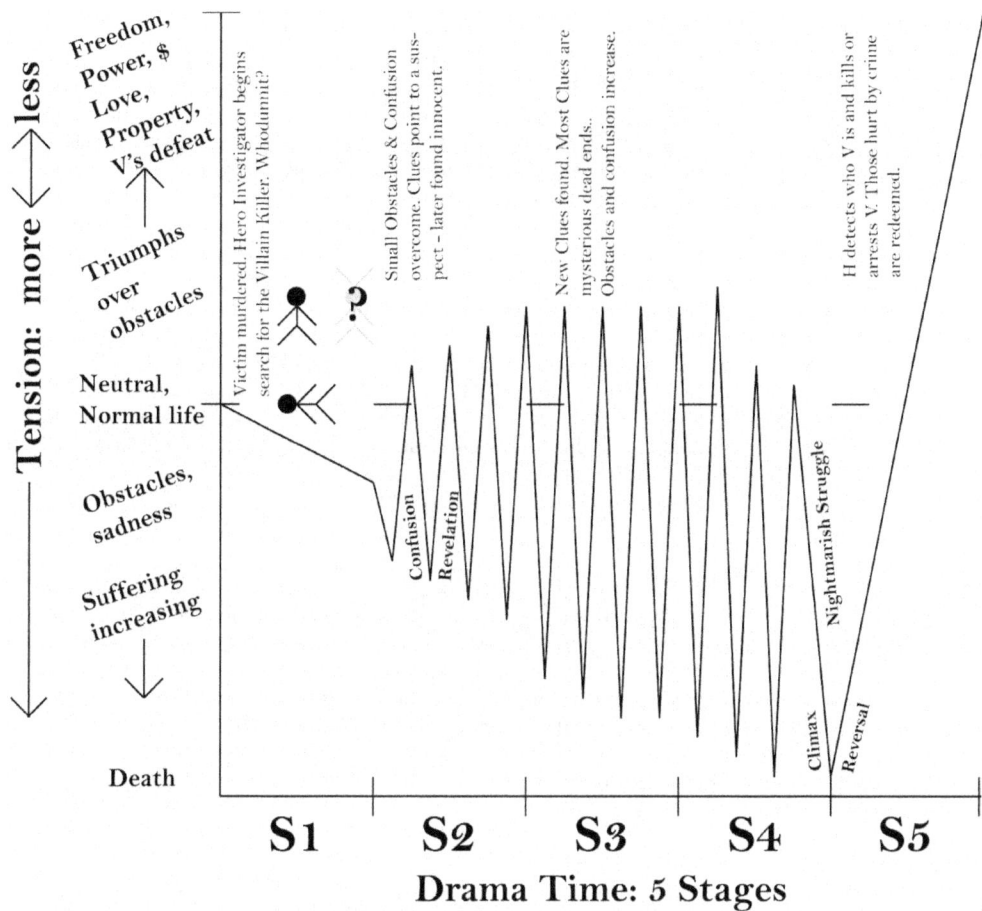

Figure 26. Mystery Plot Diagram.

In *The Troubled Man*, Sten, Hakan's wife and other friends and enemies are considered as potential Russian spies and murderers before Hakan is finally (and surprisingly) revealed as the American spy. These realizations do indeed typically happen in the second movement, though while Holmes has his suspicions, he does not point to a clear suspect until the end; the suspicions in both Conan Doyle's and Christie's works are made by the police, while the detective typically refrains from naming the murderer until he or she is certain they've got their man.

The theory goes that in modern mysteries the reader does not know "whodunit" until the end. The uncertainty of whodunit is the major cause of tension and suspense across the plot.[28] While stronger suggestive clues are offered to determine whodunit in the first pages of Christine's novel than in the other two works, in all three the solution to the murder is presented in the last movement. The trouble with *Mysterious Affair* is that Christie's early revelations detract from the reader's ability to feel a sense of suspense. And in *The Troubled Man*, Wallander's deep depression and lethargy mean that Wallander is sleeping, driving, or trying to remember where he is for the bulk of the story, and as a result suspense and tension also suffer. Additionally, the fact that Mankell does not tie up loose ends in the end means that the readers who

Plot Movement	*A Study in Scarlet* Part 1 (Conan Doyle)	*Mysterious Affair at Styles* (Christie)	*Troubled Man* (Mankell)
S1: Murder Committed, Investigation Begins	Holmes and Watson meet and move into a flat together, W solves mystery of what H does, new case found, W convinces H to do it	Hastings narrates Mrs. Inglethorp's family history, Poirot is in Styles (funded for stay by I) and is called to investigate case of I's murder	Wallander is depressed and tired of his detecting job, he learns of Hakan's disappearance, travels to other jurisdiction to interrogate his wife
S2: Minor Obstacles, Clues Point to Innocent Man	H, W and detectives investigate the crime scene, body (Drebber) and the house, garden and road around it, and find some clues: poisoning, murderer's appearance/ trickiness	Poirot investigates details of the day of the murder and prior days through questioning, Alfred and John suspected in bad argument, document case & new will missing	W makes connections between case to the Swedish submarine crisis of the 1980s (Soviet espionage), but is suspended for leaving a loaded gun to a restaurant (Alzheimer's)
S3: Mid-Roller Coaster: More Confusion and Dead End Clues	H and W meet with constable that found body, who saw a drunk (murderer) at scene, returning for the ring; H reports it found and a man disguised as an old woman comes, but escapes H in a cab	A was away at time of murder and bought strychnine poison, but P stops arrest and proves he didn't buy it	H's wife found dead after her disappearance, W does a more thorough investigation: reads history, speaks with friends and enemies (traveling as far as America), including Sten Nordlander
S4: Steep Roller Coaster	G arrests a suspect, Alice Charpentier's brother, who tried to defend her violently when Drebber tried to kiss her; L found Stangerson's body (whom he suspected)	Police arrests J because he would get money under the will, and that he bought poison	W figures out H is alive and finds him on an island house, promises to keep secret, but then figures out that H is an American spy
S5: Detective Catches Villain, Resolution	H tests pills on terrier: one nothing, second poison; Wiggins has found guilty cabby, H has him bring Jeff Hope up, and arrests him as the guilty murderer (explanation offered in Part 2)	P solves case: A and his lover did it and tried to plant false evidence to later not be prosecuted due to double-jeopardy	W returns to island with S and they interrogate H, who confesses to being a spy, and that Americans killed wife to keep her quiet, W leaves, H and S shoot each other

Figure 27. Mystery Plot Table.

felt a little bit of suspense and attempted to figure out how the various "clues" were connected are disappointed and feel cheated of the guarantee made in detective fiction—that while it is formulaic, readers can expect that the mystery will be neatly tied up and explained in the end.

Another distinguishing characteristic of the mystery plot that should be (but occasionally is not) present in detective fiction "is that the hero—the detective or investigator—is in a peculiar way not directly involved in the central drama of the story. He or she stands outside it, as a kind of voyeur, only intervening, if at all, as a detached, superior *deus ex machine* to sort out what has happened."[29] Poirot knows Mrs. Inglethorp because she is helping to fund his stay in Styles, and while he is not staying in the house with the narrator, Hastings and Mrs. Inglethorp when the murder happens, he is not a stranger to the family. Similarly, Wallander begins investigating Hakan's disappearance because he had met him when Wallander's daughter introduced them, announcing her engagement to Hakan's son. In Christie's novel, Poirot is licensed to do detective work in a different country, Belgium. In the same way, Wallander is out of his jurisdiction (and even leaves Sweden a few times) when he investigates Hakan. The relationships the private detectives have with those who have been killed allow for melodramatic dialogues, in which they can express a personal interest in solving the case. However, while Wallander and Poirot are familiar with the victims, they do not know them closely, which allows for some uncertainty and mysterious speculation about the victim's character. While detached distance works for Conan Doyle, who spends the bulk of his story examining the scientific elements of detective work, this approach would not work as effectively for the more flighty and less logical Christie or Mankell.

Another assumption about all detective and mystery fiction is that the responsible killer (or thief) has to have a "motive" for the crime. The crime is never an accident. The crime is never committed by a madman who got high and has no idea why he ran in someplace and killed a bunch of random people. This theory holds mostly true for all three works. Conan Doyle gives Jefferson Hope the motive of committing two murders out of revenge for lost love. Christie gives the simple, modern motive for murder—that the younger man, Alfred, was dissatisfied with his older wife and wanted to get the money and unite fully with his lover, Evelyn. Probably the only glitch in this theory regarding "motive" is *The Troubled Man.* Mankell explains that the American Secret Service killed Hakan's wife to keep her quiet, but then it appears as if Sten and Hakan killed each other because of a blind mad rage, and not because of any logical or selfish motive. This lack of a clear, logical tying up of loose plot lines at the end leaves Sten and Hakan without a motive for murder, while it only theoretically blames the Secret Service for Hakan's wife's murder, without showing clear proof of this or the true motivation for such an extreme action.

The deviations from the standard formula above seem like weighty evidence for anti-formulaic trends, but they are only glitches or mistakes the authors made as they tried to follow the exact formula set up in the Sherlock Holmes mysteries. When several current best-selling mysteries are compared, they have significantly more similarities than divergences in their plot lines.

In a chapter called "Recipes for Mystery" Karen Hubert asks several questions and gives multiple writing assignments that most writers should think about either before or while writing a mystery novel. Here is a list of some of her key writing prompts, ideas, questions and suggestions: 1. "Make a list of possible crimes." 2. "How do you hire a good detective?" 3. "What does a detective's office look like?" 4. "What does a detective look like?" 5. "Imagine a room ... something just doesn't seem right to you." 6. "An object has been stolen or defaced...." 7. "Write an interior monologue of the victim before, during and after the crime." 8. "You are a witness reviewing a police lineup." 9. "You committed the crime! Now write your confession." 10. "Describe the detective from the viewpoint of his sidekick and his nemesis." 11. "Prepare a list of characters [with] personality traits [including] routine upon waking, favorite foods, daily schedule, quirks and eccentricities, physical description, temperament, weaknesses, etc." 12. "Write a biography of a victim." 13. "You are on trial for your life...."[30] While these can be prompts for short writing assignments in creative writing classes, the answers to all of these should also be included in any standard formulaic mystery novel.

Mysterious Characters

While Booker is right in most of his plot calculations, his conclusions should not be taken as requirements within each of these genres. Another example for how Booker's conclusion about mysteries can have variations is that he thought that the most essential character in a mystery is the "calmly confident, all-seeing detective who has worked out how the crime was committed long before anyone else in the story."[31] All three detectives in the analyzed works do figure out how the crime was accomplished before the reader, and Wallander does not even explain before the end some of what he has understood. But some objections can be made to the idea that Wallander is "calm" or "all-seeing." He is certainly confident, like Holmes and Poirot. However, Wallander is constantly panicking as he starts to lose his mind to Alzheimer's, and he also has fits, throwing objects at co-workers. In addition, Wallander is not "all-seeing" and ultimately cannot tie all the ends together. Between the recent popular television show, *Monk,* and Wallander, eccentric and panicky fictional detectives are currently fashionable. Perhaps Booker spoke before these characters became popular and maybe in a few decades the new standard detective type will be blind and illiterate, and will not be able to solve the crime in the end, while the readers will be shouting the solution at the book.

Hubert, another generic critic, came closer to summarizing the standard detective character type: "Crime solvers are quirky, eccentric, always individualistic. We love them for being down and out, or glitteringly rich and snobbish, even if we hate the same types in all other genres. Nick Charles (of *The Thin Man*) was a socialite-alcoholic, Harriet Vane was a precursor of the women's rights movement.... But all have the ability to ferret out discordant facts and observations and deduce from them the truth *as it really happened.*"[32] The fact that in mysteries the protagonist is formulaically "ugly" can be explained as a major "flaw," which might be present in the other genres, but is exaggerated here because the mystery plot line is driven by the challenges that the detective has to overcome in order to solve the mystery. If the detective or protagonist does not have major problems of character that might stand in his or her way, he or she would solve the mystery too quickly and there would not be enough material for a novel. For example, one of the sharpest detectives in the genre's history, Sherlock Holmes, solved his cases in the span of multiple short stories and only four novellas—never a lengthy novel. Holmes looks around, takes in all of the clues, and just needs to do a bit more digging, perhaps a couple of visits to some witnesses or mysterious places, and he has his man and the motive and is hearing a confession or summarizing the case to Watson. Still, even Holmes has problems: he uses cocaine and he is extremely snobbish. If readers temporarily put themselves in place of the victim and their family, they are likely to want a detective who will help solve the case and bring justice into the world of the novel.

In a romance suspense comes from the attraction between the couple, so beauty is essential for us to trust in the character's ability to attract the designed mate. It is very unusual and perhaps impossible for a detective to fall in love with and enter a stable and happy relationship with an ideal mate. The detective has to be suspicious of everybody he meets, as they might be suspects in the case. The detective is also extremely observant and notices flaws and problems in others with uncomfortable closeness, which typically stops him from turning a blind eye to the problems of char-

Character Types	*A Study in Scarlet* Part 1 (Conan Doyle)	*Mysterious Affair at Styles* (Christie)	*Troubled Man* (Mankell)
Hero	Sherlock Holmes (highly educated, eccentric, tall)	Monsieur Hercule Poirot (Belgian, "mad," short)	Kurt Wallander (police inspector, diabetes, Alzheimer's)
Villain	Jefferson Hope (American, revenge over love)	Alfred Inglethorp and Evelyn Howard (I's companion and A's lover)	Håkan von Enke (top Swedish naval officer, spy for US), Sten Nordlander
Sidekick(s)/ Partner	Dr. Watson/ narrator (invalid from war), detectives Gregson and Lestrade, and founder constable, Wiggins and street urchins	Hastings/ narrator (invalid from war)	Linda Wallander (police officer, daughter, married with child to Enke's businessman son), Latvian Baiba (old lover, re-appears), Jussi (barking dog)
Killed Victim(s)	Enoch Drebber and Joseph Stangerson (both visitors from America)	Mrs. Inglethorp (wealthy, 70s, remarried)	Enke's wife, Hakan von Enke, Olof Palme (Swedish prime minister assassinated), Sten Nordlander (friend)
Suspects	Alice Charpentier's brother, Joseph Stangerson, Jefferson Hope	Alfred (I's husband, 50s), John (and his wife, Mary) and Lawrence Cavendish (stepsons), Evelyn	Sten Nordlander, Håkan von Enke and wife, other friends and spying governments

Figure 28. Mystery Characters Table.

acter in the individuals he would otherwise potentially date or marry. Most detectives are loners, and while they might have sidekicks, they do not seek out love or romance amid a mystery. The mystery itself has to engulf all of their (and the reader's) attention.

The title of the hero depends in part on the subgenre we are reading. A detective novel might focus on a formal police detective, while a mystery can be solved by a relative or another interested party. In general, within the larger umbrella of all types of mysteries, the crime solvers do not have to be police officer detectives. They can also be a "private citizen, curious neighbor or relative. Their motive for taking on the case may be personal interest, love, familial responsibility, curiosity, money or sentiment."[33] Once again, Hubert is more on the mark here than Booker, as the actual character descriptions for these three stories show that frequently the investigators are relatives or friends of the victims, and not fully detached observers.

All mysteries have to have at least one witness to the crime or some of the events or facts surrounding the crime. The "witnesses are accidental or purposeful observers who have seen a crime or a very suspicious occurrence. Very rarely does a witness see the crime as it happened. More often she sees or hears part of it."[34] Conan Doyle introduces as a witness the constable who saw the murderer when he returned to the scene of the crime for the ring that he had lost. In other words, the constable only saw a small part of the crime, not even realizing that he saw the murderer. Christie allows several people to be in the same house with the victim at the time of the murder, and as a result John, his wife, and his brother all observe some details that help in the investigation, but none of them actually saw how the poison could have been administered or know who could have done it. This pattern is once again somewhat broken in Mankell's novel, as Hakan's wife is killed on an abandoned road without being seen by anyone. And even Hakan's naval friend does not have any suspicion that he might be an American spy, leading to the two killing each other in the end. The lack of witnesses here stretches out the investigation and lengthens the novel, but it also leaves an open ending to the story. From a different perspective, Wallander is himself a witness to the shoot-out between Hakan and Sten, but no new detective comes along to interrogate him and solve this mystery for the public.

The second essential character-type in a mystery is the suspects, "those seemingly guilty characters any one of whom had motive and opportunity enough to commit the crime. Some suspects seem more obviously guilty than others, but there is no way of identifying the real culprit from outward appearance alone. A character becomes a suspect because she is found near or at the scene of the crime, or because she has no alibi at the time the crime was committed. But, most important, she must have a motive."[35] In Conan Doyle's plot, detectives suspect Alice Charpentier's vengeful brother and Joseph Stangerson before settling on the real criminal, Jefferson Hope. In *Mysterious Affair*, the police suspect Alfred based on initial false evidence, and then John and Lawrence before returning back to Alfred as the guilty villain. Wallander interrogates over a dozen friends and other potential suspects before finally reaching a conclusion and hearing Hakan's confession. Detectives typically spend most of the novel looking for who had a motive to kill the victim because it would be too easy if forensic evidence or evidence from easily accessible witnesses solved the case.

To return to Hakan's confession, in general, the criminal's confession is typically essential at the end because the detective has found the right motive and has guessed who must have done it, but he might not yet know exactly how, or the intricate details as to why. Jefferson Hope explains the history that led him to commit the murders in the entire second half of *A Study in Scarlet*. The villain of *Mysterious Affair* confesses in a letter he thought he had destroyed, which. Poirot reads out to the gathered family and friends:

> *Dearest Evelyn:*
> You will be anxious at hearing nothing. It is all right—only it will be to-night instead of last night. You understand. There's a good time coming once the old woman is dead and out of the way. No one can possibly bring home the crime to me. That idea of yours about the bromides was a stroke of genius! But we must be very circumspect. A false step—[36]

The letter clearly indicates the writer's intent to kill Mrs. Inglethorp and Alfred seals himself as the author and key murderer when he jumps out and tries to tackle Poirot moments after he finishes reading. In the third story, no resolution at all would be possible without Hakan von Enke's final confession in front of Wallander and Sten Nordlander. If Hakan did not confirm Wallander's vague and unproven suspicions, the novel would have no solution to the mystery.

When done correctly, "motive" is a "case history," or "a study in human behavior," that reveals the criminal's "secret self," which had something in it that served as a drive to commit the crime. Motive should be something that can be simplified into an emotion or a basic need, but can also be expanded into a complex backstory: "Motives may include revenge, jealousy, lust, greed, altruism, fear of blackmail, fear of exposure of one's past, abnormality."[37] The villain's motive in *Study* is revenge for love, in *Affair* it is greed and lust, and in *The Troubled Man* it is a barely explained political urge to spy.

It is amazing how many formulaic rules *The Troubled Man* breaks without actually becoming anti-formulaic. Among other oddities, its narrator occasionally switches from the standard third-person to a sudden first-person voice for a sentence or more, typically a few lines out of a paragraph written in third person. William Nolan warns that, "unless you are after a special shock effect, never switch viewpoints within a scene. To have the narrative viewpoint change in the middle of ongoing sequence is very jarring to the reader."[38] The two classical detective stories are both told in the first-person by the sidekick of the detective. The use of mixed voices and of the first person voice is unusual across the majority of other formulaic, modern mysteries.

Mysterious Settings

Most detectives, from Dupin to Holmes to Poirot, live in apartments. Wallander's move into a house on the beach breaks this pattern of the middle-class working detective. On the other hand, unlike the others on this list, Wallander is an official detective with the police department and has had a very long career in law enforcement, so it would have been highly unrealistic if he did not buy a house before he retired. In addition, the comparative salaries of police officers are higher today than they were in the nineteenth or early twentieth centuries. Dupin, Holmes and Poirot also live with others, and frequently with or near the sidekick, which allows them to talk with the sidekick constantly throughout the novel.

Setting Type	*A Study in Scarlet* Part 1 (Conan Doyle)	*Mysterious Affair at Styles* (Christie)	*Troubled Man* (Mankell)
Hero's Home	221 Baker Street, London, England – a flat for 2 with a spacious living room	Shares house in Styles with other Belgians, offered to him by Mrs. Inglethorp	Apartment on Mary Street in Ystad, then moves into isolated house near the ocean
Mysterious Setting	Uninhabited suburban manor	Isolated mansion in Styles	Isolated island house where Hakan hid
Time	1881	Present	Present
Scene of the Crime	Uninhabited suburban manor, Hotel	Country manor	Forest near highway, isolated island house
Mysterious World	London, England	Styles Court, England	Swedish, American, other towns/cities

Figure 29. Mystery Settings Table.

The common element between the scenes of the crime is that all three are isolated and far from city centers. Isolation and loneliness are key elements in creating death threat suspense as the detectives search through these gothic locations. All three locations are also stand-alone houses or abandoned units that are physically separated from any other buildings. Although the second victim in *A Study in Scarlet* is killed in a hotel, the killer is caught soon afterwards, for he is seen exiting the hotel and otherwise acts sloppier in this more public location than he did in the isolated house for the first murder. A murder in an apartment building allows for too many possible suspects, and too many characters that need to be interrogated.

The time setting for all of these works is the present, though *A Study in Scarlet* looks back around six years prior to its publication. For some reason, there are once again two works set and written in England, and a third foreign work, though this one is not by an American, but rather by a Swiss citizen who manages to visit America in the course of the plot. The pattern continues to be that English authors dominated the world's best-seller lists from 1814 to the present day.

Best-Selling Writers in Mysteries from Conan Doyle to Mankell

Conan Doyle, Christie and Mankell had unique backgrounds, and studying their biographies, as well as their writing methods, will help to explain the different mysteries that they created.

ARTHUR CONAN DOYLE
(1859–1930; FIRST NOVEL, A STUDY IN SCARLET, 1887)

Arthur Conan Doyle's Sherlock Holmes books and a variety of other novels and short stories made him one of the top best-selling authors in the period between 1900 and 1918, and they are still selling well in their original print format, not to motion as adaptations into film, television and various other mediums. The best-known novel from the Sherlock Holmes series is *The Hound of the Baskervilles* (1902). Conan Doyle was a doctor who wrote fiction when he was not busy with patients. He was born in Edinburgh into a family of respected artists, and he corresponded with other great Edinburgh writers, including Robert Louis Stevenson (*Treasure Island, Kidnapped*), and even borrowed some elements from Stevenson's stories. Conan Doyle's family was staunchly Tory, and rebels. For example, "His grandfather was the highly talented artist HB, or John Conan Doyle, whose political lampoons graced the Regency."[39] Political fiction and art were thus a family tradition for the Conan Doyles.

Figure 30. "Conan Doyle" (George Grantham Bain Collection: Library of Congress Prints and Photographs Division, Washington, D.C.; Bain News Service, 27 January 1913).

Arthur Conan Doyle changed focus from national politics to the criminal deeds and trials of the upper class, shaping the new genre of detective fiction. Several earlier authors had started moving toward detective stories, but in varied directions. For example, Edgar Allan Poe wrote gothic stories about several murders, some of which were solved by the police, but the focus was on studying the nature of the criminal mind and its motivations, rather than on solving a mystery. After Sherlock Holmes, numerous mimics began duplicating Conan Doyle's formula until it became the detective genre due to the abundance of similar works. There are many parallels between Conan Doyle and even his most critically respected followers, including Agatha Christie. "Enthusiasts talk of 'Sherlockiana' to describe the vast literature, both serious and ephemeral, that has come into being" from borrowings from the Holmes stories.[40]

Conan Doyle deliberately returned to the golden age of detective fiction for his inspiration, rather than using more contemporary examples. For Conan Doyle, Holmes was "a new and unique hero figure, a scientific detective who would succeed as a result of his exceptional skills,"[41] rather than because of a mistake on the criminal's part or an accident. The scientific skill of detection heightened the drama above the cheap adventure thrill of formulaic (and obvious) police inspection stories; even the name of the first successful Holmes story sounds scientific, *A Study in Scarlet* (1887), as if it is a part of a laboratory experiment, which in part reflected Conan Doyle's medical background. However, while Conan Doyle's creation was "unique," it did follow many of the generic elements that Poe set up half a century earlier. Holmes' detective techniques mimic Poe's, including Holmes' ability to follow footsteps, determining the "significance of dust ... lifted almost verbatim from Gaboriau." Still, the key similarity in the detective character types is that "both Dupin and Holmes were outsiders, both were prone to periods of moody reverie, both were accompanied in their investigations by pliant companions courageous in dangerous situations, both had a low opinion of their official police colleagues and both employed newspaper advertisements to trap their quarries."[42] Conan Doyle also borrowed plot points such as the "code" left by the notorious pirate Captain Kidd that had to be deciphered in Poe's "The Gold Bug" (1843) "on the basis that 'e' is the most commonly used letter in the English language," which was also utilized in Conan Doyle's "The Adventure of the Dancing Men."[43]

These detective stories were exercises for Conan Doyle in his attempts to be published, and he tried to turn to the more respected (at the time) genre of the "historical novel" after the success of *A Study in Scarlet,* publishing *Micah Clarke* in 1889, taking two years to complete this complex work. *Micah Clarke* was part of a curious phenomenon from across the nineteenth century of rebellion genre novels being published by British literary giants, and especially classical writers from Scotland. For example, Conan Doyle might have been prompted to write *Micah Clarke* by the successful release of Robert Louis Stevenson's 1886 *Kidnapped,* which looked back to the eighteenth-century Jacobite rebellions, a topic shared by *Waverley* (1814) from Sir Walter Scott and a long list of other novels that depicted historical rebellions. *Micah Clarke* was based on the Monmouth Rebellion from around 1685; this rebellion laid the roots for the tension between Scotland and England and the later Jacobite rebellions. While Scott, Dickens and Stevenson made a lot of money from their dramatic historical rebellion novels, Conan Doyle's attempt was not successful (in fact, it was only published when he offered to forgo payment). This failure refocused his career away from history and into detective fiction, to the delight of Sherlock Holmes admirers.

The Sherlock Holmes venture really took off in 1889–1990, when Joseph Marshall Stoddart came on the heels of *A Study in Scarlet* being popularized in pirated form in the United States to create a British edition for his *Lippincott's Magazine*. He chose to publish in his new magazine Oscar Wilde's *The Picture of Dorian Gray* and Conan Doyle's second Sherlock Holmes mystery novella, *The Sign of the Four,* both of which were widely reviewed and read and eventually raised both authors to a canonical status in British literature.

By 1891, Conan Doyle started to make a small fortune from the Sherlock Holmes venture, quit his medical practice and moved from the center of London to a more isolated country estate in South Norwood. In this setting, Conan Doyle returned to historical romances with *The Refugees: A Tale of Two Continents,* a work clearly influenced both by Alexandre Dumas' novel on a similar theme and by Charles Dickens' revolutionary *A Tale of Two Cities.* A year later, Conan Doyle began a Napoleonic-era historical novel, *The Great Shadow.* Conan Doyle worked under the continued assumption that these historical novels would establish him as a literary figure, while his Sherlock Holmes stories were exercises he did solely for money and to expand his popularity. Conan Doyle even attempted to sabotage the publication of 12 Holmes stories by asking Greenhough Smith for an enormous amount for them, £1,000, but Smith saw gold in Sherlock Holmes and agreed to these terms.

Because Conan Doyle had a financially oriented view of his Sherlock Holmes stories, he wrote them in a hackneyed style, unlike the meticulous research and editing he invested in his historical novels. Conan Doyle never spent "more than a week to complete a Sherlock Holmes story.... His technique was to map out the problem and its solution, draw up a rough outline and sketch in the characters before sitting down to write the finished story." This technique is shared by some of the formulaic speed of the romance writers twentieth century, including Heyer and Cartland, and reflects the new trend toward formulaic writing techniques. The concept of formulaic or genre-specific writing was very new in 1891, and a part of Conan Doyle's contribution is not only the establishment of a formulaic detective story but also his popularizing of professional formulaic writing itself.

> It was his habit to write from breakfast until lunch every morning, then from five to about eight o'clock in the evening, usually averaging 3,000 words a day—a prodigious output any writer would envy. Many of his ideas were dreamed up in the afternoons, walking or cycling with Touie, or playing tennis or cricket. Once he finished a story he had no further interest in it. As he would explain in a letter to G. K. Chesterton, his work might be improved by editing, but not by him. He had given all in his first effort and any further tinkering would be "gratuitous and a waste of time."

In contrast to these writing habits, Charles Dickens ran several literary magazines and had a busy lecture series in parallel with his writing. Sir Walter Scott worked as a judge in Scotland throughout the peak of his literary career. Both of these literary giants had to keep their day jobs because writing was not yet professionalized and could not generate enough money to support their families. But within a few years, Conan Doyle made a large enough income from writing even short stories to abandon medicine, and to write quickly, but at his leisure. Writing was further enhanced in Conan Doyle's literary peak by the introduction of the typewriter, but Conan Doyle did not use it, "writing by pen in a neat legible script, with few corrections."

Conan Doyle also kept an "annotated" "Ideas Book," where he wrote ideas in the format of a sentence-long plot summary, followed by a note of whether he already used the idea or planned to use it, or no such note (if he had not used it yet). One example of this was as follows: "The old nun who in her extreme old age sees the man for whose sake she entered the convent. (Used)." Beginning with a short plot summary, and subsequently building a more complex plot with character studies, and then just writing the story is a technique that has been very popular with professional writers across this past century. And as with most examples of this formulaic writing approach, Conan Doyle left numerous inconsistencies and errors in his Sherlock Holmes stories because he failed to reread or edit them after he knocked each of them off in under a week. Conan Doyle's biographer, Russell Miller, has found and listed several of the most noticeable inconsistencies: (1) Holmes puts on a disguise in minutes to the point of being unrecognizable by his partner, Watson; (2) in *A Study in Scarlet* Watson has a "bull pup," but this animal is never seen again; (3) John Watson's wife calls him James in "The Man With the Twisted Lip"; (4) Holmes' habits change across the stories, from him always "rising early" to him rising "usually very late in the mornings"; (5) Holmes' colleague at Scotland Yard, Inspector Lestrade, "transmutes" from being "rat-faced" to being a "wiry bulldog"; (6) Holmes is reincarnated in Tibet in "The Adventure of Wisteria Lodge" when he is supposed to be "dead"; and (7) Conan Doyle "made" a railway line that did not exist in the place he has it in his story. One of these glitches is particularly telling and giggle-inspiring: "In 'The Adventure of the Speckled Band'—Conan Doyle's favourite Sherlock Holmes story—a 'swamp adder ... the deadliest snake in India,' trained by bowls of milk and recalled by a whistle, slithers down a bell pull, kills a sleeping woman and returns to its master by climbing up the bell pull and entering the adjoining room through a ventilator. There is no such reptile as a 'swamp adder,' there are no adders in India, snakes do not like milk, are completely deaf, and no snake could climb a bell pull."[44] While these details show how unrealistic the components of a Sherlock Holmes mystery are, the intricate details still are incredibly unique, imaginative and innovative, and they are told with such precision that an average reader is likely to speed through them without noticing the inconsistencies (unless they are an expert in Indian wildlife). However, some literary critics still place Conan Doyle outside of the top literary canons because these inconsistencies are too hack-like and beneath the standards necessary to merit an outstanding literary achievement.

Conan Doyle had a lot in common with classical authors from the United Kingdom's nineteenth century. Similar to Sir Walter Scott and Charles Dickens, he not only published his stories but also started publishing-related businesses, including opening the Psychic Bookshop (with a small museum of spiritual artifacts in the basement and a subscription library) at 2 Victoria Street, as well as the Psychic Press in London in 1925. Conan Doyle was compelled to start these ventures, like Scott and Dickens, not for the money but for political, spiritual and literary reasons. While modern writers like Stephen King are happy to sell their laundry lists, nineteenth-century authors felt a need to write and publish great literature, even if they had to fund these ventures with their income from other jobs. Conan Doyle's Psychic Press was created to "churn out much of his spiritualist writings as mainstream publishers were showing less and less interest despite his fame as a writer."[45] Instead of capitalizing further on Sherlock Holmes or writing similar formulaic detective stories, Conan Doyle had killed Holmes prior to 1925. While Scott was concerned with the Scottish Insurrection and Dickens pondered the living conditions of the poor, Conan Doyle was keenly involved in the spiritualist movement that was blooming during this period in London. His biographer explains, "It was Conan Doyle's hope that he would recoup the £1,500 annual running costs from sales, but the venture never made money. He was unconcerned and would tell friends that while other successful writers enjoyed yachts and racehorses, he chose to have a psychic bookshop. Conan Doyle estimated that, including the profits from his spiritualist books and lecture tours, he probably contributed around £250,000—a phenomenal sum now equivalent to many millions—to the movement."[46] This expense shows the very different priorities that writers had a century ago in Britain; in contrast to modern-day American anti-intellectualism, authors back then had "fun" with and enjoyed intellectual literary pursuits. Of course, Conan Doyle's quest was not as "honorable" as those of Scott and Dickens, as many of his contemporary critics questioned the point of having séances with dead authors, including Charles Dickens himself and Joseph Conrad, during which both of these authors asked Conan Doyle to complete their last, unfinished novels. His publication of *The History of Spiritualism* with his own Psychic Press was extremely quixotic and showed passion for a criticized cause, instead of an attempt to capitalize on the spiritualist movement. Conan Doyle's genuine concern for his chosen causes is evident from the fact that, among his other political activities, back in 1908 he had assisted the Congo Reform Association when even Joseph Conrad, who "witnessed the genocide at first hand as the captain of a Congo steamer and who had used the experience in his novella, *The Heart of Darkness*," had refused to help the African cause.[47]

The Structure of Conan Doyle's Mysteries

There are five key Sherlock Holmes stories that laid the foundations for Arthur Conan Doyle's future detective fiction, and which are the most frequently cited stories by critics and mimicking authors from the genre. Three of these works are also the longest Holmes stories Conan Doyle wrote, as most of his Holmes pieces are short stories; these significant long works are *A Study in Scarlet* (1887), *The Sign of the Four* (1890)[48] and *The Hound of the Baskervilles* (1901).[49] I am not looking at the fourth complete novel, *The Valley of Fear* (1915), as it is less critically commented on and was written during Conan Doyle's "spiritualism" phase, rather than at the peak of his powers. The key short stories I reviewed are "A Scandal in Bohemia" (1891)[50] and "The Adventure of the Dancing Men" (1903).[51] I began by reading a 1915 edition of *A Study in Scarlet* and *The Sign of the Four*,[52] but there were too many pages missing from this ancient book, including most of the title page, and it smelled like it had been through a dust storm. In addition, I started to feel like I was desecrating what was in fact a first edition of these novels collected under a single cover as I wrote in the margins with a pencil. Thus, I looked at the electronic Project Gutenberg eBook editions of these works instead.

It is clear from the first of these works, *A Study in Scarlet*, that Conan Doyle was not consciously attempting to invent the detective mystery genre. There are more similarities between the plot structure of this work and Charles Dickens' *Bleak House* and *Barnaby Rudge* than even with Poe's tales (which Conan Doyle acknowledged he consciously mimicked in their style and formula). *A Study in Scarlet* is split into two parts; the first of these is the story of how Sherlock Holmes and Dr. Watson meet and how they catch the perpetrator of two horrible crimes, and the second part is the story of why the perpetrator traveled all the way to London to find these two men and kill them. The second part is written in a very different style and follows a realistic novel plot structure, in which life in a western American desert is described, with its various hardships, and close character studies are drawn of the principal actors. Similarly, half of Dickens' *Barnaby Rudge* depicts the Gordon Riots and the other half a murder mystery. Mixing plot lines from different types of stories created "thicker" plots in the nineteenth century and was a common practice in literary novels. If writers used a single plot line or kept reusing the same plot line across several stories, they would have been accused of the sins of mimicry, unoriginality, and possibly plagiarism. In contrast, today there might not be any top publishers willing to publish anything that does not follow a set generic formula. Either the editor or Conan Doyle himself must have realized after the unsuccessful release of *A Study in Scarlet* that the first part with the murder mystery was more engaging and a more complete plot line, for Conan Doyle only wrote mystery plots for the remainder of his Holmes stories,

Figure 31. "The suicide, a poorly dressed laborer, had staggered around in a circle nearly ten feet in diameter after gashing his own throat," George Hand Wright (Cabinet of American Illustration: Library of Congress Prints and Photographs Division, Washington, D.C., "Is Sir Oliver Lodge Right?" by Arthur Conan Doyle, *Metropolitan Magazine*, 47:20, Sept. 1917).

without mixing them with other genres. Over the decades he polished the detective mystery genre and became known as its key founder, despite many writers making major contributions in this field before and after him.

In addition to having a double-plot structure, *A Study in Scarlet* also has a denser introduction than the rest of the Holmes stories because it offers Dr. Watson's detailed biographical background, and the details of how Dr. Watson and Sherlock Holmes met and started living and working together. The remaining Holmes stories have a very quick pace from the start because they do not have to fill in all of this information, and instead focus on the details associated with each new mystery. In the nineteenth century it would have been unthinkable for a writer to begin a novel without giving sufficient biographical detail to make the readers feel as if they know the main heroic characters, whereas most modern generic stories fail to give sufficient biographical background even in the first book in a series because a biography is viewed as a distraction from the main narrative. In contrast to this view, the biography that Dr. Watson relates is one that is highly engaging. He explains that he finished his Doctor of Medicine degree at the University of London in 1878, then studied to become an army surgeon and subsequently joined the Afghan war, where he was hit in the "shoulder"; he later caught "enteric fever" and was allowed to return to England for "nine months" to recuperate his health. In London, he first tried staying at an expensive hotel, but when money ran out a friend of his, Stamford, introduced him to somebody to share a flat with to lower their living costs. This man is Mr. Sherlock Holmes, who is doing research at the laboratories in the University of London, where Dr. Watson previously studied, and who, it turns out, is working as a private investigator, instead of studying to complete a medical degree. All of this information might not make these two heroes "sympathetic," but it does give them multiple dimensions through which the reader can understand the motivations behind their actions and behaviors. Mr. Holmes is self-important and rude, or, in Stamford's words, "cold-blooded" and likely to test the "latest vegetable alkaloid" on one of his friends or even himself. Later in the story, Holmes does test a poison on a dying dog and the group watches it expire, so these criticisms are well founded. At the same time, Dr. Watson was not a good army doctor and struggles to keep up with Holmes' genius. These character traits do not inspire sympathy; the attraction of the Holmes stories is rather in the thick plots and unique adventures and character studies presented. In contrast, modern authors work to create "sympathy" for the heroes by making them pathetic or giving them sob-story biographies.

Suspense is the key ingredient that speeds *A Study in Scarlet* along. Suspense is created not only about the murders but also about the key heroic characters. When Stamford explains to Dr. Watson the personality of Sherlock Holmes, he expresses great hesitancy in advising that Dr. Watson should actually move in with him, at one point saying, "You proposed this arrangement, so you must not hold me responsible." To which Watson replies, "Is this fellow's temper so formidable, or what is it?" The reader is left wondering how horrible Holmes can be as a fellow flat-mate. This a form of suspense intended to interest readers in the heroic character studies the writer provides later in the story.

Another clue that *A Study in Scarlet* is anti-formulaic is that when Dr. Watson first meets Sherlock Holmes, he is engrossed in running a very precise scientific experiment that tests whether a stain is blood or another chemical. Holmes is perhaps more excited about this scientific discovery than he is when he later solves the murders, which is easy in comparison to a scientific breakthrough. There are certainly no modern mysteries that I can think of in which the detective has time to spend in the lab searching for new ways to solve crimes. Since Conan Doyle was a doctor by profession when he wrote these early stories, it is likely that he might have first conceived of writing a story on this topic because there was a scientific element involved, rather than simply because murder makes for an interesting tale. This background information is also crucial to the central plot of the story because Holmes explains that he specializes in the scientific study of all chemicals, with a particular focus on various deadly poisons, and it is in fact a poison that kills the first murdered man in the mystery. Making sure that all asides tie into the central plot is a key principle of classical nineteenth-century novel writing.

The interrogation dialogue technique is another unique feature of the Holmes stories. Even when Holmes and Watson discuss living together, they do it in the style of a "cross-examination," with each of the speakers firing questions at the other and replying by confessing their "worst" faults in order to foretell in advance if they would be a good match. (This is when Watson mentions the "bull pup" that later becomes an inconsistency because it's never seen again in the Holmes adventures.) Holmes here confesses his love for playing the violin, and later in the story he goes to a concert, so music is set up as one of Holmes' humanizing characteristics, which is both an occasional pleasure and harassment for Watson. Interrogative dialogues continue between Watson and Holmes across the stories. In *A Study in Scarlet* Watson's questions are aimed at determining what Holmes does for a living and what sort of a man Holmes is. Throughout all of the stories Watson is used as a mirror of admiration that explains to readers what is so fascinating about Sherlock Holmes' ability to deduce the solutions to mysteries. Without Watson, there would be no narrator, and nobody to build up the thrilling nature of Holmes' detective studies. And if Watson and Holmes didn't interrogate each other about the mysteries they are working on, the information would come at the readers more like the outcome in a criminal report than as a dynamic interaction between two investigators. There are no casual dialogues in Sherlock Holmes, or at least not in any scenes where Holmes and Watson are present; if one of these two is around, they are incapable of chatting casually and only ask and reply with significant questions and information.

Having mental and physical illnesses is a trait common to a lot of modern, eccentric, fictional detectives, including Monk and Wallander. Sherlock Holmes' character is at least in part at the roots of this trend. In the "Man with the Twisted Lip" adventure, Sherlock Holmes emerges out of an opium den, after several references to opium-smoking have been made. Holmes comments, "I suppose, Watson ... that you imagine that I have added opium-smoking to cocaine injections, and all the other little weaknesses on which you have favoured me with your medical views." Holmes does not answer this self-made query, which leaves the question of whether he has indeed added opium-smoking to his list of habits up in the air. In addition, Holmes clearly confesses in this statement to being guilty of making "cocaine injections." From the start, in *A Study in Scarlet*, Watson studies Holmes' character as if he is studying a mental patient, stressing that Holmes goes through periods of "energy" when he runs around solving crimes and performing experiments and periods of inactivity when he lies "upon the sofa in the sitting-room, hardly uttering a word or moving a muscle," which makes Watson suspect that Holmes is likely to be "addicted to the use of some narcotic." In this early story, Watson reports that Holmes' "temperance and cleanliness" forbid the idea that he is using drugs, but the later references clearly disprove this assumption. Thus, Holmes is a drug-using manic-depressive with a superiority complex and a long list of other symptoms that can be cataloged as mental illnesses (or the eccentricities of a brilliant hyperactive mind). Either way, creating mental and physical quirks in the heroic detectives is a key feature in modern detective novels that use the Sherlock Holmes formula for their inspiration.

Character descriptions in Sherlock Holmes stories have a complex pattern similar to those used by most of the other classical British nineteenth-century writers. There are a few possible patterns these descriptions take. If a character plays a significant part in the story, the description takes around a paragraph (such as Dr. Watson's description of Sherlock Holmes in Chapter II of *A Study in Scarlet*). It typically begins with a philosophical thought or an introductory sentence, such as "His very person and appearance were such as to strike the attention of the most casual observer." The rest of the paragraph then provides evidence to support this topic sentence. A full sentence might be spent on each of the key features, including "height," "eyes," "nose," "chin," and "hands." Instead of simply offering their dimensions, size and other basic characteristics, an attempt is made to explain not only what they look like but also what their appearance signifies. For example, "His eyes were sharp and piercing, save during those intervals of torpor." There is no mention of whether the eyes are brown or blue because most readers probably visualize Holmes as having dark hair and dark eyes. Instead, the description of the eyes explains how they interact with the people who are looking at them and show how they reflect Holmes' manic-depressive character. This description also acts as support for the statement that Holmes' character is striking. If, however, a character is merely one in a throng of other minor characters, their description typically comprises three to five words in the middle of a sentence. Thus, for example, when listing Holmes' "acquaintances," Watson describes them as "little sallow rat-faced, dark-eyed fellow," "young girl ... fashionably dressed," "grey-headed, seedy visitor, looking like a Jew pedlar," "a slip-shod elderly woman," "an old white-haired gentleman," and "a railway porter in his velveteen uniform." Instead of choosing this short route or the long character study, a typical formulaic modern novel might spend several sentences saying that a girl was wearing a long, blue skirt, a short, red shirt and the like, instead of simply saying that she was "fashionably dressed," when the specific details are insignificant to the plot or the story's meaning.

Aside from the physical descriptions, Conan Doyle's Holmes stories specialize in close studies of characters. The observation of character types, habits, abnormalities and the like is basically what Sherlock Holmes' detective profession asks of him. Dr. Watson tries to gather character details from his own observations and adds Holmes' insights to deduce the crimes they are investigating. Conan Doyle applies the same close investigative method to describing the detectives and supporting characters in the Holmes adventures. Making a topic sentence that summarizes a person and then offering evidence to support this point is a form of this type of investigative description. Another example is found in Chapter II of *A Study in Scarlet* when Watson makes a list of the subjects that Holmes knows and those that he is ignorant of as he is trying to determine what Holmes does for a living without rudely asking him directly:

1. Knowledge of Literature.—Nil.
2. Philosophy.—Nil.
3. Astronomy.—Nil.
4. Politics.—Feeble.
5. Botany.—Variable. Well up in belladonna, opium, and poisons generally. Knows nothing of practical gardening.
6. Geology.—Practical, but limited. Tells at a glance different soils from each other. After walks has shown me splashes upon his trousers, and told me by their color and consistency in what part of London he had received them.
7. Chemistry.—Profound.
8. Anatomy.—Accurate, but unsystematic.
9. Sensational Literature.—Immense. He appears to know every detail of every horror perpetrated in the century.
10. Plays the violin well.
11. Is an expert singlestick player, boxer, and swordsman.
12. Has a good practical knowledge of British law.

Here Conan Doyle is publishing a segment of the biographical notes he made when he was designing Holmes' character. In contrast to similar lists from the more modern Georgette Heyer (for example, "*Horatia Winwood*. A stammering heroine, of the naïve & incorrigible variety. 17 ..."[53]), Conan Doyle's character summary for Holmes stretches over a large portion of this first novel, and Conan Doyle considered all aspects of Holmes' education, knowledge, physical appearance and political views before putting him into the plot and having him act as a detective in these stories. Knowing what Holmes does not know was just as important for Conan Doyle because Watson typically helps Holmes out with these blind spots, and they are what makes having a sidekick indispensable for Holmes rather than an inconvenience.

Description of houses, rooms, nature and most of the other key elements in the Holmes stories is treated in the same way as the description of characters. Objects and places are studied closely and logically for practical clues to a specific committed crime, or they are examined to determine the character of those who live or have visited each of these specific places or used a given object. When several paragraphs are spent on describing the street, the front yard, the house and a specific room in "Number 3, Lauriston Gardens," in Chapter III of *A Study in Scarlet*, small details from this description are later used by Holmes to determine the identity of the killer and to visualize the steps the criminal and the victim took around the time of the murder. Readers are likely to read through these descriptions closely across the Holmes stories because they hold clues to the mystery that might help them to figure out who the murderer was. Of course, the telling clues are typically mixed with general descriptions to disguise them; for example, Watson mentions that the exterior of Number 3 was "very sloppy from the rain" during the night, and that there were "many marks of footsteps upon the wet clayey soil." These hints later indicate the time when the murderer and victim came in and out, as Sherlock finds imprints of a horse and tracks from a cab, and he identifies the footprints of the victim and murderer and the murderer's approximate size after studying these under a magnifying glass (an instrument that Conan Doyle is credited with inserting into the genre). Holmes deduces from the clues that the murderer "was more than six feet high, was in the prime of life, had small feet for his height, wore coarse, square-toed boots and smoked a Trichinopoly cigar. He came here with his victim in a four-wheeled cab, which was drawn by a horse with three old shoes and one new one on his off fore leg. It all probability the murderer had a florid face, and the finger-nails of his right hand were remarkably long." The initial descriptions are inadequate because frequently Watson does not see some of the details in the scene that Holmes notices, so Watson's first-person account of what he sees typically is not enough for the reader to find the murderer from the descriptions alone. Regardless, readers are drawn to reading descriptions closely if the writer imprints them with significance, a task at which most current formulaic writers fail.

A Study in Scarlet utilizes many genres to convey its points, including newspaper articles, letters, and scientific descriptions, as well as detective and realistic novel genres. Among these there is also a summary and discussion of a scholarly essay that Sherlock Holmes published in a "magazine" on March 4, which has the "ambitious title" of "The Book of Life." There is no equivalent academic theory of detection in any other popular detective or mystery story that I looked at, but this type of explanation for the theory and meaning behind the key character's technique was a standard element of classical nineteenth-century novels. This piece is a self-conscious assessment of Sherlock Holmes' fictional detection method by Dr. Watson, who is reading Holmes' essay: "The writer claimed by a momentary expression, a twitch of a muscle or a glance of an eye, to fathom a man's inmost thoughts." The article explains that the "'Science of Deduction and Analysis" is acquired by "patient study," and that to initially test one's ability at deduction and analysis, a trainee should attempt, "on meeting a fellow-mortal, learn at a glance to distinguish the history of the man, and the trade or profession to which he belongs.... By a man's finger nails, by his coat-sleeve, by his boot, by his trouser knees, by the callosities of his forefinger and thumb, by his expression, by his shirt cuffs—by each of these things a man's calling is plainly revealed." In classical literature, it has been a standard practice for the narrators to make deductions about characters that the hero comes in contact with by closely studying that new character's appearance and deducing what it suggests about his or her personality and profession. Here Conan Doyle is applying this "art" to an analytical method a detective can use to make judgments about the criminals he encounters. Watson expresses his realistic doubts, which are likely to prevent deductions similar to Holmes' in the real world, as, for example, a coal miner can put on a fancy suit, or a businessman can buy second-hand clothing to disguise his identity. Regardless of whether this method of deduction is "absurd," as Watson initially concludes, or potentially useful, as Holmes argues, the discussion of its techniques and elements allows readers to consciously evaluate it, instead of simply suspending their disbelief. Thus, there are elements in this story that can be of use to students of deduction and science, and the story acts as a teaching tool, as well as simply entertainment.

Dead bodies, human blood and other death-related elements are typically described in the gothic horror style in the Holmes mysteries. For example, in Chapter III of *A Study in Scarlet*, "On his rigid face there stood an expression of horror ... of hatred." Watson reports, "I have seen death in many forms [during the Afghan War, when he worked as an army doctor] but never has it appeared to me in a more fearsome aspect than in that dark grimy apartment." Watson cannot sleep, or at least not well, until this murder mystery has been solved because he is horrified by the image of this death. The revulsion and horror that the narrator expresses add a glum and tragic tint to the Holmes adventures, which was an appropriate portrayal of death in the nineteenth century. The Holmes stories are not purely analytical, but have an element of gothic horror in them to evoke more violent emotions in their readers. Thus, in Chapter IV, Holmes explains the term "a study in scarlet" by using "jargon" to say, "'There's the scarlet thread of murder running through the colourless skein of life, and our duty is to unravel it, and isolate it, and expose every inch of it." Murder is horrifying and it is the duty of honorable intellectuals like Watson and Holmes (and as a reflection the author himself, Arthur Conan Doyle) to study murderers and the ways in which they are discovered, not only in reality, but also in detective fiction. The drama of detection is intensified by the "scarlet thread" of horror that runs through the Holmes stories.

Chapters in Holmes mysteries frequently end with cliffhangers or with surprise conclusions that Holmes reaches after working through a portion of the case. For example, Chapter III in *A Study in Scarlet* ends with Holmes' deduction of exactly how the murderer looked, and his certainty that the victim was murdered with poison and that the word "Rache" written on the wall does not stand for "Rachel," as the police detectives concluded, but is a German word that means "revenge." Detectives Lestrade and Gregson are then left "open-mouthed" as Holmes exits. Chapter V ends with a young man disguised as an old woman managing to escape from Holmes, who followed him, out of a moving cab, and both Holmes and Watson not being able to fall asleep afterward, as they are trying to figure out who this young murderer's assistant might be. At the end of Chapter VI, we find out that there has been a new murder, this time of one of the suspects—the secretary, Mr. Joseph Stangerson, who was killed shortly before Detective Lestrade found him in his hotel room. At the end of Chapter VII, Mr. Jefferson Hope is led into Holmes and Watson's apartment by the street urchins to pick up bags for a cab fare, and Holmes suddenly announces that Hope is the "murderer of Enoch Drebber and of Joseph Stangerson"; a squabble results in Hope's successful capture, after which Holmes asks the two detectives and Watson if they have any questions about the mystery he just solved. Their questions are then answered in the second part of the novel, with a study of how Hope came to hate these two men and how he committed the murders. Some plot points and tension are typically resolved at the end of these chapters, and a new question or concern for suspense is raised to keep readers interested in reading the following chapter. The cliffhangers and twists are a part of Conan Doyle's technique of adding numerous levels to the plot, or, as Sherlock Holmes says in Chapter V and Chapter VII of *A Study in Scarlet*, "The plot thickens."

Holmes consciously only selects murders that are difficult to crack in order to challenge his intellect and to allow for enough plot twists to carry the story to the end without losing the readers' interest and excitement. If Holmes manages to trick the murderer or his accomplice to come to his house, the murderer then manages to escape in order to add a new twist to the plot. In contrast, in a modern mystery novel, like *Wallander*, throughout many more pages the crime appears to go unsolved primarily because of the detective's incompetence and lack of speedy investigation, and the plot stretches on, describing how the detective sleeps and how he eats breakfast, rather than focusing on the practical elements of detection or adding new plot elements. In most modern, formulaic mysteries, the plot is very thin.

AGATHA CHRISTIE/MARY WESTMACOTT (1890–1976; FIRST NOVEL, *THE MYSTERIOUS AFFAIR AT STYLES*, 1920)

While Conan Doyle developed one sticking character in Sherlock Holmes, Agatha Christie made two. The first is Hercule Poirot, who was born in her first novel, *The Mysterious Affair at Styles* (1920). The second is Miss Jane Marple, who came on the scene in *Murder at the Vicarage* (1930). Conan Doyle was still publishing Sherlock Holmes stories when Agatha Christie entered the genre. Female detective and mystery writers are uncommon to this day, as there is a gender divide between romance and detective novel writing. The other major best-selling female detective writers are Ruth Rendell, P. D. James, and Ellis Peters (the last two changed their names to more male-sounding ones). Ruth Rendell (1930–) is second after Christie as "the most famous British female crime writer,"[54] known for her psychological Inspector Wexford series. P. D. James, or Phyllis Dorothy James (1920–), is best known for the tragic and politically minded detective story called *Cover Her Face* (1962). Edith Pargeter, or Ellis Peters (1913–1995), is known for her medieval monk detective, Brother Cadfael, and her work mixes the detective and historical medieval romance genres.[55] All three gained fame in the 1960s and 1970s, reaching top sales ratings before 1999, so clearly their success was helped by the earlier strides made by Christie, and their popularity grew exponentially when a gap was left with Christie's death in 1976.

Thus, Agatha Christie has not had any significant competition for the title of Queen of Mystery. She has also outsold Conan Doyle and all other mystery male writers, as the *Guinness Book of World Records* puts her overall book sales at 4 billion copies, more than the 1 billion that the top romance writer, Barbara Cartland, achieved in her lifetime. Cartland might still catch up to Christie, though, as she only passed away in 2000, while Christie died in 1976 and sold more books after her death than during her lifetime. Overall, romance has a larger market share than mysteries, but Christie's wider appeal might be due to the fact that, as a woman, she managed to "combine the novel of manners (with a strong hint of women's romance) with the classic 'locked room' mystery."[56] Her novels do not follow the standard romance novel formula, relying primarily on the mystery formula. Christie even tried publishing six pure romance novels under the pseudonym Mary Westmacott, but these did not do nearly as well as her romantic mysteries.

In *The Mysterious Affair at Styles* characters are described in a minimalist style. The key hero of the novel, Poirot, is handled thus:

> Poirot was an extraordinary looking little man. He was hardly more than five feet, four inches, but carried himself with great dignity. His head was exactly the shape of an egg, and he always perched it a little on one side. His moustache was very stiff and military. The neatness of his attire was almost incredible. I believe a speck of dust would have caused him more pain than a bullet wound. Yet this quaint dandyfied little man who, I was sorry to see, now limped badly, had been in his time one of the most celebrated members of the Belgian police. As a detective, his flair had been extraordinary, and he had achieved triumphs by unraveling some of the most baffling cases of the day.[57]

In comparison, many chapters are spent describing Holmes' appearance when he is first introduced. Here the character portrait is completed in a single paragraph. The characteristics are those of an extreme cartoon rather than a multi-dimensional character.

An egg-headed dandy seems more like an alien time traveler from the nineteenth century than a retired detective from the Belgian police. But this is an interesting and somewhat detailed description when compared with others in the same book. For example, Mrs. Inglethorp is described as "a handsome white-haired old lady, with a somewhat masterful cast of features."[58] There is a repetition of "old" in both that word and "white-haired," thus leaving only "handsome" and "masterful" as the other two defining adjectives. Mrs. Inglethorp's young husband, the murderer, Alfred, is described with these words:

> I looked with some curiosity at "Alfred darling." He certainly struck a rather alien note. I did not wonder at John objecting to his beard. It was one of the longest and blackest I have ever seen. He wore gold-rimmed pince-nez, and had a curious impassivity of feature. It struck me that he might look natural on a stage, but was strangely out of place in real life. His voice was rather deep and unctuous. He placed a wooden hand in mine.[59]

This description is significant for the plot, as Mrs. Inglethorp calling a man in his fifties "Alfred darling" is suggested to inspire resentment in him, and becomes one of the motives for the later murder. In addition, since this is a character study, the fact that Alfred has a "wooden hand" (and as a result a stiff handshake) suggests that he is distant, cold, calculating, and therefore capable of a murder. Thus, these descriptions are not devoid of all meaning and plot significance, but they are weaker than the close character and location studies in Conan Doyle's mysteries.

It is not surprising that there is an echo of Conan Doyle's description method in the work of Christie. The formulaic parallels with Sherlock Holmes are stressed, rather than hidden, by both the narrator and the author. Hastings, the narrator, has a curiosity about detective work similar to that of Dr. Watson. When the Hastings is questioned about what, besides serving in the army, he is passionate about doing, he explains that he has always wanted to be a detective, to which the woman who is later found out to be one of the murderers, Miss Howard, asks if he wants to be "The real thing—Scotland Yard? Or Sherlock Holmes?" Hastings replies by explaining, like Sherlock Holmes before him, who said the same about Poe's Dupin in *A Study in Scarlet*, that he is better than this fictional predecessor in his method of detection:

> Oh, Sherlock Holmes by all means. But really, seriously, I am awfully drawn to it. I came across a man in Belgium once, a very famous detective, and he quite inflamed me. He was a marvelous little fellow. He used to say that all good detective work was a mere matter of method. My system is based on his—though of course I have progressed rather further. He was a funny little man, a great dandy, but wonderfully clever.[60]

The murderer then comments on the formulaic nature of "a good detective story.": "Lots of nonsense written, though. Criminal discovered in last chapter. Every one dumbfounded. Real crime—you'd know at once."

Indeed, *The Mysterious Affair* is definitely not as mysterious as Conan Doyle's Sherlock Holmes stories. For example, Conan Doyle does not reveal any of the background that might have motivated the killer until the long second half of *A Study in Scarlet*. By contrast, Christie explains with her background information that Alfred has a motive to kill his older wife for the money on the first couple of pages of the novel. This exchange suggests that this is intentional by the writer, perhaps because she is attempting to allow her readers the satisfaction of solving the mystery for themselves after the suspected man is convicted. A few other potential murderers are later suspected to cover up this track, but even Alfred's more surprising companion in the crime, Miss Howard, leads the line of questioning about detective work that leads another character to foreshadow the criminal technique she will later use. She explains that she would be able to spot the murderer, as a member of the family of the deceased, right away: "Mightn't be able to prove it to a pack of lawyers. But I'm certain I'd know. I'd feel it in my fingertips if he came near me." Because she assumes that the family would know that Alfred, the younger husband, did the deed, they decide to plant false evidence against themselves to get off despite the fact that everybody knows they did it. To this Hastings replies that violent crimes are typically committed by men, and in reply Mrs. Cavendish makes an objection that foreshadows how Mrs. Inglethorp will be killed a bit later in the story: "Not in a case of poisoning ... owing to the general ignorance of the more uncommon poisons among the medical profession, there were probably countless cases of poisoning quite unsuspected."[61] In fact, this foreshadowing might have also given the killers the idea of how they could disguise the poisoning in Mrs. Inglethorp's medicine, which had a small amount of inactive poison. There is so much foreshadowing and background information offered that suspense is diminished, and the reader is left with a minor curiosity.

The introduction to *The Mysterious Affair* is much less dense than the long biographies and character studies offered in Conan Doyle's *A Study in Scarlet*. The paragraphs are comparatively shorter and there are fewer syllables in words on average. This shortening of paragraphs and syllables is a trend that can be seen in popular fiction between 1880 and this work in 1920, and even further into 1973 and beyond. While literary fiction probably retained the same density or might have even become more complex, popular fiction was steadily watered down and diluted. Some key elements are present in the introductions of both mysteries, but all of them are choppier in *Affair*. Instead of beginning with a detailed biography, Hastings starts with a statement that the "affair" in question was a popular and curious case, then offers a sentence autobiography, and subsequently goes on to explain "the circumstances which led to my being connected with the affair." These circumstances are at first related through a dialogue with John Cavendish, in which Hastings finds out the news of Mrs. Inglethorp's marriage and decides to join her in Styles. In *A Study in Scarlet* background information is conveyed in narrative, and only essential conversations that create conflict in the story or explain intricate relationships between characters are offered in dialogue. In *Affair* little information is offered in narrative, and dialogue carries the story. Even action is negligent, as folks sit around resting in the garden. For unliterary readers, it is probably easier to read conversational dialogue that they are familiar with from their daily lives than condensed, long narrative paragraphs, so this style of writing steadily gained popularity.

Another divergence between the two works is that there are certainly no scientific experiments in Agatha Christie's books, as she was not a scientist; she rather focused on figuring out who bought or created the poison in *Affair*, instead of explaining in detail how it was made by a scientist (though this information is mentioned in passing). For example, Poirot finally solves the case with this semi-scientific deduction:

> The strychnine that killed Mrs. Inglethorp was the identical strychnine prescribed by Dr. Wilkins. To make that clear to you, I will read you an extract from a book on dispensing which I found in the Dispensary of the Red Cross Hospital at Tadminster:
> The following prescription has become famous in text books:

Strychninae Sulph	gr. i
Potass Bromide	3 vi
Aqua ad	3 viii
Fiat Mistura	

   This solution deposits in a few hours the greater part of the strychnine salt as an insoluble bromide in transparent crystals. A lady in England lost her life by taking a similar mixture: the precipitated strychnine collected at the bottom, and in taking the last dose she swallowed nearly all of it![62]

While it is explained that Poirot figures this out from looking at a textbook and a prescription bottle, and that he has some understanding of its texture and familiarity with a news story that involved this poison, it is clear that the author is not herself a scientist, but is trying to emulate Conan Doyle's scientific approach to detection (which was natural to him, as he received the best possible scientific and medical university education). Because the public at large had an easier time grasping simplified science than theoretical science, Christie rose in popularity, and Conan Doyle fell in the middle of the twentieth century.

   The two authors also differ in the way they portray mental illness, though both try to stress that the detective-hero is insane. In *The Mysterious Affair,* Poirot becomes excited about an idea and begins to "run and leap he did, gambolling wildly down the stretch of lawn outside the long window." He keeps running past the gate, and at this Mr. Hastings replies to Mary's questions by saying, "I honestly don't know. Sometimes, I feel sure he is as mad as a hatter; and then, just as he is at his maddest, I find there is method in his madness."[63] While Conan Doyle spends a great deal of time explaining various elements of Holmes' peculiarities, Christie just has Poirot gallop away.

   Also, in comparison with Conan Doyle's close descriptions of the house where a murder has been committed, Christie only offers the phrase "fine old house"[64] to describe Mrs. Inglethorp's home. The interior of the house is treated with a short description and a picture, which is meant to replace a thousand words: "The servants'

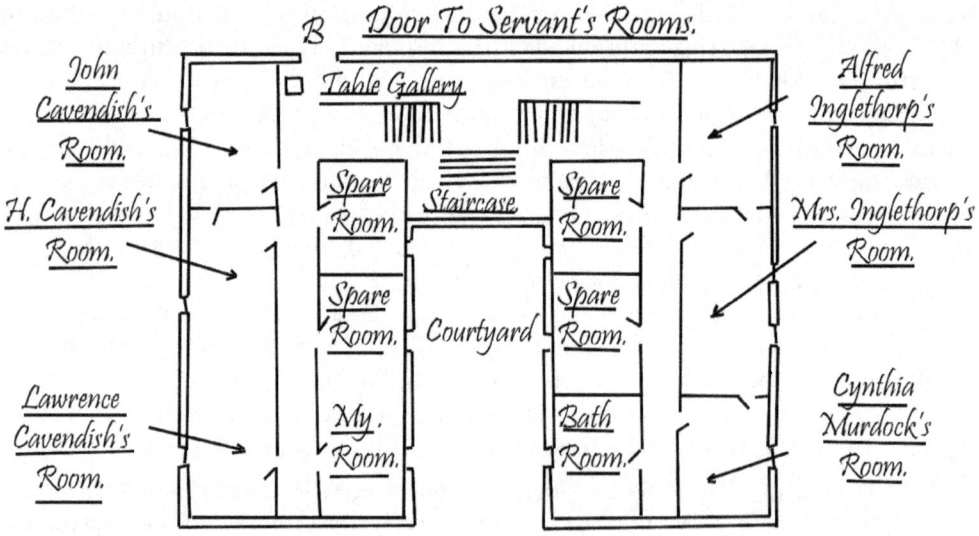

Figure 32. Map of Inglethorp's First Floor Plan.

rooms are reached through the door B. They have no communication with the right wing, where the Inglethorps' rooms were situated."[65] Later on in the story, a diagram of Inglethorp's bedroom is offered.

Of course, some descriptions of the murder scene are inserted, including this summary: "A small purple despatch-case, with a key in the lock, on the writing-table, engaged his attention for some time. He took out the key from the lock, and passed it to me to inspect. I saw nothing peculiar, however. It was an ordinary key of the Yale type, with a bit of twisted wire through the handle."[66] In a method similar to that of Holmes, Poirot examines the objects at the murder scene. But this study is done briskly, rather than scientifically. And a great deal of attention is given to the "key," which does not later turn out to be the most important clue that solves the mystery.

Similarly, instead of the gothic descriptions of the dead body seen in Conan Doyle's work, Christie executes the description of the body and the scene of her death with quick strokes, writing that Dr. Bauerstein discovered a "figure on the bed, and, at the same instant, Mrs. Inglethorp cried out in a strangled voice, her eyes fixed on the doctor: 'Alfred—Alfred—' Then she fell back motionless on the pillows."[67] First, the body is described with nothing other than the noun "figure." Second, instead of giving Mrs. Inglethorp a dramatic exiting line, Christie settles for having her solve the case and name the perpetrator with her final two repeating words. The repetition echoes a lot of formulaic romances that employ the multiple use of "significant" words like "love" for supposed emphasis. The only "scientific" detail that suggests a murder is the fact that her voice is "strangled."

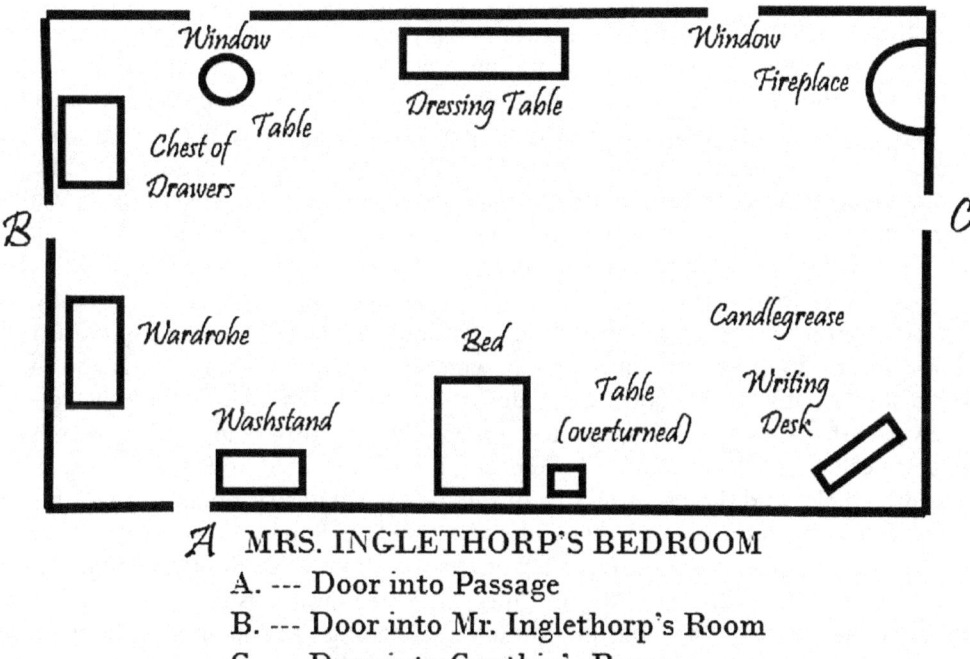

Figure 33. Map of Inglethorp's Bedroom.

HENNING MANKELL (1948–; FIRST NOVEL, *VETTVILLINGEN*, 1977)

The top Swedish best-selling author Henning Mankell recently released the latest, tenth, and final volume in his Wallander series, *The Troubled Man*,[68] and while the reviews have been mixed, I found one review that aligned with my perspective on the work. Such frank reviews are rare in today's mainstream American media, but this is a review from Sweden (I translated it into English with Google Translate). While *The Troubled Man* is not the worst formulaic offender among the books that I studied, its sins are more apparent because they come from a writer who had apparently done better work with the prior volumes in the series and appears to have given up on this piece because there was no motivation to attract readers to future volumes that would not materialize. The Swedish reviewer's name was Lotta Olsson, and the headline of her peace reads, "An absent-minded writer who writes about a tired commissioner." She continues: "*The Troubled Man* is absent-minded, as if told by a person with concentration elsewhere." Olsson further explains why the prior nine books in the Wallander series were attractive for readers by saying that Wallander is a unique and interesting character: "He is one of those difficult people you come across; he is a lout who often ... behaves badly towards women. But he works on all of the cases for his job—except when he has temper tantrums and throws phones that fly at a colleague. Henning Mankell had a shoestring budget, and sometimes had unruly qualities that created a very real person."

Olsson does not object so much to Wallander losing his mind in this book but rather to the fact that random clues are offered without being resolved, a major problem that I also noticed in my reading. "It is more difficult to accept" that the case is solved with the clues offered. "Here we have a mystical fabric tape, here is a stranger, here we hear pattering outside the window, and here we have obscure phone calls. The reader ponders with the blues: what can all these pieces mean? Yes, as you see, we never got any explanations, says Henning Mankell happily at the end of the book, when at least two prominent clues have been brushed aside. Long-time [formulaic] mystery readers grind their teeth: so you just did not [insert any explanations]!" While Olsson then makes an attempt to say that the lack of explanations might reflect reality, she only manages a harsher criticism of Mankell as an author: "Life is full of loose threads and of the incomprehensible; there is always a plethora of things that can never be unraveled. Even so, you cannot get away from a nagging suspicion that Mankell started typing without really knowing where the story was going, and then to his surprise discovered some clues do not fit at the end. Whereupon, he rather sagely says that such is life, too bad for you who thought it was logical." This is very accurate criticism—it does indeed seem that Mankell started typing without a predetermined plot and then refused to edit the book once he was done typing to make it conform to the chopped-together ending he typed up. Somehow Mankell managed to choose a formulaic plot line, but forgot to plan ahead for the plot twists that would lead him to the intended conclusion. Thus, the idea that a mystery can be logically composed when the writer does not know what is going to happen next clearly only leads to illogical, nonsensical mysteries. In addition, Olsson concludes that "Wallander's personal life has gone from terse descriptions to the directly scanty. The new house, terrier, or grandchildren do not fundamentally change anything—which of course is a completely logical progression. But Mankell does not portray Wallander's increasing inner desolation, but lets the text just fade into a tired avalanche of events."[69] Thus, the writer becomes the Weary Giant, instead of merely writing for a Weary Giant audience.

Kurt Wallander is just over sixty, has diabetes (which he developed during one of the previous novels), and is slowly developing senility or Alzheimer's (from which his father died in an earlier volume). Kurt is not a "good" character or a "good" police investigator. The author does try to create sympathy with his problems as an explanation for his constant failures, but these excuses are barely convincing.

In *The Troubled Man*, Wallander learns that his daughter's future father-in-law, Hakan von Enke, suddenly disappeared during his regular walk. Hakan lived in a different jurisdiction, but piqued Wallander's curiosity in the case when he mentioned possible spying Russian submarines during a chat the two had at a gathering shortly before Hakan's disappearance. Wallander looks around Hakan's house; finding no significant clues, he goes back to work. But shortly afterward he is put on suspension for forgetting a loaded gun in a restaurant (an early sign of his Alzheimer's). During his long suspension, Wallander has more time to explore this case. His interest is further roused when Hakan's wife also disappears and is later found dead. He reads up on the history of the period and speaks with several friends, relatives, and enemies of the retired high-ranking naval officer. The clues turn out to be just stories from the past until they are all brought to a speedy resolution at the very end. Wallander discovers that Hakan was alive and in hiding the whole time because he was the suspected spy himself—only he was spying for the Americans and not for the Russians, as previously assumed. When faced with this, Hakan's friend, Sten Nordlander, asks to see him on his island retreat, and then, after a discussion, shoots both Hakan and himself. Apparently Americans had murdered Hakan's wife just to keep his secret, and Hakan might have been involved in the murder of a major Swedish diplomat, Olof Palme. Throughout the novel the reader was misdirected from this conclusion by Hakan telling many of his friends about his paranoia that his wife might have been a Russian spy, or that Russians might have had officials in the Swedish navy spying on military affairs. The narrator points out in the conclusion that many of the minor plot points and clues offered across the novel were not resolved, uncovered or explained in the book, and does not offer plausible explanations. Wallander runs away from the crime scene, covering traces of his presence, and never explains what he found to the world because he is afraid he will be blamed for a potential double homicide.

In the 1994 Collins vs. Random House New York trial, "tangles" being "far from resolved" was one of the faults that Random House editor Leah Boyce believed was sufficient (along with problems of genre mixing, "disjointed scenes" and inconsistences) cancel the $2 million contract with Joan Collins. *Troubled Man* is definitely written in a single genre, and while there are some disjointed scenes and inconsistences, they do not overwhelm an editorial eye with overpowering dread. These problems might have been avoided in *Troubled Man* because of the work put in by "needed 'editors,' 'book doctors' or 'ghost writers,'" as Judge Ira Gammerman in the Collins vs. Random House case advised Random House to do.[70] The Collins case and other decisions have made it difficult for publishers to refuse to produce a book based on its quality after a contract has been issued, so authors who have had earlier best-sellers occasionally force publishers to go through with a costly publication even if there are major problems with the book.

The historical information offered in the opening pages and at key moments throughout the plot is frequently informative, though it is often too casual to be educational: "It is possible that the name and the suspicions had been mentioned in passing when the minister of defense held one of his infrequent information sessions with the prime minister, but not in connection with anything serious, anything specific."[71] Sentences like this one do not say anything "serious" or "specific" and just add air to the historical paragraphs.

There is an odd grammatical glitch in this novel (which might be more logical in the original Swedish version of the book): sometimes the perspective of the narrator changes from third-person to first-person. Occasionally this switch happens grammatically in italics, which explains that the first-person voice is a thought. But at other times, no italics are used, as in this example: "He went to his car, a Peugeot he'd had for the last for years, and drove off. How many times have I driven along this road?"[72] As you can see, the pronouns change from "he" to "I" in these two neighboring sentences. I have noticed similar glitches in a few other recent novels, so I think this is a new stylistic anti-grammatical revision, which happens when several writers keep repeating a mistake until they convince themselves and their readers that it is not a mistake because it appears so frequently.

One of my favorite parts of the book is Wallander's extreme political and legal apathy: "He usually dismissed politics as a higher authority that restricted the ability of the police to enforce law and order, and that was it."[73] Similar political apathy is common to almost all novels published in the last twenty years, unless they were strictly political, biographical dramas. Being apathetic about politics is currently fashionable, while political passion is fanatical and frowned upon. I liked the sections that described Wallander's extreme disinterest because they were so detailed that they reached the roots of this apathy, as well as its symptoms and outcomes. The portrayal of a political and legally apathetic investigator rings true with the investigators whom I have met. Thus, Mankell succeeds when he refrains from creating a false, melodramatic sympathy in the heart of the investigator, and just paints a realistic portrait.

The most frustrating and negative element in the book, as mentioned earlier, is the fact that there is a new clue to the main and supporting mysteries on every other page, but almost all of these clues are never explained and fail to form a logical pattern that agrees with the events in the conclusion or the final revelation. Thus, a reader who is trying to solve the mystery before the investigator does cannot succeed because the clues are all misleading. There are no clues that Hakan might have been spying for the Americans until this fact is revealed at the end in his confession, unless having an American naval friend can be considered a clue. This trick is intended to surprise the reader at the end with an outcome they did not expect, but upon rereading a Sherlock Holmes or Edgar Allan Poe mystery, one is likely to see how the clues all fit together and to go "Aha!" or "Eureka! That's what it all meant!" Instead, here the reader is left confused, uncertain and sleepy. Many of the sections and chapters end with Wallander falling asleep and then awakening at the beginning of the next section, as if the writer fell asleep over his work and let the readers know that at that point of the story he made himself sleepy.[74]

Conclusion

The popularity of the novel stems from the roots of popular fiction at the beginning of the nineteenth century, when Sir Walter Scott and Alexandre Dumas became popular best-sellers with their historical romances. As the reading public grew over the century following 1814, literary novels maintained dominance. But since the 1950s both the reading public and the quantity of books each reader reads have declined, despite continued population growth. As films, video games and other genres became popular, they took a market share away from the publishing industry. When this happened, even big literary publishing houses started to lose money because they were taking risks that were not paying off. Publishers merged across the twentieth century until five giant corporations had engulfed most of the popular fiction publishers. The oligopoly publishing climate that we are in now has meant a further pull from the literary to the unliterary. A publishing business that operates with a profit-motif alone calculates the reading level of the most buyers willing to buy books and then prints books at the third-grade level or so; because this strategy works, these titles reach the top of best-seller lists and remain at the top, at the expense of any literary fiction that might be attempting to compete for those spots.

While literary novels require educated authors who labor for years to perfect them, unliterary novels can be created by mechanizing the process with the use of simple generic formulas. Long before the 1970s romance publishers offered guidelines for the age, class and other elements of their preferred heroines and suggested key plot points. Writers might be asked to insert an ending in which the lovers marry by one publisher, while they might have to insert a positive sexual intercourse experience for a different company. One publisher might want a Cinderella story, and another a rich girl overcome by brute elderly man scenario. As publishers merged further and realized that formulaic fiction sells because the books can be marketed in bulk to a group of readers that want it, they added details to their required formulas. Georgette Heyer objected when Barbara Cartland and her publisher took not only Heyer's plot lines but also character names, linguistic elements, and even whole paragraphs in the 1950s. The problem was that Heyer failed to file charges, so while Cartland stopped these extreme plagiarisms of Heyer's work, she could have mimicked another writer and settled on continuing with her patented Cinderella formula for the rest of her long career. In more recent times, there have been lawsuits by Nora Roberts and J. K. Rowling against those who produce works similar to their own. While the formulas for most literary fiction are complex and cannot be represented with simplified plot lines and plot summary tables, the four genres in this study include works that are so similar to each other that predictable types of events almost always happen at predictable moments in the plot. Readers are attracted to the handsome men and women or beautiful magical images on the covers of these formulaic novels, and they gravitate toward the larger sections in a bookstore where these works are housed. Studies of reader behavior have found that a reader might become addicted to reading works in a single genre, like romance or mysteries, but after reading a significant quantity of them readers often realize the formulaic similarities and stop reading in that genre. It is likely that these disappointed readers might exit the reading market, further decreasing the quantity of readers who read for pleasure.

To make a formulaic novel, the publisher or the writer begins with a basic plot outline, examples of which I provided in the four genre chapters. Then questions that need to be answered about the characters, setting and plot twists are inserted into this timeline at the appropriate parts. The writer might closely read a specific novel that is in the genre he or she wants to join. Elements are added into the timeline or the pre-writing plan that identify if there should be cliffhangers or life-threatening situations at the end of each chapter, or if the main character should constantly be sleepy, or if the word "breasts" should appear on every page. These particularities are subgenre specific and each author typically develops their own list that they repeat across their novels. Frequently, if an author follows another writer's pattern too closely, comparing their works shows the family resemblance. Writers who fail to develop a full plan at the beginning but attempt to write a formulaic genre novel typically create hilarious flops—failing to tie up loose ends in a mystery, bringing together two people in a romance who could never unite in reality, proving an anti-religious position in religious novels, or keeping readers from being able to suspend their disbelief in fantasies in which characters have illogical magical powers. However, writers who take an element in a generic formula and insert it too repetitively, end up with character descriptions that are nearly identical to those of other writers who make this mistake. A writer might come up with a description like this: "Sam had blue eyes, brown hair, a medium nose, and yellow pants." The description does not identify Sam as unique and does not explain why his appearance is significant in the story. The classical convention, especially apparent in the Sherlock Holmes stories, is to study human characteristics to draw conclusions about one's character, and not to simply name basic shapes and colors of the standard facial, body and clothing features. These problems are the result of writers taking shortcuts and mimicking previous formulas, instead of taking time to think about the construction of generic formulas and designing unique formulas that fit each new project. There are infinite formulaic variations. Instead of following unique routes, modern best-selling writers only work in one of the four best-selling generic formulas, simplifying their language, plots and all other elements to the basic skeletons, and creating unliterary fiction that continually repels the reading public away from reading.

I began this study with the fantasy and science fiction genre because I have read more speculative fiction than romances, mysteries or religious novels. In each of the genres I started by looking at the founders of the genre, whom I admired more than their mimickers, in order to be able to study the genre elements closely. It is occasionally difficult to look closely at a work that is a tenth-generation imitation of the founding works in the genre because the quantity of repeating elements overwhelms statistical calculations. On the other hand, by starting with H. G. Wells in science fiction,

I recognized an interesting, key divergence in this genre between the two-world static, unresolved anti-formulaic stories and the single-world, good versus evil formulaic ones. Writers are typically grouped into the "literary" category when their work is anti-formulaic, and as working in the genre when their work is formulaic.

Recently the *New York Times* had to create a separate category for children's literature, which is mostly full of fantasy novels, and overall science fiction, fantasy and horror have been climbing steadily on best-seller lists. Therefore, I wanted to explore more recent novels in the fantasy, science fiction and horror genres than in the other genres. In addition, running this plot, character and setting comparison for a large number of recent works in this genre shows the repetitions between these works. If I looked at a dozen mysteries, romances or religious novels from the last decade and compared them with a similar table, they would be much closer together formulaically than the works I ended up comparing in these other genres. I only looked at key works at different parts of a century for the other genres because there I was more interested in the decline from literary to unliterary formulaic fiction, rather than in the quantity of repetitions in the most recent works.

Because I looked at novelists from different centuries and noted the differences between the focal authors, I inserted historical summaries for how each of the genres changed from its founding roots to the present. Typically these summaries also explained the elements that are repeated in a given genre. For example, the roller coaster plot line became especially important in thrillers and sensation fiction, as plots that rely on thrills took over the narrative depth that was popular in earlier historical fiction and other description-thick genres. When I was thinking about this, I recalled Christopher Booker's plots and realized that thrillers simply exaggerated the roller coaster device that has been an element of fiction since the earliest fictional texts, like the *Odyssey*.

Now that I have looked at the key formulaic principles that operate within each of these genres, I will explain the principles that I believe govern all four genres. The repeating curves of formulaic fiction can be clearly seen when they are put in a diagram that measures tension versus story time. In formulaic fiction, tension is created with the death threat, sexual suspense and spiritual quest. When a character's life is endangered, the reader feels tense or under threat. When a character constantly dreams of a positive sexual experience, the reader feels the constriction or tension and hopes the hero will reach this goal. The same can be achieved with a spiritual, religious, or financial goal that the hero wants desperately to reach. These goals or threats are based on the principle that when the hero does not have what he wants, his and the reader's happiness is at a low point, and that both the hero and the reader want to fight with the monster or with the novel to reach a happy ending. Happiness of the hero has an inverse curve with the tension that the hero and the reader feel. The unhappier the hero is, the more tense he is. The happier the hero is, the less tense he is. According to this theory, a hero who has attained the goal he is after will be completely happy and fully relaxed. However, the theory goes that if the hero moves steadily upward toward happiness from misery, the reader will lose interest, as the route the hero is taking will be too obvious and the reader will be deprived of the surprise that is necessary to continue to feel suspenseful about the unhappiness of the hero. To create a constant state of uncertainty and suspense across the drama, the roller coaster device is utilized. The hero is repeatedly put under the threat of death, seems further away from attaining a sexual goal, or suddenly loses all of his money or morals. Each time a "constriction" or a challenge is presented, the hero overcomes it with varying degrees of success, suddenly climbing higher on the happiness scale and temporarily lower on the tension scale.

The roller coaster plot has several other rules that govern its physics. For example, the story cannot begin at a roller coaster low point or high point. The first chapters have to gradually present the hero with growing obstacles, which he typically does not begin to overcome until the second plot movement. The death threat and the other tension devices are not as effective before the reader begins sympathizing and identifying with the hero. In addition, to avoid an untidy resolution, things have to improve for the hero gradually from the near-death climax. The story cannot end immediately after the climax unless the writer wants to be intentionally absurd (or has grown tired of typing). The third key law is that obstacles have to intensify across the three central movements of the plot. The hero cannot face and kill the most horrifying monster between the first and third movements. The biggest challenge has to be reserved for the end of the fourth act.

All of the above "rules" can and have been broken in anti-formulaic and classical literary works. For example, the Torah begins in the emptiness before the creation of the world, which then appears suddenly in seven days, bringing the story from a low point (death or lack of life) to a high point (abundance of life). Obviously, in Greek drama there were as many tragedies with unhappy endings as comedies with happy endings. And in absurd or nonsensical literature, such as James Joyce's *Ulysses*, tension is neutralized throughout by the unpredictable jumps in the narrative that spike and fall without any clear patterns. Robert Louis Stevenson's *Kidnapped* begins with an abduction and the assassination of an English official in Scotland; the official is the biggest monster killed in the plot, with the remainder of the story focused on the hero's escape from prosecution. In all of these cases the stories are complete and do not break literary conventions. They do, however, break formulaic genre fiction conventions and similar plot lines cannot be engaged in formulaic fiction.

The "rules" that govern character types in formulaic fiction are just ridiculous. For example, in speculative fiction the heroes I studied were Bilbo, the tiny, hairy hobbit; Jack, the memory-loss patient; Harry, the tragic orphan; Percy, the dyslexic demigod; and Bella, the sexual-assault-loving vampire girl. If a reader in the Middle Ages met this group in fictional works, he or she would assume they are sidekick villains due to their overall ugliness, stupidity, vulnerability, and pathetic backgrounds. These heroes have these absurd characteristics due to the formulaic principle that vulnerable characters are more sympathetic. Sympathy can also be created by isolating the hero from society and, if the audience allows it, stripping the hero and allowing him to spend at least some part of the novel in the nude. While typically a formulaic hero is not simultaneously ugly, stupid, orphaned, naked, and alone, according to this formula, the hero has to be at least one of these for a significant part of the formulaic novel. Holmes, Gulliver and even the four Musketeers had some character flaws, but if their authors had set out to make them pathetic, they would not have captured the respect of their contemporary readers.

This is not a book that offers congratulations to formulaic genre writers, like so many critics who enter the field of modern art do. If more critics wrote about plagiarism, plot repetitions and bare-bones monosyllabic writing, we would once again be able to buy modern literary fiction. Despite making an intense effort to find some well-executed formulaic recent fiction, I have not found a single soundly written formulaic novel from the last two decades. Instead of focusing on this key field that contributes to literacy rates and reading habits of the lower class, critics write postmodern absurdist deconstructive or poststructuralist criticisms that are themselves works of fictional absurdity and not helpful additions to the study of fiction. I hope that more critics will stop buying the publishing industry's propaganda that too many critics have already looked down at lowbrow formulaic fiction, and will join a critique of this field, which has been overgrown with plagiarisms and repetitions that are cheating the public.

Chapter Notes

Introduction

1. James P. Allen and Peter Der Manuelian, eds., *The Ancient Egyptian Pyramid Texts. Volume 23 of Writings from the Ancient World* (Atlanta: Society of Biblical Literature, 2005), 4.
2. Clive Bloom, *Bestsellers: Popular Fiction Since 1900* (New York: Palgrave Macmillan, 2002), 86.
3. Ibid., 86.
4. *An Annual Comprehensive Study of the U.S. Publishing Industry: BookStats 2011* (New York: Association of American Publishers and the Book Industry Group, 2011), 15.
5. Ibid., 23.
6. *Statistical Abstract of the United States: The National Data Book 2003* (Washington, DC: U.S. Census Bureau, Bureau of the Census, 2003).
7. Albert N. Greco, *The Book Publishing Industry*, second edition (Mahwah, NJ: Lawrence Erlbaum, 2005), 255.
8. "Romance Literature Statistics: Industry Statistics: 2010 ROMStat Report" (New York: Romance Writers of America and Simba Information, 2010).
9. Hibah Yousuf, "Microsoft Profit Soars," *CNN Money*, June 28, 2010.
10. "US Movie Market Summary 1995 to 2012," *The Numbers: Box Office Data, Movie Stars, Idle Speculation* (New York: Nash Information Services, 2012).
11. Bloom, *Bestsellers*, 5.
12. Karen M. Hubert, *Teaching and Writing Popular Fiction: Horror, Adventure, Mystery and Romance in the American Classroom* (New York: Virgil Books, 1976), 8.
13. Stephen King, *Bare Bones: Conversations on Terror with Stephen King*, edited by Tim Underwood and Chuck Miller (New York: McGraw-Hill, 1988), 70.
14. Ibid., 88.
15. Ibid., 172.
16. Ibid., 47–48.
17. Ibid., 96.
18. Ken Gelder, *Popular Fiction: The Logics and Practices of a Literary Field* (London: Routledge, 2004).
19. Hubert, *Teaching and Writing Popular Fiction*, 16.
20. Michael Williams, "Preface," in *Literary Structures, Character Development, and Dramaturgical Scenarios in Framing the Category Novel*, by Robert N. St. Clair (Lewiston, NY: Edwin Mellen Press, 2004), v.
21. Ibid., vii.
22. Ibid., viii.
23. Ibid.
24. Ibid., xiii.
25. Ibid., xiv.
26. Ibid., xv.
27. Ibid., xviii.
28. Robert N. St. Clair, *Literary Structures, Character Development, and Dramaturgical Scenarios in Framing the Category Novel* (Lewiston, NY: Edwin Mellen Press, 2004), 45.
29. Orson Scott Card, *How to Write Science Fiction and Fantasy* (Cincinnati: Writer's Digest Books, 1990).
30. *Guinness Book of World Records*, "Highest Earning Adult Fiction Writer," 2013, http://www.guinnessworldrecords.com.
31. *Guinness Book of World Records*, "First Author to Sell More than 1 Million E-Books."
32. *Guinness Book of World Records*, "Most Published Works by One Author."
33. *Guinness Book of World Records*, "Youngest Author of a Bestselling Book Series."
34. *Guinness Book of World Records*, "Best-Selling Copyright Book."
35. *Guinness Book of World Records*, "Oldest Mechanically Printed Book."
36. *Guinness Book of World Records*, "Best-Selling Book of Non-Fiction."
37. *Guinness Book of World Records*, "Longest Novel."
38. Bloom, *Bestsellers*, 6.

Chapter 1

1. William Nolan, *How to Write Horror Fiction* (Cincinnati: Writer's Digest Books, 1990), 29.
2. Ibid., 51.

3. Catherine W. Griffin, "Interview with Carrie Ryan, Author of the Forest of Hands and Teeth Series," *Pennsylvania Literary Journal* IV, no. 3 (Fall 2012), 40.
4. Larry Niven, "Rammer," *Playground of the Mind* (New York: Tom Doherty, 1991), 25.
5. Anna Faktorovich, "Interview with Larry Niven, Author of *The Draco Tavern*," *Pennsylvania Literary Journal* V, no. 2 (Summer 2013), 17.
6. Larry Niven, "Collaborations," *Niven's Laws* (Philadelphia: Philadelphia Science Fiction Society, 1984), 92–96.
7. Faktorovich, "Interview with Larry Niven," 12.
8. Nolan, *How to Write Horror Fiction*, 73–74.
9. Clive Bloom, *Bestsellers: Popular Fiction Since 1900* (New York: Palgrave Macmillan, 2002), 10.
10. Nolan, *How to Write Horror Fiction*, 96.
11. Ibid., 30–31.
12. Ibid., 53.
13. Ibid.
14. Larry Niven, "Niven's Laws," *Niven's Laws* (Philadelphia: Philadelphia Science Fiction Society, 1984), 56.
15. Faktorovich, "Interview with Larry Niven," 15.
16. Niven, "Niven's Laws," 56.
17. Karen M. Hubert, *Teaching and Writing Popular Fiction: Horror, Adventure, Mystery and Romance in the American Classroom* (New York: Virgil Books, 1976), 25.
18. Anne Rice, "Let the Flesh Instruct the Mind: A Quadrant Interview with Anne Rice, by Katherine Ramsland," *The Anne Rice Reader* (New York: Ballantine Books, 1997), 71.
19. Hubert, *Teaching and Writing Popular Fiction*, 26–27.
20. John Huntington, *The Logic of Fantasy: H. G. Wells and Science Fiction* (New York: Columbia University Press, 1982), 57.
21. C. S. Lewis, *An Experiment in Criticism* (Cambridge: Cambridge University Press, 1992), 3.
22. Ibid., 5.
23. Ibid., 29–30.
24. Stephen King, *Bare Bones: Conversations on Terror with Stephen King*, edited by Tim Underwood and Chuck Miller (New York: McGraw-Hill, 1988), 74.
25. Lewis, *An Experiment in Criticism*, 32.
26. Ibid., 34.
27. Ibid., 68–69.
28. Ibid., 116–17.
29. C. S. Lewis, *The Lion, the Witch and the Wardrobe*, deluxe edition (New York: Macmillan, 1983), 6.
30. Ibid., 3.
31. Ibid., 9.
32. Ibid., 10.
33. Henry James, "The Art of Fiction," *Longman's Magazine* (London) 4, September 1884; see http://public.wsu.edu/~campbelld/amlit/artfiction.html.
34. Ibid.
35. Albert N. Greco, *The Book Publishing Industry*, second edition (Mahwah, NJ: Lawrence Erlbaum, 2005), 66.
36. Arthur T. Vanderbilt II, *The Making of a Bestseller: From Author to Reader* (Jefferson, NC: McFarland, 1999), 51.
37. Ibid., 196.
38. Ibid., 72–73.
39. Ibid., 79.
40. Ibid., 138.
41. Greco, *The Book Publishing Industry*, 141–42.
42. Vanderbilt, *The Making of a Bestseller*, 179.
43. Greco, *The Book Publishing Industry*, 51.
44. Vanderbilt, *The Making of a Bestseller*, 180.
45. Ibid.
46. Ibid., 188.
47. Greco, *The Book Publishing Industry*, 37.
48. Jason Epstein, *Book Business: Publishing Past Present and Future* (New York: W. W. Norton, 2001), 173.
49. Ibid., 74.
50. Ibid., 47.
51. Ibid., 157.
52. Ibid., 7.
53. Ibid., 35.
54. Ibid., 11.
55. Ibid., 33.
56. Ibid., 29.
57. Ibid., 17.
58. Ibid., 18.
59. Ibid., 19.
60. King, *Bare Bones*, 158.
61. Ibid., 50.
62. Vanderbilt, *The Making of a Bestseller*, 80–81.
63. Ibid., 84.
64. King, *Bare Bones*, 94.
65. Ibid., 110.
66. Vanderbilt, *The Making of a Bestseller*, 89.
67. Ibid., 153.
68. King, *Bare Bones*, 109.
69. Ibid., 159.
70. Ibid., 194–97.
71. Ibid., 207.
72. Vanderbilt, *The Making of a Bestseller*, 116.
73. Ibid., 125.
74. Ibid., 133.
75. Ibid.
76. Ibid., 136.
77. Christopher Booker, *The Seven Basic Plots: Why We Tell Stories* (London: Continuum, 2004).
78. Ibid., 216–28.
79. Gustav Freytag, *Technique of the Drama: An Exposition of Dramatic Composition and Art* (New York: Scott, Foresman and Company, 1894 [orig. 1863]).
80. Ibid., 115.
81. Booker, *The Seven Basic Plots*, 18.
82. Victoria Lynn Schmidt, *Story Structure Architect* (Cincinnati: Writer's Digest Books, 2005), 55.
83. Ibid., 39.
84. Ibid., 61.
85. Ibid., 263–64.
86. King, *Bare Bones*, 78.

87. Hubert, *Teaching and Writing Popular Fiction*, 14.
88. Nolan, *How to Write Horror Fiction*, 32.
89. Ibid., 33.
90. Ibid., 34.
91. Ibid.
92. Ibid.
93. Ibid., 35.
94. Edgar Allan Poe, *Great Tales and Poems of Edgar Allan Poe* (New York: Simon & Schuster Paperbacks, 2009), 30.
95. Nolan, *How to Write Horror Fiction*, 35.
96. Ibid., 36.
97. Ibid., 41.
98. Poe, *Great Tales*, 41–42.
99. Stephen King, "Introduction," *The Arbor House Treasury of Horror and the Supernatural*, edited by Bill Prozini, Barry Malzberg, and Martin H. Greenberg (New York: Arbor House, 1981), 18.
100. Rice, "Let the Flesh Instruct the Mind," 64–65.
101. Nolan, *How to Write Horror Fiction*, 42.
102. Ibid., 43.
103. Ibid., 44.
104. Ibid.
105. Ibid., 46.
106. Ibid., 33.

Chapter 2

1. Douglas E. Winter, *Stephen King*, Starmont Reader's Guide 16 (Mercer Island, WA: Starmont House, 1982), 102.
2. Clive Bloom, *Bestsellers: Popular Fiction Since 1900* (New York: Palgrave Macmillan, 2002), 157.
3. Ibid., 157.
4. Christopher Booker, *The Seven Basic Plots: Why We Tell Stories* (London: Continuum, 2004), 23.
5. Ibid., 40.
6. Stephen King, *Bare Bones: Conversations on Terror with Stephen King*, edited by Tim Underwood and Chuck Miller (New York: McGraw-Hill, 1988), 49.
7. Ibid., 9.
8. Ibid., 74–75.
9. Ibid., 50.
10. Ibid., 51.
11. Anne Rice, *The Mummy, or Ramses the Damned* (New York: Ballantine Books, 1989), 3.
12. Ibid., 4.
13. Ibid., 9.
14. Ibid., 14.
15. Ibid., 15.
16. Ibid., 427.
17. Booker, *The Seven Basic Plots*, 31–32.
18. Ibid., 32.
19. Garci Rodríguez de Montalvo, *Amadis de Gaula* (1508), translated by Robert Southey (London: J. R. Smith, 1872), http://www.donaldcorrell.com/amadis/index.html.
20. Miguel de Cervantes Saavedra, *Don Quixote* (1605–1615), translated by John Ormsby (Chicago: Project Gutenberg eBook, 2004), Chapter X.
21. Booker, *The Seven Basic Plots*, 356–57.
22. William Nolan, *How to Write Horror Fiction* (Cincinnati: Writer's Digest Books, 1990), 9.
23. Catherine W. Griffin, "Interview with Cinda Williams Chima, Author of the Heir Series," *Pennsylvania Literary Journal* IV, no. 3 (Fall 2012), 16.
24. Ibid., 18.
25. King, *Bare Bones*, 127.
26. Ibid., 128.
27. Ibid., 207.
28. H. G. Wells, *Experiment in Autobiography: Discoveries and Conclusions of a Very Ordinary Brain (Since 1866)* (New York: Macmillan, 1934), 238.
29. Ibid., 426.
30. Ibid., 239.
31. Ibid., 411–13.
32. Ibid., 414–15.
33. Ibid., 416.
34. Ibid.
35. H. G. Wells, "The Contemporary Novel," delivered to the Times Book Club (1912), http://www.online-literature.com/wellshg/englishman-looks-at-the-world/11/.
36. Wells, *Experiment in Autobiography*, 417.
37. Ibid., 421.
38. Carol Thurston, *The Romance Revolution: Erotic Novels for Women and the Quest for a New Sexual Identity* (Urbana: University of Illinois Press, 1987), 131.
39. Wells, "The Contemporary Novel."
40. H. G. Wells, "James Joyce" (review of *Portrait of the Artist as a Young Man*), *The New Republic* (1917), http://www.james-joyce-music.com/wells031017.html.
41. H. G. Wells, letter (*James Joyce's World*, Letters of Note, 1928), see "Vast Riddles," http://www.lettersofnote.com/2012/11/vast-riddles.html, for the full text of this letter.
42. Wells, *Experiment in Autobiography*, 420.
43. Gene K. Rinkel and Margaret E. Rinkel, *The Picshuas of H. G. Wells: A Burlesque Diary* (Chicago: University of Illinois Press, 2006), 188–90.
44. Wells, *Experiment in Autobiography*, 428.
45. Ibid.
46. H. G. Wells, "The Island of Doctor Moreau," *World Classics* (New York: Oxford University Press, 1996).
47. John Huntington, *The Logic of Fantasy: H. G. Wells and Science Fiction* (New York: Columbia University Press, 1982).
48. Ibid., 22–23.
49. Ibid., 27.
50. Larry Niven, "Five Years to Infinity," *Niven's Laws* (Philadelphia: Philadelphia Science Fiction Society, 1984), 97–108.
51. Anna Faktorovich, "Interview with Larry Niven, Author of *The Draco Tavern*," *Pennsylvania Literary Journal* V, no. 2 (Summer 2013), 17.

52. Larry Niven, "Niven's Laws," *Niven's Laws* (Philadelphia: Philadelphia Science Fiction Society, 1984), 55.
53. Faktorovich, "Interview with Larry Niven," 13.
54. Huntington, *The Logic of Fantasy*, 55.
55. Ibid., 57.
56. Ibid., 116.
57. Gustav Freytag, *Technique of the Drama: An Exposition of Dramatic Composition and Art* (New York: Scott, Foresman and Company, 1894 [orig, 1863]).
58. Huntington, *The Logic of Fantasy*, 141.
59. Ibid., 143.
60. Ibid., 58.
61. Ibid., 61.
62. Ibid., 62.
63. Booker, *The Seven Basic Plots*, 49–50.
64. Bloom, *Bestsellers*, 161–62.
65. J. R. R. Tolkien, *The Hobbit or, There and Back Again* (Boston: Houghton Mifflin, 1984), 8.
66. Ibid., 9.
67. Ibid., 11.
68. Ibid., 16.
69. Larry Niven, *The Draco Tavern* (New York: Tom Doherty, 2006).
70. Faktorovich, "Interview with Larry Niven," 14.
71. Ibid.
72. Niven, *The Draco Tavern*, 93.
73. Bloom, *Bestsellers*, 209.
74. Ibid., 210.
75. King, *Bare Bones*, 116.
76. Les Daniels, *Living in Fear: A History of Horror in the Mass Media* (New York: Charles Scribner's Sons, 1975), 118–19.
77. Bloom, *Bestsellers*, 215.
78. Winter, *Stephen King*, 6.
79. Ibid., 102.
80. King, *Bare Bones*, 43–44.
81. Bob Spitz, "Interview: Stephen King," *Penthouse* (April 1982), 160.
82. King, *Bare Bones*, 55.
83. Stephen King and Peter Straub, *Black House* (New York: Ballantine Books, 2001), 1.
84. Ibid.
85. Ibid., 7.
86. Ibid., 9.
87. Ibid., 11–12.
88. Ibid., 14–16.
89. Ibid., 17–20.
90. Ibid., 452.
91. Ibid., 453.
92. Ibid., 520.
93. Ibid..
94. Ibid., 641.
95. Ibid., 546–48.
96. Ibid., 658.
97. Ibid., 633.
98. Ibid., 658.
99. Stephen King, *The Dark Tower V: Wolves of the Calla* (New York: Simon & Schuster, 2003), xv.
100. Ibid., 2.
101. Ibid., 4.
102. Ibid., 3.
103. Ibid., 6.
104. Ibid., 7.
105. Ibid., 5.
106. Ibid., 6.
107. Ibid., 9.
108. Ibid., 31.
109. Ibid.
110. Ibid., 706–9.
111. *Guinness Book of World Records*, "First Billion-Dollar Author," 2013, http://www.guinnessworldrecords.com.
112. *Guinness Book of World Records*, "Highest Initial Print-Run for a Fiction Book."
113. J. K. Rowling, *Harry Potter and the Half-Blood Prince* (New York: Arthur A. Levin Books/Scholastic, 2005), 18.
114. Ibid., 3.
115. Ibid., 16.
116. Ibid.
117. Ibid., 22.
118. Ibid., 23.
119. Ibid., 45.
120. Ibid., 4.
121. Ibid., 45.
122. Ibid., 69.
123. Ibid., 2.
124. Ibid., 5.
125. Ibid., 9.
126. Ibid., 594.
127. Ibid., 15.
128. Ibid., 31.
129. Ibid., 446.
130. Ibid., 15.
131. Ibid.
132. Ibid., 24.
133. Ibid., 25.
134. Ibid., 17.
135. Ibid., 18.
136. Ibid., 85.
137. Ibid., 20.
138. Ibid., 21.
139. Ibid., 83–84.
140. Ibid., 84–85.
141. Ibid., 89.
142. Ibid., 98–100.
143. Ibid., 46.
144. Ibid., 46–47.
145. Ibid., 47.
146. Ibid., 48.
147. Ibid., 49.
148. Ibid., 50.
149. Ibid., 51.
150. Ibid., 58.
151. Ibid., 72.
152. Ibid., 76.
153. Ibid., 77.
154. Ibid., 451.
155. Ibid., 35.
156. Ibid., 39–43.

157. Ibid., 149–53.
158. Ibid., 321.
159. Ibid., 409.
160. Ibid., 646.
161. Ibid., 412.
162. Ibid., 508.
163. Ibid., 522–23.
164. Ibid., 588.
165. Ibid., 585.
166. Rick Riordan, *The Battle of the Labyrinth: Percy Jackson & the Olympians, Book Four* (New York: Hyperion Books/Disney, 2008), 25.
167. Ibid., 23.
168. Stephenie Meyer, *Breaking Dawn* (New York: Hachette, 2008), 13.
169. Ibid., 50.
170. King, *Bare Bones*, 184.
171. Meyer, *Breaking Dawn*, 24.

Chapter 3

1. Nora Roberts, "The Romance of Writing," in *North American Romance Writers*, edited by Kay Mussell and Johanna Tunon (Lanham, MD: Scarecrow, 1999), 200–201.
2. Kay Mussell, *Fantasy and Reconciliation: Contemporary Formulas of Women's Romance Fiction* (Westport, CT: Greenwood, 1984), 6.
3. Karen M. Hubert, *Teaching and Writing Popular Fiction: Horror, Adventure, Mystery and Romance in the American Classroom* (New York: Virgil Books, 1976), 124.
4. Carol Thurston, *The Romance Revolution: Erotic Novels for Women and the Quest for a New Sexual Identity* (Urbana: University of Illinois Press, 1987), 196.
5. Ibid., 188.
6. Ibid., 188–89.
7. Ibid., 198.
8. Ibid., 215.
9. Ibid., 214.
10. Hubert, *Teaching and Writing Popular Fiction*, 163.
11. Roy Caston Flickinger, *The Greek Theater and Its Drama* (Chicago: University of Chicago Press, 1918), 2.
12. Ibid., 12.
13. Ibid., 16.
14. Ibid., 36.
15. Ibid., 39.
16. Henry Augustin Beers, *A History of English Romanticism in the Eighteenth Century* (New York: H. Holt, 1916), 2.
17. E. H. Blackmore, A. M. Blackmore, and Francine Giguere, "Introduction," *The Devil's Pool and Other Stories by George Sand* (Albany: State University of New York Press, 2004), 4.
18. Ibid., 7.
19. Pam Morris, *Realism: The New Critical Idiom* (New York: Psychology Press, 2003), 3.
20. Georgette Heyer, "Georgette Heyer," *The Black Moth. Moby Classics Series* (Boston: Mobile Reference, 2010).
21. Clive Bloom, *Bestsellers: Popular Fiction Since 1900* (New York: Palgrave Macmillan, 2002), 156.
22. Vladimir Nabokov, *Lolita* (New York: Random House Digital, 2010), 3–4.
23. Vladimir Nabokov, "First Love," in *The World Treasury of Love Stories*, edited by Lucy Rosenthal and Clifton Fadiman (Oxford: Oxford University Press, 1995), 401–8.
24. Kay Mussell and Johanna Tunon, *North American Romance Writers* (Lanham, MD: Scarecrow, 1999), 196–97.
25. Mussell and Tunon, *North American Romance Writers*, 2.
26. Thurston, *The Romance Revolution*, 46–47.
27. Ibid., 5.
28. Ibid., 4.
29. Ibid.
30. Ibid., 3.
31. Hubert, *Teaching and Writing Popular Fiction*, 126.
32. Ibid., 136.
33. Albert N. Greco, *The Book Publishing Industry*, second edition (Mahwah, NJ: Lawrence Erlbaum, 2005), 255.
34. Thurston, *The Romance Revolution*, 23.
35. "Frequently Asked Sexuality Questions to the Kinsey Institute," The Kinsey Institute for Research in Sex, Gender, and Reproduction, July 21, 2012.
36. "Women in the Labor Force: A Data Book," *BLS Reports: Report 1040* (Washington, DC: U.S. Bureau of Labor Statistics, February 2013).
37. Thurston, *The Romance Revolution*, 35.
38. Bloom, *Bestsellers*, 70.
39. C. S. Lewis, *An Experiment in Criticism* (Cambridge: Cambridge University Press, 1992), 36.
40. Bloom, *Bestsellers*, 175.
41. Lucy Rosenthal and Clifton Fadiman, eds., *The World Treasury of Love Stories* (Oxford: Oxford University Press, 1995), 332.
42. D. H. Lawrence, "The Horse Dealer's Daughter," in *The World Treasury of Love Stories*, edited by Lucy Rosenthal and Clifton Fadiman (Oxford: Oxford University Press, 1995), 333–45.
43. Bloom, *Bestsellers*, 72.
44. Ibid., 73.
45. Ibid., 74.
46. Ibid., 80.
47. Thurston, *The Romance Revolution*, 4.
48. Ibid., 134–35.
49. Ibid., 135.
50. Mary Balogh, "Do It Passionately or Not at All," in *North American Romance Writers*, edited by Kay Mussell and Johanna Tunon (Lanham, MD: Scarecrow, 1999), 24.
51. Alison Hart, "The Key Formula in Romance," in *North American Romance Writers*, edited by Kay Mussell and Johanna Tunon (Lanham, MD: Scarecrow, 1999), 96.
52. Catherine W. Griffin, "Interview with Cinda

Williams Chima, Author of the Heir Series," *Pennsylvania Literary Journal* IV, no. 3 (Fall 2012), 22.

53. Stephen King, *Bare Bones: Conversations on Terror with Stephen King*, edited by Tim Underwood and Chuck Miller (New York: McGraw-Hill, 1988), 22.

54. Ibid., 78.

55. Stephen King, *The Dark Tower V: Wolves of the Calla* (New York: Simon & Schuster, 2003), xvi.

56. Hart, "The Key Formula in Romance," 98.

57. Roberts, "The Romance of Writing," 199.

58. Ibid., 200.

59. Ibid., 198.

60. Rebecca York, "Romance Writing 101," *Writer* 124, no. 12 (December 2011): 34–36.

61. Thurston, *The Romance Revolution*, 128.

62. Ibid., 129–30.

63. Mary Cadogan, *And Then Their Hearts Stood Still: An Exuberant Look at Romantic Fiction Past and Present* (London: Macmillan, 1994), 2.

64. Bloom, *Bestsellers*, 96.

65. Christopher Booker, *The Seven Basic Plots: Why We Tell Stories* (London: Continuum, 2004), 144.

66. Ibid., 110.

67. Ibid., 116.

68. Ibid., 107.

69. Ibid., 274.

70. Thurston, *The Romance Revolution*, 225.

71. Hart, "The Key Formula in Romance," 97.

72. Ibid., 96–98.

73. Hubert, *Teaching and Writing Popular Fiction*, 25.

74. Ibid., 164–75.

75. Roberts, "The Romance of Writing," 199.

76. Thurston, *The Romance Revolution*, 56.

77. Ibid., 52.

78. Ibid., 55.

79. Ibid., 167.

80. Hubert, *Teaching and Writing Popular Fiction*, 125.

81. Ibid.

82. Jennifer Kloester, *Georgette Heyer: Biography of a Bestseller* (London: William Heinemann, 2011), 45.

83. Bloom, *Bestsellers*, 153.

84. Kloester, *Georgette Heyer*, 130–31.

85. Ibid., 131–32.

86. Ibid., 279–80.

87. Ibid., 280.

88. Ibid., 353.

89. Ibid., 281–82.

90. Ibid., 282–83.

91. Ibid., 353.

92. Ibid., 353–54.

93. Ibid., 283.

94. Ibid.

95. Ibid., 284.

96. Ibid., 284–85.

97. Thurston, *The Romance Revolution*, 37.

98. Ibid., 38.

99. Barbara Cartland, "Back to Basics and the Search for Love," *Rewriting the Sexual Contract*, edited by Geoff Dench (New Brunswick, NJ: Transaction, 1999), 257.

100. Ibid.

101. Ibid.

102. Henry Cloud, *Barbara Cartland: Crusader in Pink* (New York: Everest House, 1979), 137–38.

103. Barbara Cartland, *Barbara Cartland Bookclub Presents: The Cruel Count; Desire of the Heart* (London: Stonehouse, 1974), 6.

104. Barbara Cartland, *Diane de Poitiers* (London: Hutchison, 1962), 10.

105. Cartland, *Barbara Cartland Bookclub Presents: The Cruel Count*, 1.

106. Cartland, *Barbara Cartland Bookclub Presents: Desire of the Heart*, 2.

107. Ibid., 1.

108. Cartland, *Diane de Poitiers*, 15.

109. Cartland, *Barbara Cartland Bookclub Presents: The Cruel Count*, 2.

110. Ibid., 3.

111. Cartland, *Barbara Cartland Bookclub Presents: Desire of the Heart*, 174.

112. Cartland, *Barbara Cartland Bookclub Presents: The Cruel Count*, 2.

113. Cartland, *Barbara Cartland Bookclub Presents: Desire of the Heart*, 1.

114. Cartland, *Diane de Poitiers*, 16–17.

115. Cartland, *Barbara Cartland Bookclub Presents: The Cruel Count*, 2.

116. Cartland, *Diane de Poitiers*, 15.

117. Cartland, *Barbara Cartland Bookclub Presents: The Cruel Count*, 5.

118. Ibid., 6.

119. Ibid., 82.

120. Ibid., 121–22.

121. Cartland, *Barbara Cartland Bookclub Presents: Desire of the Heart*, 2.

122. Ibid., 175.

123. Cartland, *Diane de Poitiers*, 21.

124. Cartland, *Barbara Cartland Bookclub Presents: The Cruel Count*, 104–6.

125. Ibid., 122.

126. Kathleen E. Woodiwiss, *The Flame and the Flower* (New York: Avon Books, 1972).

127. John Charles and Shelley Mosley, eds., *Romance Today: An A-to-Z Guide to Contemporary American Romance Writers* (Westport, CT: Greenwood, 2007), 329.

128. Ibid., 331.

129. Ibid., 332.

130. Nora Roberts, *The Inn BoonsBoro Trilogy: The Last Boyfriend* (New York: Berkley Publishing Group, 2012), 53.

131. "Frequently Asked Sexuality Questions to the Kinsey Institute."

132. Hubert, *Teaching and Writing Popular Fiction*, 162.

133. Roberts, *The Last Boyfriend*, 32.

134. Ibid.

135. Ibid., 38.

Chapter 4

1. Clive Bloom, *Bestsellers: Popular Fiction Since 1900* (New York: Palgrave Macmillan, 2002), 146–47.
2. James P. Allen and Peter Der Manuelian, eds., *The Ancient Egyptian Pyramid Texts. Volume 23 of Writings from the Ancient World* (Atlanta: Society of Biblical Literature, 2005), 4.
3. Ibid., 7.
4. Wendy Doniger, ed., *The Rig Veda* (New York: Penguin, 2005).
5. Soeng Mu, *Diamond Sutra: Transforming the Way We Perceive the World* (Boston: Wisdom Publications, 2000), vii.
6. Peter Joseph, dir., *Zeitgeist: The Movie* (New York: G.M.P., 2008).
7. Stephanie Dalley, "Altrahasis," *Myths from Mesopotamia: Creation, the Flood, Gilgamesh, and Others: Oxford World Classics* (Oxford: Oxford University Press, 1989), 1.
8. Bloom, *Bestsellers*, 12.
9. "Religious Preferences: [US]," Association of Religious Data Archives, 2008.
10. "Cross-National Socio-Economic and Religion Data, 2005: I-Religion [World]," Association of Religious Data Archives, 2005.
11. Victoria Lynn Schmidt, *Story Structure Architect* (Cincinnati: Writer's Digest Books, 2005), 24.
12. Christopher Booker, *The Seven Basic Plots: Why We Tell Stories* (London: Continuum, 2004), 83.
13. Marie Corelli, *The Sorrows of Satan: Or, The Strange Experience of One Geoffrey Tempest, Millionaire. A Romance* (Philadelphia: J.B. Lippincott, 1900; Google eBook, 2009), 470.
14. John P. Ferre, *The Religious Bestsellers of Charles Sheldon, Charles Gordon, and Harold Bell Wright* (Bowling Green, OH: Bowling Green University Popular Press, 1988), 9–10.
15. Ibid., 1.
16. Ibid., 11.
17. Ibid., 13.
18. Ibid., 22.
19. Ibid., 17.
20. Lloyd C. Douglas, *Wanted—A Congregation* (Chicago: The Christian Century Press, 1920; Google eBook, 2006), 11.
21. Bloom, *Bestsellers*, 116.
22. Corelli, *The Sorrows of Satan*, 5.
23. Ibid., 7.
24. Ibid., 8.
25. Ibid.
26. Ibid., 9.
27. Ibid.
28. Ibid., 10.
29. Ibid., 11.
30. Ibid., 22.
31. Ibid., 143.
32. Ibid., 405.
33. Ibid., 439.
34. Ibid., 456.
35. Ibid., 471.
36. Florence Louisa Barclay, *The Rosary: The Mistress of Shenstone* (New York: G. P. Putnam's Sons, Knickerbocker Press, 1911; Google eBook, 2009).
37. Bloom, *Bestsellers*, 110.
38. Ibid., 89.
39. Anonymous, *Life of Florence L. Barclay: A Study in Personality* (London: G. P. Putnam's Sons, 1921), 240.
40. Ferre, *The Religious Bestsellers*, 41.
41. Barclay, *The Rosary*, back matter.
42. Ibid., 4.
43. Ibid.
44. Ibid., 388.
45. Bloom, *Bestsellers*, 146–47.
46. Douglas, *Wanted—A Congregation*, 52.
47. Ibid., 79.
48. Ibid., 96.
49. Ibid., 91.
50. Ibid., 122.
51. Ibid., 210.

Chapter 5

1. Russell Miller, *The Adventures of Arthur Conan Doyle* (London: Harvill Secker, 2008), 109–10.
2. Warren Chernaik, Martin Swales, and Robert Vilain, eds., *The Art of Detective Fiction* (London: Institute of English Studies, 2000), xii.
3. Ibid.
4. E. T. A. Hoffmann, "Volume II," *Weird Tales: Two Volumes in One* (Freeport, NY: Books for Libraries Press, 1970), 156.
5. Ibid., 160.
6. Ibid., 163.
7. Ibid., 149.
8. Ibid., 240.
9. Miller, *The Adventures of Arthur Conan Doyle*, 107.
10. Ibid., 107–8.
11. Ibid., 41–42.
12. Sir Arthur Conan Doyle, *A Study in Scarlet* (1887) (New York: Project Gutenberg eBook, 2008).
13. Edgar Allan Poe, *Great Tales and Poems of Edgar Allan Poe* (New York: Simon & Schuster Paperbacks, 2009), 94.
14. Ibid., 95.
15. Miller, *The Adventures of Arthur Conan Doyle*, 109.
16. Matthew Sweet, "Introduction," *Wilkie Collins: The Woman in White* (1860) (New York: Penguin Books, 1999), xiii.
17. Ibid.
18. Rob Warden, *Wilkie Collins's "The Dead Alive": The Novel, the Case, and Wrongful Convictions* (Evanston, IL: Northwestern University Press, 2005), vii.
19. Ibid., viii.

20. Sweet, "Introduction," *Wilkie Collins: The Woman in White*, xiv.
21. Ibid., xxiv–xxvi.
22. Ibid., xxx–xxxi.
23. Warden, *Wilkie Collins's "The Dead Alive,"* vii.
24. Ibid., viii.
25. Miller, *The Adventures of Arthur Conan Doyle*, 109–10.
26. Christopher Booker, *The Seven Basic Plots: Why We Tell Stories* (London: Continuum, 2004), 505.
27. Ibid., 506.
28. Ibid.
29. Ibid., 511.
30. Karen M. Hubert, *Teaching and Writing Popular Fiction: Horror, Adventure, Mystery and Romance in the American Classroom* (New York: Virgil Books, 1976), 109–16.
31. Booker, *The Seven Basic Plots*, 506.
32. Hubert, *Teaching and Writing Popular Fiction*, 95.
33. Ibid., 99.
34. Ibid.
35. Ibid., 99–100.
36. Agatha Christie, *The Mysterious Affair at Styles* (1920) (Champaign, IL: Project Gutenberg eBook, 2008), Chapter XII.
37. Hubert, *Teaching and Writing Popular Fiction*, 99–100.
38. William Nolan, *How to Write Horror Fiction* (Cincinnati: Writer's Digest Books, 1990), 59.
39. Clive Bloom, *Bestsellers: Popular Fiction Since 1900* (New York: Palgrave Macmillan, 2002), 117.
40. Ibid., 118.
41. Miller, *The Adventures of Arthur Conan Doyle*, 110.
42. Ibid., 113.
43. Ibid., 113–14.
44. Ibid., 144–47.
45. Ibid., 450.
46. Ibid., 450–51.
47. Ibid., 281–82.
48. Sir Arthur Conan Doyle, *The Sign of the Four* (1890) (New York: Project Gutenberg eBook, 2010).
49. Sir Arthur Conan Doyle, *The Hound of the Baskervilles* (1902) (New York: Project Gutenberg eBook, 2008).
50. Sir Arthur Conan Doyle, "A Scandal in Bohemia" (1891), *The Adventures of Sherlock Holmes* (New York: Project Gutenberg eBook, 2002).
51. Sir Arthur Conan Doyle, "The Adventure of the Dancing Men" (1903), *The Return of Sherlock Holmes: A Collection of Holmes Adventures* (New York: Project Gutenberg eBook, 2007).
52. Sir Arthur Conan Doyle, *Tales of Sherlock Holmes* (New York: Grosset & Dunlap, 1915).
53. Jennifer Kloester, *Georgette Heyer: Biography of a Bestseller* (London: William Heinemann, 2011), 130–31.
54. Bloom, *Bestsellers*, 224.
55. Ibid., 220.
56. Ibid., 132.
57. Christie, *The Mysterious Affair at Styles*, Chapter II.
58. Ibid., Chapter I.
59. Ibid.
60. Ibid.
61. Ibid.
62. Ibid., Chapter XII.
63. Ibid., Chapter X.
64. Ibid., Chapter I.
65. Ibid., Chapter III.
66. Ibid., Chapter IV.
67. Ibid., Chapter III.
68. Henning Mankell, *The Troubled Man: A Kurt Wallander Novel* (New York: Alfred A. Knopf, 2011).
69. Lotta Olsson, "Book Reviews: Henning Mankell: 'The Troubled Man,'" *Dagens Nyheter* (August 18, 2009), Swedish.
70. Bloom, *Bestsellers*, 80–81.
71. Mankell, *The Troubled Man*, 4.
72. Ibid., 13.
73. Ibid., 85.
74. Ibid., 149.

Bibliography

Allen, James P., and Peter Der Manuelian, eds. *The Ancient Egyptian Pyramid Texts. Volume 23 of Writings from the Ancient World.* Atlanta: Society of Biblical Literature, 2005.

An Annual Comprehensive Study of the U.S. Publishing Industry: BookStats 2011. New York: Association of American Publishers and the Book Industry Group, 2011.

Balogh, Mary. "Do It Passionately or Not at All." In *North American Romance Writers*, edited by Kay Mussell and Johanna Tunon. Lanham, MD: Scarecrow Press, 1999.

Barclay, Florence Louisa. *The Rosary: The Mistress of Shenstone.* New York: G. P. Putnam's Sons, Knickerbocker Press, 1911; Google eBook, 2009.

Beers, Henry Augustin. *A History of English Romanticism in the Eighteenth Century.* New York: H. Holt, 1916.

Blackmore, E. H., A. M. Blackmore, and Francine Giguere. "Introduction." In *The Devil's Pool and Other Stories by George Sand.* Albany: State University of New York Press, 2004.

Bloom, Clive. *Bestsellers: Popular Fiction Since 1900.* New York: Palgrave Macmillan, 2002.

Booker, Christopher. *The Seven Basic Plots: Why We Tell Stories.* London: Continuum, 2004.

Cadogan, Mary. *And Then Their Hearts Stood Still: An Exuberant Look at Romantic Fiction Past and Present.* London: Macmillan, 1994.

Card, Orson Scott. *How to Write Science Fiction and Fantasy.* Cincinnati: Writer's Digest Books, 1990.

Cartland, Barbara. "Back to Basics and the Search for Love." In *Rewriting the Sexual Contract*, edited by Geoff Dench. New Brunswick, NJ: Transaction, 1999.

———. *Barbara Cartland Bookclub Presents: The Cruel Count; Desire of the Heart.* London: Stonehouse, 1974.

———. *Diane de Poitiers.* London: Hutchison, 1962.

Cervantes Saavedra, Miguel de. *Don Quixote* (1605–1615). Translated by John Ormsby. Chicago: Project Gutenberg eBook, 2004.

Charles, John, and Shelley Mosley, eds. *Romance Today: An A-to-Z Guide to Contemporary American Romance Writers.* Westport, CT: Greenwood, 2007.

Chernaik, Warren, Martin Swales, and Robert Vilain, eds. *The Art of Detective Fiction.* London: Institute of English Studies, 2000.

Christie, Agatha. *The Mysterious Affair at Styles* (1920). Champaign, IL: Project Gutenberg eBook, 2008.

Cloud, Henry. *Barbara Cartland: Crusader in Pink.* New York: Everest House, 1979.

Conan Doyle, Sir Arthur. "The Adventure of the Dancing Men" (1903). *The Return of Sherlock Holmes: A Collection of Holmes Adventures.* New York: Project Gutenberg eBook, 2007.

———. *The Hound of the Baskervilles* (1902). New York: Project Gutenberg eBook, 2008.

———. "A Scandal in Bohemia" (1891). *The Adventures of Sherlock Holmes.* New York: Project Gutenberg eBook, 2002.

———. *The Sign of the Four* (1890). New York: Project Gutenberg eBook, 2010.

———. *A Study in Scarlet* (1887). New York: Project Gutenberg eBook, 2008.

———. *Tales of Sherlock Holmes.* New York: Grosset & Dunlap, 1915.

Corelli, Marie. *The Sorrows of Satan: Or, The Strange Experience of One Geoffrey Tempest, Millionaire. A Romance.* Philadelphia: J.B. Lippincott, 1900; Google eBook, 2009.

"Cross-National Socio-Economic and Religion Data, 2005: I-Religion [World]." Association of Religious Data Archives, 2005.

Dalley, Stephanie. "Altrahasis." *Myths from Mesopotamia: Creation, the Flood, Gilgamesh, and Others: Oxford World Classics.* Oxford: Oxford University Press, 1989.

Daniels, Les. *Living in Fear: A History of Horror in the Mass Media.* New York: Charles Scribner's Sons, 1975.

Doniger, Wendy, ed. *The Rig Veda.* New York: Penguin, 2005.

Douglas, Lloyd C. *Wanted—A Congregation.*

Chicago: The Christian Century Press, 1920; Google eBook, 2006.

Epstein, Jason. *Book Business: Publishing Past Present and Future*. New York: W. W. Norton, 2001.

Faktorovich, Anna. "Interview with Larry Niven, Author of *The Draco Tavern*." *Pennsylvania Literary Journal* V, no. 2 (Summer 2013).

Ferre, John P. *The Religious Bestsellers of Charles Sheldon, Charles Gordon, and Harold Bell Wright*. Bowling Green, OH: Bowling Green University Popular Press, 1988.

Flickinger, Roy Caston. *The Greek Theater and Its Drama*. Chicago: University of Chicago Press, 1918.

"Frequently Asked Sexuality Questions to the Kinsey Institute." The Kinsey Institute for Research in Sex, Gender, and Reproduction, July 21, 2012.

Freytag, Gustav. *Technique of the Drama: An Exposition of Dramatic Composition and Art*. New York: Scott, Foresman and Company, 1894 (orig. 1863).

Gelder, Ken. *Popular Fiction: The Logics and Practices of a Literary Field*. London: Routledge, 2004.

Greco, Albert N. *The Book Publishing Industry*. Second edition. Mahwah, NJ: Lawrence Erlbaum, 2005.

Griffin, Catherine W. "Interview with Carrie Ryan, Author of the Forest of Hands and Teeth Series." *Pennsylvania Literary Journal* IV, no. 3 (Fall 2012).

_____. "Interview with Cinda Williams Chima, Author of the Heir Series." *Pennsylvania Literary Journal* IV, no. 3 (Fall 2012).

Guinness Book of World Records. 2013. http://www.guinnessworldrecords.com.

Hart, Alison. "The Key Formula in Romance: A Woman's Quest." In *North American Romance Writers*, edited by Kay Mussell and Johanna Tunon. Lanham, MD: Scarecrow Press, 1999.

Heyer, Georgette. "Georgette Heyer." *The Black Moth*. Moby Classics Series. Boston: Mobile Reference, 2010.

Hoffmann, E. T. A. "Volume II." *Weird Tales: Two Volumes in One*. Freeport, NY: Books for Libraries Press, 1970.

Hubert, Karen M. *Teaching and Writing Popular Fiction: Horror, Adventure, Mystery and Romance in the American Classroom*. New York: Virgil Books, 1976.

Huntington, John. *The Logic of Fantasy: H. G. Wells and Science Fiction*. New York: Columbia University Press, 1982.

James, Henry. "The Art of Fiction." *Longman's Magazine* (London) 4, September 1884. http://public.wsu.edu/~campbelld/amlit/artfiction.html.

Joseph, Peter, dir. *Zeitgeist: The Movie*. New York: G.M.P., 2008.

King, Stephen. *Bare Bones: Conversations on Terror with Stephen King*. Edited by Tim Underwood and Chuck Miller. New York: McGraw-Hill, 1988.

_____. *The Dark Tower V: Wolves of the Calla*. New York: Simon & Schuster, 2003.

_____. "Introduction." In *The Arbor House Treasury of Horror and the Supernatural*, edited by Bill Prozini, Barry Malzberg, and Martin H. Greenberg. New York: Arbor House, 1981.

_____, and Peter Straub. *Black House*. New York: Ballantine Books, 2001.

Kloester, Jennifer. *Georgette Heyer: Biography of a Bestseller*. London: William Heinemann, 2011.

Lawrence, D. H. "The Horse Dealer's Daughter." In *The World Treasury of Love Stories*, edited by Lucy Rosenthal and Clifton Fadiman, 333–45. Oxford: Oxford University Press, 1995.

Lewis, C. S. *An Experiment in Criticism*. Cambridge: Cambridge University Press, 1992.

_____. *The Lion, the Witch and the Wardrobe*. Deluxe edition. New York: Macmillan, 1983.

Life of Florence L. Barclay: A Study in Personality. Anonymous. London: G. P. Putnam's Sons, 1921.

Mankell, Henning. *The Troubled Man: A Kurt Wallander Novel*. New York: Alfred A. Knopf, 2011.

Meyer, Stephenie. *Breaking Dawn*. New York: Hachette, 2008.

Miller, Russell. *The Adventures of Arthur Conan Doyle*. London: Harvill Secker, 2008.

Montalvo, Garci Rodríguez de. *Amadis de Gaula* (1508). Translated by Robert Southey. London: J. R. Smith, 1872. http://www.donaldcorrell.com/amadis/index.html.

Morris, Pam. *Realism: The New Critical Idiom*. New York: Psychology Press, 2003.

Mu, Soeng. *Diamond Sutra: Transforming the Way We Perceive the World*. Boston: Wisdom Publications, 2000.

Mussell, Kay. *Fantasy and Reconciliation: Contemporary Formulas of Women's Romance Fiction*. Westport, CT: Greenwood, 1984.

_____, and Johanna Tunon, eds. *North American Romance Writers*. Lanham, MD: Scarecrow Press, 1999.

Nabokov, Vladimir. "First Love." In *The World Treasury of Love Stories*, edited by Lucy Rosenthal and Clifton Fadiman, 401–8. Oxford: Oxford University Press, 1995.

_____. *Lolita*. New York: Random House Digital, 2010.

Niven, Larry. "Collaborations." *Niven's Laws*. Philadelphia: Philadelphia Science Fiction Society, 1984.

___. *The Draco Tavern*. New York: Tom Doherty, 2006.

___. "Five Years to Infinity." *Niven's Laws*. Philadelphia: Philadelphia Science Fiction Society, 1984.

___. "Niven's Laws." *Niven's Laws*. Philadelphia: Philadelphia Science Fiction Society, 1984.

___. "Rammer." *Playground of the Mind*. New York: Tom Doherty, 1991.

Nolan, William. *How to Write Horror Fiction*. Cincinnati: Writer's Digest Books, 1990.

Olsson, Lotta. "Book Reviews: Henning Mankell: 'The Troubled Man.'" *Dagens Nyheter* (August 18, 2009). Swedish.

Poe, Edgar Allan. *Great Tales and Poems of Edgar Allan Poe*. New York: Simon & Schuster Paperbacks, 2009.

"Religious Preferences: [US]." Association of Religious Data Archives, 2008.

Rice, Anne. "Let the Flesh Instruct the Mind: A Quadrant Interview with Anne Rice, by Katherine Ramsland." *The Anne Rice Reader*. New York: Ballantine Books, 1997.

___. *The Mummy, or Ramses the Damned*. New York: Ballantine Books, 1989.

Rinkel, Gene K., and Margaret E. Rinkel. *The Picshuas of H. G. Wells: A Burlesque Diary*. Chicago: University of Illinois Press, 2006.

Riordan, Rick. *The Battle of the Labyrinth: Percy Jackson & the Olympians, Book Four*. New York: Hyperion Books/Disney, 2008.

Roberts, Nora. *The Inn BoonsBoro Trilogy: The Last Boyfriend*. New York: Berkley Publishing Group, 2012.

___. "The Romance of Writing." In *North American Romance Writers*, edited by Kay Mussell and Johanna Tunon. Lanham, MD: Scarecrow Press, 1999.

"Romance Literature Statistics: Industry Statistics: 2010 ROMStat Report." New York: Romance Writers of America and Simba Information, 2010.

Rosenthal, Lucy, and Clifton Fadiman, eds. *The World Treasury of Love Stories*. Oxford: Oxford University Press, 1995.

Rowling, J. K. *Harry Potter and the Half-Blood Prince*. New York: Arthur A. Levin Books/Scholastic, 2005.

St. Clair, Robert N. *Literary Structures, Character Development, and Dramaturgical Scenarios in Framing the Category Novel*. Lewiston, NY: Edwin Mellen Press, 2004.

Schmidt, Victoria Lynn. *Story Structure Architect*. Cincinnati: Writer's Digest Books, 2005.

Sherborne, Michael. *H. G. Wells: Another Kind of Life*. London: Peter Owen, 2010.

Spitz, Bob. "Interview: Stephen King." *Penthouse* (April 1982).

Statistical Abstract of the United States: The National Data Book 2003. Washington, DC: U.S. Census Bureau, Bureau of the Census, 2003.

Sweet, Matthew. "Introduction." *Wilkie Collins: The Woman in White* (1860). New York: Penguin Books, 1999.

Thurston, Carol. *The Romance Revolution: Erotic Novels for Women and the Quest for a New Sexual Identity*. Urbana: University of Illinois Press, 1987.

Tolkien, J. R. R. *The Hobbit or, There and Back Again*. Boston: Houghton Mifflin, 1984.

"U.S. Movie Market Summary 1995 to 2012." *The Numbers: Box Office Data, Movie Stars, Idle Speculation*. New York: Nash Information Services, 2012.

Vanderbilt, Arthur T., II. *The Making of a Bestseller: From Author to Reader*. Jefferson, NC: McFarland, 1999.

Warden, Rob. *Wilkie Collins's "The Dead Alive": The Novel, the Case, and Wrongful Convictions*. Evanston, IL: Northwestern University Press, 2005.

Wells, H. G. "The Contemporary Novel." Delivered to the Times Book Club, 1912. http://www.online-literature.com/wellshg/englishman-looks-at-the-world/11/.

___. *Experiment in Autobiography: Discoveries and Conclusions of a Very Ordinary Brain (Since 1866)*. New York: Macmillan, 1934.

___. "The Island of Doctor Moreau." *World Classics*. New York: Oxford University Press, 1996.

___. "James Joyce." Review of *Portrait of the Artist as a Young Man*. *The New Republic* (1917). http://www.james-joyce-music.com/wells031017.html.

___. "Vast Riddles." *James Joyce's World*, Letters of Note, 1928, Web.

Williams, Michael. "Preface." In *Literary Structures, Character Development, and Dramaturgical Scenarios in Framing the Category Novel*, by Robert N. St. Clair. Lewiston, NY: Edwin Mellen Press, 2004.

Winter, Douglas E. *Stephen King*. Starmont Reader's Guide 16. Mercer Island, WA: Starmont House, 1982.

"Women in the Labor Force: A Data Book." *BLS Reports: Report 1040*. Washington, DC: U.S. Bureau of Labor Statistics, February 2013.

Woodiwiss, Kathleen E. *The Flame and the Flower*. New York: Avon Books, 1972.

York, Rebecca. "Romance Writing 101." *Writer* 124, no. 12 (December 2011): 34–36.

Yousuf, Hibah. "Microsoft Profit Soars." *CNN Money*, June 28, 2010.

Index

Aristophanes 98, 115
Aristotle 2, 4, 11, 71, 97
Austen, Jane 100, 122, 128

Ballantine Books 26, 106, 202–4, 210–11
Barclay, Florence Louisa 152, 156–8, 207–10; *Guy Mervyn* 156
Bildungsroman 2, 61, 120
Black House 57, 79–82, 204, 210
The Black Moth 101, 124, 205, 210
Bloom, Clive 8, 18, 21, 26, 72, 78, 109, 141, 151–2, 156, 201–9
Brown, Dan 29, 106; *Da Vinci Code* 106

Carrie 4, 59, 76, 78, 157
Cartland, Barbara 78, 96, 103, 105, 111, 115, 124, 126–36, 151, 177, 187, 195, 206, 209
Chima, Cinda Williams 56, 111, 203, 206, 210
Christie, Agatha 1, 160–2, 167, 169, 172, 174–5, 187–91
Chronicles of Narnia 18–21, 46
Collins, Wilkie 160, 162, 164–5, 207–8, 211; *The Moonstone* 162, 165
Conan Doyle, Arthur 160, 162–3, 165, 167, 169, 172, 174–80, 182–91, 207–10; Sherlock Holmes 6, 17, 154, 160, 162–7, 169–71, 173, 175–9, 181–91, 194, 196, 198, 208–9
Cookson, Catherine 103, 110
Corelli, Marie 78, 144, 150, 152–5, 158, 207, 209

Dark Tower 79–81, 112, 204, 206, 210
The Da Vinci Code 106

Dickens, Charles 3, 11, 13–5, 61–3, 65, 67, 79, 106, 137, 164–5, 176–9
Disraeli, Benjamin 3, 11
Don Quixote 7, 55, 98–9, 109, 122, 137, 203, 209
Douglas, Lloyd 149–50, 152, 158–9, 203, 207, 209, 211
Draco's Tavern 70
Dracula 16, 77
Dumas, Alexandre 82, 99, 140, 176, 195; *The Three Musketeers* 100

Epic of Gilgamesh 98, 142–3, 207, 209

Finnegans Wake 65–6
Fitzgerald, Scott 23, 30
The Flame and the Flower 105–6, 109, 115–6, 131, 136, 138–9, 206, 211
Frankenstein 56, 78
Freytag, Gustav 32–4, 38, 71, 202, 204, 210

Gone with the Wind 101
Greco, Albert 24–5, 144, 201–2, 205, 210
Guinness Book of World Records 7–8, 104, 106, 187, 201, 204, 210
Gulliver's Travels 46, 54, 99
Guy Mervyn 156

Harlequin Books 23, 102, 104–6, 111
Harry Potter 6–7, 21, 48, 54, 59, 82–9, 91–2, 108, 128, 204, 211
Heinemann 103, 124, 206, 208, 210
Heyer, Georgette 13, 96, 101, 105, 111, 115, 124–9, 131–2, 177, 184, 195, 205–6, 208; *The Black Moth* 101, 124, 205, 210; *These Old Shades* 115–6, 129

Hoffmann, E.T.A. 162–3, 207, 210
Homer 54, 143; *Odyssey* 54, 80, 143, 148, 197
Hubert, Karen M. 5, 16–7, 95–6, 105, 120, 140, 169–70, 172, 201–3, 205–6, 208, 210

The Island of Doctor Moreau 56–7, 59, 63, 66–7, 70–2, 203, 211

James, Henry 21–22, 61–7, 71, 202, 210
Joyce, James 64–66, 198, 203, 211; *Finnegans Wake* 65–6; *Ulysses* 64–6, 198

King, Stephen 3–4, 12, 19, 26–30, 38, 42, 45, 47, 51, 57, 59, 74, 76–8, 81–2, 93, 111, 157, 178, 201–4, 206, 210–1; *Black House* 57, 79–82, 204, 210; *Carrie* 4, 59, 76, 78, 157; *Dark Tower* 79–81, 112, 204, 206, 210; *The Shining* 28, 51, 59
Knopf 7, 25–6, 208, 210

Lady Chatterley's Lover 103, 108–9
Last Boyfriend 115–6, 123–4, 139, 206, 211
Lawrence, D.H. 103, 108–9, 151, 210; *Lady Chatterley's Lover* 103, 108–9
Lewis, C.S. 18–22, 27, 29, 46, 64, 73, 108–9, 202, 205, 210
Lolita 3, 25, 102–3, 105–6, 205, 210

Metamorphoses 143
Meyer, Stephenie 47, 60, 92, 205, 210; *Twilight* 39, 43, 48, 67, 83, 92–3
Mills & Boon 101, 104
Mitchell, Margaret 101–2; *Gone with the Wind* 101

The Moonstone 162, 165
Murders in the Rue Morgue 162–4

New York Times 8, 24–5, 29–30, 93, 138, 197
Niven, Larry 12, 15, 70, 75–6, 137, 202–4, 210–1; *Draco's Tavern* 70
Nolan, William 11–4, 40–1, 43–4, 56, 173, 201–3, 208, 211

Odyssey 54, 80, 143, 148, 197
Ovid 143; *Metamorphoses* 143

Patterson, James 7
Pennsylvania Literary Journal 12, 15, 56, 111, 202–3, 206, 210
Percy Jackson 6, 48, 54, 57, 67, 84, 91–2, 205, 211
Playboy 3, 52, 78, 106
Pocket Books 26, 106
Poe, Edgar Allan 40, 42, 77, 162–4, 175–6, 179, 188, 194, 203, 207, 211; *Murders in the Rue Morgue* 162–4
Proust, Marcel 8, 27, 130
Pyramid Texts 141–3, 201–2, 209

Random House 23, 25–8, 103, 106, 110, 193, 205, 210
Rice, Anne 4, 16, 42, 51–3, 82, 94, 104, 136, 150, 202–3, 211

Riordan, Rick 47, 91, 205, 211; *Percy Jackson* 6, 48, 54, 57, 67, 84, 91–2, 205, 211
Roberts, Nora 95–6, 112–3, 115–6, 120–1, 123–4, 138–40, 195, 205–6, 211; *Last Boyfriend* 115–6, 123–4, 139, 206, 211
Robinson Crusoe 99
Romeo and Juliet 100

Sand, George 99, 205, 209
Schmidt, Victoria Lynn 34–8, 145, 202, 207, 211
Scott, Sir Walter 1–3, 13–4, 61–63, 67, 77, 106, 124, 127–8, 162, 176–8, 195, 201; *Waverley* 11, 106, 124, 127, 162, 176
Shakespeare, William 51, 100, 114–5, 162; *Romeo and Juliet* 100
Shelley, Mary 56, 61, 206; *Frankenstein* 56, 78
The Shining 28, 51, 59
Silhouette Books 104–6, 111, 118, 122
Steel, Danielle 27–8
Stoker, Bram 7, 16, 77
Straub, Peter 3, 12, 79, 204, 210
Swift, Jonathan 46, 54; *Gulliver's Travels* 46, 54, 99

These Old Shades 115–6, 129
The Three Musketeers 100

Tolkien, J.R.R. 4, 7, 19, 21, 29, 46–7, 53, 72–4, 111, 204, 211
Twilight 39, 43, 48, 67, 83, 92–3

Ulysses{e64–6, 198

Viacom 26

Wallander series 161, 167, 169–70, 172–3, 182, 186, 192–4, 208, 210
The War of the Worlds 45, 63, 66–7, 70, 72
Waverley 11, 106, 124, 127, 162, 176
Weary Giants 11, 15, 64, 112
Wells, H.G. 1, 9, 17, 43, 45–7, 51, 53, 56, 60–72, 76–77, 137, 151, 161, 196, 202–3, 210–1; *The Island of Doctor Moreau* 56–7, 59, 63, 66–7, 70–2, 203, 211; *The War of the Worlds* 45, 63, 66–7, 70, 72
Wilde, Oscar 61, 63, 77, 108, 154, 176
Woodiwiss, Kathleen E. 67, 81, 95–6, 102, 105–6, 109, 114–6, 124, 131, 135–8, 206, 211; *The Flame and the Flower* 105–6, 109, 115–6, 131, 136, 138–9, 206, 211

www.ingramcontent.com/pod-product-compliance
Lightning Source LLC
Chambersburg PA
CBHW081555300426
44116CB00015B/2886